# A Market Town through Time

Also by Andy Reid

Cromer and Sheringham: The Growth of the Holiday Trade 1877-1914 (Creative History from East Anglian Sources No 3, Centre of East Anglian Studies, UEA, 1986)

The Union Workhouse: A Study Guide for Teachers and Local Historians (Phillimore, 1994)

Harriet Kettle: Pauper, Prisoner, Patient and Parent in Victorian Norfolk (Poppyland, 2021)

A Rural Community Through Time: Ashill, Norfolk (Poppyland, 2024)

# A Market Town through Time

## Watton, Norfolk

## Andy Reid

Poppyland Publishing

Copyright © Andy Reid.

This edition 2025 published by Poppyland Publishing, Lowestoft, NR32 3BB.

www.poppyland.co.uk

ISBN 978 1 869831 44 8

All rights reserved. No part of this publication may be reproduced, stored in a retrieval system or transmitted by any means, mechanical, photocopying, recording or otherwise, without the written permission of the publishers.

Designed and typeset in 10.5 on 13.5 pt Gilgamesh Pro.

Credits can be found in the captions accompanying each image.

Front Cover: High Street 'en fete' possibly for the coronation of King Edward VII, 1902 (Lesley Cowling).

Back cover: The town centre as shown on the enclosure map, 1803 (Norfolk Record Office, C/Sca 2/316).

# Contents

| | |
|---|---|
| Preface | vi |
| Acknowledgements | vii |
| What's in a Name? | 9 |
| The Wild Middle Ages | 19 |
| The Land: Enclosures, Open Fields and Commons | 31 |
| The Market Place and the Street | 40 |
| People of Early-Modern Watton | 52 |
| Christopher Hey, the Fire and the Clock Tower | 67 |
| Ingenious Tradesmen | 83 |
| Being Poor in Watton | 99 |
| The Improving Market Town | 109 |
| The George: the Hub of Watton | 119 |
| A Walk around the Town in 1841 | 137 |
| George Jacobs and the Crown | 163 |
| Maltsters and Brewers | 171 |
| Piety and Scandal | 181 |
| Learning, Private and Public | 195 |
| Celebrating and Campaigning | 208 |
| Connections and Diversions | 219 |
| A Walk around the Town in 1911 | 233 |
| The Last Hundred Years | 263 |
| A Watton Bibliography | 265 |
| Index | 266 |

# Preface

This book, like all histories, is a product of its time. The process of historical research never ends. More evidence will come to light. Errors will be discovered and corrected. People in the future will have different interests, bring new perspectives to bear and revise the version of Watton's history presented here. This book is a statement for now and will, in time, be superseded.

I started researching Watton's history in the 1970s and 1980s, while a teacher at what was initially Watton Secondary Modern School and then became Wayland High School in 1976 (and is now Wayland Academy). The purpose was to find resources that could be used in teaching, but I became interested in the subject for its own sake and continued to gather material, on and off, after moving away. Retirement has brought the opportunity to write it all up.

Several themes stand out from the pages that follow. Although its rural setting was always a significant influence and farms took up much of the area of the parish, the core of Watton was its market and many of the prime movers in its history were business people and shopkeepers. They showed ambition and enterprise, inter-married and competed with each other and sometimes over-reached. Business involved risks. The history of Watton is littered with bankruptcies.

'A Present from Watton', manufactured in Lowestoft between 1780 and 1820.
*(Norman Phillips.)*

But the people of Watton were also a community. The 'principal inhabitants' met to discuss and agree important decisions and the whole population gathered for celebrations. For the most part, they looked out for each other. The people were patriotic and showed deference to their rulers but there were also times when some of them embraced radical ideas. Women featured strongly in Watton's story; widows, in particular, often played a key part in its economic and social life. And throughout its history, people have moved into and out of the town, connecting it to the county, the country and the world. This book tells some of their stories.

# Acknowledgements

I owe a huge debt to Julian Horn, whose vast knowledge of, and enthusiasm for, the history of Watton have enriched our correspondence and conversations over 30 years. Julian's generosity in sharing documentary sources, images from his own and others' collections, insights and information has been exceptional. This book has benefited immeasurably from the material he has provided, from his observations on the draft text and from our numerous explorations and discussions of sites around the town.

Very many thanks are due to Chris Hutchings, of the Museum4Watton, for his unfailing interest and support, and for generously making available the documents in the museum's care, including a digital copy of the court books of the manor of Watton Hall. Thanks also to Kathryn Stallard, of Watton Town Council, for kindly providing a digital copy of the council's minute books and other information about the history of the town.

I am grateful to Norman Phillips, a friend since before we left Norfolk in 1988, for urging me to write this book, and for sharing his extensive knowledge of archaeological and other finds in Watton.

Thanks to the staff of the Norfolk Record Office, the Norfolk Heritage Centre, the National Archives and the British Library for all the assistance they have provided over the years. Thanks also to Heather Hamilton of the Norfolk Historic Environment Record for making available air photographs and archaeological records relating to Watton; and to Geoff Kimbell for providing images from the National LiDAR Programme (which contain public sector information licensed under the Open Government Licence v3.0), and Julian Horn for passing them on to me.

Many other people provided information, resources and insights on which I have drawn in writing this book. They are too numerous for all to be mentioned individually but I am particularly grateful to the following: Michael and Paul Adcock; Tom Bauwens and Alice Gilsenan; Linda Benton; Lesley Cowling; Bronwen Tyler; Peter and Janet Walmsley; Lord Walsingham; and Elizabeth Wright (née Harvey). In the 1970s and 1980s, I also received valuable assistance from Robert Chalmers, Ann Durrant, Lionel Fleet, Garnett Mitchell, Anne Stimpson, Peter Watts and, not least, from my pupils at Wayland High School and their parents. I express my thanks to Gareth Davies, who has been a most sympathetic and supportive publisher.

Finally, I am grateful to my wife, Alison, not only for reading and commenting on drafts of the text but also for her encouragement and her willing participation in numerous trips to Norfolk during its writing.

## Note On The Text And Sources

In quotations from contemporary sources, punctuation and capitalisation have been modernised but the original spelling retained, except that contractions such as wth (with) and '&' have been expanded. Original sources in Latin have been translated by the author. Dates before 1752, when the calendar was modernised, are given in the 'old style', according to which the new year began on 25 March. Money is expressed in £, s and d (pounds, shillings and pence; 20 shillings to the pound and 12 pence to the shilling), as in the original sources. In some cases, equivalent modern values have been added using the National Archives' currency converter (nationalarchives.gov.uk/currency-converter), which takes account of the relative prices of a range of items at ten- or five-year intervals, although it has to be said that the valuations given in 2017 (when the website was last updated) would be lower than those that would apply now, in 2024. The meanings of unfamiliar terms provided in square brackets [] and footnotes are derived from the Shorter Oxford English Dictionary and, in some cases from David Yaxley, A Researcher's Glossary (The Larks Press, 2003). Genealogical information has been gathered from the census returns from 1841 onwards, from parish registers, from the records of civil registration and from other records accessed through findmypast.co.uk, freereg.co.uk and freebmd.co.uk. This information has not been individually referenced. Newspaper material has been collected, for the most part, using the online British Newspaper Archive (britishnewspaperarchive.co.uk).

A source for the history of Watton which, largely thanks to the intervention of Julian Horn, has become available recently is an archive of documents from the former solicitors' office in Dereham Road. This material is now in the Norfolk Record Office but has not yet been catalogued, and so references to it (as ACC 2023/12) are, perforce, imprecise.

## Abbreviations

| | | | |
|---|---|---|---|
| BCE | Before the common era (BC) | NHER | Norfolk Historic Environment Record |
| BNP | Bury and Norwich Post | NM | Norwich Mercury |
| CE | The common era (AD) | NN | Norfolk News |
| DMG | Downham Market Gazette | NRO | Norfolk Record Office |
| LA | Lynn Advertiser | TNA | The National Archives |
| LNCP | Lynn News and County Press | TWT | Thetford and Watton Times |
| NC | Norfolk Chronicle | | |

# What's in a Name?

Why is Watton called Watton? The name dates from the Anglo-Saxon period, which lasted from about 1,600 to a little under 1,000 years ago. Exactly when during that long period of time people began to use the name 'Watton' is unknown and unknowable but the 'ton' element suggests that the name originated in the later Saxon period, sometime after the mid-8th century.

What is known for sure is that William 'the Conqueror', after the Battle of Hastings in 1066, ordered a huge survey of every landholding in England to be undertaken, mainly for taxation purposes. The results were compiled in the Domesday Book in 1086, and they include an entry for a place called Wadetuna. The name meant Wada's enclosure, or homestead, or village, or estate: in short, Wada's place.[1] In the past, it was suggested that the 'wade' element came from the Anglo-Saxon word for ford, *wadan*, but this is implausible because any fords over the stream known as the Little Wissey[2] were some distance from the original centre of Watton, presumed to be on the higher ground in the vicinity of the church.

Much later, but certainly by the 16th century, people in Watton adopted the hare and barrel as symbols of the town. This was a bit of fun; a 'wat' was an old name for a hare and a 'tun' was a barrel. The symbols are a rebus, or pun, on the name of Watton. They are not what the name 'Watton' actually means.

৸৶

Although it was the Anglo-Saxons who gave Watton its name, people had lived in the area long before the first Anglo-Saxon settlers arrived.

The earliest humanly-made artefact found in Watton is a hammerhead or mace-head dating from the Mesolithic period, or Middle Stone Age (c 10,000 BCE to 4300 BCE)[3]. The Mesolithic people who left their traces in Watton may just have been passing through, perhaps hunting the animals that inhabited what was probably a wooded landscape. More evidence has been found from the following period, the Neolithic or New Stone Age (c 4300 to 2500 BCE), when people began to clear land for farming. The finds comprise worked flints including polished axe-heads from several locations around the parish, including Wayland Wood.[4]

More substantial evidence survives from the Bronze-Age (c 2500–700 BCE), in the form of a burial mound or barrow that stood where the RAF constructed a radar station in the 20th century. Seven copper alloy socketed axe-heads were found nearby.[5] Other evidence of a Bronze-Age presence was found on the site of the former officers' mess at RAF Watton.[6] Bronze-Age arrow-heads have been found, including one with barbs and tangs from Watton Green.[7]

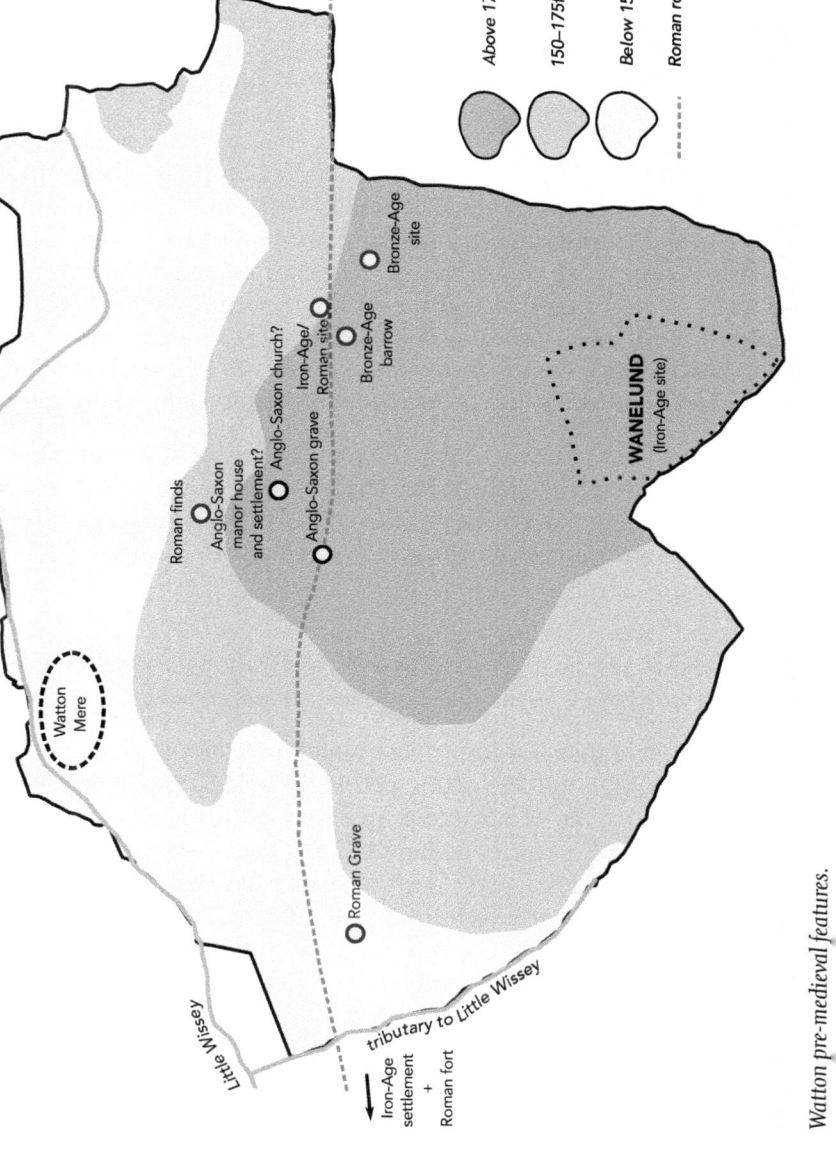

*Watton pre-medieval features.*

Next came the Iron-Age (c 700 BCE—43 CE). Two important sites associated with this period have been found in Watton. One is in Wayland Wood, where large quantities of Iron-Age pottery sherds have been found, suggesting the presence of a settlement of some kind.[8] The other is a site investigated in 1991, near the junction of Norwich Road and the road to Watton Green, not far from the Bronze-Age barrow, where the finds included Iron-Age pottery. The Iron-Age people, like their Bronze-Age predecessors, were farmers and the orientation of some of the present-day fields in the parish probably dates back to Iron-Age times. In Threxton, a mile or so west of Watton, was a major Iron-Age settlement, evidenced by finds of coins and brooches. A very fine silver coin of this date has also been found in Watton.

When the Romans occupied Britain after 43 CE, they referred to the Iron-Age people they found in this part of the island as the Iceni.

୪୦୦୪

The most significant Roman presence in the Watton area was around where the Roman road, Peddars Way, crossed the Little Wissey. On a raised promontory south of the stream in Threxton, where the Iron-Age settlement had been located, a Roman fort was constructed in about 47 CE, probably to guard the river crossing. Finds of coins and metalwork on this site indicate that it was only occupied for a brief period, until about 54 CE.

Under the leadership of their celebrated queen, Boudicca, the Iceni rebelled against the Roman occupation in 61 CE. After they had been defeated, the Romans established another fort, on the north side of the stream, in what is now the south-western corner of Saham Toney. Surrounded by triple ditches, it could provide accommodation for about 800 legionaries. An adjacent enclosure was probably a compound for their horses. Although, once again, the military occupation was brief, the area north of the stream remained an important civil settlement until the 4th century CE.[9]

The people of the area become Romanised and are often referred to as Romano-British. Roman

*Iceni silver coin, found in Watton.*
*(Museum4Watton)*

pottery and metalwork have been found in several locations within Watton itself, including near Wayland Wood and, at the other end of the town, at Stokes Avenue, where two graves were found in a garden, one containing the burial of a woman.[10] Considerable numbers of Roman coins, along with brooches and other metalwork, have been found in the area north of St Mary's Church.[11]

Evidence of Roman as well as Iron-Age occupation was found on the site north of Norwich Road, near the turn-off for Watton Green. The investigation carried out in 1991 yielded evidence of pits and ditches, and Roman coins of the 2nd to 4th centuries CE. The conclusion was that the site was probably domestic in nature, perhaps a house or a farm.[12]

The most prominent feature in Watton that is likely to date from the 400-year Roman occupation, although there is no definitive proof that it does so, is the road that runs through the town from west to east, forming Brandon Road, the High Street and Norwich Road.[13] It may have formed part of a long-distance route from the Fen Causeway and Denver, via the settlement at Threxton/Saham Toney, to the town of Venta Icenorum at what is now Caister St Edmund, south of Norwich, although no supporting evidence has been found for the central section of the route, from Scoulton to Crownthorpe.[14]

The alignment of Watton High Street cuts across the orientation of the earlier, Iron-Age fields. The field boundaries follow the contours of the land, whereas the High Street rises gently from west to east, crossing the contours,[15] until it reaches what was occasionally referred to in the 19th century as the 'market hill'. The reason why there is a bend half way along George Trollope Road is that North, South, East and West Roads were laid out parallel to the earlier, Iron-Age field boundaries rather than the 'Roman' road. The High Street was called 'the street' until very recent times, which might be suggestive of its Roman origins although it may also have reflected its long-established importance as a 'thoroughfare'. The road through Neaton, also, was referred to as 'Neaton Street' in the 17th century[16] but has never been proposed as a Roman road—although it could, conceivably, have been part of an alignment continuing through the western end of Ashill, where there was an important Roman site.

ഔരു

After occupying southern Britain for almost 400 years, the Roman legions left these shores in the early 5th century. People from across the North Sea, the Angles, raided and came to settle, establishing the kingdom of East Anglia, while Saxons and others occupied other parts of what had been Roman Britannia. These people, who became known as Anglo-Saxons, gave Watton its name.

The 'ton' element in 'Wadetuna', Wada's place, or Watton as we know it now, makes it likely that the name of the settlement was coined in the mid to late Anglo-

*The roof-lines in the market place preserve the alignment of earlier market stalls (Julian Horn).*

Saxon period. 'Tons' were subsidiary to 'hams', which were founded earlier and tended to be more important.[17] Our local 'ham' was Saham and Watton probably formed part of, or was dependent on, a large estate centred on Saham. Watton Wick, in turn, may have been established in the Anglo-Saxon period as an outlying settlement to Watton, 'wick' being derived from 'vic', an Old English term for a farm, often meaning a dairy farm.

Some evidence from early in the Anglo-Saxon period, including a cruciform brooch, has been found north of St Mary's Church, in the area where much Romano-British material has also been collected. There may, therefore, have been an Anglo-Saxon presence here, perhaps of a transient nature, from the 5th or 6th century onwards.[18] Much more evidence survives from the middle and late Anglo-Saxon periods, including pottery sherds, coins and metalwork, and so it seems likely that there was an Anglo-Saxon settlement of some kind north of the church, perhaps a manor house and farm. A LiDAR (light detection and ranging) image certainly suggests the presence of a building or buildings in this area.[19]

Other items of metalwork have been found elsewhere in the parish, including brooches, weaponry and a Middle Saxon coin.[20] The most dramatic discovery from this period was a grave found in front of 35, Norwich Road in 1952 which contained the skull of a young male and a sherd of early Anglo-Saxon pottery.[21]

East Anglia was invaded by an army from Denmark in 865 and again in 869,

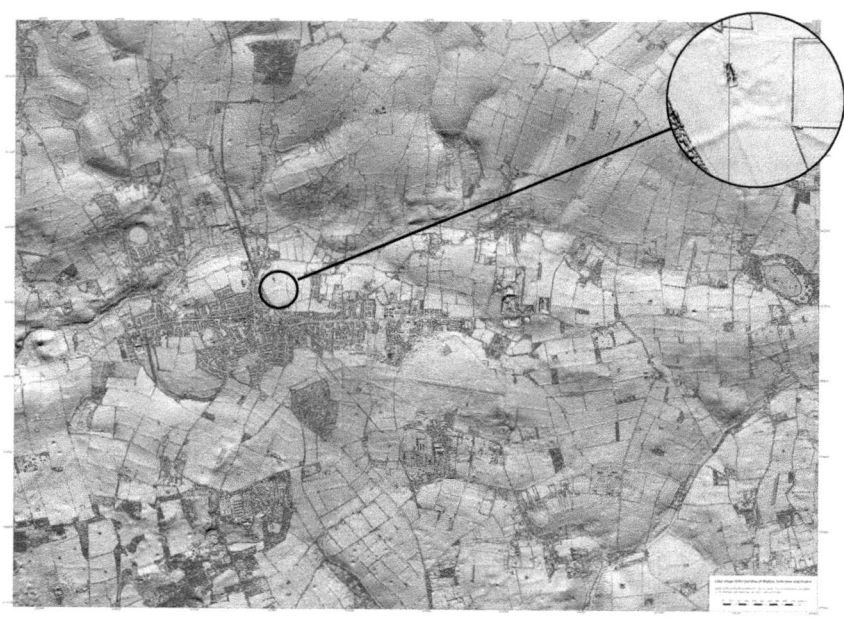

*LiDAR image of Watton, from the National LiDAR Programme.*
(With thanks to Geoff Kimbell and Julian Horn.)

The disturbed area north of St Mary's Church (circled) may be the site of the Anglo-Saxon and medieval manor houses.

and Danish settlement occurred during the following two centuries. There was certainly Danish influence in the Watton area, although it was less strong than in some parts of Norfolk, such as Flegg and the area south of Norwich. The village of Thompson has a name originally derived from the Old Danish personal name Tumi, hence 'Tumi's ton, or farm'.[22] The name of Waite Farm in Saham comes from the Old Norse term 'thwaite', meaning a clearing or cleared land. In Watton itself, several furlongs and closes in the fields contained the Scandinavian place-name element 'wong', meaning a piece of land or meadow. Two brooches in a 10th century Scandinavian style have been found in the area north of St Mary's Church.

ೞ⚬ಇ

The 'hundred' was a unit of local government established in East Anglia after its reconquest by the Anglo-Saxons.[23] The area around Watton was known as Wanelund, or Wayland Hundred. The name 'Wayland' is of Scandinavian origin, the 'land' part being derived from the Old Norse 'lundr' meaning a wood or grove, often with the sense of 'sacred grove'. Oliver Rackham suggested that Wayland Wood was a 'grove of assembly, perhaps even of heathen worship, long before the Norman Conquest'.[24] The 'Way' element in Wayland was probably derived from an Old Danish personal name, Waghn.[25]

Wayland Hundred took its name from the wood and the hundred court met there. Thetford Priory was represented at a 'turno' (tourn, or court) in 'Waylonde Woode' in 1498/99 and regularly thereafter up to 1540.[26] As late as 1749, a document referred to an entrance to the wood called the 'hundred oake gate'.[27] The hundred oak was probably a particularly large and conspicuous tree which served as the assembly point for the court.

An intriguing connection exists between the two names Wayland and Wada in Anglo-Saxon mythology.[28] Wada was a Germanic mythological character, a king or god said to be descended from a king and a mermaid, who lived in Denmark and was strongly associated with water. According to a tale related by the Brothers Grimm, he once waded through Groenasund (Gron Sound, S.E. Denmark), in water nine yards deep, carrying his infant son whose name was…Wayland.

Versions of Wayland's name occur in Anglo-Saxon, Norse and German. He is generally known as Wayland Smith, a craftsman with supernatural powers, often regarded as a god. References to Wada occur in various place-names in Yorkshire, and there is a Wayland's Smithy, a bronze-age barrow near the White Horse at Uffington in Oxfordshire, but Watton and Wayland Wood and Hundred appear to be the only references to them in Norfolk. It is tempting to speculate that it was this Wada in honour of whom Watton took its name, and that Wayland Wood was somehow associated with Wayland Smith.

In early-modern times, Wayland Wood was claimed as the setting for the legend of the 'Babes in the Wood', first published as a ballad by Thomas Millington in Norwich in 1595, with the title: *The Norfolk gent his will and testament and how he committed the keeping of his children to his own brother whoe delte most wickedly with them and howe God plagued him for it.*[29] The story has interesting echoes of that of the princes in the tower, allegedly murdered by their uncle, King Richard III in 1483. Francis Blomefield, the 18th century historian of Norfolk, noted that Wayland Wood was 'commonly called Wailing Wood from a tradition of two infants murdered by their uncle in this place, of which the ballad or old song of *The Two Children in the Wood* is said to be made; the original of which tradition I do not find'.[30]

༄༅

Apart from Wada, the only other individual Anglo-Saxon associated with Watton whose name is known is Aldreda,[31] a freewoman. She was named in the Domesday Book of 1086 as the person who had held the two manors, or estates, that existed in Watton in the reign of King Edward the Confessor, shortly before the Norman Conquest in 1066. The Domesday Book also recorded that Watton had a church with 20 acres of land, worth 20d. This church is very likely to have stood on the site of the present St Mary's church.

According to the Domesday Book, the two manors that had been held by Aldreda, which were worth £4 each, had been united by 1086 into one worth £7 which was held by a Norman called Ranulf son of Walter (otherwise known as Ranulf Fitzwalter), whose overlord was Roger Bigod, one of William I's barons. Other inhabitants recorded in 1086 included 23 'sokemen', eight more than at the time of King Edward, with 82 acres of land. The sokemen did not have to work for Ranulf but probably had to attend the court of outsoken in Saham. There were no villeins, people who held land from the lord of the manor but had to work for him in exchange for it, although previously there had been nine. The number of 'bordars' who held small plots of land and, like the villeins, had to provide 'labour services' for the lord of the manor, had increased from 11 to 12. Three serfs, or slaves, who were landless, had lived on the manor throughout. All told, in 1086, 38 inhabitants of Watton were mentioned.

The manor of Watton contained five 'ploughlands', that is to say, about 600 acres of arable land, plus the 82 acres held by the sokemen. The land was worked by 11 plough teams, comprising oxen: four on the demesne, the lord's own land; three (previously four) owned by the bordars; and four which ploughed the land of the sokemen. Three riding horses had been kept throughout, but the number of cattle had fallen from 13 to five. Sheep, however, had increased from 17 to 62. There were 30 acres of meadow. Domesday Book also recorded that Watton had a mill in 1086, which it appears not to have had previously. The location of this mill, which would have been a watermill, is a matter of speculation; it may have been on the Little Wissey, which probably formed the boundary between Watton and Saham, or perhaps more likely, on the even smaller stream which flows north along the boundary between Watton and Merton before joining the Little Wissey.

Watton contained a considerable area of woodland, enough to support 400 swine. Wayland Wood may have been bigger then than it is now. It would have been an important resource in the Anglo Saxon and medieval economy, not just as pasture for pigs (Domesday Book records that there were actually 30 swine in Watton in 1086, against 35 in 1066) but also as a source of timber (oak, ash and maple) and underwood (hazel and bird cherry). The timber and underwood were valuable; at the time of the 'Peasants' Revolt' in 1381, a man from Merton was prosecuted for cutting down and taking away underwood to the value of 40s (equivalent to about £1,250 today) 'at Waylond.'[32] Large boundary banks which divided the portions of the wood belonging to different landowners, probably of medieval date, can still be seen. In the medieval period, most of Wayland Wood became the property of the De Grey family of Merton Hall and in 1428–29 a man was fined at the De Greys' manor court of Merton for trespassing there.[33] One of the boundary banks divided off an area of four acres known as 'Threxton Nab' (a piece which jutted out) and alternatively as 'Colledge Close,' as it belonged to the college at Thompson.[34]

It has to be said that Watton was not a very important place in the 11th century. It was not big: a league (about three miles) in length and half a league in breadth. The church that was to be built, or rebuilt, in the parish was small and remained so; as Blomefield noted seven centuries later, it was only 20 yards long and, including its aisles, 11 yards broad.[35] Saham, a royal manor and the principal place in Wayland Hundred, was three times bigger, almost three times more valuable and paid more than twice as much in 'geld' (tax). It was also to acquire a much more impressive church.

But Watton was to acquire a market, and that changed everything.

## Notes

1. Eilert Ekwall, *The Concise Oxford Dictionary of English Place-Names* (Fourth edition, Oxford, 1960); Victor Watts, *The Cambridge Dictionary of English Place Names* (Cambridge, 2004). Francis Blomefield, in *An Essay towards a Topographical History of the County of Norfolk*, volume 2 (William Miller, 1805), suggested that the name derived from 'Wadan' and the same interpretation has been offered by later authors.
2. The stream that runs between Watton and Saham Toney is sometimes referred to as the Watton Brook. I refer to it as the Little Wissey throughout.
3. NHER 8778. The approximate dates for periods in prehistory in Norfolk are taken from John A Davies and David M G Waterhouse, *Exploring Norfolk's Deep History Coast* (The History Press, 2023).
4. NHER 8771-4, 21584.
5. NHER 42674, 8777.
6. G Trimble, *An Archaeological Evaluation – Former Officers' Mess, Watton* (Pre-construct Archaeology, 2011).
7. NHER 8769, 8770.
8. NHER 36300.
9. Robin A Brown, 'The Iron Age and Romano-British Settlement at Woodcock Hall, Saham Toney, Norfolk', in *Britannia*, 17 (1986); Megan Dennis, *Early Roman Forts Resource Pack* (Norfolk Heritage Explorer, Norfolk Museums and Archaeology Service, 2007).
10. NHER 8779, 17251, 35347, 11500, 35348, 25014, 25827, 20401.
11. NHER 1031.
12. Heather Wallis, *Report of Archaeological Evaluation at Norwich Road, Watton* (Norfolk Archaeological Unit, 1991).
13. David Gurney, 'Roman Norfolk', in Trevor Ashwin and Alan Davison (eds), *An Historical Atlas of Norfolk, Third Edition* (Phillimore, 2005).
14. James E Albone, *Roman Roads in the Changing Landscape of Eastern England, c.AD 410-1850* (PhD thesis, University of East Anglia, 2016, accessed via ueaeprints.uea.ac.uk).
15. I owe this insight to Julian Horn.
16. For example, in the manor court book, Manor of Watton Hall, 17 April 1671; Museum4Watton, M4W/2016/8A.
17. Tom Williamson, 'Place Name Patterns', in Trevor Ashwin and Alan Davison (eds), *An Historical Atlas of Norfolk, Third Edition* (Phillimore, 2005).
18. NHER 1031.
19. I am grateful to Geoff Kimbell for making available images from the National LiDAR Programme and to Julian Horn for passing them on to me.
20. NHER 25827, 39299, 36300.

21. NHER 8781.
22. David Boulton, Viking *Migration and Settlement in East Anglia: The Place Name Evidence* (Windgather Press, 2023).
23. Tom Williamson, The Origins of Norfolk (Manchester UP, 1993).
24. Oliver Rackham, *Trees & Woodland in the British Landscape*, revised edition (Phoenix, 1990).
25. O. Arngart, 'The Hundred Name Wayland', in the *Journal of the English Place-Name Society, 12* (1980).
26. The Register of Thetford Priory, (ed) David Dymond, Norfolk Record Society (2 vols, 1994-6).
27. NRO, WLS XXXI/9 417x6.
28. The connection of Wada and Wayland Smith was first brought to my attention by John Newton of Saham Toney in the 1980s. This account given here is derived from Wikipedia.
29. Wikipedia.
30. F Blomefield (1805).
31. In the Penguin edition of the Domesday Book (published by Alecto Historical Editions in 1992 and by Penguin in 2002), Aldreda's name was given as Ealdthryth. Comparison with the original text demonstrates that this was an error.
32. Plea roll, Court of Common Pleas; TNA, CP40/483.
33. George Crabbe, 'Report on the Muniments at Merton Hall, Norfolk', in Walter Rye (ed), *Norfolk Antiquarian Miscellany*, Volume II (1883).
34. Rental of Walsingham properties, 1624; NRO, WLS IX/7.
35. F Blomefield, (1805).

# The Wild Middle Ages

Ranulf Fitzwalter, who held the manor of Watton at the time when Domesday Book was compiled in 1086, granted part of it shortly afterwards to Thetford Priory, along with the rectorial tithes of the church and the 'advowson' (the right to nominate the vicar). The priory's part of the manor became known as Monk's-Wick. In 1540, after the dissolution of Thetford Priory by Henry VIII, it was reunited with the main manor of Watton Hall, but the name 'Wick Farm' survived, as it does to this day.

The rest of the manor passed from Ranulf Fitzwalter to the family of Richard D'Engaine (1035-1100), the man who had made the weapons used by William the Conqueror at the Battle of Hastings. His grand-daughter, Ada, married Robert de Vallibus, or de Vaux, sometime before 1115. He was her second husband and the manor of Watton Hall passed to their descendants, remaining in the de Vaux family until 1282, when John de Vaux settled it on his daughter Maud on her marriage to William de Ros. Members of the Ros, or Roos, family, several of whose members fought in the Hundred Years' War with France, then held the manor until the 16th century.

In 1364, Margery, widow of William de Roos (perhaps the grandson of Maud and her husband), died holding a life interest in the manor of Watton Hall. A jury was convened to enquire into her properties, and swore that the manor comprised a messuage (house), 140 acres of arable land, six acres of meadow, eight acres of pasture and a dovehouse (location unknown). Early in the medieval period, in exchange for land they held in the common fields, the 'bond' or 'native' tenants, the successors to the villeins and bordars of Domesday Book, had to perform various services for the lord of the manor, such as haymaking and harvesting on his demesne land. In 1364, they no longer provided labour services but instead paid rents in money, amounting to 26s 8d, plus four hens and two capons, per year. Margery also held land, meadow and pasture from the manor of Saham Toney.[1] Although there was a house on the manor of Watton Hall, it seems unlikely that any members of the de Roos family, whose main residence was at Helmsley in North Yorkshire, or indeed any of the de Vaux family before them, had ever lived in Watton. The manor house was a modest dwelling which initially may have provided accommodation for the lord's steward when visiting the manor and, later, provided living accommodation for the 'farmer', the person who leased the manor in exchange for an annual rent. In 1422, the manor house comprised no more than a hall, kitchen and a 'house for steers' (cowshed),[2] and in 1422-23 the whole manor was leased to John Doket for £5 10s 8d per year (equivalent to about £3,600 today).[3]

In 1237, part of the manor of Watton Hall had been granted by Oliver de Vaux to Richard de Rupella or Rokele, establishing the manor of Rokeles Hall. Rokele had extensive land-holdings in Ireland and served as justiciar on the island under Henry III; he also went on a crusade with the future Edward I in 1270.[4] Rokeles Hall remained in the hands of members of the Rokele family into the 14th century, after which it changed hands regularly. There was another small manor in medieval Watton, called Curson's, which was made up of properties purchased piecemeal from the manors of Watton Hall and Rokeles Hall. Curson is a name that occurs in the local area in 14th and early 15th century sources. The 'manor' of Curson's, which was probably located near Curson's Cross at the west end of the main street, was bought in the 17th century by the lord of the manor of Watton Hall.[5]

ഉരു

The game-changer for Watton's development was the establishment of the market. Watton's first charter, for a Friday market, was obtained from King John in 1202. It was challenged and withdrawn in 1204 on the ground that it was prejudicial to the market of Saham, but in the same year the lord of the manor, Oliver de Vaux, succeeded in obtaining another charter for a market on Wednesdays.[6] These charters appear not to survive, although Horace Crawshay Frost, son of Thomas Crawshay Frost of Watton Brewery, claimed to have seen one of them on display in 1929.[7] Initially Saham people were exempt from paying tolls at Watton market, but in the course of time they appear to have lost this privilege.

The establishment of Watton's market was not only crucial to the town's economic importance but also determined its physical shape. It is just possible that, originally, the market was in the vicinity of the old manor house[8] but it is much more likely that it was established at, or at a very early stage moved to, the space that it now occupies, on relatively high ground on the north side of the 'Roman' road. It was certainly located there well before the fire of 1674, almost certainly as a result of a conscious decision rather than happenstance. Watton, as the landscape historian Tom Williamson has argued, is a 'possible example of a true planted town...The earliest property boundaries here seem to indicate a measure of planning.'[9]

During the medieval period, the market place gradually became the focus for a community. Buildings were erected around it and spread down the 'Roman' road, which developed into the 'street' of Watton, the High Street, as it now is. The area around the market place became the town centre, at some distance from the parish church and manor house.

The parish church is the one surviving medieval building in Watton. Its round tower dates from the early 12th century, with the octagonal belfry being added in the 15th century. The tower previously had a small spire (taken down in 1878). The chancel and south arcade date from the 13th century and the north arcade from the 15th.[10] The church was originally dedicated to St Giles and continued to

*St Mary's Church, 1834.*
*(Museum4Watton.)*

This image shows the church as it was before the rebuilding of the nave aisles in 1842.

be referred to as St Giles' Church until the mid-16th century.[11] The precise date of its re-dedication to St Mary is unknown.

The addition of aisles to the parish church was a response to the growth of the town, Nevertheless, the population of medieval Watton remained relatively small. The poll tax assessment of 1380 listed the names of 67 people in the parish. They were all assessed at fairly small sums: no one very wealthy, and none of the lords of the manors, resided in the town. In contrast, 108 people were assessed in Saham Toney, which had a resident lady of the manor: Philippa de Beauchamp.[12]

Apart from the market place and the street, the other foci of settlement in Watton

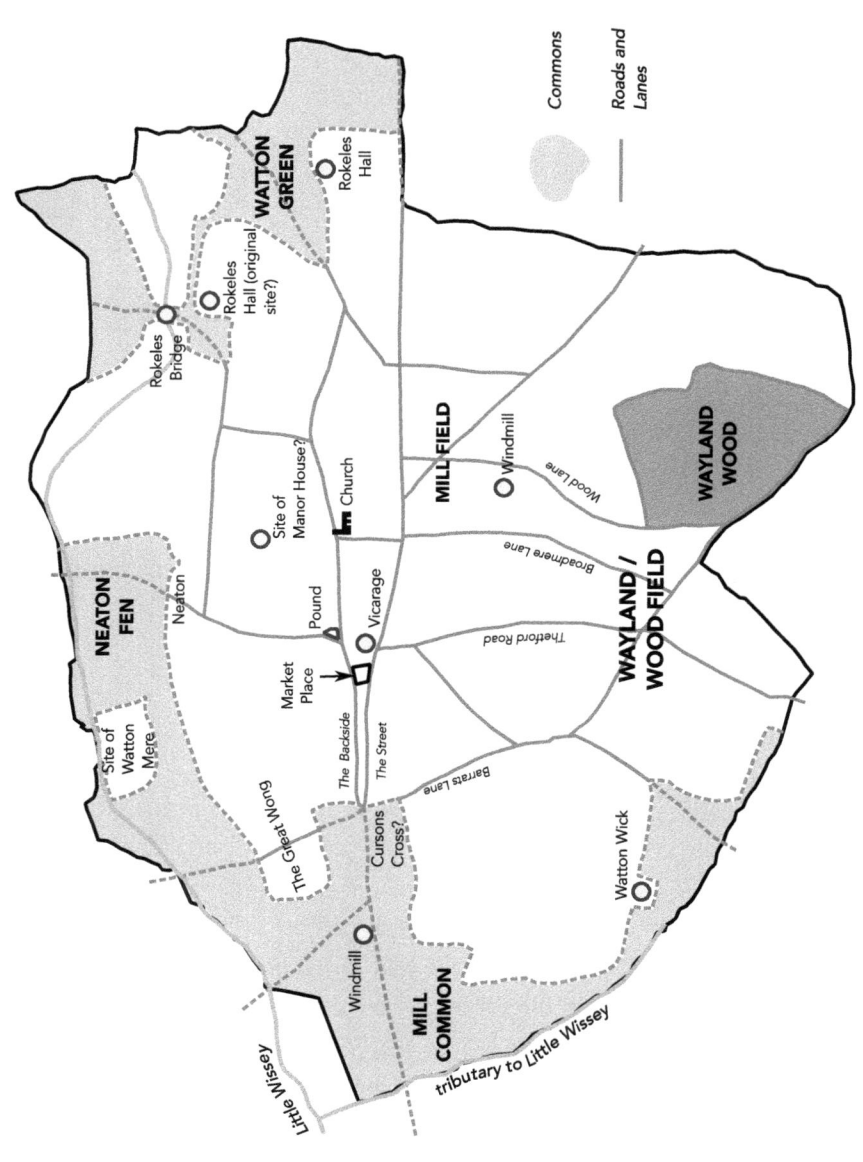

*Watton medieval and early-modern features*

included the area around Watton Green and Rokeles Hall; Watton Wick; and the hamlet of Neaton. There may also have been a few dwellings near the church and manor house.

☙❧

A little information about the geography of Watton in the 14th century is provided by a document, of which a 16th century copy survives, describing a perambulation of the 'mettes and boundes perteynyng to the common of Saham Thony.'[13] Saham, as a royal manor at the time of the Domesday Book, claimed rights over a wide area of common land stretching into the adjoining parishes. A section of the claimed boundary ran: 'by the dyke to a brygg called Rokelles Brygg and be Rokkelsmedow to Wasshbrygg and return towards the south to Eton and so by the northend of the lond of the lord of the manor of Watton and so by Wolbyswong to Cursunz and so by the dyke to the Wykestok'.

Most of these names can be placed. Rokelles Brygg (Rokeles Bridge) carried Redhill Lane across the Little Wissey to Ovington. Rokkelsmedow (Rokeles Meadow) was a large area of meadow adjacent to the bridge. The precise location of Wasshbrygg is unknown but it may have been where the current road to Dereham crosses the Little Wissey. Eton could be interpreted as Neaton and Wollbyswong may have been a piece of land on the east side of Saham Road later referred to as 'the Great Wong'. Cursunz was at the west end of the street and 'Wykestok' was almost certainly Watton Wick. We are, therefore, walking from east to west along the Little Wissey, and then turning south, following what remained the edge of the common until parliamentary enclosure in 1803.

The same document also specified where the people of parishes other than Saham were allowed to pasture their animals. 'Watton,' it stated, 'begynnyth to pasture ther cattell at the Steppellz and be the water which doth come from the watermill of Watton and be the grett well unto Tolisepytt and so to Fle to the Wasshbek between Ovyngton and Watton and ther pasture by the Grene and ye gates of Story and be all Sandwade to Wollydam'. Some of these features cannot be located but it seems that the description moves from west to east through the same low-lying area between Watton and Saham.

The steppellz may have been stepping stones over the little stream between Watton and Merton, the grett well could conceivably have been one of the springs shown on the Ordnance Survey map immediately to the west of the Watton parish boundary and Sandwade would have been a sandy ford across the Little Wissey. Fle, from the Old English word 'fleot' (stretch of river or water with fishing rights),[14] may have been a reference to Watton Mere, referred to in an inquisition on the death of John Lord de Roos in 1422, as a 'fishery' worth 18d per year (equivalent to about £50 today).[15] It lay on the south side of the Little Wissey, west of where the track of the railway line from Watton to Swaffham was laid in the 19th century.[16] The

Wasshbek may have been associated with the Wasshbrygg mentioned earlier and could have been a place for washing sheep. The Grene is probably Watton Green. The document provides evidence that the watermill mentioned in the Domesday Book was still in existence in the 14th century and gives a rough indication of its location, in the west of the parish, possibly on the tributary stream that follows the parish boundary.

ೞಚಿ

From time to time in the 14th century, Watton, like many places, was affected by serious disorder. In 1350, Margery, the widow of William de Roos, lady of the manor of Watton Hall, complained that 22 named men, including Edward de Monte Acuto [Montagu] and John Dunche, 'took her cattle at Whaddon [Watton]…and drove them to places unknown, to prevent her from repl[e]vying [recovering] them…whereby her land at Whaddon has remained untilled, and assaulted her men and servants, whereby she has lost their services for a great time.'[17] Edward de Montagu, who had fought at the Battle of Crecy in France in 1346, was the youngest son of William, second Baron Montagu. In 1352, he was indicted for assaulting his wife, Alice of Norfolk, causing her death.[18] A thug, to say the least.

Eleven years later, in 1361, William Dunche, perhaps a relative of the John Dunche mentioned in 1350, in recognition of 'good service done in the war of France', was pardoned for, among other things, having stolen 11 horses and 20 cows belonging to Margery Roos, and driving away other horses and cows, some belonging to Margery Roos, some to the master of the Commandery of the Knights of St John at Carbrooke, and some to the Prior of Thetford, at Watton, Kerbrok [Carbrooke] and Merton, and for having detained them 'until they made fine with [paid a ransom to] Edward [de Montagu] for their deliverance'. William Dunche came from Bungay in Suffolk and was pardoned for many other crimes, including his part in the death of Edward de Montagu's wife Alice, as well as for the incidents in Watton. It sounds as though he was part of a raiding party, perhaps of ex-soldiers, orchestrated by Edward de Montagu, which performed acts of pillage over a wide area. Edward de Montagu died in 1361 and that may have been what occasioned the pardon for William Dunche.[19]

More violent incidents occurred in the following years. In 1367 several Watton men 'conspired…to beat and wound certain persons of the township of Kerbrok [Carbrooke]'. They 'came to the town of Great Kerbrok on Sunday night, the eve of All Saints' and assaulted six people, including two women, 'so that some of them despaired of their lives'.[20] In 1375, a group of 12 named men from Watton, including Robert de York, bailiff of Watton[21] (perhaps the leader) and Robert Hurthaunt, who had been involved in the attack on Carbrooke eight years earlier, made a raid on the property of Lady Philippa de Beauchamp of Saham Toney and 'broke her closes and houses at Watton…took away her goods and assaulted her men and servants'. They were ordered to be detained in the gaol at Norwich Castle pending trial, along with others, including another two, and possibly four,[22] of those involved in the 1367 incident. There seems to have been something of a Watton mafia at the time.

Saham Toney's revenge followed later in the same year. Margery de Roos had died and the lord of the manor of Watton Hall was now her son, Thomas de Roos, another war veteran who had fought in the Battle of Poitiers in 1356. In April 1375, he complained that a large group of named individuals from Saham Toney, with others from Carbrooke, Ovington and Griston, had descended on the manor of Watton and ransacked it. They 'broke the doors and windows of his houses in the manor, fished in his fishponds and several fisheries there…took away… fish from the stews and fisheries, and goods found at Watton…trod down and consumed with cattle his crops and grass at Watton…hindered his servants and ministers from holding his market at Watton and collecting toll and other profits there, and so threatened his men, servants and tenants, and afflicted them with such injuries, hardships and grievances, breaking their houses and carrying away their goods, that the tenants have withdrawn from his lordship and tenure and his men and servants from his service'.[23] Even though such complaints were routinely exaggerated by those making them, it nevertheless sounds as though the manor of Watton had been ransacked. Watton market had been disrupted and the people had fled. Perhaps the men from Saham Toney continued to harbour resentment of the market at Watton.

In a separate incident in 1375, a man named Thomas Warner was murdered in Watton. The killer was Thomas Everard of Watton, a blacksmith who, with Nicholas Canoun, also of Watton, had come to notice as a debtor in 1365.[24] He was pardoned on the ground that he acted in self-defence.[25] These were violent times.

ℰ⚭ℛ

The 'Peasants' Revolt' followed a few years later, in 1381. During the disturbances, Thomas Smyth of Letton came to Watton and threatened to destroy the buildings of the commandery of Carbrooke unless the master paid him an outstanding debt. Judging discretion to be the better part of valour, the master promptly complied.[26] There were several other incidents in the surrounding area. It is not known how many Watton people actually participated in the Rising, although it seems likely that some at least of the 'Watton mafia' got involved. One who definitely did is John Payn, who participated in the attack on Saham in 1375 and, as 'John Payn of Woton', was listed in an indictment of those who attacked the house of a wealthy merchant of Norwich, Henry Lumenour, during the Rising.[27]

Someone who played an ambivalent role in this disturbed period was Thomas Neve of Watton. Already noted as a debtor in 1366,[28] he was one of those ordered to be detained in the gaol of Norwich Castle in 1375. His name headed the list of those assessed for the poll tax in Watton which, although the assessment was low, suggests that he was an important figure in the town. He also served as a member of the jury that presented the indictments of those who participated in the Rising of 1381.[29] The following year, he was prosecuted by the Prior of Pentney (who owned land in Watton) because, allegedly, he 'took and carried away the goods and chattels of the said prior to the value of 40 marks found at Watton, and took and abducted Matilda Canon, his native tenant [someone who held land from him in exchange for various services and payments], who was there, by which the said prior lost the services of his said servant for a great time, and other enormities'.[30] Despite his allegedly unruly behaviour, a later source, of 1404, described Thomas Neve as a chaplain and referred to his ownership of lands and tenements not only in Watton but in several other parishes.[31] In 1411 he granted land in Ovington to another chaplain, William Rokel of Saham, perhaps a relative of the family that had given its name to Rokeles Hall.[32] John Neve, probably a descendant, was recorded as a landholder on the manor of Rokeles Hall in 1469.[33]

The impression gained from all these episodes is of a breakdown of state authority and a free-for-all among those who could command sufficient support to take the law into their own hands. At the same time, however, the economic and social life of the country continued. The basic unit within which that happened was the manor. Little evidence survives from the manor of Watton Hall in this period, but there are a few documents from the manor of Rokeles, or Rokells as it was often written, at the end of the 15th century which yield useful information about the parish as a whole.

ℰℭ

The earliest document relating to the manor of Rokeles that has been found so far contains the accounts of John Hobbys, the bailiff, for the two years ending 3 March 1469.[34] The accounts listed the rents due to the lord of the manor and a few items of manorial expenditure. It would seem that the normal administration of the manor was being re-established following a period of disruption (perhaps owing to the Wars of the Roses, raging at the time), as the landholders had to pay four years' arrears of rent as well as what they owed for 1468-69. The accounts recorded the names of the manor's tenants, providing, for example, the first evidence for the Ficket family, discussed later. They also referred to places in the eastern part of Watton, including 'myllefeld' and some of the furlongs and enclosures. The 'site of the manor' was rented out, which could indicate that the original manor house, which may have stood on a moated site nearer to the Little Wissey than the present Rokeles Hall, no longer existed but had not yet been replaced by the present building. John Hobbys paid the lord of the manor some of the arrears of rent due to him 'at Watton Mere'. Perhaps they had arranged to go fishing there.

More informative than the accounts of 1469 are those compiled by a later bailiff of Rokeles Hall, Ralph Platfoot, for the years ending Michaelmas 1482, 1483, 1484 and 1486, the last being incomplete.[35] At the time, Platfoot's employer was receiving not only the rents due to the lord of the manor of Rokeles but also those owed to the manor of Watton Hall and the manor of Woodhouse in Saham and Ovington.

The rents received by the manor of Watton Hall included the profits of the fairs and markets in Watton. There were three fairs: on the feast of St Peter and St Paul (29 June), the feast of St Michael the Archangel (Michaelmas, 29 September) and the feast of St Simon and St Jude (28 October). The fair held on the feast of St Michael was the most profitable. In 1482, it yielded 4s (equivalent to about £140 today) in tolls and other payments, while the other two fairs realised 3s 4d each.

In the market, there were 16 stalls in 1482 and 1483, 17 in 1484 and 16 in 1486, the annual rental of each being 8d (equivalent to about £23 today). There were also 'strangers' stands in the market place' but apparently no rent was collected from them. Money had to be spent on repairing some of the stalls and carrying wood for the purpose from Saham. Rents amounting to 20s were also received for 'divers shoppez…situated in the row', probably a reference to more permanent buildings that had developed along the street in Watton. There were ten shops and their tenants were 'drapers and rafmen'. Rafmen were probably candle-makers and grocers, and were a recognised group in Norwich.[36] The drapers facilitated the local textile industry, Watton having been 'a small worsted weaving centre from the fourteenth century'.[37] In 1483, William Edrich was paid 20d 'for daubing in defective places on the shops', indicating that these were probably timber-framed structures with walls of wattle and daub. In 1486, two additional shops had appeared, with higher rents.

A clerk of the market was employed to collect the rents. The stallholders also had to pay tolls, additional to their rents. Thomas Davy of Wymondham paid 7s for the use of a 'house called Le Tolhous' [tollhouse], which was in what is now Middle Street. It was here that the market traders would have paid their tolls, which would have enabled Thomas Davy to make a profit on his rent of the building. He was the 'farmer' of the tolls.

The greater part of the income of the manor came from the rents paid by the tenants for their lands. Much of the manorial land was now leased, usually for seven but sometimes for five, ten or more years. Payments in money had been substituted for the haymaking and harvest work formerly undertaken by the 'bond' or 'native' tenants and for the hens and capons that they had supplied. There was still one important distinction between free and 'native' tenants, however. If the latter wished to bequeath or sell their land, they had to conduct the transaction in the manor court and pay a small fine, the deeds to their properties being copies of the manor court roll recording the transaction. They became known as customary or copyhold tenants and the land was known as copyhold (as distinct from freehold) land. By the 16th century, many landowners, large and small, owned or leased both freehold and copyhold land, with the copyhold land often held from more than one manor.

In 1482, the proceeds of the 'farm' (renting out) of the manorial lands of Watton Hall were over £8 11s (equivalent to about £6,000 today), of which over £5 10s came from the lease of closes, meadows, pasture and a foldcourse (the right to graze sheep on the commons and common fields) to Sir Robert Wingfield, a member of a powerful family based in East Harling. The lands of Rokeles realised £6 11s 5d, and so Watton Hall, which also benefitted from the income from the market and fairs amounting to £2 8s 4d (equivalent to about £1,700 today), was the larger and more profitable manor.

The accounts provide further evidence of the names given to some of the different pieces of land in the parish. Some are readily identifiable. 'Weylond Wode' was mentioned, as was 'the field of Weylond', otherwise 'Weylond Feld', an area of open arable land in the southern part of Watton. As in 1469, reference was also made to Millefeld and several names connected with Rokeles Hall: Rokell Clos, Rokell Yerd, Rokelhill and Rokell Medwe (Rokeles Meadow), the last having also been noted in the 14th century perambulation of Saham common and in the accounts of 1469. In 1482, Robert Platfoot recorded that it was 'previously mown for the use of the lord' but yielded nothing for him in 1482 'because of rainy weather in the summer' (some things never change). Other names mentioned included Brygwong, Longlond, Wetlond, Sondhill (sand hill), Sexiswong and Salteresmoor. Much of the arable and meadow land was still held in small pieces of an acre or so, but some had already been consolidated into larger units and several pasture closes had been created.

As well as the repair of the market stalls, Ralph Platfoot also had to arrange payment for the maintenance of other assets on the manors. The hedge around one of the pasture closes needed attention in 1482, as did the pinfold (the pound, located at the junction of Church Walk and Dereham Road, where stray animals were penned), for which wood, and hooks and hinges for the gate, were required. The following year, more work was done on the hedges and a drain at 'Rokell Medwe' was unblocked, no doubt to prevent the meadow from flooding.

※

In 1485, the Wars of the Roses came to an end with the defeat of King Richard III at the Battle of Bosworth. The victor was Henry Tudor, Henry VII. The manor of Rokeles Hall may have come into the new king's hands, explaining why the accounts for 1481-86 have been preserved in the National Archives.

Watton now entered the 'early modern' period, the 16th and 17th centuries' during which England was ruled by the Tudors and then, after the union of the crowns of

England and Scotland in 1603, the Stuarts. Apart, that is, from the period 1649–1660, when, following the execution of Charles I, it had no monarch at all.

We will now jump forward to 1542, towards the end of the reign of King Henry VIII.

## Notes

1. Inquisition Post Mortem, Margery, late the wife of William de Ros of Hamelak (1364); TNA, C 135/179/1.
2. Inquisition Post Mortem, John de Roos, 1422; TNA, C 138/60/58.
3. Accounts for various manors, including Watton; TNA, SC 6/1121/15.
4. Ronan Mackay, 'Rochelle (Rokele, Rokesle, Rupella, Rupellis), Richard de la', in the online *Dictionary of Irish Biography* (2009). Many thanks to Alice Gilsenan for this reference.
5. The information in this and the first two paragraphs of this section comes from F Blomefield (1805) and geni.com.
6. F Blomefield (1805).
7. Many thanks to Kathryn Stallard for this information.
8. A small piece of land near the supposed site of the manor was known as 'Market Pightle' in the early 19th century but was probably the place where animals were kept prior to being taken to the market. Abstract of title of Charles Dorr deceased to freehold premises in Watton, 1801-45; NRO, MS 7858 19 D 1. Probably for the same reason, an enclosure on Back Street was called 'Market Close'.
9. Tom Williamson, The Origins of Norfolk (Manchester UP, 1993).
10. Stephen Heywood, *The church of St Mary, Watton, Norfolk: Statement of Significance* (Norfolk County Council, 2009); NHER 8795; Watton church guide.
11. For example, in the will of Thomas Ficket, 1558; NRO, ANW Hychekocke, fo 731.
12. Poll tax assessments, 1380; TNA, E179 149/48.
13. NRO, MS 20937 47 B 5.
14. V Watts (2004).
15. TNA, C 138/60/58.
16. The location of Watton Mere can be established precisely from a detailed description of the parish boundary of Watton by the parliamentary enclosure commissioners, reported in the NC, 20 November 1802; the boundary passed near 'the north-east corner of an old enclosure called Meer Meadow', and is further confirmed by the map attached to a conveyance of 1838, which shows 'First Meer Meadow' and 'Further Meer Meadow': NRO, ACC 2023/12.
17. Calendar of patent rolls, 1350.
18. Wikipedia.
19. Calendar of patent rolls, 1361.
20. Calendar of Inquisitions Miscellaneous, Vol III, 1348-77.
21. Plea rolls of the Court of King's Bench; TNA, KB27/485.
22. Two have the same surnames but different forenames.
23. Calendar of patent rolls, 1375.
24. TNA, C 241/146/17. Canoun had also been noted as a debtor the previous year: TNA, C 241/146/24.
25. Calendar of patent rolls, 1375.
26. TNA, KB 9 166/1.
27. TNA, KB 27/489.

28. TNA, C 241/146/35.
29. TNA, KB9 166/1.
30. TNA, CP40/485.
31. Charter/grant, Thomas Neve to Richard Geggh and others, 26 May 1404; NRO, WALS I/19 407x2.
32. D1273, *Catalogue of Ancient Deeds*, Vol 3.
33. Manor of Rockells Hall, bailiff's account, 1467-69; TNA, SC6/945/3.
34. Ibid.
35. Manor of Rokeles Hall, bailiff's account, 1481-82, 1482-83 and 1483-84; TNA, SC 6/945/4-6. Manor of Rokeles Hall, bailiff's account (income only), 1485-86; TNA, SC 6/HENVII/429.
36. Mary Wallace, *Medieval People of Norwich: Artists and Artisans* (King Street Publications, 1992).
37. Nigel Heard, *Wool: East Anglia's Golden Fleece* (Terence Dalton, 1976).

# The Land: Enclosures, Open Fields and Commons

It was 1542, and Elizabeth Fitzwilliam was not happy. In fact, she was hopping mad.

She had recently purchased the manor of Watton Hall with its buildings and lands from the Earl of Rutland, son of Baron Ros of Hamelak (Helmsley), the last member of the Ros or de Ros family to own the manor. Elizabeth believed her purchase to include 'a certeyn ground somtyme a meyre over flowen with water and nowe dryed upp and become a pastur'. This was the former mere, referred to in an inquisition on the death of John Lord de Roos in 1422 as a 'fishery' called Watton Mere,[1] which lay on the south side of the Little Wissey.

Elizabeth Fitzwilliam had decided to enclose the pasture where the mere used to be, 'for her moost commodyte profyt and avantage'. She 'causid a greate dyk to be cast to invyron the same parcell of land and sett the same with quyck sett for to mak ther a good sure and sufficyent hedge or inclosure to her great coste and charge as lefull [lawful] was for her to do'.

According to her account, Robert Rust of 'Nayton' (Neaton) arrived on the scene on 20 February 1542 with a group of men from Saham Toney, including Gregory Trendill, the parish constable. They came, alleged Elizabeth, 'in rytous maner' armed with 'swerds, bucklers [shields], daggers, billys, stavys and other weypeyns invasive,' and 'came and repayryd unto the said parcel of land [and] with force, strength and violence with such instruments and toolys as they then had with them ryotously and wilefully did cast downe 20 roodes [about 100 metres] of the said dyche and pullyd upp and utterly destroyed the quyck sett being in the same. And', she continued, 'not with this contented nor satisfied the said [men from Saham Toney] have at sundry times sythen [since] the breykyng downe of the said dyche fellyd cut and caryed aweye the grasse growing in and upon the same parcel of land so inclosyd and converted the same to ther owne syngler profytt and avantage'. As a result, claimed Elizabeth Fitzwilliam, she 'cannot use occupie nor inioye the said parcel of land as her several [separate, private] ground without myche difficulty and danger'. She asked that the offenders be summoned to appear before the king and his council in the Court of Star Chamber in Westminster, to answer her charges.

Robert Rust replied to Elizabeth Fitzwilliam's complaint. He claimed that he was not guilty of any of the charges other than the 'breaking downe of teene [ten, not 20] rodds of the seid dicke', which he was authorised to do because the land enclosed was part of the manor of Saham Toney, held at the time by King Henry VIII himself. At a meeting of the manor court in Saham on 13 January 1542, he said, Gregory Trendell and 13 others had sworn that John Payn, 'servant of Lady Fitzwilliam, by special order of the said Elizabeth, joined with many other unknown persons, made a dyke…called a quycke sett within the common of Saham' the previous November. The 'ditching and enclosing part of that common to the separate use of the said Elizabeth', he maintained, was 'to the disinheritance and contempt of the said lord king and the grave detriment of the tenants'. The manor court had fined Elizabeth 10s and ordered her to level the dyke, after which Elizabeth had 'cawsed parte of the seid dyche …to be plukid and caste downe'.

However, alleged Robert Rust, she had then, 'by the procurement and importune labour of oon John Jenney esquier' [who was leasing the manor of Saham at the time] caused 'another dicke within the said common to be repared and made and an other grounde nuelie to be enclosed and kept several to her owne oonlie use', to the prejudice of the king and also to, 'the great hynderance and empoverisshement of the kingez tenantez of the said manour of Saham Tonye who doon cleyme..to have common of pasture within the seid grownde soo enclosed being for the most parte medowe grounde conteigning by estimacon eightie acres at the leaste'. Rust claimed that, as bailiff of the manor, he had then consulted the surveyors of the king's estates and had been ordered to 'immediatlie cawse the seid quyck sett to be throwen downe and the seid grounde soo inclosed to be leied open ageyne'. Rust then instructed two employees 'to goo to the seid dicke…in peaseable manner with ther worken tooles to cast and throwe down the seid dicke'. Rust denied that the enclosed ground 'was at any tyme any parcel of the manor of Watton'; on the contrary, he insisted, it 'hath ben alweies demed, accepted, reputed and taken to be within the bowndez and lymittes of Saham Tonye'. Elizabeth Fitzwilliam's case, he argued, should be dismissed.[2]

And it may have been, as no 80-acre enclosure of meadow was mentioned in a rental of Watton Hall in 1595.[3] The 16th century copy of the 14th century perambulation of the boundaries of Saham common, mentioned previously, was very likely produced at this time and may have supported Robert Rust's case but the crucial factor was probably the king's ownership, at the time, of the manor of Saham Toney.

By the end of the 18th century, however, Mere Meadow had once again been enclosed and brought into the ownership of the Manor of Watton Hall.

ഇഗ

The vividly described confrontation of Elizabeth Fitzwilliam and Robert Rust illustrates the tension generated in the first half of the 16th century by the enclosing of common and open field land and their conversion into privately owned pasture grounds for grazing sheep, from which good profits could be made. This was not the first instance of the enclosure of land in Watton. As is evident from the Rokeles Hall accounts of 1482-84, pasture 'closes' had already been created, and some of the arable land and much of the meadow land had been consolidated and enclosed. For landowners and leaseholders, enclosing the land meant not only that they could convert it from arable to pasture, but also, if the land remained arable, that they could prevent other people exercising a right of 'shackage', grazing their sheep or cattle on the stubble after harvest. The value of the land would be increased.

When the government set up a commission to investigate the issue in 1517, the commissioners found that, in Watton, 'Robert Strange made a close of 77 acres which were ploughed in the time of the said commissioners and now are totally converted into pasture and the shack [right of shackage] is lost'.[4] It is possible that Robert Strange was leasing the lands of the manor of Watton Hall at the time, and that this close was the same as that named as 'Halle Closse,' with an area of 80 acres, in a rental of the demesne lands of the manor compiled in 1595.[5] By that time, almost all the demesne land of Watton Hall comprised closes or large blocks of meadow. As well as Hall Close, the rental referred to the Hill Close (20 acres of pasture), the Lord's Meadow (30 acres), 'Moore Close' (12 acres) and Moore Meadowe (20 acres). These enclosures seem to have been mainly on the west and south-west sides of Watton.

Resentment of the enclosing of open fields and commons in Norfolk was widespread, and contributed to the support shown for Robert Kett's rebellion in 1549, when a large 'camp' of rebels was established at Watton and remained there for two weeks before moving on to join Kett at Mousehold Heath. At least one rebel is known to have come from Watton;. He was John Bougion, husbandman, who was imprisoned after the rebellion but was pardoned on 8 March 1550.[6]

೫ಙ

The tensions caused by competing demands on the land continued into the 17th century. They are illustrated by a case in the Court of Chancery in 1620, in which Henry Palmer, the leaseholder of the Wick Farm estate, issued a complaint against tenants of the manor of Watton Hall, and specifically against Edward and Charles Hey, sons and heirs of the deceased Christopher Hey (grandfather of his namesake who built Watton's Clock Tower), who had been one of the principal shopkeepers in Watton.

Wick Farm, at Watton Wick, formerly known as Monk's Wick, occupied the land given to Thetford Priory by Ranulf Fitzwalter shortly after Domesday Book was compiled. The small estate remained in the monks' possession until, following Henry VIII's break with the Pope, the priory was dissolved in 1540. The monks had kept sheep. For a period in the early 16th century, the priory leased the foldcourse of the manor of Watton Hall at 10s per year. Subsequently, it rented pasture called 'le waste grownd' for 13s 4d. Shepherds were employed to care for the 200 sheep that were grazed there. In 1521-22, the monks purchased oats and rye for feeding the animals during a 'great freeze' that winter. Barley was grown on the farm and was malted, presumably for brewing.

Shortly before they lost it, the monks had invested heavily in the premises at Watton Wick. Repairs were made to the stable in 1532-33 and then, in 1535-36, a new barn was erected, at the considerable cost of £26 6s 10d (equivalent to over £11,600 today). Payments were made for bricks, for 'rede' for thatching the roof, for clay and for 'dawbynge', suggesting that the barn was partly of brick and partly timber-framed, with the spaces between the timbers filled with wattle and daub. In 1536-37, two men were employed, with their assistants, for 20 and 15 days respectively for 'redyng' or thatching the roof. The priory also used the Vicar of Watton as their agent to arrange the 'rammyng and levelyng' of the ground outside the barn.[7] Regrettably, no trace remains of what, in its day, must have been an impressive structure, but it would, no doubt, still have been there when Henry Palmer made his complaint.

After the dissolution of Thetford Priory in 1540, its property at Watton Wick came into the ownership of Thomas de Grey of Merton Hall, who, in 1561, leased it for 900 years to Thomas Palmer, vicar of Watton from 1528 to 1557. The estate comprised 160 acres of land, meadow and pasture, along with a 'shepes course, common and shacke for sheepe'.[8] The lease was inherited by Thomas Palmer's nephew, Henry Palmer and then by Henry's son, also called Henry.

In his complaint to the Court of Chancery, Henry Palmer junior stated that for several years he had been in possession of a 'capitall messuage called the Wike and divers lands to the same belonging' and claimed that, attached to this property, had been 'a libertie of fouldcourse and common of pasture for fowre hundred sheepe…at all times of the yeare and in and upon the arable feildes of Watton… at such times of the yeare as the same lye unsowne'. That is, until about 30 years previously, when Henry Palmer, his father, was 'very younge and ignorant of his estate', and was worried about the prospect of conflict with the tenants of the manor of Watton Hall, who had claimed (falsely, according to Henry junior) that 'manye lands belonging to the said capital messuage were by Thomas Palmer [the former vicar]…latelye inclosed and kept severall', thus depriving the tenants of their rights of shackage.

Henry senior had agreed to submit the matters in dispute to arbitration and the arbitrators had decreed that he should keep no more than 80 sheep on the common and fields but that, in compensation, he should also be allowed to pasture his 'great cattell' there, as the tenants of the manor did. But, according to Henry Palmer junior, the tenants had abused the award, putting great numbers of not only cattle but also of their own sheep on the pasture and 'shack' of the common fields. They even, he alleged, threatened to impound Henry's own cattle.

As one of the tenants against whom he had complained, Christopher Hey, had died,[9] Palmer sought to subpoena his sons and heirs, Edward and Charles Hey, because they 'oppresse and overcharge the said common and shacke wt their sheepe as their father Christopher Hey had used to doe'. The outcome is not known but the case illustrates the tensions that enclosure was still causing, the pressure on the remaining common lands from both leaseholders and manorial tenants, and perhaps also the growing power of Watton's commercial elite, in the early 17th century.[10]

ఎరాస

The process of enclosure continued, slowly but inexorably, in a gradual and piecemeal manner, throughout the 16th and 17th centuries. Many of the new closes were quite small. In 1597, for example, Henry Ficket referred to 'five acres new enclosed in the fields of Watton called Dunsburrowe,'[11] William Jarvys, who died in 1608, had three enclosures in different parts of the parish: 'one arable close conteyninge by estimacion three acres lyinge in the [open] feild of Watton'; 'one acre of coppihould ground inclosed lyinge att watton greene'; and 'my inclosse lying nigh Wayland woode'.[12] Robert Brett (died 1614) and Richard Lincoln (died 1620) both referred in their wills to their pasture closes.[13] A later Henry Ficket (died 1650) bequeathed 'one close of pasture conteyning by estimacion...seaven acres and a half, parte whereof is not inclosed lyeing in a place called Shorne Hill Bush'.[14] Ambrose Dunn surrendered 4 acres of land 'lately enclosed' in Bridge Wong in 1671.[15]

Over time, some of the larger enclosures created previously were subdivided. Stephen Dunham (who died in 1625), provided an example of the sub-division of a close, referring in his will to 'one close called the Bushy Close...in Neton Street in Watton and half the errable close lyeinge at the south end of the Bushy Close as it is now parted with railes'.[16] Mayses Close, formerly Wong Close, a pasture close on the east side of Cley Lane said in 1583 to have been 18.5 acres,[17] had been divided into two closes by the early 18th century.[18]

ఎరాస

Although many pasture closes existed in Watton, much unenclosed common land remained, and was to remain until the parliamentary enclosure of Watton in 1803. Much of the common was low-lying; the boundary of the common that survived in 1803 followed, broadly, the 150 foot contour line, with the common lying below it. Wick Farm stood on the edge of the common that extended southwards into Merton, westwards to the stream that ran into the Little Wissey and northwards to the Little Wissey itself. This was a mixture of rough grazing land and fen, where the monks of Thetford Priory had grazed their sheep until the dissolution of the priory. Its extent had probably not changed significantly since the 'mettes and boundes perteynyng to the common of Saham Thony' had been described in the

14th century.

The boundary between the parishes of Watton and Merton, which ran across the common, became a matter of dispute in 1539-40, when the De Greys of Merton Hall complained that 'the chaplains of Watton [perhaps a reference to the monks from Thetford Priory at Watton Wick] made a certain cross at Maidswell as a new bound or division for the…town of Watton, to the detriment of the lord of [Merton], for that the said parcel of land called Maidswell is within the common of Merton and not within the bounds of the town of Watton'.[19] There were still 'controversies and disputes' about the 'ancient waste or comon [sic] called Merton and Watton Comon', as late as 1770, involving the lords of the manor of Watton and Merton and other landholders in Watton 'concerning the said waste or common and their respective rights of common of pasture and common of turbary [the right to cut turves for fuel] thereupon'.

As a result, a surveyor, Clement Overton of Watton, was commissioned to make a fair and equal division of the common and make a boundary between the two parishes.[20] The boundary was paced by the inhabitants of Watton when they 'beat the bounds' of the parish at Rogationtide (the fifth Sunday after Easter) and, in the late 18th century, the tenant of Wick Farm was expected to give a leg of pork and a barrel of beer to the participants.[21] This large area of common on the western side of Watton began at the end of the street, where the Junior School stands now. Even though what is now Brandon Road may have been a Roman road, it and Swaffham Road would have been little more than tracks across the waste land.

Common land continued along the south side of the Little Wissey, past the site of the former Watton Mere. Neaton Fen was an area of wet common north of the hamlet of Neaton. Further east, where the parish of Watton extended north of the Little Wissey, was 'the common pasture of Watton…commonly called Rockolls alias Redhill'.[22] The name of another significant area of common land lying to the north and east of Rokeles Hall has been preserved to this day as Watton Green, which was sometimes known as Rokeles Green. A scatter of farms and cottages hugged the boundaries of the Green. These areas of common were all to remain open until enclosed by Act of Parliament in 1803.

༄༅

Despite the gradual enclosure of both large and small areas of the open fields in the 16th and 17th centuries, two areas of 'common field' (open arable land) remained in Watton. They were called Mill Field, which lay in the east of the parish, and Wayland or Wood Field, which extended towards Wayland Wood in the south-east. The land in these fields was divided into furlongs. Furlongs comprised blocks of strips, long thin pieces of land of an acre or so belonging to different landholders, many of which lay unenclosed. Each furlong had its own distinctive name.

A 'terrier' (list of lands) of Rokeles Hall compiled in 1550 gave the names of many of the furlongs and other features of the landscape.[23] The evidence in this document, supplemented by that in a lease of 1650[24] and by references in wills and deeds, provides clues about the location of some of the furlongs, although most cannot be placed precisely.

Mill Field lay both north and south of the road from Watton to Hingham and Norwich. The mill after which it was named was a windmill which between two old lanes running southwards from the road, called Broadmere Lane and Wood Lane.[25] This was probably the mill recorded in the 1595 rental as held by Robert Porter. It may still have been in existence in 1641, when a piece of arable land was described in a deed as 'nigh unto the wyndemill'.[26]

On the south side of the Hingham road, moving from east to west, were Sondehill (sand hill) and Shorne Hill Bush, where Henry Ficket had a pasture close straddling the boundaries of Watton, Carbooke and Griston. After that came Overgate Furlong (the 'gate', an Old Norse term, probably referring to the Hingham road), south of which lay Upper and Lower Posterlond (or Postellon) Furlong. The next furlong to the west was Delpyt Furlong followed by Oak Furlong. South of them lay Hyllefurlong and Anowe Furlong (which may incorporate the element 'howe' and refer to a Bronze-Age round barrow). Then, after Griston Road, adjacent to Broadmere Lane, were Broadmere Field,[27] Mill Furlong and, stretching away beyond it to the south, Overmill Furlong.

On the north side of the road, after the enclosures which lay south and west of Rokeles Hall were Green Croft Furlong, Overstede Furlong, Baxterwong, Berys Pece (perhaps just after the turning for Watton Green) and Nether Mill Furlong (opposite Mill Furlong on the south side of the road). Further to the north-west was Brigwonge, described as abutting on Thetford Way, which may have meant Redhill Lane, coming from Rokeles Bridge.[28] Rokeles Meadow covered a large area on both sides of the Little Wissey. North of the river was an area of pasture ground called Hothemore. A lane called Knotts Lane ran from Rokeles towards the town centre and another ran directly from Rokeles Green to Neaton. Slight traces of these ancient routes can be seen on air photographs and a LiDAR image.

Wayland or Wood Field lay between Wayland Wood and the market town. According to a rental of the properties of Lord Walsingham of Merton compiled in 1624, Wayland Wood, which the family had purchased, comprised 65 acres,[29] plus a further 36 acres in the adjacent 'Colledge Close' and Harp Pightle, the latter being referred to in another rental of 1630 as 'my wood close'.[30] Near the wood was Wayland Reede, which abutted on Heighmere to the east.[31] Crundle (an Old English term for a chalk pit, later corrupted into 'Crowne Hill'), subdivided into Nethercrundle and Overcrundle, lay near a lane running from Wayland Wood to Watton Wick.[32] At the corner where Barn Ruche stands today was Great Spicers Close.[33] Between there and the town centre, on the east side of the road, were furlongs called Long Bradfresshe and Short Bradfresshe.[34] Lying further east were the confusingly named Long Long Furlong, Long Furlong and Short Long Furlong. Game Furlong lay west of Short Long Furlong. Wood Furlong and Dunsburgh (or Dunsburrowe, where Henry Ficket had enclosed five acres of land shortly before 1597) were other furlongs that lay in Wayland or Wood Field. Wetlond Furlong was near Watton Wick, abutting on the road from Watton to Merton, and later became a ten-acre close called Wetlands.

Such was the rural landscape in which many of the inhabitants of early-modern Watton lived and worked. But the centre of the community's economic and social activities, which was probably where the majority of the population lived, was the market place and the street to its west. This was Watton's beating heart.

## Notes

1. TNA, C 138/60/58.
2. TNA, STAC 2/15/97. This and the preceding four paragraphs are based on this source.
3. NRO, NRS 18144 33A3. There was an 80 acre enclosure, but it was not meadow.
4. I S Leadam (ed), 'The inquisition of 1517: Inclosures and Evictions', an edited edition of Lansdowne MS I153, in *Transactions of the Royal Historical Society*, Vol 7 (1893). The editor points out that Robert Strange was not the lord of the manor and may be identified with Sir Robert L'Estrange, who died in 1511.
5. NRO, NRS 18144 33A3.
6. Calendar of patent rolls, Edward VI, iii.
7. *The Register of Thetford Priory*, (ed) David Dymond, Norfolk Record Society (2 vols, 1994-6).
8. Will of Thomas Palmer, 1564; TNA, PROB11/47/148.
9. Christopher Hey the elder died in 1617.
10. Palmer v Hey, 6 February 1620; TNA, C2/Jas I/P26/19.
11. Will of Henry Ficket, 1597; NRO, ANW Lyncolne fo 185. 'Dunsburrowe' may refer to the site of a round barrow but unfortunately its location cannot be established precisely.
12. Will of William Jarvys, 1608; NRO, ANW Remaine fo 37.
13. Will of Robert Brett, 1614; NRO, ANW, fo 163; will of Richard Lincoln, 1620; NRO, NCC Williams 155.
14. Will of Henry Ficket, 1650; NRO, ANW, 1648-52, fo. 331, no. 309. This piece of land was described similarly in the will of John Fecket, 1624; NRO, ANW 1626-29, fo 226.
15. Manor court book, Manor of Rokeles Hall; NRO, MC3243/59.
16. Will of Stephen Dunham, 1625; NRO, ANW, 1624-25, fo 551.
17. Will of James Hansard, 1583; NRO, ANW 1580-83, Reinold fo 381. Hansard bequeathed Wong Close to his wife for her life and after her death to his grandson, Thomas Mayes.
18. Admission of Thomas Younge to properties formerly of Edward Younge, Manor of Watton Hall, 1761; NRO, NRO, BL/CS 8/6/1.
19. G Crabbe (1883).
20. Articles of agreement between Thomas de Grey, lord of the manor of Merton and William Henry Fleming, lord of the manor of Watton, 30 June 1770; NRO, WLS XXXI/13.
21. Thomas Barton, *Notices of the Town and Parish of Watton*, in Norfolk Archaeology, Volume 3 (1852).
22. Robert Heighoe to Robert Scott, Lease of Rokeles Hall, 1650; NRO, WLS VII/I 408x3.

23. Terrier of the manor of Rokeles, 1550; TNA, SC 11/482.
24. Robert Heighoe to Robert Scott, Lease of Rokeles Hall, 1650; NRO, WLS VII/I 408x3.
25. An enclosure here was called 'Mill Piece'; Sale Particulars of the estates of Charles Dorr, 1845, in private possession.
26. Margaret Turner and George Lawes to Christopher Hey, 1641; NRO, BL/CS 8/6/1.
27. Mentioned in the Watton glebe terrier of 1706; NRO, DN/TER 159/4; and also in Sale Particulars of the estates of Charles Dorr, 1845, in private possession.
28. Manor court book, Manor of Rokeles Hall; NRO, MC3243/59. Church Walk was described in an early 19th century deed as 'formerly the road from Watton to Dereham'.
29. Today, the area of Wayland Wood is 76 acres: woodlandtrust.org.uk.
30. Rentals of properties belonging to the Walsinghams of Merton, 1624 and 1630; NRO, WLS IX/7; G Crabbe (1883).
31. Will of Henry Lincolne, 1640; NRO, ANW 1640-43, fo 99.
32. Blomefield (1805) stated that, before the dissolution of the monasteries, the Prior of Pentney held 15 acres in Watton called Crundale.
33. As shown in the map book of the estates of Thomas de Grey, 1723; NRO, MF/RO 90/2.
34. It is tempting to equate Bradfresshe with Broadflash, although the present Broadflash Farm lies further to the south, in Merton parish.

# The Market Place and the Street

In 1384, an inquisition was conducted at 'Watton Market',[1] the earliest use of that phrase encountered so far.

Throughout the 16th century, the inhabitants of Watton often described themselves as being from 'Watton Market'. Had the appellation stuck, we might be calling the town 'Watton Market' today, like 'Downham Market' and 'Pulham Market', but it didn't. Nevertheless, the use of the phrase highlights how important the market had now become and how central it was to the community's identity and sense of itself. 'Watton Market' also distinguished the area around the market place from the outlying parts of the parish: Watton Green, Neaton and Watton Wick.

It is impossible to say exactly how many people lived in Watton in the 16th and 17th century but several sources give a rough indication. A detailed analysis of the data from the registers of baptisms and burials kept by Watton's vicars from 1539 onwards, undertaken by Julian Horn, led him to the conclusion that: 'up to 1580, the size of the town was fairly constant at around 300 souls [which could be consistent with the 56 names of adult men recorded in the muster list of 1577.[2] There was then a period of expansion, particularly rapid over the first 25 years continuing thereafter at a slower rate'.[3] The growth of the population would have been slowed by the high death rate in certain periods: in 1545 and 1555-65; in 1635-50; and for ten years after 1657, probably owing largely to epidemic disease. In 1635-50, the Civil War between the supporters of King Charles I and parliament would also have been a contributory factor.

The hearth tax assessment of 1664[4] recorded 60 households, while the assessment of 1667[5] added 45 more, the homes of the poor who were 'not chargeable'. Taking the figure of 105, and assuming the average household size at this time was about 4.5, this might provide a total for the population of 460–480.

ஐ൪

Most of these people lived around the market place and in the street. The market place was larger than it is now, including the whole of the area between what are now Middle Street and High Street, and extending to Dereham Road.

A focal point for the people of the town was the market cross, which stood on the west side of the market place. The authors of several 17th century wills specified that legacies were to be paid to their recipients there, which would have added

*The town centre as shown on the enclosure map, 1803.*
(Norfolk Record Office, C/Sca 2/316)

to the solemnity of the transaction. A deed of 1786 referred to 'the market house or cross' and to the rights of 'setting and fixing stalls…within the market cross of Watton', which suggests that the market cross was a fairly substantial structure.[6] It was supported on wooden pillars, between two of which were the stocks, the place of punishment for those who misbehaved. A payment was made in 1786 for 'stocks mending and painting', which indicates that they were still in use at that time, possibly for the public humiliation of unmarried mothers.[7] In earlier times there had also been a pillory, described as 'old' in 1605[8] but it or a replacement was still in use in 1712 when Nicholas Whisker of Great Cressingham, miller, was ordered to be placed in it for substituting chalk for a third of the corn he had ground for a widow from Saham Toney.[9]

The market cross was demolished in 1820 and replaced by a 'neat obelisk'.[10] The obelisk did not remain for long; it was still there in 1864[11] but had been removed by 1869, according to testimony given by an elderly inhabitant of the town in 1899.[12] When the Clock Tower was renovated in the 1820s, one of the lintels connecting the pillars of the market cross, featuring a carved hare and a barrel (the pun on the name of Watton), was incorporated into its façade. It remained until the 1980s, when it was replaced by a modern piece of wood of the same shape, but without the hare and barrel.

Another building which stood in the market place was the tollhouse referred to in the accounts of 1482-84, where the holders of market stalls paid their tolls. The building was also mentioned in a will of 1503 as 'the tollhows'[13] and in a rental of the manor of Watton Hall in 1595, as 'the towlehouse',[14] at which time the rent paid for it had fallen to 4s per year. It stood on the north side of the market place, in what is now Middle Street.[15]

Around the market place stood several inns and houses, the latter often fronted by shops where trade was conducted. The buildings were not all continuous; some adjoined each other but others were separated from their neighbours by gardens. Behind them were yards and stables and, in some cases, pasture closes.

The inns provided hospitality for people visiting the market. The earliest known reference to one of Watton's inns is to the *Swan*, mentioned as 'oon capitall measse [messuage] callyd the Swanne' in a plea to the Lord Chancellor submitted sometime between 1533 and 1538, during the reign of Henry VIII.[16] The *Swan* was on the south side of the market place, at what is now 13 High Street. It was referred to in the 1595 rental, when it was held by Edward Goffe, one of Watton's benefactors, who built the almshouses that stood where the Methodist Church car park is now. It is tempting to identify the *Swan* with a large property occupied by John Howard, gentleman, at the time of his death in 1662, as the inventory of Howard's possessions referred to a 'Swan chamber', but that is speculation.[17] Ownership of the *Swan* had passed to Richard Callibutt of Saham Toney before his death in 1668.

Another inn, which became Watton's premier hostelry, was the *George*, also on the south side of the market place, west of the *Swan*. It was referred to in 1591 as the 'capital messuage' of John Bettes, mercer (a dealer in textile fabrics),[18] and noted in 1595 as having 'groundes behind the howse'[19] amounting to about five acres.

The *Angel* was a property which stood immediately to the west of the market place. In 1595, John Bettes held half of this, too, and most of a close belonging to it, the other half of the house and the remainder of the close being held by Christopher Hey, grandfather of the builder of the Clock Tower. Another inn in Bettes' hands in 1595 was the *Christopher*, 'late Websters,' which John Webster, yeoman, had referred to in his will of 1567 as 'the house and the land therto belonging that I now dwell in commonlye called the Christover.'[20] The building had a parlour and a brewhouse.

Other inns recorded in 1595 were the *Gryffen* (on the site on which, later, the *Crown* was built) and the *Bull* (not the present *Bull*, but the forerunner of the *King's Arms*). Another was the *Dove*, formerly known as the *Westell* or *Wassell*, the location of which has not yet been discovered.[21]

༄༅

Several of the houses and shops around the market place were occupied by prosperous and influential business people. In 1595, Christopher Hey, who described himself in his will as a 'wollendraper', occupied a shop 'on the ste [south?] sid of the markytt place'[22] although his main residence was on the north side of the street and the west side of the market place.[23] This, his 'mansion howse with the shoppes ajoyninge unto yt against the market', had, he stated in his will, a hall and parlour and a chamber above 'where my menn lyeth' which contained 'all my brewing vesselles and copper with the maulte mill'.[24]

A grocer and mercer, William Jarvys, held a shop 'near the markytt crosse' in 1595. The will made before his death in 1608 provided an insight into the appearance of his premises, referring to 'my shop...wth all the shelves saltbings shopchists and other things going with the said shopp'. He also referred to 'all my wares in my shopps, warehouses or wheresoever'.[25]

Thomas Blumfeilde, who died in 1600, had a 'shoppe' but his premises also included a hall, a 'kitchyn' and a 'buttry', with chambers over them. Over the shop were two chambers, an upper and a lower, and so this part of the property had three storeys. Outside were a yard and stable. The shop contained many varieties of cloth, mostly in small quantities. 'Carsey' (Kersey), a coarse woollen cloth, was sold in a range of colours: willow green, sky, sage, milk and water, russet, woded russet,[26] tawny, red, 'graney' (scarlet) and mixed ('mingled' or 'medly'), the values ranging from 12d to 3s per yard (equivalent to about £7 and £21 today, respectively). 'Northern', also stocked by Blumfeilde, at around 5s per yard, was a more expensive variety of this cloth. Other woollens for sale in the shop included fearnought and rugg (thick fabrics), pampilion (a coarse and very cheap cloth), frieze (a rubbed cloth used for petticoats and linings), bayes and twill. Perhaps surprisingly at this early date, cottons, presumably imported, were stocked in white, black, green and 'coloured'; they were valued at 5d to 14d per yard. Like many shopkeepers throughout Watton's history, Thomas Blunfeilde was owed a lot of money when he died: over £100 in loans (equivalent to about £14,000 today) and over £180 'by the booke' for the sale of merchandise. Over half his debts were thought to be 'desperate' (not recoverable).[27]

George Francke was a humbler person, a cooper, who had a shop and a house in the street. Before he died in 1598, he asked his executors to 'white my howse and paven it on the streate syde';[28] which makes it tempting to imagine that, if others had the same wishes, the buildings facing the street were whitewashed and had a pavement in front of them.

Over time, reflecting the pressure of a rising population, many of the houses in the town were sub-divided and multi-occupied. Katherine Bywater, who died in 1640, left her son Thomas, 'my shoppe wherein he now dwelleth, and all the toolles and utensiles thereunto belonging. And also the greatest parte of the chamber of the shoppe...and one little roome called the parlor wherein Richard Nelson nowe dwelleth. And also parte and parcel of one yarde belonging to the shopp and parlor...extending from the ende of the parlor...eastwards to Sir

Edward Barkham's house with free ingresse and egresse and regresse acrosse and passinge...from the north gate of the said yard'.[29]

ഩര

One of the houses in the market place whose history can be reconstructed in detail stood immediately to the east of what is now the *King's Arms* in Middle Street. It was known as 'Paines' or 'Paynes' and was probably built by John Payne, who died in 1549 and referred in his will to 'my howse and yerdes that of late I new buyldyd'.[30] John Payne was the servant of Elizabeth Fitzwilliam, the lady of the manor of Watton Hall who had tried to enclose Mere Meadow in 1542, and he had clearly done well for himself. His property passed to his son Thomas Payne who, when he made his will in 1571, left what he called his 'mansion houses' to his wife, Alice, but reserved for his son, Henry, 'the little chamber that I doe nowe lye in to make him a shoppe withal when he come out of his apprentishood'.[31]

Later, 'Paines' was owned by Henry Ficket, who died in 1597,[32] after which it appears to have passed to John Fecket, who died in 1627. John bequeathed two adjacent parts of the property to different people: 'the howse...with the yard on the backe side so farr as the particion between the same howse and the howse where the wedow Browne dwell', and the 'howse where the wedowe Browne dwell... with the shop...with the yarde on the backside against the howse'.[33]

Subsequently, the property came into the possession of Thomas Bettes (possibly in 1654, when he acquired what was then called the *Bull*, now the *King's Arms*). Bettes' daughter, Anne, married Ralph Ives in 1656 and, in 1657, the latter was admitted at the manor court to a 'messuage built, that is to say one hall with twoe chambers built over the said hall and a yard to the same adioyninge...and one stable...and liberty to drawe, take and carrie watter in and from the well nowe or late apperteyneinge to the messuage...And also one cytchyn...conteyninge in length twenty and twoe foote and in bredth twenty and fower foote. And also one entry leading from the shop late Robert Tebold towards the aforesaid citchyn. And one garden called a yard as the same is divided by pales and other fences'. Anne was also admitted to 'one shop with a chamber thereupon built called a pikewall'[34] with access to the same well; to another shop 'on the east part of the messuage late Thomas Browne'; to 'one chamber above the said shop; and to 'percell of the west part of a stable...conteyninge in length nyne foote and in breadth one and twenty foote together with liberty of passuage and repassage to draw watter at the said well'.[35]

All very complicated! These details demonstrate, again, how properties were subdivided, added to and amalgamated over time. They also illustrate the importance of wells, from which the water supply of the people of Watton was derived. The *Bull*, next door to 'Paines', had a yard behind it, with access 'to a certain well late Thomas Paines'. A brewhouse, stable and barn opposite stood in the yard. Water from the well belonging to 'Paines', therefore, also supplied the water for brewing the beer sold at the *Bull*.[36]

༺༻

Occupying the whole of the market place were stalls. In 1486, there had been 16 stalls; in 1595, there were 45.[37] Although three had 'decayed' and were not tenanted at the time, the market of late 16th and early 17th century Watton was thriving.

And it was getting crowded, which led to disputes. Thomas Bettes, 'gentleman', probably son of the John Bettes mentioned in 1595, was alleged by William Jarvis, mercer (perhaps a son of the William Jarvis who died in 1608) to have confiscated, on 30 September 1620, 'two tilting cloathes [awnings], two trussells [trestles], five poales, six crutches, seaven fathome [about 13 metres] of small lyne and other things…apperteyninge to his stalls'. The reason, as Bettes explained in a complaint to the Court of Chancery, was that, according to custom, the spaces in front of the houses around the market place were reserved for stalls belonging to the owners and occupiers of those houses, 'to erect…and sett up at every market and fayre…stalls for petty chapmen [small traders] and others…to open and show there wares'. William Jarvis (unlike his possible father) did not have a house in the market place and had set up his stall in front of Thomas Bettes' dwelling, which may have been the *George* Inn. Bettes considered that he was within his rights to pull the stall down.[38]

The market stalls may once, as Thomas Bettes claimed, have been erected only in front of the houses but by the late 16th century most of them were arranged in rows, on an east-west alignment (parallel with the street). Among those in the market place in 1595 were three selling fish, sometimes referred to collectively as the 'fishmarket'. They were held by Christopher Hey and later by his son Charles Hey,[39] and were first referred to in 1570 in the will of Thomas Spicer, grocer, who held both the fish stalls and another stall 'next the merkett crosse'.[40] Two glovers' stalls were held by John Bowgen, or Bougeon, who followed the trade of glover himself.[41] Meat was sold in the market; in 1526–27 Thetford Priory had paid for 'meat bought at the market of Watton'[42] and one of the tenants of a stall listed in 1595, Robert Brett, was a butcher.[43] A later tenant, John Childerhouse of Saham (died 1637) had butchers' stalls in both Watton and Swaffham. The area where butchers carried on their trade was sometimes known as 'le butchery' or the 'butchers' shambles', and the descriptions of the stalls given in the manor court books indicate that they lay in the northern and western parts of the Market place. A stall in the butchery was described in 1714 as abutting on the market cross to the west.[44]

Like John Childerhouse, George Deney, grocer, who died 1622, had a stall in Swaffham market as well as a shop in Watton. Christopher Hey, too, had a shop in

Swaffham. By the same token, a number of the stallholders in Watton market may well have come from elsewhere, and made a living by selling their wares in different towns.

Over time, some of the stalls evolved into shops. In 1595, Christopher Hey held 'one shop somtymes two stalls'. The shops in the market place were also increasing in size. Francis Avenall paid rent for 'two shops now made into one'. George Deney (died 1622) mentioned in his will, 'one shop or stalls...lying in Watton marketstead',[45] and also ground that he had purchased from the lord of the manor for another shop at the east end of his original one. Such processes of consolidation and expansion may explain why the 1595 rental mentioned only nine shops, while in 1484 there had been ten. The shops for which separate rents were paid were probably free-standing, whereas the majority of shops were part of the buildings in which their owners resided.

The process of converting stalls into permanent structures continued over the centuries; William Thompson, who died in 1785, referred in his will to his 'stall... which I purchased from Nathaniel Stagg and is now a dwellinghouse'.[46] The eventual result, by the end of the 19th century, was the rows of permanent buildings, lying parallel to each other between what are now Middle Street and High Street, the west ends of which are now concealed by a façade facing the remaining, much-reduced market place in front of Wayland Hall.

ഗ്രര

From the market place, the built-up area of Watton extended westwards along the 'street'; that is, along what, today, is the north side of the High Street. John Turnor, for example, held 'a shop howse in Watton Streete'.[47] The buildings in the street had facades facing southwards, looking into the street, with ranges at right angles to them behind and yards, in some cases extending to 'the backside', which became Back Street and is now Harvey Street.

A passageway which still exists, next to what is now Edwards' newsagents, led from the street through to the backside. This was sometimes referred to as 'Middle Row', a name recalled as late as 1880, when the passage was referred to as 'formerly called Middle Row'.[48] Confusingly, however, the name Middle Row was also used in a broader sense to refer to the whole block of buildings stretching from the market place to and a little way beyond the passageway, the earliest known use of the phrase in this sense being in 1636.[49]

The plot immediately to the west of the passageway was owned by the Hornigold[50] family in the 17th century. It comprised 'a tenement called Le Barrell in Middle Row...viz a hall, a parlour, a shop, a buttery, a bakehouse, a mill house, a small stable'.[51] Immediately to its west was a garden on which the *Green Man* inn was to be built at the turn of the 17th and 18th centuries.

Beyond Middle Row, the street continued westwards, although much of this stretch was probably not built up until the second half of the 17th century and later. It was known as 'Rotten Row', the first known reference to the name being from 1672.[52] Occasionally, 'Rotten Row' was also used as a synonym for the 'backside' or 'backsideway'.[53] The origin of the name, 'Rotten Row' is unclear. A Rotten Row ran across Hyde Park in London, from Whitehall to Kensington Palace, from the late 17th century, its name possibly a corruption of 'route du roi' ('road of the king' in French),[54] and so one possibility is that the Watton version acquired its name in ironic imitation of its more illustrious namesake.[55]

Beyond the immediate vicinity of the market place, there were very few buildings on the south side of the street in the 16th and 17th centuries, an exception being the almshouses erected by Edward Goffe before his death in 1612, on the site now occupied by the car park of the Methodist Church.

ഽഐ

The market place and the street must have been a hive of activity, filled with the noises and smells of all the trades carried on there. They would have been especially busy on market days, and even more so on the days of the three fairs, which continued to take place on the same dates as in the late 15th century. No documentary evidence of the location of the fairs has been found so far. Finds from metal-detecting suggest that they may have taken place on a field adjacent to the minor road from Watton to Thompson but, additionally, stalls would have been erected in the market place on fair days. The fairs were profitable; in 1595, the bailiff of the manor of Watton Hall paid no less than 66s 8d (equivalent to over £500 today) for the power to collect the tolls and other charges levied on those who attended, which in 1484 had amounted to only 11s 8d.[56]

The lord of the manor of Watton Hall continued to collect dues from the town's market and fairs for another four centuries. In 1854, the Revd W H Hicks, lord of the manor, 'owner of the bailiwick [the area under the jurisdiction of his bailiff], fairs and markets of Watton…and of the ground and soil whereon such fairs and markets are held', had handbills printed warning 'that no person or persons will be allowed to place or fix any tent, booth, stall, table or stand, in or upon the Market-Place of Watton…without having previously paid the piccage and stallage dues'. Another handbill published the following year stated that temporary stalls or similar structures could only be erected in the Market Place on the day of the fair and had to be taken down by midnight, which suggests that the action continued well into the evening. Perhaps the same was true in the 16th and 17th centuries.[57]

ഽഐ

The centre of Watton was home to many trades, small industries and crafts. Several involved the processing of agricultural products.

Wool and linen were spun and woven. Thomas Blumfeilde, when he died in 1600, had six stones of wool 'for the dier [dyer]'[58] while William Heighoo of Rokeles Hall had four stones of wool on his death in 1632.[59] Roger Caudwell had three stones of wool when he died in 1674, along with one and a half stones of hemp, the raw material for producing linen.[60] The processes of combing, spinning and weaving were sometimes mentioned in 17th century sources. The occupation of John Vincent, who lived in a cottage in the town until his death in 1685, was given as woolcomber.[61] Inventories of the period sometimes referred to spinning wheels. Philip Toole, who died in 1682, had one, as well as a pair of cards for combing wool.[62] Three people identified themselves in their wills as weavers; one was a worsted weaver and one a linen weaver. John Godwyn, who died in 1633, left his youngest son his tenters, which were frames on which cloth was stretched to dry (hence the phrase, 'on tenterhooks'), and all his 'working tooles which belonge or any wise appertaine to the trade of a clothworker'.[63] The picture is of a small-scale industry using local raw material, with spinning carried on largely in people's homes, a few specialists in the other stages of cloth manufacturing and several mercers and woollendrapers who may have marketed the output of the local industry as well as selling products manufactured elsewhere.

Malting and brewing were important industries in 16th and 17th century Watton. The larger houses, such as William Heighoo's and Christopher Hey's, contained facilities and equipment for brewing beer, but the more significant brewhouses were probably those attached to inns, owned by people who were described as maltsters and brewers. John Webster, who died in 1567, owned the inn called the *Christopher* and referred in his will to the implements in its brewhouse.[64] Thomas Betts, who died in 1659, left to his heirs 'the copper, mash fatte, coolers, breweing vessels and all other the breweing vessels and utensils to the brewhowse now being or belonging'.[65] Although he had wider interests, Roger Caudwell was described in his will as a 'beerebrewer';[66] when his possessions were valued after his death in 1674, they included malt worth £7 in one of the chambers of his dwelling, and he was owed substantial sums of money for beer supplied: £15 18s 8d (equivalent to over £1,800 today) for 'strong beere' and £2 for 'small beere'.

Dairying was another Watton industry in the 17th century, although it was to become more significant in the 18th century. The inhabitants of the larger houses had dairies on the premises and when inventories were compiled after their deaths they contained references to the equipment for making butter and cheese. Thomas Bettes (died 1632) had a cheese press and three cheese fattes (vats). William Heighoo of Rokeles Hall also had a cheese press. His equipment included 35 milk bowls, 14 cheese fattes, 'a lead to set milk', a salting trough, and other equipment suggesting that he was engaged in production for sale on a fairly large scale. His house also contained 'twoe waie of cheese and a halfe' (560 lb or 254 kilos) worth £5 (equivalent to over £600 today).

Candle-making used another animal product: tallow. George Deney, who died in 1622, bequeathed 'to Thomas Canham my man, my candle mould and my press that I presse my tallowe withall',[67] while ten years later Thomas Bettes also referred specifically in his will to 'one copper, one press and one mould belonging to the making of candle'.[68]

Many other crafts and trades could be found in 16th and 17th century Watton. Millers, bakers, butchers and fishmongers helped to keep the people fed, while tailors, glovers, cordwainers and shoemakers kept them clothed and shod. Blacksmiths, wheelwrights and collar-makers kept their means of transport moving, while coopers produced the barrels in which beer was stored. Many of these tradesmen were also small farmers, with an enclosure or two, or a few acres in the open fields.

During the early modern period, other professions began to be represented in Watton's population. Lawyers, for example; there was plenty of work for them, as this was a litigious age. And medical men: Alexander Ames, 'practisioner of phisacke,' Thomas Goodrich, 'chiruigion' [surgeon] and Francis Cuffard, apothecary, whose possessions included 'a parcell of books', 'a case of lancetts' and 'a parcel of potts, glasses, waters, sirroups, drugs and other things in the shopp'.[69]

These were the people who lived in the market town in the 16th and 17th centuries. But what went on in their minds, and how did they get on together? They were like us in many ways, but very different in others.

## Notes

1. Calendar of Inquisitions Post-Mortem, vol XVI.
2. P Millican (ed), *The Musters Returns for Divers Hundreds in the County of Norfolk, 1569, 1572, 1574 and 1577, Vol II* (Norfolk Record Society, Volume VII, 1934).
3. Julian Horn, *Watton: Some Snapshots of its History* (The Wayland Partnership Development Trust, 2011).
4. Norfolk Genealogy, vol 15 (1983).
5. TNA, E179/253/45; NRO, NAS 1/1/25/Watton/13.
6. Assignment of mortgage of property in Watton, 5 December 1786; NRO, MC2364/2/24.
7. Watton overseers' accounts; NRO, PD218/3.
8. Watton Town Book; NRO, PD 218/1.
9. Susan D Amussen, *An Ordered Society* (Columbia University Press, 1988).
10. White's Directory of Norfolk, 1836.
11. It is shown on the plan included in a conveyance of 1864 (in private possession).
12. John Hicks Thompson stated that it had been removed during the period when the Revd W H Hicks was lord of the manor, and therefore before he sold the manor in 1869.
13. Will of William Pollard, 1503; NRO, ANW Fuller alias Roper fo 351.
14. Rental of the manor of Watton Hall, 1595; NRO, NRS 18144 33A3 (hereafter '1595 rental').
15. This is apparent from references in the court books of the manor of Watton Hall.
16. TNA, C 1/803/8.

17. Inventory of John Howard, 1662; NRO, DN INV/50A/84.
18. Edward Flood of Carbrooke to John Bettes, sale of two pieces of land in Watton, 1591; NRO, WLS VII/3.
19. 1595 rental.
20. Will of John Webbester, 1567; NRO, ANW Mendham fo 245.
21. It is mentioned in the will of Margaret Besowthe, 1588; NRO, ANW James fo 228.
22. 1595 rental.
23. His will, written in 1617, referred to an orchard on the west side of 'the messuage or tenement wherein I nowe inhabit and dwell in', which abutted on the 'common streete' to the south. TNA, PROB 11/131/778.
24. Will of Christopher Hey, 1617; TNA, PROB 11/131/778.
25. Will of William Jarvys, 1608; NRO, ANW Remaine fo 37.
26. Meaning unclear. Russet dyed with woad?
27. Inventory of Thomas Blumfeilde, 1600; NRO, INV 17/46. See also J Horn (2011) for discussion of this inventory.
28. Will of George Francke, 1598; NRO, ANW Lyncolne fo 42.
29. Will of Katherine Bywater, 1640; NRO, NCC Gibson 33. The reference to the house of Sir Edward Barkham, lord of the manor of Watton Hall, is significant, suggesting that he may already have moved out of the original manor house near the church. Unfortunately, the precise location of Katherine Bywater's property cannot be determined.
30. Will of John Payne, 1549; NRO, ANW 1545-51, Aleyn fo 289.
31. Will of Thomas Payne, 1571; NRO, ANW Busbye fo 258.
32. Will of Henry Ficket, 1597; NRO, ANW Lyncolne fo 185.
33. Will of John Fecket, 1624; NRO, ANW 1626-29 fo 226.
34. Possibly, a pointed wall, the chamber lying between the two sides of a pitched roof.
35. Copy of court roll, manor of Watton Hall, 2 April 1657; in private possession.
36. Copy of court roll, manor of Watton Hall, 21 December 1654; Museum4Watton, ms 2017-29.39.
37. 1595 rental.
38. Bettes v Jarvis; TNA, C 2/JasI/B8/39.
39. Court roll of the Manor of Watton Hall; NRO, Bradfer Lawrence IXa.
40. Will of Thomas Spicer, 1570; NRO, ANW Busbye fo 219.
41. As mentioned in the will of Thomas Bowgeon, his cousin, in 1587; NRO, Ives fo 193.
42. David Dymond (ed), *The Register of Thetford Priory*, Norfolk Record Society (2 vols, 1994-6).
43. Will of Robert Brett, 1614; NRO, ANW 1614-15 fo 163.
44. Manor court book, Manor of Watton Hall, 1714; Museum4Watton, M4W/2016/8B.
45. Will of George Deney, 1622; NRO, ANW 1621-23 fo 69.
46. Abstract of title in private possession.
47. 1595 rental.
48. Indenture of 24 April 1880 between William Clubb, innkeeper and William Meek, harness maker, in private possession.
49. Will of John Olley, senior; NRO, ANW Bankes fo 109.
50. The spellings of this surname vary: Hornigold, Horningold, Hornygold and Hornigoe being some of the variants. They have been standardised as 'Hornigold'.
51. Manor court book, Manor of Watton Hall, 1710; Museum4Watton, M4W/2016/8B.
52. Manor court book, Manor of Watton Hall, 1672; Museum4Watton, M4W/2016/8A.

53. As at the court held on 25 November 1714, for example; manor court book, Manor of Watton Hall, Museum4Watton, M4W/2016/8B.
54. Royalparks.org.uk.
55. Manor court book, Manor of Watton Hall, 1673; Museum4Watton, M4W/2016/8A. Another possibility is that the name derived from 'Rattan', meaning the undressed timber of which houses were sometimes constructed; see E Patricia Dennison, *The Evolution of Scotland's Towns* (Edinburgh University Press, 2018).
56. 1595 rental.
57. NRO, HIL 2/60/1-3.
58. Inventory of Thomas Blumfeilde, 1600; NRO, INV 17/46.
59. Inventory of William Heighoo; NRO, INV 38/102.
60. Inventory of Roger Caudwell, 1674; NRO, ANW 23/3/159.
61. Will of John Vincent, 1685; NRO, ANW 1681-82 fo 375.
62. Inventory of Philip Toole, 1682; NRO, DN/INV 60A/104.
63. Will of John Godwyn, 1633; NRO, ANW Gray fo 231.
64. Will of John Webster, 1567; NRO, ANW Mendham fo 245.
65. Will of Thomas Betts, 1659; TNA PROB 11/295/408.
66. Will of Roger Caudwell, 1674; NRO ANW 1674-75 fo 155.
67. Will of George Deney, 1622; NRO, ANW 1621-23 fo 69.
68. Will of Thomas Bettes, 1632; NRO, NCC Morse 70.
69. Inventory of Francis Cuffard, 1682; NRO, ANW 23/1/115.

# People of Early-Modern Watton

John Westonne must have cut a fine figure.

His clothes, all mentioned in his will of 1556, included a 'dublett of blew satton', a 'russet jerkyn with lether sleves', russet hose, a pair of shoes, a cap and a 'gowne furred with blake cony' (rabbit). He carried a dagger, as a weapon, or fashion accessory, or both. We can picture him, thus attired, striding across Watton market place.[1]

John Westonne was not unique among Wattonians of the 16th century in mentioning his clothes in his will. Thomas Ficket, in 1572, was another. His 'best hatt' and 'best hoass' (hose) were given to one of his sons and his 'best duble' and my best jerken' to another, while a godson had to make do with his 'old freise [coarse woollen] jerkein' and 'olde dublett'.[2] The apparel of William Delfe, who died in 1591, included a 'black grograine [worsted, mohair and silk] dublett', a 'black cote', a 'red tawnye cote', a 'black dublett with skurtes' and 'buve [buff] lether brytches'.[3]

Women, too, occasionally mentioned clothes in their wills. In 1511, Isabel Borgopp left her daughter 'my best gowne and my best kyrtyl' and her sister 'a gowne and a kyrtyl next the best'. Agnes Bougeon, who died in 1555, had more elaborate outfits. Her daughter in law received her 'new kirtill with the fustian [wool and linen] overbodie' and her 'seconde raile [dress]', while one daughter was given her 'best gowne', her 'frocke', her 'best hatt' and her 'best girdle' and another, her 'kirtill with the worsted overbodie' and her 'best apron' or her 'best raile at her choise'. Her sister was to have her 'gowne lined with cottonne'. Elizabeth Girth, a single woman and probably a domestic servant, had fewer possessions. She bequeathed to Anne Smythe, perhaps a sister or friend, her 'redd petticoat and a little box with all the linen and a hatt'.[4]

In the 17th century, clothes were mentioned much less, perhaps because, under the influence of Protestantism, they became plainer and finery was less valued. But personal adornment still mattered, to some at least. Margaret Turner made no mention of clothing in her will of 1645, but she bequeathed several gold rings to different people, including 'one gould ringe with blue turkie stones sett in itt' and 'my little gould ringe sett with 3 rubies in itt'.[5]

༄༅

For the inhabitants of Watton in the 16th and 17th centuries, Christian burial and religious observance during life were vital priorities. They were reverent, God-fearing folk; the church played a central part in their lives and many left legacies for the maintenance of the building. However, how their piety was expressed changed significantly during the early-modern period.

Until the mid-16th century, most of the inhabitants of Watton were Roman Catholic. They revered the Virgin Mary and celebrated the traditional festivals on the saints' days. In their wills, they used formulations such as, 'I commend my sowyll to Almyty God, to owr lady Seynt Mary and to all seyntes in hevyn'.[6] Isabel Borgopp (died in 1511) was not alone in wanting 'a preste to sing for me by the space of a yere';[7] that is, to have a mass celebrated in her name. St Giles' church, as St Mary's church was known until the mid-16th century, housed three guilds, of St Giles, St Mary and St John the Baptist, which helped the poor and to which people left money in their wills.[8]

After King Henry VIII's break with Rome, Protestant ideas spread, and the content and wording of the wills made by the inhabitants of Watton changed. Thomas Palmer was the vicar of Watton from 1528 until his resignation in 1557.[9] He served for the last four years of his incumbency during the temporary swing back to Roman Catholicism under Queen Mary but, on the evidence of his will, was a strong Protestant whose views were influenced by Calvinism. This may have been why he resigned. Palmer bequeathed his soul to God, 'most humblie beseechinge the most holie and blessed trinitie to have mercie on my sowle and to forgive me my synnes so that after this mutable worlde and transitory life I maie arise with the ellecte and have the eternall life and fuision of the godhed according to my trew faithe'.[10] No mention of Mary and the saints here.

Margaret Besowthe (died 1589) commended her soul, 'into the mercyfull hands of God the father, God the son and God the holly ghost, trusting most assuredly that I, by and thoroughe the merittes, bitter death and passion of my lord and onely savior Jesus Christe, shall be saved, and at the latter day have and possesse a joyfull and blessed resurrection, amongst the elect people of God'.[11] The latter was a Calvinist formulation, the product of the intense personal faith of a person who, like many in Watton at the time, would have been known as a 'Puritan'.

Whereas, in the early 16th century, people might ask the parish priest to sing for them, in the 17th century requests were made occasionally for sermons. Margaret Turner, for example, stated that her 'will and desire is that Mr William Foster may preach a sermon at my funeral if it may be without offence.'[12] She left him ten shillings to buy a ring in memory of her, a common custom at the time.

Changes made inside the church reflected the changing views of the inhabitants of the town. The 'holy water stoppes' had been pulled down by 1560 and in 1567 a mason and his 'server' were paid for laying brickwork and 'whytinge the place wheare the awter stood'. The altar had been replaced by a 'communion bord' or table.[13]

The vicar in 1626-32, Robert Taylor, was probably a Puritan and appears to have been a scholarly man. The inventory of his goods, compiled after his death, included '47 books in the chest' and another three 'which are lent out'. The vicarage at this time was a modest dwelling with a hall and kitchen and chambers over them: a two-up, two-down.[14] In 1636, it was described as the 'viccaradge house with a hey house and a stable'.[15] In 1725, it had acquired, in addition, a 'hogs' court', three gardens and an orchard.[16]

William Foster was vicar and 'minister of God's word'[17] from 1632 until 1660, during the Civil War between the supporters of King Charles I and Parliament and subsequently during the Commonwealth and Protectorate. He appears to have resigned on the restoration of Charles II in the 'glorious revolution' of 1660, perhaps unwilling to comply with new religious legislation. He was replaced by Henry Tooley, who had a much more luxurious lifestyle, eschewing the vicarage for 'my great dwelinge house at Watton Greene'. When he died in 1681, Tooley left legacies amounting to over £1,400 (equivalent to over £160,000 today) to family members but only 20 shillings (equivalent to £114) for the poor of Watton.[18]

ഈരു

The leading inhabitants of Watton competed with each other commercially but collaborated as members of the community. A small group of farmers, shopkeepers and tradesmen formed an oligarchy, from among whose number individuals were chosen to perform the role of churchwardens, one selected by the vicar and the other by the principal inhabitants. Details of their activities and decisions were recorded in the pages of the 'Town Book' kept by the churchwardens from the mid-16th century onwards.[19]

On Hallowmas, or All Hallows (All Souls) Day, which today is usually called Hallowe'en, they gathered at a 'drynkin' to consume refreshments, collect money to meet the needs of the church and community, identify the churchwardens for the ensuing year and present their accounts for the previous year. Drynkins also took place at other times, for example 'Wissin (Whitsun) Monday' in 1566. For a drynkin in 1560, payments were made for apples, white herrings, raisins, aniseed, honey, butter, pepper, bread and cakes – quite a feast. The town also had a 'greate spete', a spit for roasting meat, which was lent to George Franke on the occasion of his marriage in 1583. Another occasion on which eating and drinking took place was the 'plowlet' (Plough Monday, the first Monday after Epiphany, 6 January). Plowlets were recorded in 1561, when malt and beer were purchased in considerable quantities, and in 1568. After that, however, drynkins and plowlets seemed to have ceased, perhaps because such indulgence was at odds with the increasingly puritanical attitudes of the townspeople.

There was much else for the churchwardens to do. They managed the routine maintenance of the church, including the bells and the ropes and baldricks that enabled them to ring, the lead of the roof and the glass of the windows. Anyone who wished to bury their relatives within the church was charged the sum of 6s 8d (equivalent to about £35 today) for the lifting of the 'pavment' on the floor, with the money being given to the poor. Among those who paid were Richard Hamond, for the burial of Rose Salter in 1658 and Ralph Ives for the interring of his child two years later; both are names that will be encountered again in later chapters. In 1659, the churchwardens even paid 'old William Mayes' 10s for the year to 'put out the bells keeping and to keepe out the doggs of the church and to awake all sleapers which sleape in devine servis'.

The churchwardens' duties were not confined to the church. Individuals were paid for 'laying the towne for noyfull vermen and fowles' and in 1579 six men, including Christopher Hey, Henry Ficket and Nicholas Cock, were given this responsibility. In 1589, Nicholas Cock was paid 1s 8d for 20 moles' heads and others received unspecified payments for 29 dozen sparrows' heads and 18 cadows' (jackdaws') heads. The churchwardens had the custody of Watton's armour and armaments, used to equip the men that the town was obliged to contribute to the militia (a reserve force, rather like the Territorial Army). In 1587, John Betts was paid for providing a sword, a scabbard, a dagger and a pair of hangers (belts from which swords were hung), while in 1603 the town armour included a corselet, a pike, a sword, three daggers and a 'calyver' (light musket), together with girdles and head pieces for protection. The churchwardens also arranged the letting of the town lands (pieces of land that had been donated to the parish over the years), mostly for four years at a time, specifying that if the land was arable it should be laid down to 'somerlay' (fallow) in one of the years. The rents were used to relieve the poor. The churchwardens even lent parishioners money from the town funds, charging them interest, thereby raising more money for the poor. Henry Ficket, for example, received a loan of 32 shillings in 1627 and was still paying interest on it over 15 years later.

The parish was responsible for the maintenance of the roads and bridges. In 1561, work had to be done on the 'pyssel bryg' (referred to in later sources as the Postle Bridge), which was in the vicinity of the market place and may have crossed the ditch which ran behind the properties fronting the street. In the same year, 8d (equivalent to about £8 today) had to be spent on 'mendyng of Rockelles bridge', the ancient crossing point on what is now Redhill Lane. The parish officials of 1622 neglected their duty to maintain bridges, causing the town to be fined at the sheriff's court 'for not keeping a sufficient causaye at the southe end of Sametonye bridge leading from Watton to Swafham'. The same bridge, referred to as 'Sahamtony Great Bridge' (now known as Story's bridge) needed more attention in 1660, when both ends were repaired, and in 1567, when its south end was 'new sett'.

In the 17th century, an annual meeting of the chief inhabitants of the town took place at Easter and it was then that they chose the churchwardens, 'questmen' (sidesmen), people to represent the town at the sheriff's court and the other officials that the parish was now required to identify: overseers of the poor and surveyors of the highways. The latter were able to draw on donations for the repair of the roads that people occasionally made in their wills. In 1549, for example, John Payne gave 'to the mendinge of the heywayes in Watton that lyeth betwyn my mese [messuage] and the cawuseys ende 10 loades of gravell'.[20] He may have been referring to what is now Church Walk, which others were also keen to keep in repair. Thomas Palmer, formerly vicar of Watton, left 10 shillings 'towards the mendinge of the highe wais leading from the towne to the church of Watton' when he died in 1564.[21] Christopher Hey the elder, in his will of 1617, gave 20 shillings (equivalent to about £134 today) 'towards the repayringe and amending of the church path between the gate at the ponde [pound, at the corner of Dereham Road] and soe towards the church'.[22] It was important that the people of the town were able to get to their parish church.

৪০০৪

After Henry VIII's break with Rome, the guilds in the parish church, like the monasteries, were dissolved. From the middle of the 16th century onwards, legacies which might previously have been given to the guilds were now left to the poor. The sums given by individuals ranged from a few shillings to as much as £5. The instructions given for the use of the money varied. Matilda Palmer, in her will of 1561, left five shillings 'towards the comfort of my poore christen brethren and sistren…where most need is and to be distributed amongeste them when they have most need therof'.[23] Henry Ficket, in 1597, gave each of seven widows 'halfe a bushel of rye apece to be paid everie yeare during ther natural lives… upon Ash Weddnesdaye.'[24] Robert Alden (died 1601) gave 20 shillings to the poor, but additionally bequeathed 'unto three poore old widowes, viz the Wedow Stephinson, Wedow Joyner and Wedow Turner and to every of them, a freese [coarse woollen] gowne, to be made new and delivered unto them immediately after my decease.' Thomas Lincolne, in 1686, distinguished between the different parts of Watton: 'two shillings to the poore at the Greene and three shillings to the rest of the poore about the towne and Newton [Neaton] Streete'.[25]

The 'poor menes boxe' received donations from several people. This box predated the present 'poor box', which features the figure of a man and inscribed 'Remember the Poore', which was installed in Watton church in 1639. The Revd Benjamin Armstrong, diarist and vicar of Dereham, visited the church two centuries later, in 1855, and commented: 'Mr H[icks, vicar of Watton] said a workman in the church once stole this figure, which looks like the idol of the place, and settled afterwards at Liverpool. Failing there, he sold off his stock at auction, among which was the 'idol' aforesaid; this was recognised by a Norfolk man who was present, who purchased it, and sent it back to Watton, where he is perched, as grim as ever, with his nose knocked off and a malevolent scowl on his countenance like a heathen god....I confess it would have been as well had he been shipped off to America instead of being sent to Watton'.[26] He survives to this day.

At the end of the 16th century, the growth of the country's population and rising prices meant that increasing numbers of people fell into poverty and required assistance, some of whom, termed the 'idle poor', travelled from place to place as vagabonds and were seen as a threat. Legislation of 1597 and 1601 mandated the appointment in each parish of overseers, responsible for the relief of the poor. The churchwardens and overseers were empowered to charge rates. In the year ending 24 March 1599, the postholders in Watton gathered over £12 (equivalent to over £1,650 today) in three instalments, which funded expenditure on the poor, 'for howse fearme [rent], for hempe to sett them on worke, for the binding forthe of an apprentice and other contribusions as they had neede'.[27]

The collection of poor rates continued, but so also did charitable donations for the benefit of the poor. Two acts of charity in the 17th century stand out as particularly generous. Edward Goffe of Threxton, who died in 1612, bequeathed to trustees, four houses 'which I have built for almshouses in Watton', and declared: 'I will that four of the poorest aged couples dwelling in Watton, shall have their dwelling in the alms-houses during the term of their natural life, and also an annuity of £5 [equivalent to about £670 today] per annum'.[28] Goffe also bequeathed a recently-purchased house in Saham Toney for use 'for a school house', with annuities for the inhabitants of the almshouses, for the schoolmaster's stipend and to provide 'good cheer' for the trustees, who were to meet yearly to 'examine the scholars, how they profited'. The schoolmaster was to teach, for no charge, all the pupils from Saham, one from Threxton and six from 'out of the town of Watton if so many shall be sent'.[29]

These bequests were remembered. The almshouses were reported, in 1815, to provide accommodation for 'four ancient couples'.[30] In 1834, when the trustees of the parish lands, buildings and charities in Watton submitted an account to the Charity Commissioners, they reported that the almshouses, which had been rebuilt by Robert Harvey (a Watton lawyer) in 1820, were inhabited by 'four of the poorest aged [single] men and women or, for the want of such, the poorest aged couple dwelling in Watton'. The annuity of £5 was still paid. The entitlement to send six children to the 'free school' in Saham was also recalled but 'none have been sent for several years'. Edward Goffe's munificence was not confined to the almshouses and the school; he also bequeathed to the parish an income of 10s per year out of land in Griston, 'to be given in bread to the poor not taking collection' (not receiving regular poor relief from the parish) and by 1834 this still helped to fund the distribution of bread on St Thomas's Day (21 December), 'to all the poor belonging to the parish...a 4d loaf to each man and woman and a 2d loaf to each child'.[31]

The second particularly generous bequest was by Richard Turner who, by his will of 1641, bequeathed a four-acre enclosure called 'Oake Close...in ye feild of Watton' to the town, the rent to be used to provide 'six pence in bread and beer given and distributed on every Sunday weekly to six of such of the poore men and women of the aforesaid towne as ye...Minister and Churchwardens for ye tyme being... shall think to stand in most need thereof'.[32] Turner's bequest, and its terms, were recorded in the Town Book in 1644 and were remembered almost two centuries later, in 1834 when the then trustees reported that part of the land bequeathed by Turner had been exchanged for an allotment on the former Mill Common at the time of parliamentary enclosure in 1803, and that the churchwardens had 'of late years allowed 9 poor widows 1d each every week...for bread'.[33]

There may have been more to Richard Turner's bequest than first appears. A very elderly man when he died, with great-grandchildren but no direct heirs, he was the brother of Hugh Turner, vicar of Watton from 1571 to 1609. Their father, Henry Turner, had submitted complaints against Robert Alden, yeoman of Watton, to the Court of Chancery in the 1570s to recover 11 acres of land he believed to be his, the deeds of which Alden refused to yield. Alden claimed that the land had been granted to the inhabitants of Watton in the reign of Queen Mary I so that the churchwardens could use the proceeds to mend the roads and to provide employment for the poor. Henry Turner claimed that the land had originally been granted to fund annual 'obits' (commemorative services for the deceased) but had come into the Crown's possession following the dissolution of chantries (endowments for the singing of masses) and that Elizabeth I had granted it to a private owner, from whom it had eventually come into his hands.[34] He appears to have won his case, as there were no further references to the 11 acres of land in the possession of the parish. It seems possible, therefore, that the gift made by Richard Turner was by way of atonement for the acquisitiveness of his father.

The tradition of philanthropy continued in subsequent centuries. Thomas Scott of Rokeles Hall, who died in 1729, was commemorated in the parish register as 'an honest, just, good, charitable man, a great benefactor both to ye church and poor', and was buried 'to ye great loss and inexpressible lamentation, particularly of the minister of the parish and all the inhabitants'.[35] Scott gave the churchwardens of Watton a 'pightle' of pasture of about an acre, the rent accruing to be distributed in bread to the most needy inhabitants twice a year, the first distribution to be on St Thomas's Day after his death, supplementing the bequest left by Edward Goffe for the distribution of bread on the same day that remained in force in 1834. Scott also left £5 to be distributed to 'the most indigent and necessitous persons' in Watton 'who do not receive or take the public parish collection'. He provided an additional £20 (equivalent to about £2,360 today) 'to be laid out for and towards cloathing in blew [blue] fifteen of the poorest and most aged inhabitants', no more than two people in any one family, and again excluding those who received the 'public collection'. Thomas Scott excluded those on 'collection' in order to target those 'virtuous' poor people who did not become a burden on the parish. But why he insisted on blue clothing for the poor of Watton can only be a matter of speculation.[36]

෴

The people of early-modern Watton were not only devout and charitable to the poor. Like people today, they also cared for their own families.

Men were concerned to make suitable provision in their wills for their wives and young or unborn children. Widows and widowers, in particular, tended to spread their property around among family members as they contemplated their own mortality. The assets they bequeathed included animals, especially cows and horses; Watton was still a rural community as well as a market town. Bedsteads and bedding often featured, as did other domestic furnishings and utensils, especially those in silver, brass, latten (an alloy of copper, tin and a little lead) and pewter. And, in the 16th century, clothes mattered too.

A touching example of the provision made by a man for his daughters is provided by the will of Thomas Chirnell in 1553. As well as giving Agnes, Johan and Margerie 40 shillings each, he gave each of them a cow, a ewe and a lamb, 'to be delivered at thage of 12 yeris'.[37] Similarly, Richard Magges, who died in 1547, was keen to make provision for all his children, boys and girls alike. He bequeathed to 'every one of my children…a bedstedd, a mattres, 2 payer of shetes, a payer of fyne and thother paier of corse, a paier of blanketes, a coverlight with a pylowgh bolstere and covering or pylowgh beres to the same…a cowe..2 pewter platters, 2 pewter dysshes, 2 pewter sawcwers, an honest candelstyke, a pewter salte'. Just about everything they would need in life.[38]

Edward Childerhouse, a brewer, was concerned that his grandson should be educated, enjoining his daughter Faith, in his will of 1626, to bring him 'upp to schoole until he be able to wright and read English well and perfectlye'.[39] A widow, Elizabeth Hatley, who died in 1696, left £10 to a nephew, to be paid when he was 15 'to bind him forth an apprentice'.[40] William Chrashell, who died in 1588, wanted to make specific, if limited, provision for his wife Alice, stipulating that, as well as a cow, a mare, a bed and six pewter dishes, she should have, 'hir dwelling in the chamber behind the chimny during her widowhood', although the rest of his property, including 'the proffitt of two appell trees in the west side of my close', was divided between his two sons.[41] Similar provision for his wife Bridget was made by John Mirrill, yeoman, in 1652. She was to have 'my parlor and chamber over it with two rooms at the south end of the parlor with her ingate and outgate into the entry to goe up and downe into the said chamber and also one house in the yueard called the newe house with free ingresse and regresse to the same with horse and cart and any other carriages with a convenient roome to sett her wood at the south end of the newe house, and alsoe to take her water at the usuall pitt during her natural life if she keepe herselfe a widdowe'.[42] But, as was not uncommon, if she remarried, she would lose everything. Her new husband would have to take care of her.

❦

The lives of a few of the individuals and families who lived in Watton in the 16th and 17th centuries can be reconstructed in more detail. Here are four examples from different parts of Watton society: William Heighoo, Nicholas Cock, the Fickets and the Hornigolds.

William Heighoo, who died in 1632, was a yeoman: someone who owned his own land but did not have enough of it to qualify as a member of the gentry. He lived at Rokeles Hall, the nearest thing to a country house that existed in Watton, which he had owned since 1615. Heighoo seems to have had a chequered past. As a young man, he may have been associated with plots against Elizabeth I, for which he was pardoned by King James I in 1604.[43] In 1618, he was accused of having harboured a 'great recusant' (a Roman Catholic) but he denied the charge, which had been made by someone who was contesting his ownership of some of the property he occupied.[44]

William Heighoo seems to have settled down to enjoy a prosperous and comfortable life at Rokeles Hall. He left a will referring to 'my mannor of Rockells'[45] and a detailed inventory of his possessions was compiled after his death in 1632.[46] The house had three stories and contained an 'entry', hall, parlour, kitchen and pantry, all with chambers over them. On the second floor were a further chamber over the entry chamber and a garret where four stones of wool were stored, with a pair of 'stock cardes' to comb it and a spinning wheel. 'A paier of clypping shears' had been left in the chamber over the kitchen and another spinning wheel stood in the pantry. Four sides of white leather and four stones of hemp were found in the chamber over the entry chamber, and some linen yarn in the chamber below (along with two rat traps). Below the ground floor was a cellar, containing three hogsheads, three beer stools and five half barrels. A backhouse, dairy and 'little butteries' provided facilities for brewing, grinding mustard and making butter and cheese, the utensils listed including firkins and cheese presses.

The house was well furnished and suitably equipped to provide hospitality. The parlour contained four chairs, 11 stools, eight cushions, two carpets and 'a drawing curteyne for the window'. A 'chyldes chayer' stood in the pantry. There were numerous bedsteads, including at least two four-posters. The stock of linen, kept in the chamber over the parlour, included no fewer than 40 pairs of sheets, four dozen napkins and eight table-cloths. Eight dozen trenchers (plates), eleven kettles and many other items for preparing and serving food were found in the kitchen but the 22 silver spoons were kept in the hall.

The estate associated with the hall was not large, comprising 27 acres in pasture closes, two closes in Rokeles Meadow, and 12.25 acres of arable dispersed in small pieces across Mill Field and Wayland Field.[47] William Heighoo also owned land in Holme Hale and Saham Waite. These properties were sufficient to support a comfortable lifestyle. William Heighoo's clothes were worth £8 (equivalent to almost £1,000 today) and he possessed books valued at £2. He enjoined his executors to 'educate and bring upp my…sonne James Heighoo at schoole until hee be fit to goe to Cambridg. And then that they educate and maineteine him at Cambridg, soe long tyme as they…shall thinke fit'.

When he died, William Heighoo had wheat, rye and a large quantity of barley 'on the chamber' and rye and peas stored in the barn. The inventory was taken on 10 April 1632, at which point there were '27 acres of corne upon the grounde' worth £27. Also on the property was malt worth £120 (equivalent to approaching £15,000 today), no doubt destined for Heighoo's 'brewhouse at Watton towne', which he had purchased from Charles Hey, of the influential Hey family. Horse mills provided traction at both the hall and the brewhouse. The most valuable animals on the farm were sheep, worth £37, but there were also 30 steers; four heifers; six bullocks; 15 cows; seven weaned calves; eight 'shotes' (weaned piglets) and two sows; and turkeys, geese, ducks, capons, cocks, hens and 'other poultry in the yeards'. Eight flitches of bacon were found in the hall at the house, along with fishing nets two 'fowling peces' and an old musket. Six working horses were kept, along with a gelding, eight colts and six yearlings. William Heighoo's wife Marie probably rode, as a 'syde sadle with the cloth' was found in the house. The equipment for use on the farm included two carts and a plough, along with rakes, scythes and muck-forks.

The manor of Rokeles Hall was sold by William Heighoo's son Edward in 1643. The purchasers were Thomas Scott, yeoman (probably the grandfather of the philanthropist of 1729), and his son Robert. They paid £680 (equivalent to about £80,000 today). The house was described as 'all that messuage called… the mannor house…with the homestalls and crofte thereuto adioyning', lying between the highway from Watton to Hingham to the south and Watton Green to the north.[48] In 1653, Thomas Scott altered the house, perhaps largely rebuilding it, setting the date in a panel in its north gable end.[49] Ceiling beams in rooms on the ground floor of the house are similar to those on the first floor of 30 High Street, which experts have dated to the 16th century, and so the core of the building may well date from then. Further changes were made in the 18th century (a new pedimented west front) and the 19th century (rebuilding of the south gable wall).

༄༅

Nicholas Cocke, who died in 1595,[50] lived more modestly than William Heighoo. He was a husbandman, a small farmer. In his will, he mentioned 11 cows, all different, including a 'red bull,' and specified that they were all to be 'wintred upon the groundes, with the stuver [fodder] in the barnes'. Nine horses were kept, again individually described. The farming equipment included a 'greate cart' and an 'other cart' along with two sets of 'thillers geare' with fore- and hind-horse traces and cart traces, and halters. At least two of Nicholas Cocke's horses were employed, either in single file or side by side, to pull his carts.

Nicholas Cocke's house was smaller than William Heighoo's, comprising a hall and parlour with chambers over them, and a backhouse behind. But he had plenty of furniture, including two posted bedsteads, two 'trendle' beds to fit under them and a boarded bed, with bolsters, blankets and 18 pairs of sheets. There was a cupboard and a round framed table, with chairs, stools and cushions. Basins and candlesticks of latten', described as the 'best' and 'worst,' were listed and numerous utensils were available for cooking and serving food. Nicholas Cocke made cheese and brewed beer. He was listed as a 'selected person' in the muster of 1577,[51] and so perhaps had had occasion to use what he described as 'my blacke bill and my bowe and sheaf of arrows.' He also part-owned a 'callyver' (light musket). He may have been of modest means but Nicholas Cock was not a man to be trifled with.

∞☙

The Ficket family was long established in Watton but Thomas Ficket, who died in 1572, was the first member who is known to have been a cooper, a barrel-maker. He bequeathed an oak tree to his stepfather, and two ash trees, all his 'clapplord' (clapboard, split oak or deal) and 'all the tooles in my shoppe' to his brother Henry.[52] Thomas also leased land and among his bequests was a combe of malt.

Henry Ficket, Thomas's brother, described himself as a yeoman when he wrote his will in 1597. He owned several pieces of land including five acres newly enclosed. Other people, however, referred to him as a cooper. An educated man, it is fairly certain that he wrote his will himself, as he had been the scribe for the wills of several other people over the preceding few years. He also served frequently as one of Watton's churchwardens. Henry and his wife Margaret lived at Paines, on the north side of the market place in Watton. They had no children and Henry left to his brother George, 'all my coopers tooles and my timber fit for coopers ware wrought or unwrought except my hatchet and hooke.' Henry also left George a cart, a 'bayd meare', a year-old colt, two steers, and, after Margaret's death, most of his land.[53] George Ficket, lived until 1624 and he, in turn, bequeathed to his son Henry 'all my coopers tools and my tymber wrought and unwroght'.[54] For a craftsman, the tools of the trade were prized possessions.

When Henry died in 1650, apparently without issue, he bequeathed to 'William Howard my apprentis cooper certain working tooles. Item I give unto him a joynr, a thicksell, a passer and a cliver, a paire of compasses and a croyse, a hand sawe.'[55] With these, William Howard was equipped to make a living, manufacturing barrels for the town's brewers. Henry's wife Mary died only four months after her husband

and among her possessions was 'one greate bible.'[56] Mary was illiterate but her husband had signed his will and so can be presumed, like his uncle Henry, to have been able to read and write. The Ficket family had been significant members of the community in Watton for well over a century.

༄༅

William Hornigold, who died in 1630, was a tailor who lived in the street of Watton. He and his wife Margery, who died three years later, on the evidence of the wording of their wills, were both Puritans.[57] They had two surviving children: Edmund, baptised in 1623, and Elizabeth, in 1630, the latter being born just months before her father died. When Margery died, all her unbequeathed moveable goods were given to her brother-in-law, Thomas Hornigold, 'towards the education and bringing up' of Edmund and Elizabeth. From Margery's will and the inventory of her goods compiled after she died, it is apparent that her house contained a hall, parlour and shop with chambers over. There was probably a bakehouse, or backhouse, as well, since several items used in the preparation of food, such as two spits, tongs and cobbirons, were mentioned without being assigned to a particular room. No reference was made to the buttery, mill house and stable mentioned in a later conveyance of the property, and so these may have been added later by their son Edmund.

Margery divided her possessions carefully between Edmund and Elizabeth. Earmarked for Edmund were a posted bedstead in the parlour, with bedding including a 'birdey covering',[58] two framed tables, two chairs, two forms, a cupboard, a chest and 'my two middle skillettes'. Elizabeth was to have a livery (non-posted) bedstead with bedding, a cupboard, a little framed table, two small chairs, four cushions, a chest, all the linen and all the brass and pewter not otherwise bequeathed. All these items were listed in the inventory of Margery's goods,[59] along with many others besides, including a stone of wool, 'certeine remnants of stuffe', and a collection of 'buttons, silk, garters, lace and such lyk', relics of her late husband's trade as a tailor.

The value of Margery's assets (excluding real estate but including £22 in debts owing to her), was over £40 (equivalent to nearly £5,000 today), which indicates that the family was moderately prosperous. The most significant debt she was owed was £16, provided as a mortgage to a weaver, John Wilkinson. When he reached adulthood, Margery's son Edmund married Mary Merrill and from 1645 onwards they had several children. The tenement in which they lived was called 'Le Barrell' and lay immediately west of the passageway from the street through to the 'backside'. Edmund died in 1664, ten years before the house was destroyed in the great fire of 1674 but Mary lived on as a widow until 1709. She sold some of her late husband's property and had little to bequeath when she died. The fire had reduced the family to relative poverty.

None of these people were members of the nobility or gentry, although some of the lands and pastures in Watton were owned by people of these classes. In neither the medieval nor the early-modern period did Watton's population include a great landowner or wool merchant prepared to pour money into building a grand church, and so the town's place of worship remained small.

The 'movers and shakers' of Watton were the yeomen farmers and those involved in commerce, the mercers, grocers, brewers, tradesmen and, increasingly, the lawyers. These groups overlapped; the businessmen and lawyers also owned land and houses and received income from rents, while the yeomen often had business interests. The same was true of some of the humbler people, who combined a craft or trade with land ownership on a small scale. Others, however, like Nicholas Cock, the husbandman, had interests that were confined to farming, while many of the craftsmen and small tradesmen held no land. Servants and labourers were employed by the more prosperous people, while craftsmen and tradesmen took on apprentices.

Now, it's time to meet properly another important Watton family: the family of Christopher Hey, builder of Watton's iconic landmark, the Clock Tower in the High Street.

## Notes

1. Will of John Westonne, 1556; NRO, NCC Jagges 393.
2. Will of Thomas Ficket, 1572; NRO, ANW, Busbye, fo 407.
3. Will of William Delfe, 1591; NRO, ANW Burre fo 227.
4. Will of Elizabeth Girth, 1617; NRO, ANW, Weavers fo 164.
5. Will of Margaret Turner, 1646; NRO, NCC Cally 63.
6. Will of William Pollard, 1503. NRO, NCC 362 Popy.
7. Will of Isabel Burgopp, 1511; NRO, NCC Johnson 93.
8. For example, William Pollard in 1503 and William Snellyng in 1479; NRO, NCC NCC 362 Popy.and NCC Aubrey 8.
9. F Blomefield (1805).
10. Will of Thomas Palmer, 1564; TNA PROB11/47/148.
11. Will of Margaret Besouthe, 1588; NRO, ANW James fo 228.
12. Will of Margaret Turner, 1646; NRO, NCC Cally 63.
13. Watton Town Book; NRO, PD218/1.
14. Inventory of Robert Tayler, 1639; NRO. The date is a puzzle, as Robert Tayler died in 1632.
15. Watton glebe terrier, 1636; NRO, DN/TER 159/4/1.
16. Watton glebe terrier, 1725; NRO, DN/TER 159/4/6.
17. Will of John Olley, yeoman; TNA, PROB 11/238/479.
18. Will of Henry Tooley, 1681; NRO, ANW 1681-82 fo 318.
19. Watton Town Book; NRO, PD218/1. The book is worn and many of the early pages are damaged or very faint and difficult to read. Fortunately, many of the earliest entries were transcribed by Thomas

Barton in 1851 when, presumably, the book was in somewhat better condition, and were printed in *Norfolk Archaeology*, Volume 3 (1852). Entries were also transcribed by the anonymous author of a typescript history of Watton, preserved by Wilfrid Harvey from the clearance of the premises of Harvey and Sons, n.d. (but before 1958 since Goffe's almshouses are referred to as still in existence; hereafter cited as anonymous typescript, pre-1958); by the present author in the 1980s; and by Julian Horn in the 1990s. This and the next two paragraphs are based on the evidence in the Town Book.

20. Will of John Payne, 1549; NRO ANW 1545-51 Aleyn fo 289.
21. Will of Thomas Palmer; TNA, PROB11/47/148.
22. Will of Christopher Hey, 1617; TNA, PROB 11/131/778.
23. Will of Matilda Palmer, 1561; NRO, ANW Ayer fo 10.
24. Will of Henry Ficket, 1597; NRO, ANW Lyncolne fo 185.
25. Will of Thomas Lincolne 1686; NRO, ANW 1685-86 fo 193.
26. Christopher Armstrong (ed), *Under the Parson's Nose* (Larks Press, 2012).
27. Summary of poor accounts 1598-99 and 1600-01; NRO, NAS 1/1/25/Watton/14.
28. Quoted in F Blomefield (1805).
29. Extracts from the will of Edward Goffe, n.d. (but watermarked 1827); NRO, PD566/152. See also Robin A Brown with John Newton and Andy Reid, *Shadows on the Summer Grass: some essays on aspects of a Norfolk parish from prehistory to the 20th century* (Woodcock Hall Publications, 1998).
30. *Abstract of Returns relative to the Expense and Maintenance of the Poor*, Parliamentary Papers, 1815.
31. Copy of an account of town lands, etc, delivered to the Charity Commissioners, 17 March 1834; NRO, ACC 2023/12.
32. Will of Richard Turner, 1641; NRO, ANW 1640–43 fo 427.
33. Copy of an account of town lands, etc, delivered to the Charity Commissioners, 17 March 1834; NRO, ACC 2023/12.
34. Turner v Alden; TNA, C 3/179/50, C 3/181/76.
35. Watton parish register, 1539-1730; NRO, PD 218/26.
36. Will of Thomas Scott, 1729; TNA, PROB 11/631/352.
37. Will of Thomas Chirnell, 1553; NRO, NCC Wilkins 240.
38. Will of Richard Magges, 1547; NRO, ANW 1545-51, Aleyn fo 101.
39. Will of Edward Childerhouse, 1626; NRO ANW 1626-29 fo 108.
40. Will of Elizabeth Hatley, 1696; NRO, ANW 1695-96 fo 227.
41. Will of William Crashill, 1588; NRO, ANW Ives fo 56.
42. Will of John Mirrill, 1652; TNA PROB 11 269.
43. NRO, MS 12173 RYE 125 34B6.
44. Dunthorne v Heighoo, 1618: TNA, C 2/JasI/D9/38.
45. Will of William Heighoo, 1632; NRO, NCC Morse 58.
46. Inventory of William Heighoo; NRO, DN/INV 38/102.
47. Robert Heighoe to Robert Scott, Lease of Rokeles Hall, 1650; NRO, WLS VII/I 408x3.
48. Conveyance from Edward Heighoe to Thomas Soctt and Robert Scott, 2 November 1643; NRO, BL/0/I/2.
49. Some sources suggest 1652; see NHER 8788. In recent times, the panel became too eroded to read.
50. Will of Nicholas Cocke, 1595; NRO, ANW Holmes fo 285.
51. P Millican (ed), *The Musters Returns for Divers Hundreds in the County of Norfolk, 1569, 1572, 1574 and 1577, Vol II* (Norfolk Record Society, Volume VII, 1934).
52. Will of Thomas Ficket, 1572; NRO, ANW, will register, Busbye, fo. 407.

53. Will of Henry Ficket, 1597; NRO, ANW, will register, Lyncolne, fo. 185.
54. Will of George Ficket, 1624; NRO, will register, 1624–1625, fo. 75.
55. Will of Henry Ficket, 1650; NRO, will register, 1648–1652, fo. 331. A joynr was a jointer, a large plane mounted at an angle; a thicksell was an adze; a passer was a hoop of steel used for aligning the barrel staves; a croyse was a croze, used for making grooves at the end of the staves. Information from R A Salaman, *Dictionary of Tools used in the Woodworking and Allied Trades c1700-1970* (George Allen and Unwin, 1975).
56. Will of Mary Ficket, 1650; NRO, ANW, will register, 1648-1652, fo. 362, no. 339.
57. Will of Margery Hornygold, 1633; NRO, NCC Tuck 3.
58. 'Cloth with a pattern resembling birds' eyes, particularly that called Pulham work'; D Yaxley, *A Researcher's Glossary* (Larks Press, 2003).
59. Inventory of Margery Horneygold; NRO, DN/INV 39/4.

# Christopher Hey, the Fire and the Clock Tower

Christopher Hey's family can be traced back to the mid-16th century.

Thomas Hey, aka Thomas Heath, great-grandfather of the builder of the Clock Tower, held land from the manor of Rokeles in 1550[1] and served as one of the churchwardens of Watton in 1570.[2] His son Christopher Hey aka Heath married Mary Alden at St Mary's Church on 15 May 1574. Mary was the daughter of Robert Alden of Watton, a yeoman whose possessions included a long lease of eight and a half acres of meadow 'at or neare Rockelles brigge' and other property in the Diss area. He left Mary a legacy of £10 (equivalent to about £2,000 today) when he died in 1578.[3]

Christopher and Mary's first son, Edward, was baptised on 8 August 1574, and so the marriage may have been a forced one. Nevertheless, the couple went on to have 12 more children before Mary died in 1593, possibly as a result of the birth in that year of their final child, Robert. Of the 13 children, three died in infancy and two more failed to reach their fifth birthdays. Six of the eight who survived were sons: Edward, Christopher, Thomas, Charles, John and Robert.

Christopher Hey, who became known as 'the elder' to distinguish him from his son, described himself as a 'wollendraper'[4] and his business gave him a good enough living to employ servants.[5] He was a prominent figure in Watton, serving as churchwarden in 1579[6] and, as recorded in the 1595 rental, holding several copyhold properties in the town, including half the *Angel*, which lay west of the market place. Among Christopher Hey's other properties were a shop on the south side of the market place; the three fish stalls in the market; 'Bens Pytle', which was a close 'at the westende of Watton markett';[7] (the former Youth Centre playing field); half 'the great close called the Great Wonge somtymes Magges' (the Wong Close, or Mayses Close adjacent to Cley Lane); and more.[8] By 1617, his portfolio had expanded further; in his will, Hey referred to more closes, 'my meadow called Rockles meadowe', a shop in Swaffham, the 'mansion house with the shoppes ajoyninge yt against the market with three fishe stalls' (the house possibly incorporating his half of the *Angel*), 'one tenement and howse newe built' and 'the messuage wherein I nowe inhabit', which had an old barn, an orchard and a new garden attached to it.[9] The mansion house may now have been occupied by Christopher's son and executor, Charles.

Christopher Hey 'the elder' died in 1618. Much of his estate went to Charles but he gave legacies to his sons Edward (who died shortly afterwards), Robert and

Thomas. He did not mention his second son, Christopher Hey junior, who died two years after his father, in 1620; perhaps they had fallen out. He did, however, leave £5 (equivalent to about £660 today) to another Christopher Hey, his grandson, to be paid on his 21st birthday. This was the Christopher Hey who was to build the Clock Tower.

ಸಂಚ

Christopher Hey, the grandson, had been left fatherless at a tender age. His father, John Hey, 'berebrewer', was born in 1586 and married Ann Scott on 24 July 1614. Their son Christopher was baptised on 4 November 1615. John died less than two years later, aged only 31, after just three years of marriage.

John left most of his real estate and goods, with permission to sell them, to his elder brother Charles. Charles duly sold John's brewhouse to William Heighoo of Rokeles Hall.[10] The proceeds were to go to John's widow Ann, to provide an income for her and to pay for Christopher's education. John also left Ann 'all my beds, bedding, brasse, pewter and lynnen and all other my howsehold stuffe whatsoever used in my dwelling howse'. For Christopher, who was yet to reach his second birthday, John reserved 'such implements as shall belong to the brewhouse and the bed in the parlour as it now standeth furnished and two paier of sheets, one boulster, one pillowe, two pillowbeeres [pillow cases], two blankettes and one covering now upon the said bed. And also the plate in the said house used'.[11]

The young Christopher Hey had been carefully provided for. His mother, Ann, lived as a widow for over 50 years, until 1668 and so was able to care for and guide him in his tender years. Christopher established himself as a mercer and began to acquire property in the town. Sometime before 1641, he had got married. Between 1641 and 1660, he and his wife Mary[12] had 12 children, of whom no fewer than six, including the first two, both named John after Christopher's father, died in infancy. Of the other six, one died aged 12 and another aged 24. Mary died in 1673 and when Christopher himself died in 1682, just three of his children survived: two daughters, Lucy and Jane, and his sole heir and executor, his son, Thomas Hey, who had been educated at Gonville and Caius College in Cambridge.

ಸಂಚ

Christopher Hey lived through a period of religious and political conflict in England culminating in the civil war between Crown and Parliament which began in 1642, followed by the execution of Charles I in 1649, the Commonwealth and Protectorate and, eventually, the restoration of the monarchy in the 'Glorious Revolution' of 1660. It was a time when, unsurprisingly, some took advantage of the situation to pursue their own interests.

One such, in 1664, was Ralph Ives who, like Christopher Hey, was a mercer, and lived at 'Paines' on the north side of the market place. Ralph's wife Anne was the daughter of John Bettes (son of the John Bettes mentioned in the 1595 rental), who had died when she was about eight years old. Bettes had conveyed his 18-acre close called Mayses Close (formerly owned by Christopher Hey the elder) to John Olley in 1635 as security for a loan of £100 (equivalent to over £11,000 today). He failed to repay the money when agreed and so Olley seized the close, cut the corn and trees growing there and, according to Ives, 'the late unhappy warres then breaking out whereby those that were well affected to his late Majestie of blessed memory [Charles I] and to his cause and interest as the said John Bettes…was, were lyable and obnoxious to sequestracons and other penalties inflicted by the late usurped powers'.

In the circumstances, the Royalist Bettes, no doubt wisely, took no action and on his death in about 1646, his daughter 'beinge younge and noe ways understanding her own right or affaires of that nature' was in no position to respond. Following the restoration of Charles II in 1660, however, Ives, opportunistically perhaps, sought to recover the close for his wife by bringing a case in the Court of Chancery. He did not succeed.[13]

If Ralph Ives and his father-in-law John Bettes were supporters of the Crown, Christopher Hey's sympathies, very likely, lay with Parliament and, although the evidence about the property is conflicting, this may have helped him to gain control of the half of the *Angel* owned by the Bettes family in 1646.[14] Hey had been an active member of the Watton community in the 1640s and 1650s, serving as churchwarden on numerous occasions and, on 29 March 1656, providing a new cover for the 'Town Book' but, as Julian Horn has noted, with the exception of a year as surveyor of the highways, he then seems to have withdrawn (or been excluded) from parish affairs for eight years after the Restoration in 1660 before once again serving as churchwarden for several years from 1669 onwards.[15] The situation may have parallelled that in Thetford, where, after 1660, 'an Anglican Tory faction…began to reassert itself following ten years of dissenter supremacy'.[16]

Christopher Hey's business, however, appears not to have been unduly affected by the national conflicts. He dealt in textiles and more besides, and his customers covered a wide area. They included members of the Gawdy gentry family in West Harling, to whom he supplied 12 ells of holland[17] and ten yards of fine white thread in 1653, and fish, herrings, sugar, fruit, soap and pewter goods in 1654.[18] Hey acquired the distinction of being the only inhabitant of Watton ever to issue a coin, a small copper trade token with 'Christopher Hey' and the mercers' arms on one side and 'of Watton, Mercer, CMH' (Christopher and Mary Hey) on the other. Tokens were issued in the period from 1649 until the early 1670s in response to a national shortage of small change. Christopher Hey was one of over 350 people in Norfolk to produce them but the date when he did so is not known.[19]

When assessments were made for the hearth tax in 1664 and 1667, Christopher Hey had one of the largest houses in Watton, with eight hearths.[20] By 1670, he was referred to as a 'gentleman'.[21] His principal residence, probably inherited via his uncle Charles from his grandfather, comprised what is now 30, and probably also 28, High Street, with a wing behind and at right angles to the street frontage and a courtyard garden to its west. The first floor of the range facing the street has, a fine beamed ceiling dating from the 16th century,[22] which may have been part of the property called the *Angel*.

All must have seemed good to Christopher Hey. But then, in 1673, his wife Mary died. Another calamity affecting the whole town ensued in the following year.

ಸಿಂಡ

A huge fire broke out in Watton on 25 April 1674. The record of a manor court held on Friday 24 April began and ended with the statement, in Latin: '*Subsequente die oppidum violento igne torruit*' ('On the following day the town was burnt by a violent fire').[23]

*Trade token issued by Christopher Hey.*
*(Norman Phillips)*

The 18th century historian, Blomefield gave the wrong year for the fire but the details he provided about its extent were accurate. 'In 1673', he wrote, 'on Saturday the 25th of April, there happened a most dreadful fire in this town, which burnt down above 60 houses, besides barns, stables and outhouses, the butchers' shambles, etc.' The losses, he said, ran to £7,450 (equivalent to nearly £900,000 today) in real estate and £2,660 (equivalent to over £300,000) in goods, 'for which there was a brief granted to gather all England over till the 20th of Sep 1675'.[24]

*Ceiling beams at 30 High Street.*
*(Author)*

The brief was granted to permit the collection of money for the relief of the inhabitants. It was founded on a certificate given by the Justices of the Peace at their quarter sessions on 14 July 1674, which recorded that 'on Saturday 25 of April last past, there happened a sudden and lamentable fire at Watton…which burnt ye

*Brick panel CHA1674.*
*(Julian Horn)*

houses of Christofor Heye, Thomas Jarvis, Ralph Ives, Frances Hammond widow, Edmund Jarvis, John Howard besides above threescore houses more of the several inhabitants, with their barns, stables, outhouses, market place and butchers' shambles'. The certificate gave the same figures for the value of the losses as were quoted by Blomefield.[25]

Fires were a perennial hazard at a time when most houses were built partly of timber and were thatched. Watton's fire, which caused losses equivalent to about £1.2m, was the worst to occur anywhere in England in 1674, although it was dwarfed the following year by a fire in Northampton, which destroyed 600 houses and caused losses of over £152,000 (equivalent to well over £17m).[26]

If 60 houses were affected in Watton then most of the market town would have been touched by the fire. The hearth tax assessments of 1667 had listed 105 households but some, particularly those of the poor, were probably in multi-occupied buildings. A century later, in 1777, the market town had just 77 houses.[27] However, not all the houses affected were necessarily destroyed. The use of the word *torruit*—perhaps 'charred' might be a good rendering—suggests that the buildings were not completely consumed or, at least, that not all of them were. The fire might have taken the thatch and rafters from the roofs and the laths and window frames while leaving the main timber frame and brick chimneys in place. So much is suggested by a comment by Thomas Barton, writing in 1851: 'Traces of [the fire] can now be seen when any of the old houses in the market-place are undergoing repair'.[28] The surviving timber frames of several buildings at the east end of what is now the High Street, concealed behind later facades, are suggestive of dates of construction before the fire. And, bad as it was, there is no indication in the register of burials that anyone was actually killed in the conflagration, although some may have died as a result of poverty or disease in the aftermath.[29]

The more substantially-built houses in Watton clustered around the highest-status location—the market place. This was where the houses owned by the individuals named in the certificate stood: Christopher Hey, Thomas Jarvis (who may have been renting the *Swan*, which he was to acquire in 1702, next to the *George*), Ralph Ives (at Paines, on the north side of the market place), Frances Hamond, widow (at the *George*, facing the south side of the market place), Edmund Jarvis (who held a house and workshops on the east side of the market place, on the corner of what are now the High Street and Dereham Road) and John Howard (who held a shop and stall in the market place itself). With the exception of the last, the frameworks of these houses probably survived.

Within the market place, three stalls in the 'butchery' (the 'butchers' shambles' mentioned in the Justices' certificate), formerly held by Christopher Hey, and another stall there, did not survive. They were said in 1710 to have been 'for divers years previously…fallen and wasted',[30] very likely as a result of the fire.

Some of the humbler dwellings stretching down the street to the west were very badly affected, to the extent that they were completely destroyed or had to be pulled down. This is what happened to the property of Mary Hornigold, between the passageway to the 'backside' and the site later to be occupied by the *Green Man*. When John Hornigold, her son, took ownership of the premises following the death of his mother, Mary, at the manor court on 13 April 1710, they were described as: 'three tenements or cottages with a yard or garden, which tenements or cottages were built by the said Mary Hornigold in or since the year 1674 on a certain toft or piece of ground wasted, on which part of a tenement called Le Barrell in Middle Row in Watton, viz a hall, a parlour, a shop, a buttery, a bakehouse, a millhouse [and] a small stable formerly stood, which last-mentioned premises…were burnt and totally wasted by fire in the said year 1674'.[31] It was a similar story further down the street, in 'Rotten Row', on part of the site on which Watton Brewery was built over 150 years later, which was described in 1676, two years after the fire, as 'modo vastat' (now wasted).[32] Other buildings suffered the same fate. On 28 March 1695, reference was made to 'a piece or parcel of ground on which was a house called le post house lately burnt', this property being somewhere on the north side of the street. Another property in Rotten Row was stated in 1714 to have been 'lately burnt down and since rebuilt'.[33]

ಸಃಧ

It is not known how much money was raised by the 'brief' but in Norwich, at least, the response was generous. Less than three weeks after the fire, on 13 May 1674, the Norwich Court of Mayoralty asked the aldermen to instruct the churchwardens and overseers of the different parishes of the city to receive from the inhabitants 'their charitable contribution to the relief of the poore distressed inhabitants in Watton who suffered by the late fire and to set down in wrightinge what every person gives and to bringe the whole moniye they collect to the court on Wednesday 20th instant'.[34] The parishes subscribed a total of £143 13s 9½d (the equivalent of over £16,000 today), to which members of the city's corporation added £25 5s (equivalent to nearly £3,000).[35] The inhabitants of Watton were grateful. On 11 July, 'Mr Christopher Hay and several others of the inhabitants of Watton came to ye court and gave their humble and hearty thanks to the court for promoting the charitable benevolence of the inhabitants of the city towards the releife of the poore of that town who suffered by a great fire lately there.'[36] Other places responded generously, too; Hingham raised a total of £14 4s 3d.[37]

The people of Watton themselves had contributed to similar appeals from other places in the past, including after the Great Fire of London in 1666, when they subscribed £2 13s (equivalent to over £300 today).[38] They continued to do so, collecting £1 18s 6d for the people of Northampton in 1676 and smaller sums for places all over the country in the period up to 1683. Another notable act of generosity, unconnected with a fire, was a collection of £3 7s 0.5d for 'poor distressed prisoners in Algiers, Sally [Sale, on the coast of Morocco near Rabat] and other places in [North] Affrica' in 1680.[39]

☙❧

The market town was rebuilt rapidly. A visitor, Thomas Baskerville, noted in 1681: 'Watton is a small towne, lately burnt, but now rebuilt'.[40] Like the Hornigolds, owners of property rebuilt their houses and shops on the ground that they owned, where houses and shops had stood before, although a few sites remained 'waste' for some time. Watton did not move as a result of the fire.

One of those who rebuilt his premises was Christopher Hey. His business had undoubtedly taken a hit. His house had been damaged and his butchery stalls destroyed. Nor, despite his losses being mentioned in the certificate, would he have benefited directly from the money collected under the brief. The Justices of the Peace, meeting in quarter sessions, ordered that 'noe parte of the mony which shall be collected by virtue of any brieife to be obteyned for the losses susteyned by the great fire which lately happened at Watton…be not appllyed to the benifitt of landlords or such other persons of abilitiye who are able to live of themselves and meainteyne theire families without the charitye of the kings liege people.'[41]

Nevertheless, Christopher Hey rebuilt. He appears to have encased the north wing of his house in a brick skin, into the back gable end of which he inserted a panel bearing the date 1674 and the initials CAH, standing for Christopher and Alice Hey. Photographs taken in 2006 when the panel was removed show that it blocked a window opening in the original wall.[42] A brick skin may have been added to the front range at the same time.

Christopher had rebuilt his life in another respect, too: he had remarried, no more than a year after his first wife Mary's death in 1673. His second wife, Alice Fuller, originally Alice Wilks, was a widow from the Ely area and quite wealthy. She owned land in Ely and in the nearby village of Witchford and 'stalls…in the market place in Ely'. In the following century, merchants from Watton were to take butter from Watton to Downham Market, for onward transmission down the Great Ouse past Ely and on towards Cambridge and London. It is tempting to speculate that they were already doing so in the 17th century and that Christopher Hey met Alice or, perhaps, initially, her deceased husband, through such commercial connections, although Alice described her new husband as a woollen draper rather than a butter tracer.[43]

☙❧

Christopher Hey's most notable, enduring legacy to Watton was the iconic Clock Tower, originally known as the 'clock house'. Evidence from inside the building demonstrates that it was built butting up against the chimney stack of Hey's existing house to its east.[44] The clock house was built with red bricks, laid in a

pattern similar to that used in the brick skin of the back range of Hey's 'mansion house' and was covered with a lime wash. The clock was a novel feature; there is no evidence that Watton had ever had a public clock before. The original clock may have been mounted at a lower level than the current one, with the external face in the recess where a datestone is now mounted; traces of the mountings are detectable on the inside of the wall.[45] The clock house may not, originally, have had a cupola as it does today; the bell, installed to warn the inhabitants if fire broke out again, may have hung inside the tower, as in a church. On its west side, at first-floor level, there appears to have been an opening, probably for a window, as there was an open space immediately to the west at that time. What is now 32 High Street was not built until the first half of the 19th century.[46]

It seems likely that the clock house was built at the time when Christopher Hey rebuilt his own mansion house and premises, shortly after the fire. It was built at Hey's own cost, which he then recouped by conveying it to the town. It is possible that the town had, in effect, commissioned Hey to build the Clock Tower on the understanding that he would be reimbursed out of the moneys collected in accordance with the brief. The Town Book recorded on 12 April 1680 that the minister, churchwardens and the rest of the inhabitants of the town had agreed that: 'Mr Christopher Hey having delivered in an account of £70 19s 6d [equivalent to over £8,000 today] disbursed in building a clock house and setting up of a clock and bell, and whereas upon the account £40 was allowed out of the collection for the saide building and charges which being deducted there appeared due to the said Mr Hey £30 19s 6d'. The same entry continued: 'it is further agreed that the inhabitants of Watton shall pay 2s for the ground on which the house stands and that the said Mr Christopher Hey doe give sufficient assurances of the ground upon such a rent', which confirms that Christopher Hey erected the building on land he already owned himself.

Most of the outstanding balance of £30 owing to Christopher Hey for the building of the clock house was to be paid in five annual instalments of £6 from 1680. Two years later, on 17 April 1682, £19 was still owed. It seems likely that by this stage Christopher Hey was already suffering from the complaint that brought about his death less than three months later. His will, in which he left everything to his son Thomas, was dated 28 June 1682 and the parish register recorded his burial a week later, on 5 July.

Already, on 2 April 1682, Thomas Hey had conveyed the clock house to 'several feofees…to the use of the inhabitants of Watton', with the outstanding balance to be paid by letting the Heys have the use of all the town lands for three years free of the normal rent of £5 0s 6d, and by paying them a further 26s per year over the same period. The property was described as a 'piece of ground with a house

*Opposite: The Clock Tower, 1909.*
(Museum4Watton)

thereupon built called the clock house…between the mancion house of him the said Thomas Hey towards the east and the ground of the said Thomas Hey towards the west and abutted on the king's highway to the south'.[47] This entry provides further confirmation that the 'mansion house' belonging to Thomas and, formerly, Christopher Hey lay immediately to the east of the Clock Tower and pre-dated it, and that there was not, as yet, a building immediately to the west of the Clock Tower.

❧☙

Christopher Hey died insolvent, as became clear shortly after his death. He had sold some of his properties, mortgaged others and settled the *Angel* on his son Thomas on the latter's marriage in 1679.[48] He had failed to hand in tax revenues he had collected in his capacity as chief constable of Wayland Hundred, only £7 out of £20 owing being recovered eventually from his executors.[49] Christopher's marriage to Alice may have been driven as much by economic necessity as by a desire for company. He behaved honourably, however; when Alice died in 1681, most of her property was bequeathed to her brothers, sisters, nephews and nieces, 'by and with the consent of the said Christopher Hey.' Alice did leave small bequests to her husband's children and grandchildren. Christopher's unmarried daughter and youngest child Lucy received £5, as did his daughter Jane, the wife of Peter George. Jane's daughter Anne was promised £5 when she reached the age of 21, as were two other grandchildren, Mary and Joseph Isaak, the children of another of Christopher's daughters, Mary, now deceased.

Thomas Baskerville, in 1681, noted the presence in Watton of 'Mr High [Hey], a master of Art in Cambridge'. The following year, after his father's death, Thomas Hey sold his remaining properties and repaid his father's debts as far as he could. A close of nine acres, in the southern part of the parish, was acquired by Edmund de Grey, who resided at Merton Hall and was owed money by the Heys.[50] Thirteen years later, in 1695, Thomas Hey was ordained and became the rector of a parish in Nottinghamshire.[51] The life of a mercer and woollen draper was not for him.

❧☙

The present appearance of the Clock Tower owes much to refurbishment at different times in the 19th and early 20th centuries. In 1827, a new clock, the present one, was installed, the gift of Edward Stevens, and its predecessor removed. The installation of the new clock may have provided the occasion for the incorporation of a section of the old market cross in the façade of the Clock Tower, which had certainly happened by 1836.[52] In 1831, the Clock Tower was described as 'a small building, with a clock and one bell, the latter rung on Sundays preparatory to divine service; the lower part is used as a lock-up house'.[53] A similar portrayal was recorded in 1834: 'a building used as a clock house by the parish in which a clock was fixed and a new one has been placed there…a few years since, also a part of it is used as a lock up for disorderly persons'.[54] Another feature of the Clock Tower noted in 1834 was a 'vertical sundial' on the wall facing the street.[55] The following year, a new bell was presented to the town by Edward Stevens, engraved with the date, Stevens' name and '37 years churchwarden'.[56]

In 1844, the parish paid 'Darkins Bill for rebuild[in]g clock house, £51 7s 0d'[57] (equivalent to about £4,120 today) and White's Directory of the following year noted of the Clock Tower that: 'This building has recently been repaired and beautified'. Darkins was the builder who constructed the new National School in 1842, in which he had used white bricks, fashionable at the time. The crenelations at the top of the Clock Tower were also constructed in white bricks and so they were probably added as part of the work done in 1844. The cupola may also have been erected at this time.

In 1870, at a vestry meeting, the principal inhabitants of the town resolved to rent out the coal house and fire engine house at the west end of the street, sell the engine and use the proceeds for the maintenance of the clock and the building. Whether or not they actually did so, by 1878, the Clock Tower was again in a 'dangerous condition' and a committee was set up to establish what 'restoration and repair' would cost. The 'front of the building was in danger of falling out' and the cupola and weathervane were also in a dangerous condition.[58] The vestry meeting decided to keep the clock house as a 'public parish building' and not to let it out, and to raise the cost of repairing it, about £30, by voluntary subscription.[59] It may have been at this point, if not in 1844 or earlier, that the original twin-arched entrance was replaced by the present doorways, on a slightly different alignment.

In 1913, the Clock Tower needed attention yet again. Workmen 'stripped off the outer coating of old plaster' revealing the original entrance and the red brick of the building, which was in 'a splendid state of preservation', prompting a debate about whether the brickwork should be pointed or rendered with cement. The Parish Council decided on rendering; it was cheaper.[60] A further change occurred in 1935, when an illuminated clock face was installed to commemorate the silver jubilee of King George V.[61]

Sometime between 1669 and 1721, the manor house belonging to Watton's principal manor, the manor of Watton Hall, was abandoned, a development that had no obvious connection with the fire.

Sir Edward Barkham, son of a lord mayor of London, inherited the manor from his father in 1634. He sustained losses in the Great Fire of London in 1666, referring in his will to lands in Cheapside and St Lawrence Lane in the City, 'upon which were heretofore erected several houses or tenements which were ruinated by the late fire'[62] and instructed his executors to sell the manor of Watton Hall. Barkham died in 1667 and two years later the manor was sold to Anthony Samwell[63] for £5,300 (equivalent to over £600,000 today). In 1672, Samwell conveyed the manor to trustees for his son, William Samwell. William was an architect, responsible for designing the west wing of Felbrigg Hall, and Julian Horn has argued that he may well have had a hand in the rebuilding of Watton immediately after the fire.[64] He died in 1676 and his widow Anne Samwell married John Woodhouse in 1680, retaining ownership of the manor of Watton Hall, which she had inherited from her first husband. Anne died a widow in 1720[65] and the manor was inherited by Ann Samwell, her daughter by her first husband, who married Captain William Henry Fleming in the same year. Ann Fleming died in 1728 and her husband remarried, the manor descending to his son by his second marriage, Sir William Fleming, who sold it to Francis Hicks in 1775.[66]

When the manor was sold to Anthony Samwell in 1669, the property was said to include: 'all that capital messuage or tenement mannor house and scite of the said mannor of Watton',[67] a description that was reproduced word-for-word in a document of 1733.[68] However, when the former Ann Samwell and her husband William Henry Fleming conveyed the manor to trustees in 1721, reference was made, not to the capital messuage but to 'all that toft upon which stood formerly the capital messuage or mansion house or scite of the…manor'.[69] At some point before 1721, therefore, the old manor house had ceased to exist. It had probably gone by 1714, because an entry in the manor court book that year recorded that the property east of the Clock Tower, at the corner of the street and the market place, had been acquired by John Woodhouse and Anne his wife in 1689 and that since then 'several addicons and alteracons have been made…to convert the same into a mansion house for the said lord and lady',[70] suggesting that they had stopped using the old manor house as their residence before 1714.

Blomefield, writing in 1738, stated that 'the church was placed by the old manor house (which is now quite demolished)'[71] and at that date the toft on which the manor house stood might still have been discernible. The archaeological finds from the field north of the church support Blomefield's assertion that the manor house and church stood close to each other. As Julian Horn has pointed out, the location of the porch on the north side of the church is unusual and this might be further evidence that the manor house was on its north side.[72] The lands associated with the manor were referred to in 1764 as Manor Farm.[73] In 1801, they were purchased by Charles Dorr, as part of a farm, 'commonly called the Manor otherwise Neaton Farm', on which Dorr built himself a new house and farm buildings.[74] The new farm premises were adjacent to what is now Dereham Road, but those they replaced may have been much nearer the church and the site of the original manor house.

Watton's market revived rapidly after the fire. A rental of 1680[75] referred to only one 'stall wasted' but 28 that were in use, including the fish stalls.[76] The total number of stalls was lower than in 1595, when 45 were listed, but the market was still a going concern. Seven shops were noted, including one described as a 'shop late stalls'; again, fewer than the nine in 1595 but it seems likely that some of the stalls and shops were gradually being converted into more permanent 'tenements', an extension of the process of converting stalls into shops that was already happening in the 16th century. One property in 1680 was referred to specifically as a 'tenement late stalls'.

Subsequent rentals, for 1712 and 1726,[77] showed this process continuing. Twenty-seven stalls, (30 if three fish stalls are added) were noted in 1712 but the fish stalls were described as 'down' in 1716 and 'laid waste' in 1721. Five other stalls had gone, described as 'wast' or 'laid wast' in 1726. Although one new stall had appeared, overall the market had contracted. At the same time, however, the consolidation and conversion of market structures into permanent buildings was continuing. 'A dwelling house late Mr Hey's shop' and 'two stalls now a house' illustrate the process. Later, in 1785, William Thompson referred in his will to the 'stall which I purchased…now a dwellinghouse'.[78]

Most of the inns mentioned in the rental of 1595 remained in evidence. The *George*, the *Griffin*, the *Swan* (with a 'signe') and the *Bull* (renamed the *Labour in Vaine* by 1719) were all mentioned in these rentals but the *Christopher* and the *Dove* seem to have disappeared. The *Angel* was recorded but the name seems to have migrated from its original location to a building in the street formerly known as the *Cock*. New names that appeared by the end of the 17th century were the *White Hart* and the *Queen's Arms*, the latter having been built by James Tooley sometime between 1699 and 1712, on a plot in 'Rotten Row'. Another inn in 'Rotten Row' had probably been destroyed in the fire: the *Three Fishes*, formerly held by John Tooley, who was recorded as an alehouse keeper in 1648-1651 and 1670.[79]

The building of the *Queen's Arms* is one of several examples in the rentals of the development taking place in 'Rotten Row', towards the west end of Watton's street. Several small pieces of what had been the waste grounds had passed into private ownership and been built on. Other sources told the same story; William Dunthorne, for example, referred in his will of 1696 to a messuage or tenement 'with the outhouses thereto belonging…which I built upon the lands I purchased'.[80] Richard Tillett, a chairmaker, bequeathed to his wife 'all that my new built messuage or tenement….in Watton…with the yard, stable, outhouses and other edifices and buildings thereunto belonging' when he died in 1740.[81] On the 'backside', the house originally known as Godfrey's and later as Harvey House was built (or rebuilt) in 1720.[82]

On the south side of the High Street, Goffe's almshouses survived the fire of 1674 because they occupied what was still, at that time, a fairly isolated position. During the 18th century, however, development began to take place on the south side of the street as well.

It was driven by dynasties of shopkeepers—enterprising and ingenious tradesmen.

**Notes**

1. Terrier of the manor of Rokeles, 1550; TNA, SC 11/482.
2. Watton Town Book; NRO, PD 218/1.
3. Will of Robert Alden, 1579; NRO, ANW, Sellers fo 276.
4. Will of Christopher Hey the elder, 1617; TNA PROB 11-131-778.
5. Robert Alden (junior) gave them money in his will of 1601; will of Robert Alden, 1600; NRO, NCC Gardyner 184. Christopher Hey himself did likewise, 16 years later.
6. Watton Town Book; NRO, PD 218/1.
7. Will of Agnes Bougeon, 1555; NRO, NCC Beeles 84.
8. 1595 rental.
9. Will of Christopher Hey the elder, 1617; TNA PROB 11-131-778.
10. Will of William Heighoo, 1632; NRO, NCC Morse 58.
11. Will of John Hey, 1617; NRO, ANW Weavers f169.
12. No record has been found of their marriage.
13. Ives v Salter, 28 September 1664; TNA C 10/473/104. John Olley's executors had sold the close to Simon Salter. It was inherited by Salter's son Richard and eventually passed to Thomas Younge.
14. According to the manor court book of the manor of Watton Hall, Christopher Hey was admitted to both halves of the *Angel* on the surrender of Christopher Jay in 1646 and then surrendered them to his son Thomas Hey in 1679. In 1707, however, the daughters of Thomas and Elizabeth Jarvis were admitted to the half of the *Angel* formerly held by John and Thomas Bettes, with a barn in its backside and a garden and orchard adjoining. It may be that ownership was disputed, or that the property was now divided in a different way. Museum4Watton, M4W/2016/8A.
15. J Horn (2011).
16. Alan Crosby, '"Villaines enough": political and personal feuding within Thetford Corporation, 1658-1700', in Evelyn Lord and Nicholas R Amor (eds), *Shaping the Past: Theme, Time and Place in Local History* (University of Hertfordshire Press, 2020). See also Alan Crosby, *A History of Thetford* (Phillimore, 1986).
17. An ell was a little over a metre; holland was an unbleached linen or cotton cloth.
18. Gawdy papers, Historical Manuscripts Commission.
19. Adrian Marsden, 'Norfolk's seventeenth-century tokens and the Norfolk token project' in *The Annual: The Bulletin of the Norfolk Archaeological and Historical Research Group*, No 26 (2017).
20. 1664 hearth tax assessment, Norfolk Genealogy vol 15 (1983); 1667 hearth tax assessment, TNA, E179/253/45.
21. In the wills of Richard Linkcon and William Clements, both 1670.
22. D Gurney and K Penn (eds), 'Excavations and Surveys in Norfolk in 2004', in Norfolk Archaeology, Volume XLIV, Part IV (2005); NHER 40381.
23. Manor court book, Manor of Watton Hall, 1674; Museum4Watton, M4W/2016/8A.
24. F Blomefield (1805).

25. NRO, NAS/1/1/25/Watton. This is a copy of the brief that may have been made by Blomefield himself.
26. W A Bewes, *Church Briefs* (A and C Black, 1896).
27. T Barton (1852), referring to information in the glebe terrier of 1777. There were another 26 houses in the hamlets — Watton Green and Neaton.
28. Ibid.
29. J Horn (2011).
30. Manor court book, Manor of Watton Hall, 1710; Museum4Watton, M4W/2016/8B.
31. Ibid.
32. Surrender of a tenement by Humphrey Browne, 30 March 1676; NRO, BR156/2/6.
33. Manor court book, Manor of Watton Hall, 28 March 1695, 25 November 1714; Museum4Watton, M4W/2016/8A, 8B.
34. Minute book of the Court of Mayoralty, Norwich; NRO, NCR Case 16 Shelf A/24, quoted in J Horn (2011).
35. T Barton (1852).
36. Minute book of the Court of Mayoralty, Norwich; NRO, NCR Case 16 Shelf A/24, quoted in J Horn (2011).
37. From the catalogue of an exhibition in Hingham Church, 1978.
38. Watton Town Book; NRO, PD218/1.
39. NRO, PD 218/27. The prisoners in North Africa would have been victims of the fearsome Barbary pirates.
40. British Library, Add Mss 70523.
41. Norfolk Quarter Sessions order book, 1669-81; NRO, C/S2/3.
42. As shown in photographs taken by Julian Horn when the panel was removed.
43. Will of Alice Hey; TNA, PROB 11/366/420.
44. J Horn (2011).
45. This paragraph relies heavily on photographs taken over the past 30 years by Julian Horn, and on observations and discussions with Julian on site.
46. Although J Horn (2011) suggests that the panel on the northern gable end may originally have been mounted here.
47. Abstract of the deed for the Clock Tower, 2 April 1682; Museum4Watton mss 2017-29.29. This source indicates that £31 was paid to Christopher's son Thomas Hey in 1682, and that the annual rent was 2s 6d.
48. Manor court book, Manor of Watton Hall, Museum4Watton, M4W/2016/8A.
49. Norfolk Lieutenancy Journal, 1676-1701; Norfolk Record Society Volume XXXX (1961).
50. NRO, WLS VII/4/14-16 408x4.
51. This was discovered online by Julian Horn.
52. White's Directory of Norfolk, 1836. This piece of wood was removed in the 1980s.
53. Topographical Dictionary of England (Samuel Lewis, 1831).
54. Copy of an account of town lands, etc, delivered to the Charity Commissioners, 17 March 1834; NRO, ACC 2023/12.
55. Watton glebe terrier, 1834; NRO, DN/TER 159/4/24.
56. Cutting from TWT, August or September 1978. Many thanks to Julian Horn for sharing this.
57. Pencil addition to a note on a parish vestry meeting on 21 March 1878.
58. Draft letters to the Charity Commission and to Lord Walsingham, nd (1878); Museum4Watton mss 217-29.28.

59. Minute of vestry meeting, 21 March 1878; NRO, ACC 2023/12; Watton vestry minute book, 1842-83; NRO PD 218/89.
60. Watton Parish Council minutes, book 2, 29 August 1913; DMG, 30 August 1913.
61. Cutting from TWT, August or September 1978.
62. Will of Sir Edward Barkham, 1667; TNA PROB 11/324/466.
63. Not William Samwell, as stated by Blomefield. William was Anthony's son.
64. J Horn (2011).
65. An entry in the parish register reads: 'Mrs Ann Wodehouse, patroness of this living, was buryed in ye chancel Aug 23 [1720]; NRO, PD218/26.
66. T Barton (1852); NRO, catalogue description of HIL/1/252/1-19 875x2 and HIL/1/252/20-29, 875x3.
67. Conveyance from the executors of Sir Edward Barkham to Anthony Samwell, 28 July 1669; NRO, MC 2364/2/1.
68. NRO, MC2364/2/9/1-2 1032x8.
69. Lease and release from William Henry Flemming and Anne his wife to trustees, 1 December 1721; NRO, MC 2364/2/6/1-2 1032x7.
70. Manor court book, Manor of Watton Hall, 1714; Museum4Watton, M4W/2016/8B.
71. F Blomefield (1805).
72. J Horn (2011).
73. Lease and release, Sir William Fleming to Stephen Caesar Lemaistre, 16-17 July 1764; NRO, MC2364/2/11/1-2.
74. Abstract of title of Charles Dorr deceased to freehold premises in Watton, 1801-45; NRO, MS 7858 19 D 1.
75. NRO, BL MC/25.
76. Assuming there were three of them, as before, although the number was not given.
77. NRO, MC1819/33 844x8.
78. Will of William Thompson, 1785; NRO, ANW fo 152.
79. Alehouse recognizances, Wayland Hundred; NRO, C/Sch1/2.
80. Will of William Dunthorne, 1696; NRO, ANW, 1695-96 fo 417.
81. Will of Richard Tillett, 1740; NRO, ANW 1711-12, fo 382.
82. NHER 19202.

# Ingenious Tradesmen

On 28 June 1727, Watton was celebrating.

A local newspaper reported that 'the morning was spent in adorning the streets with boughs and garlands, and the houses with tapestry, pictures, etc. All the neighbouring gentlemen and others assembled and at three in the afternoon set forward in good order with Mr Reuben Muston as sheriff, preceded with drums, trumpets and other musick. A mile from the town we met Tho. De Grey Esq., our truly worthy representative [MP] for the county, attended with several coaches; and then we set forward with as good decorum as possible with so great a crowd; next the coaches went the town serjeants with their fine halberts; the constables, with silk streamers upon their staves, and the musick. Then the sheriff, with his white staff, the clergy in two ranks, the gentle-men and country-men with above 300 horses, and a vast number on foot with a continual acclamation of Long Live King George the Second.' The celebration was in honour of the new king's succession.

The report continued: 'In this order, with great decency, we marched to the [market] cross and proclaimed His Majesty, upon which the shouts were the loudest ever heard in so small a market town. Then we proceeded into the Cross-street,[1] and repeated the proclamation with the like shouts; there the gentlemen on horseback drank the King's health, and treated the ladies and the better sort of country-man with wine, and gave a barrel of strong beer to the populace in the street. Then the gentlemen waited upon our representative to the *George*, where they drank healths of the King, the Queen, Prince Frederick and the rest of the royal family; after which Sir Robert Walpole [the Prime Minister at the time] and an abundance of worthy gentlemen were toasted. The evening was finely illuminated and hardly one house miss'd; a handsome bonefire was made and another barrel of strong beer given to the populace; the whole was concluded about 12 at night; the bells rang without ceasing the whole time'.[2]

A fine cameo of Watton in the first half of the 18th century, with the life of the town being centred, as in the previous century, on the market cross and the *George* Inn.

ಸಂಬ

Among the prominent inhabitants of Watton in the mid-18th century were the Hicks family.

According to the parish register, Francis Hicks, buried on 3 May 1743, was 'an ingenious tradesman and a very charitable man'.[3] He was a grocer, who had built up an extensive portfolio of properties in Watton, Caston, Shipdham and Carbrooke,[4] including the *George* Inn in Watton, which he had purchased in 1731. He and his wife Jane had 12 children, five of whom died in infancy.[5] Their eldest son was Francis Hicks (1720-83) and he, with his widowed mother, took over his father's business and properties. Burden Hicks (1721-81), the second son, became a surgeon and apothecary, 'whose business was very extensive among the first families'.[6] Among the other sons, John (1731-78), was a grocer and draper and occupied property next to the *George*,[7] Thomas (1735-94) became 'an eminent attorney at law'[8] and William (1742-84) became vicar of Watton. They were a high-achieving family.

Francis Hicks, the eldest son, prospered for a time but then disaster struck. He had purchased the manor of Watton Hall and the estate associated with it from Sir William Fleming in 1775 but immediately mortgaged it. On 21 April 1781 it was announced that his estates were to be sold.[9] He was bankrupt.

His mother, Jane Hicks, perhaps affected by her son's situation, died in November of the same year.

Francis Hicks 'of Breckles', described as 'merchant, butter factor, dealer and chapman', was required to appear before the bankruptcy commissioners at the *George* Inn, which he owned, on three dates in June and July 1781 to 'make a full discovery and disclosure of his estate and effects' and face his creditors.[10] It must have been humiliating.

The *George* was one of the properties that had to be put up for sale in auctions held on 29 November and 6 December 1781, along with a 'compleat estate' of 300 acres in Watton and Carbrooke, with grazing rights for sheep. As lord of the manor of Watton Hall, Francis Hicks had also owned the advowson of the vicarage (to which he had presented his brother, the Revd William Hicks, in 1779) and the impropriation of the rectorial, or 'great' tithes of the parish.

The auction took place at the *George* and the first lot to be offered on 6 December was the inn itself and 'a dwelling house with necessary buildings' next door, described as 'late in the occupation of John Hicks', Francis's younger brother. A second lot comprised 'all that public house in Watton called the *Bull* [the earliest known reference to the *Bull* that existed until recently], with the outhouses, stable, yard and spacious garden to the same belonging' with an adjoining house. Lot 3 was another dwelling house with a yard, stable and other buildings in the occupation of John Flower. Flower was the landlord of the *Crown* but this was not the *Crown*, which was owned at the time by the Younges; it may have been Flower's private residence. Lot 4 was a butcher's stall in the market place of Watton. Properties in Caston, Rockland St Peter and Sporle comprised the remaining lots.[11]

The *George* Inn sold but the 'compleat estate' did not. It was offered again at auction on 21 March 1782, when another property was added: a 'messuage, with a shop, warehouse, chandling office, brewhouse, stables, yard, garden and two inclosures of pasture land adjoining…late in the occupation of John Kett and Samuel Ellington.'[12] This newly advertised property was the shop that had belonged to Francis Hicks the elder, which was probably the former *Swan*. John Kett had advertised a 'cheap sale' there of 'a great variety of woollen and linen drapery, grocery, ironmongery, haberdashery and divers other kinds of goods'. He gave up the shop, which was offered to let on 27 April 1782, described as previously, with the addition: 'The premises [are] fitted up in the most convenient and compleat manner for carrying on the general business of a shopkeeper. The above has been one of the best accustomed shops in the county and a very extensive butter trade carried on there'. The advertisement noted that 'there is no old stock for the tenant to take'. Obviously, the 'cheap sale' had been successful.

Francis Hicks, the younger, died in 1783. He had lost most of what he had once possessed but was able to remember family members and others close to him in his will. To one of his less-known brothers, Henry Hicks, he left 'a dozen of my best shirts and neckcloths, four of my best waistcoats and six of my best handkerchiefs (four of linen and two of silk)'; to his nephew Robert Hicks, son of his brother John Hicks, 'a set of plated buttons'; to his niece Jane Hicks, daughter of John, 'a pearl snuff box'; the same to Mr Rogers, surgeon; to another surgeon, Mr Bringloe of Shipdham, 'a leash of my best greyhounds'. Despite his misfortunes, Francis Hicks had managed to keep up appearances. He left his bed and the remainder of his linen to his servant, Sarah Frostick, and the rest of his clothing to 'Richard Margisson who now lives with me'. Finally, he bequeathed 'the residue of my personal estate, if any' to his nephew and niece. A poignant end for a man who had over-reached.

Francis Hicks' younger brother, Thomas Hicks, the lawyer, married Elizabeth Raby on 9 January 1765. He acquired the manor of Watton Hall, with the associated estate and advowson of St Mary's church after Francis's bankruptcy. He died in February 1794. Later in the same year, his widow, Elizabeth, became fabulously wealthy because her brother, John Raby, had died and she inherited the properties he had amassed, worth 'near £150,000' (equivalent to about £11.5m today).[13] As a very eligible widow, on 16 May 1796, she married Benjamin Barker, widower, of Carbrooke. As Elizabeth Barker, owner of the Watton Hall estate, her name appeared prominently on the map of Watton produced by the Enclosure Commissioners in 1803. She lived at what later became known as the 'Manor House' in Dereham Road, which she described in her will of 1807 as her 'capital messuage...with the coach house, stables, outhouses, yards, gardens and fish pond to the same belonging'.[14] She died in 1813.

☙❧

Another story of a Watton businessman who got into difficulties concerns Thomas Jarvis. At the beginning of the 18th century, he occupied the *Swan* (east of the *George*), scene of a tragic incident in 1695, recorded in the parish register of burials: 'Peter Stanguage...lost his life by falling into a copper of boyling wort at ye *Swan* [and] was buryed, Jan 4'.[15]

The *Swan* may still have been in business as an inn in 1704, when Jarvis, who had 'endeavoured to get his living by using the trade of a common brewer and by buying and selling of malt and hops', became subject to a commission of bankruptcy. He had been renting land from Richard Salter, fellow of Jesus College, Cambridge but had fallen behind with his rent. Salter was approaching 60 years of age and was 'very ill and uneasy'. Despite claiming 'I would not bee [sic] hard upon a tenant', he asked his attorney in Watton, John Muston, to 'presse' Jarvis for payment of the £22 (equivalent to about £2,400 today) owing to him, adding 'I leave him wholly to your management, whether you will seize upon ye crop in ye barn, and take ye farm from him or what else you thinks [sic] most adviseable'. Salter's condition deteriorated; in May 1705 he confided to Muston: 'I am so afflicted with my dizziness and tremblings that I am seldom able to write'. Thomas Jarvis acknowledged his debts to Salter, writing to Muston: 'I am willing to pay my landlord Salter the arrears of rent I owe him as fast as mony can be raised. And to satisfye you I am in earnest, I desire you to imploy workemen to cut down and get in all my crop of corn as fast as you can. And I do consent and agree all the charge thereof shall be first paid you and the remainder of the mony which the corne shall be sold for I desire you to apply towards payment of my landlord'. The crops of barley and peas growing on Jarvis's farm, including in a close, 'part of sixteen acres behind the Swann', were seized, along with 'two mares and a horse with the cart and the wheat in the barn, both threshed and unthreshed, the harness belonging to the horses when they were yoaked in the cart, the screen and two riddles, a parcel of wheat straw in the barn, the bushel, two fans, a casting shulve, two parcells of wheat straw, a plough and harrow, a parcel of bricks, two parcells of muck in the Barn Close and yard'.[16] This episode shows how the rural environment still penetrated right into the centre of Watton at the time.

ಜಲಿ

Among the biggest players in Watton in the second half of the 18th century and the first decade of the 19th were members of the Younge family.

Like the Hicks, the Younges developed a large grocery and drapery business and were brewers and dealers in butter. However, the first member of the family to establish a presence in Watton, Edward Younge, was initially an 'aromatarius' (a spicer or apothecary).[17] He married Elizabeth Stalworthy, daughter of Thomas Stalworthy, another apothecary (and probably Edward's employer), in 1723 and they had four sons over the following seven years. Only one, Thomas, survived his father.

One of Thomas' brothers, William, died of smallpox in 1742, aged 17.[18] Deaths from smallpox punctuated Watton's parish register of burials in the 18th century. In 1712, 21 out of the 32 people buried during the year died of smallpox. In 1737, there were four victims; in 1741, another four; and in 1742, Edward Younge's son was one of eleven more. In the second half of the century, the poor were vaccinated against smallpox and the death rate from the disease declined.

Edward Younge's wife Elizabeth died in 1731 and Edward promptly married her sister Mary Stalworthy. They had five daughters and a son, two daughters and the son dying in infancy. The other three daughters, Mary, Hester and Pleasance, survived their father.

In 1731, Edward began to acquire property in Watton. His first acquisition was just over a quarter of an acre of land on west side of the *George* Inn.[19] It was on this plot, described thirty years later as 'formerly the garden belonging to the *George* Inn', that the 'capital messuage' or chief residence of the Younge family was to be built.

Further acquisitions followed. In 1733[20] Younge bought from Ann, widow of Thomas Ives, the house called 'Paines' on the north side of the market place together with the tollhouse and two 'shops' next to the site of the former fish stalls. In 1735 he acquired from John Muston nearly 50 acres of arable and pasture land in different parts of Watton, including the two closes known as Mayses Closes and the house in 'Rotten Row' previously known as the *Queen's Arms*, then as the *King's Arms*, and later as the *Green Man*. In 1737, Edward Young was one five people who took action in the Court of Chancery to recover debts from Reuben Muston, John Muston's son, who had died. The debts owed to Edward Younge amounted to £117 for goods sold and delivered, and money lent, an indication of the extensive credit which shopkeepers were expected to provide to their customers.[21]

In 1735, Edward Younge had also acquired a small piece of land 'next Curson's Cross' (at the west end of the street, on the south side) and a 'millhouse and kiln' nearby. Further purchases took place in 1742, 1745 and 1746. The property acquired in 1746 included the half of the 'messuage or tenement formerly called the *Angel*' which had belonged to John and Thomas Bettes. Finally, in 1755, Younge obtained another part of the former garden of the *George* Inn and a 'messuage or tenement formerly Cranmer's'.[22] These acquisitions amounted to a significant portfolio of property in the town.

Edward Younge did not just buy real estate; he sold and developed it. In 1756, he offered to let: 'a convenient dwelling house new built, five rooms on a floor, with a good garden thereto belonging, and a pasture close adjoining to the same, now in the occupation of Mr Burden Hicks, apothecary'.[23] Burden Hicks, the brother of Francis Hicks, probably renewed his lease, as an agreement of 1760 between Younge and his son Thomas[24] referred to a house let to Hicks.

Edward Younge made provision in his will (drawn up in July 1760) for his wife Mary to live in 'Paines', which he referred to as 'late called the *Duke's Head*', to choose furniture for it to the value of £100 and to have an annuity of £50 per year. To the surviving son of his first marriage, Thomas, and his three surviving daughters Mary, Hester and Pleasance (the last two being minors) he bequeathed £1,000 each (equivalent to over £100,000 today).[25] Two months after drawing up the will, and 'being in a bad state of health', Edward Younge made an agreement with his son[26] by which he transferred his business to him. Thomas was to pay Edward's debts and to maintain two horses for his use. Edward was to give Thomas rent-free accommodation in his house (if Thomas married, he was to have the house occupied by Burden Hicks 'if his lease be then out' or other suitable accommodation free of charge) and provide subsistence for him and for 'his journeyman and two apprentices', an indication of the size of the business at this time. Thomas and Edward were to share the expense of 'keeping and maintaining a man servant for their equal use and benefit'. Before his death Edward made, at Thomas's expense, a journey to Bath costing £150 (equivalent to over £15,000 today), no doubt to 'take the waters' there.[27]

Edward Younge died at the end of January 1761. His widow, Mary, did not long survive him; she was buried at Watton on 29 March 1761.

ঙ০෬

Thomas Younge, Edward's son by his first marriage, married his wife Dorothy shortly after his father's death and they had eight children, six of whom survived infancy. He took over the business but did not add significantly to the real estate he had inherited from his father, although he acquired under the will of his uncle, Thomas Stalworthy of Norwich, surgeon (son of his grandfather, Thomas Stalworthy of Watton, apothecary), another house and property in Watton. The house, which stood near his 'capital messuage',[28] was in the occupation of Burden Hicks in 1763 and may have been the one referred to in the agreement of 1760.

In 1767, 'Herring's Norfolk Antidote for the Bite of a Mad Dog and other Mad Animals' was advertised as obtainable from 'Hicks and Younge' in Watton.[29] Rabies was one of the hazards of life in the town. In 1697, an entry in the parish register recorded the burial of someone who 'dyed mad after two months being bit by a mad dog', while in 1792 the parish authorities made the following announcement: 'Mad Dogs. To prevent as much as possible the dreadful and fatal consequences which at this time are likely to arise from dogs being at large within the…parish, the inhabitants are requested to confine their dogs for 40 days, from the date hereof, and to take notice that all dogs found at liberty during that time will be destroyed'.[30] The advertisement for Herring's antidote may indicate that there was a partnership between Younge and either Francis Hicks or his brother Burden Hicks.

Thomas Younge was primarily a grocer and draper but his trade as a butter factor was a significant part of his business. Twenty years or so before Thomas had taken over from his father, Blomefield recorded that the market at Watton was 'no despicable one, great quantity of butter being sent through this place to Downham-Bridge, from whence the factors return it to London by water.'[31] The butter was sent to Downham Market because there was a large butter market there on Mondays. In the mid-18th century, during spring and summer, about 3,000 firkins of butter (a firkin contained 56 lb of butter) were regularly sold to factors, who sent them by water to Cambridge and thence overland to London.[32] In 1831, the neighbourhood of Watton was still 'noted for supplying the metropolis with large quantities of butter, called Cambridge butter'.[33]

Thomas Younge incurred debts for purchases of butter and also owed money to butter tasters and butter carriers. Other sums were due for the 'landing of butter,'[34] probably at Downham Bridge where tolls had to be paid on the butter unloaded.[35] Among payments owing to Thomas Younge at the time of his death in 1770 were a number from cheesemongers, presumably for butter, amounting to £1,250 (equivalent to about £130,000 today).[36]

A desire to facilitate the transport of butter from central Norfolk to Downham Market was probably one of the motives behind a proposal to build a canal from Norwich to the river 'Ouze', via Wymondham, Hingham and Watton, floated in 1777. The thinking was that agricultural produce could be exported more easily and coal could be brought in. To establish whether a canal would pay, the proprietors of estates were invited to state the quantities of various commodities that they might wish to have conveyed, including the number of tons of butter sent to Cambridge for the London markets.[37] Their replies must have disappointed the promoters of the scheme, as no canal was ever built to or near Watton.

However, seven years earlier, in 1770, action had already been taken to improve communication between Norwich and Watton by road, when an Act of Parliament established a turnpike trust to take responsibility for the maintenance of the road from Norwich to the windmill on the common at the west end of Watton. Toll gates were set up at Colney and Hingham, where road users had to pay a fee. The initiative seems to have been successful but an attempt to 'turnpike' the road from Watton to Thetford was defeated.

ಶಿಂಡ

Thomas Younge 'gentleman', died in December 1770. He was well regarded, having just been appointed treasurer of the Wayland Association for Apprehending and Convicting of Horse-stealers and Other Robbers, a body to which most of the other 'gentlemen' of the district belonged.[38] He had, however, over-extended his commitments. He died 'greatly in debt.'[39] His debts amounted to nearly £18,000 (equivalent to nearly £1,600,000 today) and were not finally paid off until 1795.[40] Younge's will established a 'trust for sale' in order to pay his debts and provide legacies for his children.[41] To meet the demands of his creditors it was necessary to sell 'a great part of the real estate.'[42]

A detailed valuation of Younge's property, including the stock in his shop, was carried out. The results were recorded in two inventories which together ran to 57 pages;[43] the longer listing his stock and the shorter providing details of his household and other effects. These amazingly detailed documents, with other sources, take us to the heart of the Younges' business, their lifestyle, and life in Watton 250 years ago.

Thomas Younge's main premises comprised the house and shop, a warehouse and candle house, and associated outbuildings and gardens. The buildings occupied by the house and shop were erected between 1731 and 1761 and survive to this day, as 19 High Street. The shop, on the ground floor facing the street, was extensive.

A paper dated 8 October 1771 gave details of the shop, other buildings connected with it and 'the drawers, counters, shelves, writing desk and all the fixtures in the shop, counting house, backshop, chamber and all the other fixtures, which are on the premises, not mentioned in the inventory'.[44] An 'iron chest' may have contained the takings.[45]

The living accommodation for the household was above and behind the shop. A keeping room, parlour and kitchen were probably on the ground floor of the range behind the shop, with a cellar (containing wine and ale) beneath them. On the first floor were bed chambers, the nursery and the dining room. One chamber was referred to as the 'gate way chamber' probably the room that still exists over the gateway into the courtyard. On the second floor were garrets, a store room and the apprentices' chamber. The premises had sash windows: the family was billed in 1771 for sashes, lead for weights, glass and white lead (probably for painting the window frames).[46]

The rooms occupied by the family were furnished comfortably and quite fashionably. Three mahogany tables stood in the parlour, a walnut veneer table in the nursery and a 'spring clock' in the keeping room. Pictures hung on the walls of the keeping room and staircase and '14 prints glazed and framed' decorated the parlour. The dining room was carpeted, had chintz window curtains and a 'needle worked fire skreen', a 'moving fire grate polished', two mahogany tables, eight mahogany chairs, and a mahogany stand with an urn. Here, no doubt, the family entertained favoured customers in a suitably genteel style, making use of the plate valued in the inventory at over £50.[47] Other customers, perhaps, were entertained in the keeping room (also carpeted) or the parlour, where they were plied with wine or porter, tea or coffee, and cakes.[48]

In the nursery were beds, a chest of drawers and a bureau. It may have been in this room, at the walnut veneer table or small mahogany table, that Thomas

Younge's children received their education from Clement Overton, the surveyor who defined the boundary between Watton and Merton.[49] Overton also mapped the Younge estate.[50]

Five chambers, including the maid servant's chamber, boasted beds with hangings of different colours, dressing tables and mirrors. Three chambers also contained 'armed' chairs. The apprentices' chamber contained two beds with hangings, and there were two more beds in the garrets. Both apprentices and journeymen 'lived in'.[51]

The kitchen, on the ground floor, had a fireplace with three spits for roasting meat. It is likely that the larder, ironing room, brewing house and workshop were nearby, in the same range or in adjacent buildings. Among the objects in the ironing room were four trestles and three ironing boards, two 'linnen horses,' six 'ironing boxes' and the equipment for heating the irons. The workshop contained a cross-cut saw and there were two timber oaks and two ashes in the yard outside.

The warehouse stood in the yard entered through the gateway next to the shop. It does not survive, having been replaced by other buildings in the 19th century. On the other side of the yard was the stable with, beyond it, the candle house. These buildings still stand. The Younges owned several horses, including a colt called Westmorland and a gelding called Reeve, and a pair of brown geldings which pulled the 'chariot'. A chaise and the harness for it were sold after Thomas Younge's death.[52]

Other buildings included a granary, a malthouse, a drying house containing linen horses and 'twelve old salt sacks' and a garden house in which a wheelbarrow and other items of gardening equipment were stored, which may have been the structure referred to later as a summerhouse.[53] The malthouse may have been the one towards the west end of the street. The granary contained dried barley and malt, and malting was in progress at the time the inventory was compiled. Two carts and a wagon were used for transport. The inventory, which is dated 31 December 1770, referred to turnips in two 'pightles'; stacks of hay; and, in the barn, threshed and unthreshed barley and straw. Younge also possessed seven heifers.

സാര

The inventory of Thomas Younge's 'stock in trade and utensils thereto belonging' was compiled by two grocers. It listed items with a total value of £3,907 11s 11d (equivalent to over £340,000 today). The contents of the inventory confirm that Younge was a grocer, draper, tallow chandler and maltster but indicate that his trade also extended to hardware, haberdashery, shoes, stationery and more. The stock also included a considerable quantity of fleece wool, valued at £342, suggesting that Younge marketed the wool from the local flocks. The inventories contained no references to butter, perhaps because, as a perishable product, it had already been disposed of.

Cloth of over 50 different kinds, stored in the shop and the adjoining warehouse, featured prominently. Cotton cloth, white, blue, checked, striped, printed, figured and chintz, was stocked in large quantities. Woollen broadcloth was sold in 'drab' and a variety of shades and 'mixtures'. Linsey, a mixture of wool and linen, was available in plain colours, blue, green, yellow, brown, crimson, and striped. Shalloon, a light cloth for linings and women's dresses, could be bought in red, brown or black. Large quantities of linen were stocked, mostly Irish (including 'Irish housewife linen') but some from Yorkshire.

Other woollens included kersey (a coarse cloth, much of which was described as 'drab') and kerseymere, flannel (including swanskin, a fine thick variety), serge, tammy (a fine worsted cloth), durant (a variety of tammy), calamanco (a glossy cloth from Flanders), ratteen, bays, say and woolsey. Linens included holland (an unbleached linen or cotton cloth, which Christopher Hey had also sold), huckaback (used for towels), lawn, Irish dowlas, diaper and drugget (a coarse stuff used for table or floor coverings). Among the cottons were jean (a twilled cloth, from which 'jeans' are named), denim, dimity (corded or figured, used for bedroom hangings and such purposes), jaconet, beaverteen, muslin and dungaree (or 'dunjar' as it was called in the inventory). There were also silks, velvet, canvas and a variety of fustians and other mixed fabrics: camlet, velveret, poplin and barragan.

Cloth for different kinds of clothing included duck, in its natural colour and white, for men's trousers; shirting flannel; buckram, a stiffened linen for petticoats; prunella, a material used for clergymen's gowns; fearnought, a strong, thick woollen cloth used for overcoats; and bombazine, used for mourning clothes. Other types of cloth were destined for different purposes; pillow tick and tabaret (a silk cloth used in upholstery), for example.

Most of those who bought cloth from the shop would have made it up into clothes or other articles themselves or, if they could afford it, would have paid someone else to do so for them. However, Younge did sell several items of ready-made clothing and what would now be called accessories, and household linen. His stock included a small number of silk and knitted breeches, a 'fancy silk waistcoat' and several 'cardinals' (short cloaks for women) in scarlet and black silk. There were also three 'cherry derry gowns dirty'. Hats were sold; they were made of sarsenet (a fine, soft silk), satin, felt, straw (including 'leghorn' hats) or 'chip' (wood or a woody fibre split into thin strips).

The headgear stocked included the 'fantail', the 'ruff' and double cotton caps. Younge carried an extensive stock of handkerchiefs, in linen, muslin, cotton, silk, sarsenet and gauze, and including 'Manchester handkerchiefs' and 'Black Barcelona handkerchiefs'. There were stays in canvas and in leather, sometimes identified as being for children, girls or maids. Gloves were offered in a range of styles and materials: mittens for maids and women; satin and nankeen gloves for women; gloves for youths and men which were 'coloured' or had 'turned tops'; 'wash', 'bevor', 'ribbon bound' and 'lined shamy' gloves for both sexes; lamb and kid gloves in quantity; and more. Another specific item of clothing to which there were several references in the inventory was stockings, for boys, girls, men, women and maids. They were mostly of cotton or worsted, ribbed or plain, in white, grey, brown or black, but there were also silk and scarlet stockings for men, and pink and blue ones for girls. Footwear, too, was sold: there were '19 pair child's first pomps' and shoes in morocco, green, blue and black.

Among the items of household linen mentioned were table cloths and pillows. Curtains, blankets, coverlets, quilts and bed hangings were also stocked, along with rugs and carpets. The deceased were catered for: the stock included shrouds and a velvet pall, along with 'a parcel of coffin furniture' and, in the warehouse, coffin handles.

In the shop were many articles of haberdashery: ribbons (including 'a parcel of love ribbons') tape and buttons of many kinds, buckles, thread, pins and thimbles. Among the items listed were: 'all the death head buttons in the drawer' (presumably for those in mourning), and 'gold and silver trimmings, black lace and fringe'.

၈၁၀၃

Thomas Younge sold what would now be called hardware. He kept brooms and mops, brushes, wire and twine, locks and hinges, hammers and gimlets, and nails, screws and glue. Among the many miscellaneous items in the shop were hour glasses, mouse traps, rings for both curtains and pigs, spurs, knives, forks and marbles. The sources of pigments for paints and dyes were kept: smalts, nutgalls, indigo, green copperas, ivory black and red and white lead. Writing materials were available: foolscap, and 'pott' and 'post' paper for writing letters, and ink pots. Horn books and spelling books, and cards ('Harry cards' and 'Andrew cards') were for sale as well. A blunderbuss and 'a steel crossbow in a bag' were more surprising items.

The grocery stock largely comprised tea, cocoa, coffee, chocolate, spices and other dry goods. The tea, kept in tea canisters in the shop and 'on the warehouse chamber', comprised Bohea and Congou (black teas from China), Hyson (a green tea from China) and 'common green'. The spices included caraway seeds, ginger, black pepper and pepper dust, nutmegs, cinnamon, mace, pimento, coriander and cloves. Pepper and coffee mills were kept for grinding those products for customers. Capers and anchovies were kept in jars, various oils in bottles. Other items listed in the inventory included rice, almonds, 'Turkey figs', currants, raisins, mustard, sugar (lump, loaf and powder), salt and cheese. Tobacco was kept in the shop and in the warehouse behind, the varieties offered being shag, leaf, 'best saffron cut', 'Oronoco' and some 'very old damaged Spanish'. Medicines were mentioned too: 35 bottles of Daffey's Elixir (a proprietary medicine including senna and alcohol) in the shop and, in the warehouse, prunelle salt (for the throat) and '2 doz. Herrings antidotes', the product mentioned in the newspaper advertisement in 1767.

As well as tea and tobacco, the warehouse contained more supplies of salt, spices and Warwickshire, Gloucestershire and Cheshire cheese. Olive oil, linseed oil and other oils were kept there, as were spirits of sulphur and vitriol. A carboy (a large vessel of green or blue glass) contained oil of turpentine. Here, too, were brimstone, gunpowder and a barrel of saltpetre; vinegar, alum, soap and fuller's earth. The stock of spirits was considerable: 105 3/4 gallons of rum and a large quantity of brandy. The presence in the warehouse of beams, scales and weights, sieves for currants and raisins, and white and brown paper, suggests that convenient quantities of some of the products were weighed out and wrapped before being displayed in the shop. A pulley and rope were available to move the bulkier items, such as sacks and 'skepps' (large baskets).

Beyond the warehouse, in the 'chandle house', the appraisers noted the presence of tallow, moulds and other equipment required in making candles, as well as a stock of the finished product. Coal was used during the candle-making process.[54] Thomas Younge dealt in coal, as money received from its sale was recorded in the accounts of his executor.[55]

☙❧

After Thomas Younge's death in 1770, his business was carried on by his widow Dorothy and William Younge, probably a cousin. They agreed to go into an equal partnership for 15 years from 27 October 1771, each putting £1,000 into the business, taking out £10 per month (equivalent to about £900 today) for 'private use' and purchasing provisions for their own use from the stock at cost price. William was to run the business but Dorothy's son Thomas Younge was 'to be taken apprentice at a proper age' by the partners and would be entitled to buy them out in due course if he so wished.[56] The partners announced that: 'the widow of the late Mr Thomas Younge, deceased, and Mr William Younge, as partners, intend to carry on the trade of a butter factor, grocer, draper...as usual...'[57] William Younge maintained a direct involvement with the London butter market.[58]

It took time to settle Thomas Younge's affairs, paying the debts he owed and pursuing those who owed debts to him, selling off some of his real estate and providing his children with their entitlements. In October 1775, William Younge wrote to Thomas's executor, Philip Case, reporting with satisfaction that, 'we have sav[e]d this year clear of all expences and bad debts £228 (equivalent to about £20,000 today) which I am glad to find,' but also asking for more money to meet the partnership's expenses, while noting that, 'our neibours are in a bad way which will help our trade.'[59] It was dog eat dog in Watton's commercial community.

Three years later, William was upbeat, reporting to Philip Case: 'Our trade increase and we are doing well.'[60] In 1780, matters had taken a turn for the worse. 'You can not immagin how bad trade is with us our stock dead on our hands as very little can be sold being no money amongst our farmers. Times were never so bad with us.'[61]

Thomas Younge's eldest son, Thomas, was able to buy the main house and shop from his father's executor in 1787.[62] His mother, Dorothy, died in May 1804 and Thomas himself died aged 40, unmarried and intestate, in October 1805. His heir was his brother, Edward Younge, who in 1795 had bought out the interests of his other four surviving siblings in the estate. Edward had kept a shop in Shipdham but sold up there and moved to Watton in October or November 1805, just a couple of months after his brother's death.[63] By 1812, he was bankrupt.

Edward Younge's properties and their contents were sold by public auction. First, a large stock of malt, 600 coombs of it, went under the hammer at the *Crown* on 10 June.[64] Stocks of hay, clover and other fodder crops were auctioned on 24 June.[65] A sale of 'beds and bedding, household furniture, richly embossed and plain plate, fine old china' and other effects took place on Younge's own premises on 29 June.

The residence, shop and stock in trade were offered for sale at the *Crown* on 26 June 1812.[66] The press notices referred to the 'capital dwelling-house and very old established and well accustomed shop, most eligibly situated for trade, in the market-place of Watton, with a convenient compting-house and detached offices, chaise-house and stabling for four horses, extensive warehouses, chandling house, walled-in garden, with paddock and pightle of rich pasture land, called Balding's Pightle, adjoining, and containing together nearly three acres'.[67] The contents comprised large amounts of bedding, china, household utensils and furniture, including a 'clock with chimes'; a side-board 'with upwards of 300 ounces of elegant plate'; a 'capital patent mangle'; and a 'genteel gig and harness, lately new'.

The house and shop did not sell on 26 June but did so at another auction at the *Crown* on 5 August. They were accompanied by 22 other lots, including the *Crown* itself; another 'capital sashed dwelling house, near the market place'; a third 'dwelling house near the market place'; 'a very substantial new-erected and spacious malt-house, comprising an excellent kiln, drying houses, working floors, and twenty-two coombs steep, with the yard and land to the same adjoining';[68] and several other cottages, barns and pieces of land, including a butcher's shop and lime house in the market place.[69] It was the end of an era.

Being a shopkeeper in Watton was a risky business. Credit was so fundamental to commerce in the 18th and early 19th centuries, that a sudden change in economic circumstances, or in their personal situations, could leave traders vulnerable.[70]

Bankruptcies were all too common.

Business people, accustomed to a relatively affluent lifestyle, could suddenly face straitened circumstances. To mitigate, to some degree, the risks they faced, some joined friendly societies. In 1813–15, an average of 68 people in the town were members of such organisations.[71] They would pay a small sum each week and receive help if they were sick or injured.

Many of Watton's people, however, knew little other than straitened circumstances. They were the poor and, despite the rising prosperity of the country as a whole, their numbers were increasing.

**Notes**

1. Presumably the market place.
2. NM, 29 June 1727; quoted in the anonymous typescript, pre-1958.
3. Watton parish register, 1730-99; NRO, PD 218/28.
4. Will of Francis Hicks, 1742; TNA, PROB11/726/324.
5. Memorial tablet in St Mary's Church.
6. NC, 26 January 1782.
7. Will of John Hicks, 1778; NRO, ANW 1778-79 fo 125.
8. NC 15 February 1794, reporting his death on 9 February.
9. NC, 21 April 1781.
10. NC, 23 June 1781.
11. NC, 17 November 1781.
12. NC, 16 March 1782. Samuel Ellington was the tenant of the Bull and John Kett was Francis Hicks' nephew.
13. NC, 14 June 1794.
14. Will of Elizabeth Barker, 1813; NRO, ANW 1812-13 fo 109.
15. Watton parish register, 1539-1730; NRO, PD 218/26.
16. Papers and accounts of Richard Salter; NRO, BL/CS 8/6/1/2/2-44.
17. As mentioned in 1731 in the court book of the manor of Watton Hall; Museum4Watton, M4W/2016/8B.
18. Watton parish register, 1730-1799; NRO, PD218/28.
19. Cited in copy admission of Thomas Younge to properties formerly of Edward Younge, Manor of Watton Hall, 1761; NRO, BL/CS 8/6/1.
20. Ibid.
21. Young v Berney; TNA, C 11/2254/66.
22. Younge admission, 1761; NRO, BL/CS 8/6/1. The reference to 'formerly Cranmer's' may be a clue to the location on the south side of the High Street of a public house called the 'Drum and Colours' mentioned in the alehouse recognizance list for Wayland Hundred of 1789, where William Cranmer was named as the innholder. The court book of the manor of Watton Hall records that a tenement with a yard 'lately Cranmer's' was conveyed by Christopher Hey to William Candler on 7 October 1674. The publican of the Drum, called Ward, took action for defamation in 1807 against a farmer from Ovington called Lincoln, who had denounced him as 'a rogue, a thief and a liar', and won his case, as reported in the BNP, 5 August 1807.
23. NM, 28 August 1756.

24. Agreement between Edward Younge and Thomas Younge, 26 September 1760; NRO, BL/CS 8/6/6.
25. Copy of will of Edward Younge, 1760; NRO, BL/CS 8/6/1/3/1-9.
26. NRO, BL/CS 8/6/6/6.
27. Ibid.
28. Surrender by Thomas Younge to Henry Case and Edward Case in trust for Hester Younge spinster of properties in Watton, 25 November 1763, recited in a later abstract of title; in private possession. Part of a pasture close adjoining the house was annexed by Thomas Younge as a garden for his own house. NRO, BL/CS/8/6/1.
29. NM, 17 January 1767.
30. BNP, 14 March 1792.
31. F Blomefield (1805).
32. David Dymond, *The Norfolk Landscape*, 1985.
33. Samuel Lewis, *Topographical Dictionary of England* (S Lewis and Co, 1831).
34. Accounts of Philip Case as executor of Thomas Younge, 1771-1777; NRO, BL/CS 8/6/3.
35. NC, 24 February 1776.
36. Letters from William Younge to Philip Case, 1 March 1778 and 29 March 1880; NRO, BL/CS 8/6/7.
37. NC, 4 October 1777.
38. NC, 30 November 1771.
39. Abstract of title of Younge properties, 20 September 1809; in private possession.
40. Executorship accounts, nd (1792?); NRO, BL/CS 8/6.
41. Will of Thomas Younge, 1771; TNA PROB 11/969/35.
42. Abstract of title of Younge properties, 20 September 1809; in private possession.
43. Inventory of the goods, chattels and credits of Thomas Younge of Watton, deceased, 1771; NRO, BL/CS 8/6/2.
44. Loose paper signed by Nicholas Downing and Edward Slade, appraisers, 8 October 1771; NRO, BL/CS 8/6.
45. Considerations relating to Mrs Younge and Mr W Younge as Partners in Trade, nd; NRO, BL/CS 8/6.
46. NRO, BL/CS 8/6/7.
47. Considerations relating to Mrs Younge and Mr W Younge as Partners in Trade, nd; NRO, BL/CS 8/6.
48. Ibid, 'that the wine and porter for the entertainment of customers be jointly bought and set apart for that purpose...That the tea, coffee, sugar and money for buying cakes be had out of the shop, for the entertainment of customers at either party's.'
49. NM, 2 January 1773 and 27 September 1776.
50. Accounts of Philip Case as executor of Thomas Younge, 1771-1777; NRO, BL/CS 8/6/3. The map appears not to survive.
51. Considerations relating to Mrs Younge and Mr W Younge as Partners in Trade, nd; NRO, BL/CS 8/6.
52. Accounts of Philip Case as executor of Thomas Younge, 1771-1777; NRO, Younge papers.
53. Surrender by Thomas Younge to Henry Case and Edward Case in trust for Hester Younge spinster of properties in Watton, 25 November 1763, recited in a later abstract of title; in private possession.
54. Considerations relating to Mrs Younge and Mr W Younge as Partners in Trade, nd; NRO, BL/CS 8/6.
55. Accounts of Philip Case as executor of Thomas Younge, 1771-1777; NRO, BL/CS 8/6/3.
56. Articles of agreement between Dorothy Younge of Watton widow and William Younge of Watton grocer, 27 October 1771; NRO, BL/CS 8/6.
57. NC, 12 January 1771.
58. Letters from William Younge to Philip Case, 1 March 1778 and 29 March 1880; NRO, BL/CS 8/6.

59. Letter from William Younge to Philip Case, 6 October 1775; NRO, BL/CS 8/6.
60. Letter from William Younge to Philip Case, 1 March 1778; NRO, BL/CS 8/6.
61. Letter from William Younge to Philip Case, 29 March 1780; NRO, BL/CS 8/6.
62. Admission of Thomas Younge under a bargain and sale of 5 March 1787, 4 April 1793; in private possession.
63. NC, 26 October 1805. Further evidence from settlement examinations in 1816 of Thomas Simkin, who had 'let himself' as Younge's servant for the years beginning Michaelmas 1803, 1804 and 1805; NRO, PD218/12.
64. NC, 6 June 1812.
65. NC, 20 June 1812.
66. NC, 13 June 1812.
67. NC, 7 July 1812.
68. NC, 4 July 1812.
69. Edward Younge moved away from Watton and appears to have died in Essex in December 1813.
70. See Margot C Finn, *The Character of Credit: Personal Debt in English Culture, 1740-1914* (Cambridge UP, 2003).
71. Parliamentary Papers, Abstract of Returns relative to the Expense and Maintenance of the Poor, 1815.

# Being Poor in Watton

Throughout the 18th and 19th centuries, varying proportions of the people of Watton were poor and needed help from their community. How much help to give and how to provide it were sometimes matters of debate.

The system for relieving the poor continued in the first half of the 18th century much as it had been in the 17th century although, over time, it evolved. One new development was the provision of a 'town house' to accommodate some of those, mainly the elderly and widows, who could not afford to pay rent.

On 12 June 1719, about 30 of the principal inhabitants of the town agreed to contribute 'towards the building a dwelling house upon the comon [sic] pasture of Watton…for the use of the poor of the said parish'.[1] The lady of the manor, the twice-widowed Anne Wodehouse (formerly Anne Samwell), along with her unmarried daughter Anne Samwell, recognising that 17 named trustees led by the vicar, John Berry, were, 'intending out of their charitable dispositions to erect and build a dwellinghouse for the better support and habitation of such of the poor of the parish' granted them a small piece of land 'with an old house or cottage then upon part thereof built', situated 'near the end of the street of the…town' comprising a partially enclosed area 15 yards square and the 'common pasture… lying round the same'. The price was five shillings (equivalent to about £30 today) and, as the land was copyhold, the purchasers would pay an annual rent of one shilling.[2]

Careful accounts were kept of the cost of erecting the building.[3] The trustees paid for the 'old house' that stood on part of the plot to be pulled down and for the site to be cleared and levelled. Brick floors were laid and 'Stebbing and his boy' were paid for five days' work felling, hewing and sawing the 'town timber', trees that were growing on pieces of land that had been donated to the town in the past. The next tasks for Stebbing and his boy were to make a timber frame and to 'set up the hous', after which they made and installed windows, fashioned 'ledges' for the door openings and made and hung three doors. Clay was fetched for daubing the walls and more bricks were obtained and laid. Finally, three loads of straw were fetched and a thatcher was paid £1 5s 4d (equivalent to about £150 today) for thatching the roof. The building became known as the 'town house', or sometimes as the 'common house' (because it was on the edge of the common) to distinguish it from another house, acquired by the town sometime before 1722[4] in 'Rotten Row', at the west end of the street. The 'common house' may have been the building referred to in 1725 as 'an house upon our common built by contribution for ye reception of any that shall be infected with any dangerous distemper' although it is possible that this was a different building.[5]

Oversight of the town houses was one of the responsibilities of the overseers of the poor. Their accounts survive for Watton from 1769 onwards, kept in a book, inscribed with 'Town Book alias the Chronicle of Misery, F Hicks 1769'[6] on the title page. F Hicks was Francis Hicks, the businessman who became a bankrupt 12 years later. Each year, the two overseers divided the twelve months between them, keeping an account of the rates paid and the payments made to and for the poor.

The responsibilities of the overseers overlapped with those of the churchwardens. They included 'cutting the river' and 'draining the fen'; 'playing the engine' (the fire engine); cleaning and when necessary mending the clock in the clock tower; catching sparrows; and maintaining the parish property, including repairing the town houses, sweeping their chimneys and re-thatching the one on the common.

Most of the overseers' duties, however, concerned the relief of the poor. From May 13 to October 14 1772, the overseer was Francis Hicks' brother, John Hicks, grocer and draper. He made regular payments, known as the 'collection', to over a dozen people, including widows and children. Another item of expenditure was for 'cutting and landing flaggs' which were turves, cut on the common, brought into the town by wheelbarrow and given to the poor as fuel. Those who had the strength, and had common rights attached to the properties they owned or occupied, could go on to the common and gather fuel for themselves, and so those who received flags from the overseers were the propertyless and helpless. After parliamentary enclosure in 1803, neither the overseers nor the poor themselves could use the commons as a source of fuel. In compensation, the enclosure commissioners awarded the churchwardens and overseers allotments of 28 acres at Redhill, 20 acres at Watton Fen and five acres and one acre at Neaton, the rental income from which was used to provide coal for the poor who were not otherwise receiving poor relief.

John Hicks' accounts include 'Mr Hicks's bill for clothing the poor' and also payments for shoes and, in one instance, for mending them.. Several people who could not afford their rent had it paid by the overseer. Some of the payments related to the specific needs of individuals; for example, four payments were made 'for looking after Chapman's wife', followed by one to 'Mr Robinson for delivering Chapman's wife'; it sounds as though she had a difficult pregnancy. On several occasions, small sums were given to people 'in need'. Widow Clemmence received 10s 6d (equivalent to about £45 today) 'for wearing apparrell [sic] for her son', while John Tompson was paid 2s 'for carrying the widow Watson's colle'. A 'coffin and furniture' were paid for: the parish provided support from the cradle to the grave.

The parish had a stock of beds and bedding, furniture and household utensils that could be lent to those who needed them. A tow wheel (for hemp or flax) and a wool wheel could be issued to enable those who lacked employment to earn an income.[7] If illegitimate children required support, the overseers sought to establish the identity of the father and secure payment for the child's maintenance, or, if that was not possible, made regular payments themselves. The mothers received little sympathy; in a vestry meeting, the principal inhabitants ordered that 'all girls having more than one bastard child to have a complaint laid before the magistrates respecting it and punished accordingly'.[8] The boys and girls, when old enough, were 'put out' to learn trades. For example, the churchwardens and overseers agreed with Mrs Lydia Palmer that she would 'instruct…Susan Grimes a poor girl in the art of a mantua maker [a dressmaker] in the best way and manner that she can' for one year from 17 February 1806, for which she would be paid £2 2s. Mrs Palmer was to allow Susan to have 'half a day in every week…to wash and repair her apparel' and was 'to have such new apparel as shall be required for the said Susan Grimes made without expence [sic] to the parish'.[9]

༄༅

Basic medical services were provided for the poor and, each year, a surgeon was identified to deliver them. One of the earliest entries in the overseers' account book recorded an agreement at 'a town meeting att the *George*' to appoint Mr Swallow, surgeon, 'to attend all the poor of the parish who receive a weekly collection and live in the widows', the common and [the] blacksmith shop houses'. He was to be paid five guineas for the year (fractures and midwifery excepted). Similar appointments were made in subsequent years, the task of attending the poor rotating among the different surgeons in the town, the terms being negotiated from year to year. In 1775, it was the turn of Francis Hicks' brother, Burden Hicks, and, as well as providing medical services, he was required 'to badge the poor that take collection', which may have involved giving them a tattoo of some kind.

A medical man who was more forceful and specific than others in setting out his terms was Richard Dinmore. The son of a saddler turned iron-founder in Norwich, in 1787 he announced his presence, aged 22, as a surgeon in Watton.[10] The following year, the town considered 'Mr R Dinmore's proposals for attending the poor belonging to Watton within six miles of the town cross, also to supply them with all necessary medicines, dressings and attendance', for ten guineas (equivalent to over £800 today). For an additional 15s, Dinmore would also 'attend all women who shall send to him as paupers…provided they have not had a woman with them, but if any woman has had a midwife with her and she could not deliver her then the said Mr Dinmore will not attend…for less than one guinea… He also proposes to set all simple fractures…but fractur'd sculls and all compound fractures to be excepted'. Setting fractures would cost a guinea but if they occurred out of the town one and a half guineas would be charged. The inhabitants agreed to Dinmore's terms, 'with an addition of his attending the small pox'.[11] Despite vaccination, smallpox was yet to be eradicated.

Richard Dinmore married his wife Jane in January 1788 and they had six children baptised over the next six years in Watton, and a seventh in Norwich in 1795. Dinmore's skills as a surgeon, however, were insufficient to prevent six of the seven children dying in infancy. In 1797, he and Jane emigrated to the United States. Perhaps they felt the need for a fresh start. But there was another reason too: Richard Dinmore was a radical, sympathetic to the French Revolution of 1789. Either he or his father, also called Richard, was the first president of the pro-reform Patriotic Society (successor to the Revolution Society) in Norwich in 1795-1796.[12] Richard Dinmore junior published two pamphlets: *A Brief Account of the Moral and Political Acts of the Kings and Queens of England, from the Conqueror to 1688, with Reflections tending to prove the Necessity of a Reform in Parliament* in 1793, in which he argued that, among other reforms, women should have the right to vote;[13] and *An Exposition of the Principles of the British Jacobins* in 1796, in which, although disavowing the excesses of the French revolution, he called for a more egalitarian society in Britain.[14] In the increasingly repressive atmosphere generated in Britain by the wars with France he may have felt that living in the United States would be more congenial. He may also have judged, not unreasonably, that he and his family might be in danger if they stayed in Britain. In America, the Dinmores settled initially in Georgetown, District of Columbia (DC), where Richard ran a grocery store and a school, and then moved into Washington DC in 1801. Jane died in 1804[15] but Richard devoted himself to writing and publishing newspapers and books until his death in 1811.[16] An influential figure, he corresponded with, among others, the third and fourth presidents of the United States, Thomas Jefferson (1801-09) and James Madison (1809-17). Jefferson wrote a commendatory note for Dinmore's *Compilation of Select and Fugitive Poetry*, published in 1802.[17] Richard Dinmore was remembered as the 'one author connected with Watton' in an article published in 1896,[18] but has been largely forgotten since.

୫୦୬

The overseers' accounts and other parish documents show that, in the 18th century, Watton was a community that looked after its own; but, for the most part, only its own. The Settlement Laws of 1662 and 1691 determined who was entitled to receive relief in the town, because they had a 'settlement' here, and who was not. A settlement could be obtained by parentage (in the case of legitimate children); marriage (for women); birth (for illegitimate children); occupation of property worth £10 per year or over; and, from 1691, serving an apprenticeship; hiring and service for a year; and paying parish rates or serving in a parish office. The overseers issued 'settlement certificates' to those who met one or more of these criteria and wished to move elsewhere, and 'removal orders' to those who needed relief but did not have settlements in Watton.

The system gave rise to much correspondence with the officials of other parishes about the relief of individuals. The overseers normally displayed a measure of humanity, especially if the applicant was, in their view, deserving but, anxious to keep the rates down, gave short shrift to those who were not. A persistent applicant, Mrs Penelope Johnson, who was settled in Watton but living elsewhere, received a letter from Smith Hastings (overseer in 1808), expressing the hope that she would be 'as little expense to us as possible' and another, enclosing a pound note and concluding, 'I hope you will not think of troubling us any more'.[19]

More sympathetically, when William Pyman, carpenter, his wife Elizabeth and their four children were issued with a removal order in 1819, the order was suspended because Elizabeth was pregnant. Three months later, Robert Swallow, the Watton surgeon, certified that 'Elizabeth Pyman might [now] be removed without danger in a stage wagon to Clerkenwell' where the family was settled, and the churchwardens and overseers of Clerkenwell were sent a bill: a guinea for Swallow's attendance and £1 16s for nine weekly payments of 4s (equivalent to about £11.50 today) for the family's sustenance.[20]

In cases of doubt, an applicant for relief would be 'examined' (questioned) by two magistrates to determine the parish to which they belonged. Thus, for example, Erasmus Allcock was examined in 1810. He stated that he had been born at Scarning but four years previously had 'let himself to Edward Taylor of Watton… innkeeper as a post lad for one whole year',[21] served him for 14 months and not done anything to gain a settlement elsewhere. He was therefore settled in Watton, because of his hiring and service with Edward Taylor (landlord of the *Crown*). So too was Thomas Palmer of Bawdeswell, aged about 28, who was examined in 1815 and stated that he 'was born in the Industry House in the Parish of Gressenhall' (Gressenhall workhouse) and in 1803 had 'lett himself to William Pearson of Watton…postmaster' for the year and served him for two years after that. Although he had lodged in Thetford during the third year, this was because 'he rode as postman for the said William Pearson'.[22]

After the Battle of Waterloo in 1815, which brought the wars with France to an end, many servicemen were discharged and became unemployed. One was John Walker, shoemaker, who applied for poor relief in 1816. He had been born in Norwich but his father's settlement had been in Watton. In the words of his 'examination', 'when he was about eleven years of age he went to seas and continued there for about ten years. Then he was taken prisoner by the French and remained as such for seven or eight years'. Since his release, he had not done anything to gain a settlement anywhere else, and so Watton had the responsibility of supporting him.[23] Another who sought relief from the parish in 1817 was Thomas Minns, born in Watton, who had served in the West Norfolk Militia for a year and a half, 'and then volunteered into the line, wherein he served five years and an half and was discharged on account of being wounded'.[24]

༄༅༄

An Act of Parliament of 1723 allowed parishes to establish workhouses, where the poor could be set to work; to refuse relief to any who were not prepared to enter a workhouse; and to reach agreements with contractors to 'farm' the poor, to take responsibility for maintaining and employing them, for a fixed fee.

In 1774, the principal inhabitants of Watton considered the erection of a workhouse. They had funds, money received from three men 'as and for a compensation for the maintenance of their several bastard children' and agreed that the money should be 'laid out towards the building a workhouse'. One of their number, the maltster Edward Crockley, went so far as to purchase limestone and timber. However, the project didn't go ahead, Crockley was compensated and the money was invested instead.

Instead, premises were rented for use as a workhouse from John Thompson (who was the publican at the *King's Arms* in 1789-99 and possibly before that[25]). In 1780-81, a year of exceptional need because of an epidemic of smallpox, several payments were made in connection with this workhouse: Wright and Monson, for example, were paid for 'a months looking after poor at workhouse'. From the late 1780s, the overseers paid John Wright £8 per month, perhaps because he had the responsibility of both running the workhouse and serving as an assistant overseer, a post which parishes were allowed to create. In January 1788, a Mr Brett was paid a shilling for 'carring [sic] a man to the workhouse' and John Wright was given a shilling 'for the man's board'.[26]

Payments for the rent of the workhouse building and the relief of the poor accommodated there continued in the following decade. At a meeting at the *Crown* on 4 October 1796, the churchwardens, overseers and principal inhabitants of the town agreed to contract with William Jessup for 'putting out the paupers in the workhouse'. Jessup would be paid nine shillings (equivalent to about £20 today) per head per month, 'be the number more or less', or two shillings and three pence per week for any inmate who stayed in the house for less than a month, and in exchange was 'to find the paupers with sufficient meat, drink and fireing'. The diet was specified. Breakfast was broth, except on Sundays, when bread, cheese and beer would be provided. Dinner was more variable: beef pudding on Sundays and Thursdays; milk broth on Mondays, Wednesdays and Fridays; dumplings on Tuesdays; and bread and cheese on Saturdays. Supper was unvarying: bread, cheese and beer every day. The incentive for Jessup was that he was 'to be entitled to all the earnings of the paupers'.

Another subscription was organised in March 1805 'for the purpose of defraying the expences of erecting a house for the reception and residence of the poor inhabitants of Watton according to the plan and estimate of Mr Stannard of the City of Norwich builder.'[27] The sum of £525 was pledged but, once again, the idea seems to have been dropped. Watton did not acquire a large, permanent workhouse and by 1813-1815 all the poor were given 'outdoor relief', payments in money or in kind that enabled them to remain in their own homes.²⁸

⁂

The number of poor people in Watton increased rapidly in the late 18th and early 19th centuries and consequently the poor rates and the parish's outlay rose dramatically. In 1783-5, the money raised from the rates averaged £227 9s 9d and the expenditure on the poor averaged £215 17s 7d (equivalent to over £18,500 today).²⁹ By the year ending Easter 1813, these figures had more than quadrupled to £1,065 6s 4.5d and £934 0s 6d (equivalent to about £44,000), although inflation in the intervening period meant that in real terms it had roughly doubled³⁰ The parish authorities were under pressure to limit the demands on the ratepayers and to keep the rates as low as possible. The principal inhabitants even agreed 'not to allow any pauper any weekly allowance who keeps dogs etc'.³¹

The system of poor relief was under pressure nationally and, in response, parliament passed the Poor Law Amendment Act of 1834, which introduced a radical reform. Under the 'New Poor Law', parishes were grouped together in 'poor law unions', which were expected to build large workhouses, in which conditions would be sufficiently harsh to act as a 'test' of the validity of claims for relief. The old system of payments to the poor, enabling them to remain in their own homes, was supposed to end although in practice such payments continued, under the guise of giving temporary relief to the sick, which was allowed. The new system was explained to the inhabitants of Watton and the surrounding district by Sir Edward Parry, the assistant poor law commissioner responsible for East Anglia, at a meeting on 24 June 1835 chaired by John Weyland of Woodrising Hall.³² The inhabitants agreed that their parishes should form a union and in due course Watton became part of the Wayland Poor Law Union, managed by a board of guardians elected by the ratepayers, on which the magistrates of the district also sat *ex officio*. The Wayland Board met for the first time at the *Angel Inn*, Larling, on 21 September 1835. A union workhouse was erected on a site in Rockland St Andrew. It was replaced by a new building, which later became the Wayland Hospital, in 1914.³³

⁂

Watton's parish 'town house' or 'common house', erected in 1719, was still occupied in 1834 when, as a result of the enclosure award of 1803, it stood in an allotment of three quarters of an acre of former common land. An account of parish property delivered to the Charity Commissioners in 1834 stated that: 'The house is occupied by three poor families who on account of their poverty are allowed to live free of rent. The land is divided into 8 small gardens and given to the most industrious families to occupy free of all rent. There was also built upon the said land a coal house for depositing the coal for the use of the poor, [and] an engine house for the safe custody of the fire engine at the expense of the parish in the year

1819'. The coal house and engine house adjoined each other and above the coal house was a school-room.[34] The coal was given out weekly to those who came for it at the low price of 9d per bushel. If those who qualified for the coal preferred, they could have 8s per family allowed to them instead.[35] In 1820, a glebe terrier (a list of church lands – which also, on this occasion, included parish property) mentioned the other 'small town house and yard' in 'Rotten Row', occasionally referred to as the 'backsmith house' as it was next door to a smithy.[36] In 1834, it was 'occupied by two small families free of rent'.[37]

In 1842, both buildings, the 'thatched double cottage and piece of land now let as gardens' and the 'brick and tiled cottage with a yard at the back', were described by the solicitor, William Massey, writing to the Poor Law Commissioners in London, as 'in a very dilapidated state of repair'.[38] They were sold by auction at the *Bull*[39] and passed into private ownership.

The coal house ceased to be used for its original purpose after the railway opened, because the parish authorities found it more convenient to issue the coal to the poor at the station, where it arrived, but it was then rented out and was still in existence in 1911.[40] The engine house fell into disuse after 1853, because facilities for storing the engine were provided at the newly-built Wayland Hall.

Wayland Hall: just one of the developments in 19th century which entitled Watton to the accolade of being an 'improving market town'.

**Notes**

1. NRO, PD 218/6.
2. Abstract of deed of feoffment of town house; NRO, ACC 2023/12.
3. NRO, PD 218/6. See also J C Barringer, 'The Poor of Watton in the 18th and 19th centuries' in WEA (1975).
4. It was mentioned in the manor court book in 1722; Museum4Watton, M4W/2016/8B.
5. Watton glebe terrier 1725; NRO, DN/TER 159/4/6. Local tradition has it that there was a 'pest house' on what was then common land in Neaton; thanks to Peter and Janet Walmsley for this information.
6. Watton overseers' accounts; NRO, PD218/3. The following paragraphs are largely based on this source.
7. Overseers' letter book, with various memoranda, 1805-9; NRO, PD 218/15.
8. Watton vestry minute book, 1821-29; NRO, PD 218/88.
9. Overseers' letter book, with various memoranda, 1805-9; NRO, PD 218/15.
10. BNP, 27 June 1787.
11. Overseers' accounts, 1769-1802; NRO, PD 218/3.
12. C B Jewson, *Jacobin City* (Blackie, 1975); Carole Rawcliffe and Richard Wilson (eds), *Norwich since 1550* (Hambledon and London, 2004).
13. Arianne Chernock, *The Right to Rule and the Rights of Women* (Cambridge, 2019).
14. C B Jewson (1975).
15. NC, 19 May 1804.

16. Thanks to Bronwen Tyler for sharing her research on the family history of the Dinmores.
17. C B Jewson (1975).
18. By James Hooper in NN, 28 November 1896.
19. Quoted in the anonymous typescript, pre-1958.
20. Removal order with endorsements and bill and certificate; NRO, PD218/10. These sources are reproduced in J Crowley and A W Reid, *The Poor Law in Norfolk 1700-1850* (EARO 1983).
21. Settlement examination of Erasmus Allcock, 1810; NRO. PD218/12.
22. Settlement examination of Thomas Palmer, 1815; NRO, PD218/12. Two further examples of settlement examinations are quoted in full in J C Barringer, 'The Poor of Watton in the 18th and 19th centuries' in WEA (1975).
23. Settlement examination of John Walker, 1816; NRO, PD218/12.
24. Settlement examination of Thomas Minns, 1817; NRO, PD218/12.
25. Alehouse recognizances, 1789-99; NRO, C/Sch 1/16.
26. Watton overseers' accounts; NRO, PD218/3.
27. Documents in the possession of the Museum4Watton.
28. Parliamentary Papers, Abstract of Returns relative to the Expense and Maintenance of the Poor, 1815.
29. Parliamentary Papers, Abstract of Returns made by Overseers of the Poor, 1787.
30. Parliamentary Papers, Abstract of Returns relative to the Expense and Maintenance of the Poor, 1815.
31. Watton Vestry Minute Book 1821-29; NRO PD218/88. This practice was not unique to Watton; Birmingham was one of several other places where a similar approach was recorded. See C Upton, *The Birmingham Parish Workhouse, 1730-1840* (University of Hertfordshire Press, 2019).
32. NC, 27 June 1835.
33. J C Barringer, 'The Poor of Watton in the 18th and 19th Centuries', in WEA (1975).
34. Extracts from the glebe terrier of 1820; NRO, ACC 2023/12.
35. Copy of an account of town lands, etc, delivered to the Charity Commissioners, 17 March 1834; NRO, ACC 2023/12.
36. Manor of Watton Hall in Watton: abstract of the admissions of certain trustees for the church and parish of Watton to lands and tenements copyhold of the said manor, 29 November 1770; NRO, ACC 2023/12.
37. Ibid.
38. Correspondence of the Poor Law Commissioners with Wayland Poor Law Union; TNA, MH12 8616.
39. Sale particulars, 10 August 1842; NRO, ACC 2023/12.
40. DMG 8 April 1911.

*Drawing of the market place and King's Arms.*
(from a private collection, via Julian Horn)

The presence of the obelisk and the absence of Wayland Hall means that this and the other drawing showing the same area (below) can be dated to between 1820 and 1853.

*Drawing of the market place and King's Arms, 1820-53.*
(from a private collection, via Julian Horn)

# The Improving Market Town

In the mid-19th century, the phrase, 'The improving market town of Watton' was sometimes used to promote sales of property in the town.[1]

The words reflected the expansion of the town and its economy, its acquisition of new buildings and its development of public facilities that enhanced the quality of the environment for the inhabitants. For the people of Watton, the improvement of their town would also have had a social and moral dimension: the community was becoming more civilised, cultured and conscientious in upholding the ruling values of the day. For its efforts at self-improvement, Watton earned an unusual accolade in 1859. In the words of a newspaper report: 'We are not aware that any other town in the county has shewn more signs of progress during the last few years than the little town of Watton. It has fallen to our lot from time to time to chronicle a great many improvements it has undertaken in trying to adapt itself to the progressive spirit of the times we live in'.[2]

The population of Watton had probably been rising in the second half of the 18th century. In the first half of the 19th century it almost doubled, from 693 in 1801 to 1,353 in 1851. This significant rise in Watton's population was accompanied by major changes in the town's geography and economy, and drove its espousal of 'improvement'.

೫೦೦೩

In 1800, Watton still had large areas of common and wasteland and parts of the arable land still lay in the open fields inherited from medieval times. Such arrangements were increasingly seen as inefficient. Landowners could make more money by enclosing the commons and reorganising the land into separate, privately owned fields, but they required an Act of Parliament to bring that about. Ashill and Saham Toney had already been subject to the process known as parliamentary enclosure, and in 1801 an Act was passed 'for dividing, allotting and inclosing the open or common fields, half year or shack lands, lammas meadows, fens, commons and waste lands within the several parishes of Watton and Carbrooke'.

Three commissioners were appointed to implement the process. They were assisted by a Watton solicitor, Edward Harvey Grigson. Their first meeting took place at the *George* on 1 July 1801.

Much work was required. The land had to be surveyed, and the boundaries of the parishes defined. The owners of lands and common rights were asked to provide details of their properties and these were recorded. The commissioners calculated that the fragments of the open or common fields that had not already been enclosed, and the fens, common and waste lands, amounted to nearly 395 acres. The main surviving area of open or common field was east of the town and south of Norwich Road, in Mill Field, although the windmill that had given it its name had gone. There were several areas of common: Wick Common, south-west of the town; Mill Common, to the west and north-west (which took its name from the second windmill near the junction of the Brandon and Swaffham roads); Neaton Fen; and Watton Green. The commissioners had to decide how these should be divided up among the landowners and converted into enclosed fields.

The commissioners were also required to set out allotments that could be rented out to provide funds to compensate the poorer inhabitants, who would lose their rights to graze animals and gather fuel on the commons, and to define the places where gravel, clay and sand could be extracted. They laid out the public and private roads across the former commons which, in Watton, was fairly straightforward as they were all existing roads. Many of the larger landowners took advantage of the process of enclosure to negotiate exchanges of land, enabling them to concentrate their holdings into more compact and convenient estates. The exchanges were recorded in the enclosure award and map, thereby confirming the owners' title to their new lands.[3]

The commissioners met several times in 1802, and on 19 October organised an auction at the *George* of 11 pieces of land that had formed part of the commons and had been staked out with a view to their sale, to reduce the cost of the process of enclosure for the landowners.[4] Six of these pieces of land were in Watton, four on the former Mill Common, on the north side of Brandon Road, and two on the former Watton Green, on the north side of Norwich Road. As a result of the sales, only £1,519 8s 2d (equivalent to about £67,000 today) of the total costs of £3,967 10s 8d had to be found by the landowners, each one paying a share proportionate to the value of their lands. After several further meetings in 1803, the commissioners held a special meeting on 21 December to read and execute their award.[5]

The commons and open fields disappeared, to be replaced by fields hedged with quickset.

ଚ୨ଠଃ

Parliamentary enclosure influenced the development of Watton's urban landscape. The enclosure commissioners laid out small allotments along the roads over the former Mill Common, in a manner that facilitated their acquisition as building plots. As a result, Watton began to expand westwards. When the tithe map was drawn in 1839, the first houses had appeared on Mill Road (as the first section of Brandon Road, as far as the junction with Swaffham Road, was called) and, further west, on Brandon Road.[6] Building accelerated in the second half of the century. In 1858, for example, an acre of land 'well adapted for building purposes', was offered for sale, along with 'four newly and substantially erected freehold cottages, of a superior class, with wash-houses and offices and about 15 rod of garden ground to each', fronting Brandon Road 'in the improving market town of Watton'.[7]

Much of Watton's growing population, however, was still accommodated in the town centre. A good deal of infilling and rebuilding took place in the street and in the vicinity of the market place; gardens were built over, and stalls, stables and outhouses converted into living accommodation. As a result, settlement in the centre of the town became even denser and more concentrated.

ೞಌ

Parliamentary enclosure, and the adoption of the improved methods popularised by Thomas W Coke of Holkham and others, resulted in greatly increased agricultural productivity, while the growth of population, particularly in the towns, meant that the demand for agricultural products increased. Watton, with its market and fairs, was the natural focal point for the sale of the grain and animals produced by the farmers of the district.

From 1828, specialist fairs for animals, and particularly for sheep, were held on the first Wednesday in July and the first Wednesday after Old Michaelmas Day (11 October), supplementing the traditional fairs on 10 July, 11 October and 8 November. In 1829, the new fair for sheep took place on 1 July, in 'a field on the Mill Road' (Brandon Road).[8] It seems to have been very successful, prompting the comment: 'It will very soon become a mart for agriculture equal to any in the county. The influx of company to the town on this occasion filled every inn, and here we cannot but notice the magnificent preparations made by the *George* Inn for the accommodation of the worthy chairman, T W Coke Esq and his friends (147 in number) who sat down at three o'clock to a most sumptuous dinner, comprising all the delicacies of the season. The venison, so kindly presented by the Right Honourable Lord Walsingham was served up in the rich style for which the excellent hostess of the *George* Inn [Susanna Wright] is so eminently noted'.[9]

The second new fair of the year, held on 14 October, was also judged successful, 'but on account of the depressed state of agriculture, as well as the weather, there was not so much business done as anticipated'.[10] Times were hard for the farmers, but worse for their work force; while their employers were tucking in to their venison, the labourers were starving on wages of around ten shillings a week (equivalent to about £34 today).

The fairs continued for the next 40 years or so. In 1834, the first of the two sheep and lamb fairs was held on Wednesday 2 July and, again, Thomas W Coke of Holkham himself attended, along with a 'business-like and respectable company'. A reporter commented: 'We have never seen a fair in this county so well attended as this was on Wednesday about twelve or one o'clock [when] Mr Coke...made his appearance in the fair...shaking many of the agriculturists and others cordially by the hand, as he walked round to examine the various stock'. As in previous years, the fair was a social as well as a commercial event, with the *George*, once again, providing the venue: 'About two o'clock about 114 gentlemen sat down, in a booth on the bowling green, to an excellent dinner, provided by [Robert] Coe...at which T W Coke, Esq, presided.'[11]

ಬಿಡಿ

Serious riots by agricultural labourers, protesting against starvation-level wages and the threats to their livelihoods posed by new threshing machines, broke out in Norfolk in 1815, 1822 and 1830. Other manifestations of discontent, such as stack-burning and an undercurrent of rural crime, continued for several decades afterwards. There are no records of agricultural labourers in Watton, or the town's poor generally, participating in the rioting, although they may have done.

An incident of incendiarism, however, occurred in Watton in 1834. 'On the night of Monday the 31st of March last, or early on the following morning', stated a report, 'a wheat stack and a barley stack, belonging to Mr Charles Russell of Watton... were wilfully and maliciously set on fire by some evil disposed person or persons unknown'.[12] Charles Russell, at this time, was one of the largest landowners and farmers in Watton, whose home premises were at Watton Green.

A local subscription, to which both Charles Russell himself and the Norwich Union Fire Insurance Society contributed £50, raised £200 as a reward, which would have represented about 12 years' wages for an agricultural labourer. Two of the local magistrates asked the government to supplement it and to offer a pardon to any accomplices who betrayed the perpetrator.[13] Despite the reward, no conviction was secured; three young men were charged and detained but when their case came before the assizes on 26 July, it was thrown out.[14]

Other rural crimes occurred from time to time, notably poaching, particularly on the Merton estate, and there were several documented examples of poachers from Watton.

Events such as these helped to bring home to the propertied classes just how disaffected the agricultural labourers had become. In Wayland, as in other parts of Norfolk, an effort was made to reduce the threat that they posed, change their attitudes and engender more harmonious relations with them. On 15 December 1834, a meeting of owners and occupiers of land in Wayland Hundred was held at the *George* 'for the purpose of forming an association for promoting and rewarding good conduct, and encouraging industrious habits among servants, cottagers and labourers'.[15] Along with the principal farmers in Watton and the surrounding district, those associated with the initiative included Lord and Lady Walsingham, the lawyer Edward Grigson and Edward and Robert Stevens, maltsters and brewers. The meeting, 'very numerously and respectably attended', was addressed by John Weyland of Woodrising Hall, who praised the savings bank and friendly society that already existed in Watton because they encouraged the poor to be prudent and provident. He argued that the proposed association would 'bring the higher and lower orders together, and afford the former a consolation in knowing they had done what they could to improve the character of their labourers, and to make them independent and happy'. Those present agreed to offer rewards and premiums to servants, cottagers and labourers and to distribute them at an annual general meeting.[16]

From 1835 onwards, these annual meetings took place regularly. In 1843, to take one example, prizes were given in numerous categories: agricultural servants (single men and single women, separately); tradesmen's servants (likewise); shepherds, carters and labourers; savings bank (supplements being given to those who had saved assiduously); independent families (those who had not required poor relief); knitting (Mary Hartt of Watton was the champion here, having knitted 76 pairs of stockings and 4 pairs of socks in the year; her reward was 15 shillings); brewing; cultivation of gardens; swede turnip seed; white turnip seed; and ploughing. The total distributed in rewards was £70, after which the recipients listened to a speech delivered 'at great length' by the Association's vice-president, the Honourable F Baring (a major landowner in Ashill), who stressed that their rewards were passports to future service and employment. They were then 'dismissed' and 'the members adjourned to the dinner table'[17] for the usual eating, drinking, toasting and speechifying.

༄༅

The people of 19th century Watton wanted to improve their town and they wanted to improve themselves. The 'Watton Mutual Improvement Society' was founded in 1849 and quickly won support. On its first anniversary, in November 1850, a 'soiree' was arranged in the 'large room' at the *Crown*, with a varied programme of songs and instrumental music and, according to a report, 'about 190 friends, male and female, sat down to tea'.[18] Even more people, about 240, attended the third anniversary in the 'assembly rooms' at the *George*, when the chairman, Mr T Alexander, 'alluded to the necessity for young men earnestly to embrace every opportunity for cultivating their mental faculties'.[19] The programme of lectures over the first five years of the society's existence ranged widely, covering 'true manliness', phrenology, the eye, the steam engine, geology, poetry and the languages of the world.

Members of the Mutual Improvement Society had suggested the erection of a large public hall in Watton and the idea had been taken up by others, including Lord Walsingham, with the thought that it could also include a room in which the magistrates' petty sessions for the district could be held. A large sum (£1,100, equivalent to nearly £90,000 today) was speedily raised in donations and shares, and an architect was engaged: E B Lamb of London, who designed churches and other public institutions across the country.[20] The foundation stone of the building that became known as the Wayland Hall was laid by Lady Walsingham on 26 April 1853, the town being 'the scene of considerable animation and gaiety' on that day. The hall, noted a reporter, 'is intended to serve as a corn exchange, as an assembly-room for public purposes generally, and particularly for the meetings and lectures of the Young Men's Mutual Improvement Society...The edifice promises to be neat and elegant in its appearance, and an ornament to the town'.[21] Afterwards, the great and the good adjourned to the *George*, for a meal, speeches and toasts, while the workmen were provided with dinner in the humbler surroundings of the *King's Arms*.

Construction of the Wayland Hall was completed remarkably quickly. It was opened on 3 November 1853. On the ground floor was a reading room, used by the Watton Mutual Improvement Society for meetings and to accommodate its library of 150 books, and a room to which the town's (relatively new)[22] fire engine would be transferred from its previous home by the coal store under the National School. On the first floor were the hall itself, with a gallery for musicians, and the magistrates' room where the petty sessions were to be held on the first Wednesday of each month. Previously, they had been accommodated at the *George* and *Crown* hotels, alternating year by year. The overall verdict on the Wayland Hall was that: 'altogether the edifice is an ornament to the town, and cannot fail to be of great utility for business and other purposes'.[23]

Wayland Hall took some of the business that would previously have gone to the *George* or the *Crown*. On its opening day, it hosted the annual meeting and dinner of the Wayland Society for Rewarding Labourers, Cottagers and Others. The following week, it was the venue for a soiree organised by the Mutual Improvement Society. The Loyal Walsingham Lodge of the Manchester Unity of Oddfellows, a friendly society, held its 13th anniversary celebration and dinner there on 19 June 1854. On 1 December 1854 the first of many sales (on this occasion, of furniture, plate, glass and china) took place in the building. The large hall also became a venue for town meetings, theatrical productions and concerts.

On 31 May 1859, Wayland Hall was the setting for an ambitious initiative promoted by Watton's 'energetic and public-spirited vicar', the Revd W H Hicks. The event, presented

*Foresters' dinner at Wayland Hall, 1907.*
(Museum4 Watton)

as a 'conversazione', was an exhibition of objets d'art and curiosities lent by an impressive list of personages headed by the Duke of Wellington, Lord Albemarle and Lord Walsingham, a collection 'sufficient to win the attention of the dilettante and virtuoso, to raise the emulation of the studious, to arouse the apathetic, and to amaze and instruct all present'. Included were 'Russian and Chinese flags, taken in the Crimea and at Fat-Shan by Admiral Keppel…Sioux Indian weapons and costumes, sent by Lord Bury…cases of most rare and valuable Dresden and Sevres china, belonging to Mrs Hicks…medals and antiquities sent by Mr Barton, of Threxton' and much more besides, including microscopes and a printing press. Beginning at 8 pm and lasting three hours, the event was attended by 300 guests, 'in evening costume' and also featured explanations of some of the objects by their owners, the reading of prize essays, 'solos, vocal and instrumental' and 'glees and madrigals by the Watton choir'.[24]

One of those who attended was the Revd Benjamin Armstrong, vicar of East Dereham and celebrated diarist, who, with his party, had dined, 'with plenty of claret and champagne', at the Hicks' beforehand. Thus fortified, they all proceeded to Wayland Hall, the object of the event, noted Armstrong, being 'to show goodwill to the lower classes by mingling with them and providing them an agreeable evening in which amusement and instruction could go hand in hand'. Certainly, thought Armstrong, 'the object was abundantly achieved. The room was crowded and all enjoyed themselves supremely. The hall was fitted up like a Crystal Palace'. And, he concluded, 'there was tea or coffee at 6d per cup'.[25] Watton had never seen anything quite like it.

₰⃝

As well as Wayland Hall, Watton gradually acquired other facilities and public buildings that were the essential accoutrements of an 'improving' town. Main drainage had already arrived in 1851. Previously, solid waste often accumulated in dunghills at the rear of properties while rainfall and liquid waste probably flowed away in ditches, aided by the downward slope of the street to the west. A deep ditch, or culvert, ran between and parallel to the front and back streets, traces of which are often seen today when building work takes place at the rear of the shops of the High Street. The mysterious and otherwise unexplained feature called the Pyssel, or Possell or Postle Bridge, located near the market place, may have spanned this ditch.[26]

A brick tunnel-like cellar still exists underneath the rear portions of what are now 30, 32 and 34 High Street which, when constructed, lay behind the then-existing buildings fronting the street. It may have formed a replacement for, or been connected with, the ditch. According to anecdotal evidence, traces of a similar structure have been found underneath other premises adjoining the Market Place and in Middle Street. In the past 15 years, Julian Horn has observed running water in the 'tunnel' when leaks from underground mains occurred outside Khyber

House and the former Lloyd's Bank (previously the *George* Hotel). The water stopped flowing when the leaks were repaired.[27]

The process of installing main drainage in Watton was initiated by a meeting of the rate-paying inhabitants in the parish church on 3 April 1851, 'to consider the propriety of making a drain or sewer and certain branches down the public street…to contribute to the health and convenience of the…inhabitants', under the provisions of the Public Health Act of 1848. Three-fifths of the ratepayers agreed with the scheme, which duly went forward. Plans were drawn up and approved at a further meeting on 6 May, when it was agreed that the drain would be built in brick. Tenders were sought, and builders were invited to study a plan and specifications at the *George*, whose tenant at the time, Stephen Emerson, as an architect and surveyor, was well qualified to explain the particulars. He had estimated the cost of the work at £350 and the inhabitants agreed to raise the sum by a voluntary rate. Those who did not contribute would have to pay extra if they wished to be connected subsequently.[28] The sewer was built and connected to a treatment plant between Swaffham Road and Cley Lane, from which the purified water was conveyed to the Little Wissey.[29]

⁂

A county police force had been established in Norfolk in 1839, under the provisions of the Rural Constabularies Act of that year. The number of police officers employed gradually grew and in 1855 Watton acquired its own police station. It was built at the corner of Norwich Road and Thetford Roads, partly on glebe land and partly on a small piece of waste ground 'not much larger than a good-sized table cloth', according to Captain Black of the Norfolk Constabulary.[30] By May 1855, plans for a 'second class police station-house' had been drawn up.[31] The building was ready for occupation early in 1856 and served as the town's police station for many years.

In 1859, attention turned to the provision of a gas supply. Wayland Hall was the venue for a public meeting to discuss the possibility in January 1859, chaired by the vicar, the Revd W H Hicks. A large number of 'influential rate-payers' attended. They decided to form a company to take the project forward, and promised over two-thirds of the required funding on the spot.[32] The gas works were duly erected in Cley Lane, the large circular gasholder becoming a landmark, and a house for the manager was built next to it.

On 6 October 1859, another meeting agreed to go ahead with using gas to light the streets, which had previously been illuminated by oil lamps.[33] Lamps appeared along the High Street, lit by hand every evening and then extinguished several hours later.[34] In 1870, after the opening of the Thetford and Watton Railway, the gas company was approached about providing three or four extra lamps in Norwich Road.[35] The other end of the town benefited in 1882, when four lamps were installed in Brandon Road, illuminating the stretch from the National School to 'Mill Corner' (the junction with Swaffham Road).[36] Four years later, two extra lamps were installed in Brandon Road between Mill Corner and the *Jolly Farmers* public house, plus one near Walsingham Cottages in Merton Road and one near George Jacobs' house in the High Street.[37] Gas lighting was extended to other parts of the town in subsequent years and remained in use until 1932, when mains electricity arrived.[38]

Investment in public buildings and facilities was paralleled by developments in the business premises in the town. One Watton institution which benefited from improvement was the *George* Inn or, as it was now often called, the *George* Hotel.

## Notes

1. NM, 6 July 1861, and elsewhere.
2. NC, 4 June 1859.
3. Watton and Carbrooke Inclosure Award and map; NRO, C/Sca 2/316.
4. NC, 9 October 1802.
5. NC, 10 December 1803.
6. Watton tithe apportionment, 2 September 1841 (map dated 1839); NRO, DN/TA 565.
7. NM, 7 August 1858.
8. NC, 27 June 1829.
9. NC, 4 July 1829.
10. NC, 24 October 1829.
11. NC, 5 July 1834.
12. NM, 12 April 1834.
13. TNA, HO 64/4/113-4.
14. Calendar of prisoners, 1834, accessed via findmypast.co.uk; NM, 2 August 1834.
15. NM, 6 December 1834.
16. NM, 20 December 1834.
17. NM, 21 October 1843.
18. NN, 16 November 1850; photocopy of the programme in the author's possession.
19. NN, 20 November 1852.
20. Wikipedia.
21. NC, 30 April 1853.
22. It had been purchased by public subscription in 1845; G Jessup (1985).
23. NC, 5 November 1853; George Collins, *A Short History of the Wayland Hall and the Lords of Watton Manor* (2022).
24. NC, 4 June 1859.
25. Christopher Armstrong (ed), *Under the Parson's Nose* (Larks Press, 2012).
26. Watton Town Book; NRO, PD 218/1; Court book, Manor of Watton Hall, 17 April 1707; Museum,4Watton, M4W/2016/8A.
27. Thanks to Julian Horn for this information and for showing me the tunnel, with the kind permission of the owner, Paul Adcock.
28. Watton Vestry Book 1842-83; NRO, PD218/89; NM, 22 March 1851 and 10 May 1851.
29. Cecil F Chapman, *More about Grandad's Watton* (1985). A sewage tank is shown in this position on

the second edition of the 6 inch Ordnance Survey map, published 1906.
30. NRO, C/C2/165.
31. NC, 12 May 1855.
32. NM, 15 January 1859.
33. Samuel Lewis, *A Topographical Dictionary of England*, Volume IV (1831). Thanks to Julian Horn for this reference.
34. Cecil F Chapman, *More about Grandad's Watton* (1985).
35. Watton Vestry Book, 1842-83; NRO, PD 218/89.
36. NN, 23 September 1882.
37. TWT, 4 September 1886.
38. Cecil F Chapman, *More about Grandad's Watton* (1985).

# The George: the Hub of Watton

The *George* was Watton's premier hostelry and meeting place. It dated back to the 16th century and possibly earlier.

*The George.*
*(Museum4Watton, from the Studio Khyber collection.)*

In 1591, *'le George'* was the capital messuage of John Bettes, mercer, who bought a piece of land to the west of it from the lord of the manor of Watton Hall, probably for use as a garden.[1] In 1595, the inn was still held by John Bettes and was said to have an estimated five acres of 'groundes behind the howse'.[2] It may have been the residence of Thomas Bettes, probably the son of John, when he complained about the erection of a stall in front of his premises in 1620. Thomas Bettes died in 1632 and a detailed inventory of his possessions was made.[3] His property was large, comprising hall and parlour with chambers above, kitchen, dairy, a pantry chamber, a 'shop chamber' and a 'chandle house' with equipment for making candles. The reference to a 'shop' suggests that the premises were in the town centre but unfortunately there is no firm evidence to identify them with the *George*.

Thomas Bettes bequeathed all his real estate to his son John Bettes[4] and the *George* may have remained in the latter's hands until 1658, when it was acquired by

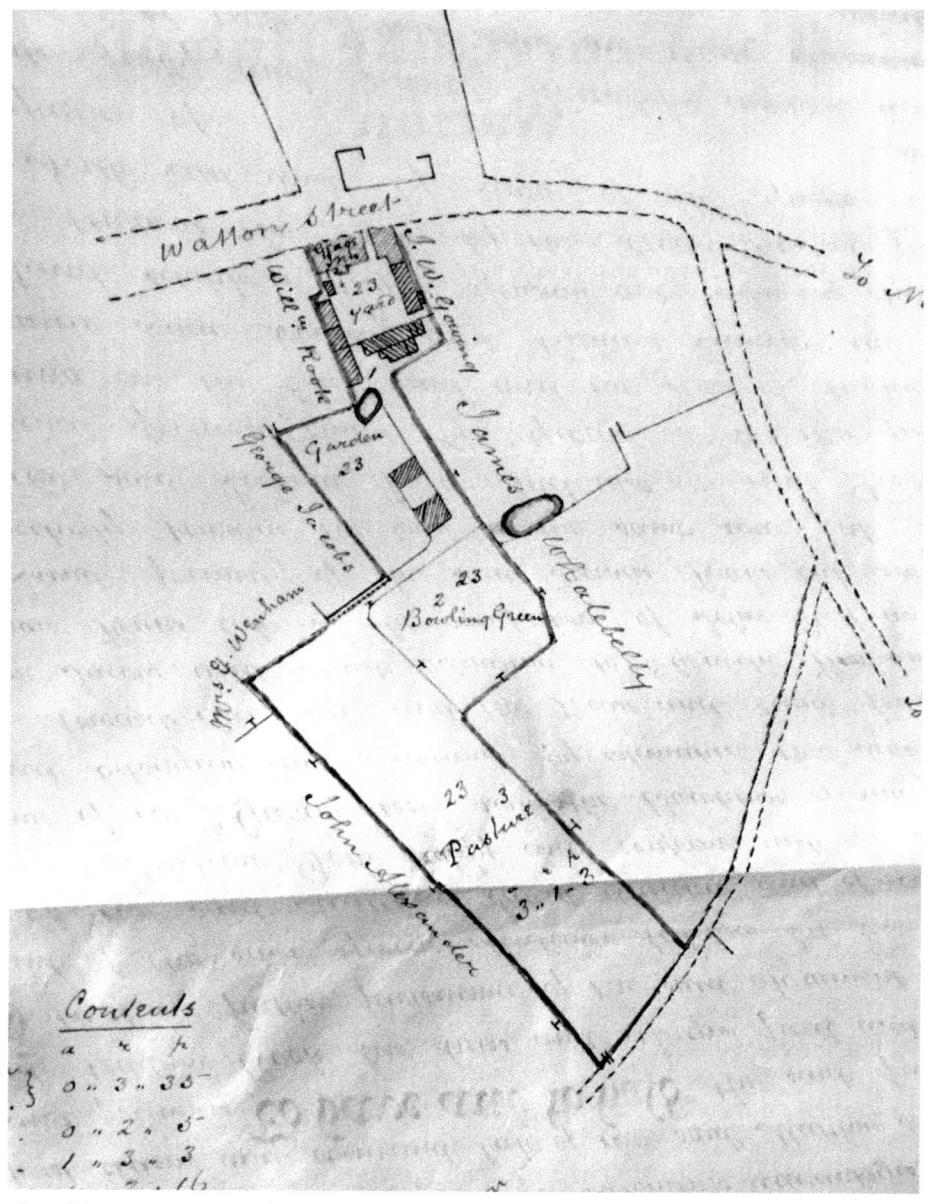

*Plan of the George premises, from a deed of 1869.*
*(Museum 4Watton)*

# The George: the Hub of Watton 121

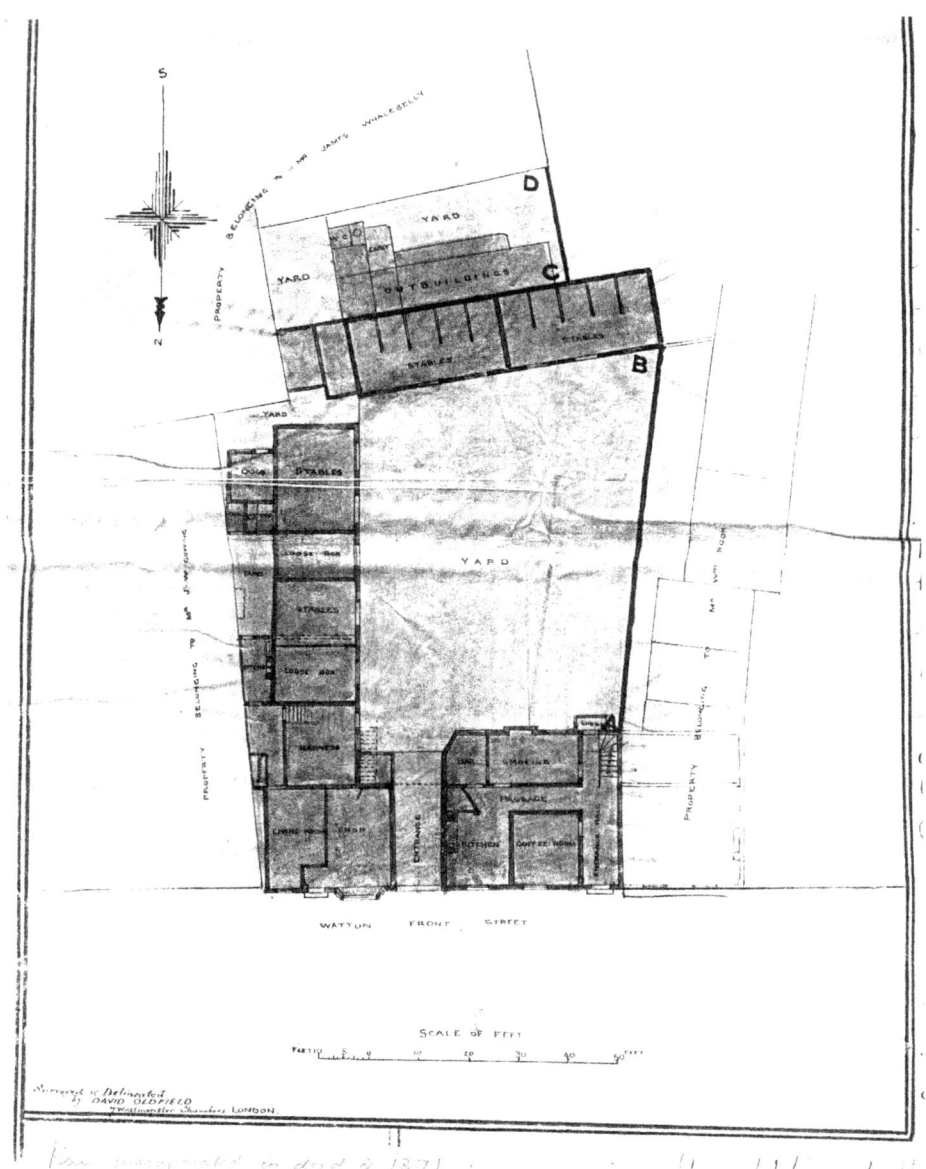

*Plan of the George premises, from a deed of 1871.*
*(Lloyd's Bank)*

Richard Hamond, who owned land in Shipdham, Cranworth, Letton and Warham. He left the *George* to his wife Frances, and then to the younger of his two sons, Charles, when he reached the age of 16, which he did in 1679. Frances Hamond, as a widow, was the owner of the *George* at the time of the fire of 1674.

Thomas Baskerville dined at the *George* when he visited Watton in 1681 and, although he found 'little remarkable' in the town, he was impressed by the 'fine new bowling green att ye *George Inn*'.[5] The landlady, he noted, was 'Mrs Jeames', who was probably Susan James, widow, who died in 1689, one of whose sons by an earlier marriage was Edward Harris of Watton, beer brewer (died 1696).[6] Harris was recorded in the manor court book as the occupier of the *George* in 1679. He was succeeded by Judith Hamond, widow, probably a relative of the owner. The bowling green was patronised by, among others, William de Grey of Merton Hall who, in 1686, 'wonne at Watton bowling greene…00 09 06' (equivalent to about £60 today).[7]

ಐಧ

In 1687, Charles Hamond went to 'overseas parts' and disappeared. The *George* seems to have become, effectively, the property of his elder brother Richard, who died in 1695 owing a lot of money, including £300 (equivalent to about £36,000 today) on a mortgage on his estate in Cranworth and Letton. Creditors to whom he was indebted for smaller amounts included Dr Samuel Walker, 'for physick'; William Candler, 'glasser'; Robert Kiddall and Widow Pooly 'for beere'; Francis Butcher, shoemaker, for shoes and boots; Francis Curson, for mending shoes; William Hill, miller, for meal; Edmund Turner, for malt; John Brett, for oatmeal and carriage; William Pattrick 'for taylor work'; Robert Brett, 'for blacksmith work'; and William Curle, 'for blacksmith's work…when he did some repairs at the *George*'; a cross-section of the tradespeople of Watton at the time, and another illustration of the centrality of credit in English commercial life.

Richard's will, recording that his estate should be sold to pay his debts, was contested by his father-in-law, acting on behalf of Richard's son Richard, aged eight, and the case went to the Court of Chancery. The plaintiff claimed that Richard, the father, 'was so disturbed in his minde, memory and understanding' that he didn't understand what he was doing when he wrote his will and was 'abused and imposed upon' by a 'confederacy' involving his sister; his mother; Reuben Duffield of Saham Toney (who had helped him write the will); and Jane, his widow and mother of his son Richard, to deprive the latter of his inheritance. The father-in-law alleged that the 'pretended will' had not been proved. He was wrong: the will was proved in the Norwich Consistory Court on 23 October 1695.[8] Nor was it true that Richard junior had been disinherited. According to his father's will, after the payment of his debts, the proceeds from the sale of his real and personal estate were to be put out at interest to provide annuities for his wife and sister, and for 'the bringing up and educating my…son' until he reached the age of 21, after which the investments would be his.

The members of the 'confederacy' maintained that the deceased had been 'a very sencible person and a good scholler having been brought upp clerke to a very eminent councellor at law', and that he had read his will through three times before signing it. The defendants gave full details of Richard's extensive debts and provided an inventory of the 'goods and chattels' in the property in which he resided. Although he had described himself as 'gentleman', his house was not extensive, comprising a hall and parlour with chambers over and a dairy—a yeoman's house. He had some good furniture including modern items such as 'an ovell table' and 'a looking glass' but the value of his personal effects was far from sufficient to cover his debts. The Cranworth and Letton property had been sold by the trustees but Richard's house in Watton and the *George Inn* (which still officially belonged to Richard's absent brother Charles), had been retained. Money had been spent on repairing these buildings and 'a copper and brewing vessels and other materiells' costing £25 had been purchased 'for the brewhouse at the *George*...without which charge the *George* would have stood tenantless' rather than being let, as it was, for £27 per year (equivalent to nearly £2,900 today). The father-in-law's case was clearly flawed.[9]

In 1706, when the absent Charles Hamond was finally presumed dead, the *George* passed to Richard junior, his 18-year-old nephew, who was already occupying the premises. However, he failed to take them up when he came of age and in 1713, now in the occupation of Henry Thompson, they were sold to John Turner.

೮⊃Q੩

John Turner became bankrupt in 1731. Described as 'late of King's Lynn, wine merchant', he had accumulated debts of over £1,000 (equivalent to about £120,000 today), including a mortgage of £400 on the *George*, which was sold by the bankruptcy commissioners to Francis Hicks (the elder), grocer, who paid off the mortgage. As well as the 'publick inn', the premises included 'the shopps, brewhouses and other outhouses, barns, stables, yards, gardens, orchards, bowling green, lands, meadows, pasture grounds and homestall to the same belonging'. It was occupied by Mary Howard, widow.[10] After the death of Francis Hicks the elder, the *George*, now occupied by Richard Stebbing, became the property of Hicks' executors, his widow Jane and son Francis. In 1746, Jane and Francis granted a ten-year lease of the house and shops adjoining the east side of the inn to Edward Crockley, described as a peruke maker. In the same year, Crockley took on an apprentice, Thomas Candler, when his trade was given as barber.[11] Later he became a maltster[12] and had extensive interests in land and trade. He died in 1795, aged 82.[13]

The lease provides interesting information about the inn and its yard. Jane and Francis Hicks agreed to 'make a door in one of the great gates belonging to the

*George Inn…bigg enough to pass…therein with a horse and to hang a lock on the same the key of which is always to be in the custody or power of…Edward Crockley'*. They also undertook to allow Crockley to come and go at night 'by the little gate with his horses and through the great gates in the day time with carts and carriages to his stable in the…*George* yard with firing or any thing he thinks proper to lay therein'. Crockley was also to have access to the well in the yard of the *George* and 'the liberty of drying linen on the hangings or hakes belonging to Richard Stebbing belonging to the said *George Inn* and the same liberty of the pew or seat in the church as the said Richard Stebbing hath'.[14]

Francis Hicks (the younger) held the *George* until his bankruptcy in 1781. His tenant at the inn from at least 1756 was Joseph Thickpenny, from whom, in January of that year, a saddler called John Brame stole a saddle, one of two that he took from the stable. Brame was sentenced 'to be publicly whipt at Watton next market day, and to have 40 lashes'.[15] Thickpenny drummed up business by offering 'a neat four wheel post chaise at nine-pence per mile, with able horses and a careful driver, to any part of England' and by offering to take in boarders.[16] However, he suffered the same fate as was to befall his proprietor, and became bankrupt in 1769.[17]

ଛଓ

The *George* was the default venue for important meetings in Watton. In 1769, it hosted a town meeting, attended by the principal inhabitants, as it was to do on a number of subsequent occasions.[18] The following year, the first known meeting of the Association for the Apprehending and Convicting of Horse-Stealers in the Hundred of Wayland and Adjacent Hundreds[19] took place there, when Thomas Younge was elected as the association's treasurer. The association offered rewards for the recovery of lost or stolen horses and a £10 bounty for a conviction. Its meetings were regularly held at the *George*, although occasionally its members gathered at the *Crown* instead. The *George* was also the site of the majority of auction sales of properties in Watton and nearby villages, and was the place where the commissioners appointed to implement the parliamentary enclosure of Watton and of surrounding parishes held their discussions.

Following the bankruptcy of Francis Hicks in 1781, the *George* was offered for sale as 'a capital and well-accustomed house, with a brewhouse, granary, stables, yard, garden, orchard, bowling green and inclosure of pasture'.[20] The purchaser was Edward Stevens. The tenancy had already been taken over by Edward Ellis, who was the innholder when a notice appeared in September 1792 advertising a post-coach service to London, via Thetford, Barton Mills and Newmarket: 'Carries four insides, sets out from…London every Monday, Wednesday and Friday mornings, precisely at seven o'clock; returns from Mr Ellis's, the *George Inn*, Watton, on Tuesday, Thursday and Saturday mornings, at four o'clock; breakfasts at Newmarket, and dines in London. The proprietors …flatter themselves this coach will merit encouragement, as it arrives in the afternoon, and the game and parcels shall be immediately delivered'.[21] Presumably, travellers had to share the journey with bags of recently-shot pheasants destined for aristocratic tables in London. According to another advertisement two years later, the fare from Watton to London was 1s 6d (equivalent to about £6 today) for those sitting inside the coach and half that if sitting outside, exposed to the elements.[22]

An indication of the *George's* role as a hub for the local gentry, and of attitudes at the time, is provided by events that took place at the inn in January 1793. The French Revolution had taken place four years previously and war was about to break out between Britain and France. Initially, opinion in Britain was divided, with some sympathetic to the ideals of the revolution and others, increasingly, appalled by its violence. A group of 21 local gentry and farmers assembled in the presence of Brampton Gurdon Dillingham of Letton Hall at the *George* on 9 January to sign a declaration of support for the government and to propose the formation of a local 'association for the preservation of the constitution and the security of the lives and persons' of the people of Britain.

W Tooke Harwood, a landowner in Thompson, was present and was not happy with what he saw and heard. He feared that those dragooned (as he saw it) into signing the declaration would help to perpetuate political and fiscal abuses 'under the plausible pretence of their country's being in danger'. Harwood claimed that Mr Harvey (Robert Harvey, a lawyer), had observed that 'the common people were too stupid to be informed'; that the Revd Thomas Scott of Rockells Hall had opined that 'they ought to sign anything that their superiors recommended'; and that Mr Hicks (probably Thomas Hicks, the lawyer) had claimed that 'the present mode of buying and selling representations in parliament was just and honest'. Many had been of the view that 'all reform of parliamentary representation was impracticable', not a view that was shared by W Tooke Harwood,[23] or by Richard Dinmore, the doctor.

Harwood challenged those present and left a declaration of his own at the *George*, supporting the constitution established by the Glorious Revolution of 1688 and advocating the reform of parliament to remove abuses. The following week saw the publication of an emollient reply from Brampton Gurdon Dillingham, acknowledging 'the propriety of a temperate and constitutional reform of some few abuses at a proper time' and maintaining that he had merely wished to give the 'gentlemen' of the district the opportunity to support 'the welfare of our country and the happiness and security of ourselves and neighbours'.[24] The controversy seems to have died down, and the gentry closed ranks in the face of the perceived threat from revolutionary France.

☙❧

Edward Ellis was still the tenant of the *George* in 1797 but by 1801 the 'innholder' was Thomas Sallitt. He died that year, aged 41, but his widow, Isabella, whom he had married in 1787, acquired the ownership of the *George* from Edward Stevens in 1802. Born in 1763, Isabella was the daughter of Robert Buxton, fellmonger (dealer in animal skins) and breeches-maker in Neaton. In 1807, six years after the death of her first husband she married John West of Breccles. Isabella remained the owner of the *George* for almost 30 years, until 1831, when she and John West sold it to Matthew Sallitt of Saxlingham, probably a relative of her first husband, for £375. In both 1802 and 1807, the *George* had been described as having a 'brewhouse, granary, stables and other outhouses, yard, garden, orchards, bowling green and one inclosure of pasture land thereto adjoining'. Isabella also owned the house, with stables and yard, next door to the east, which Edward Crockley had formerly occupied.[25]

The owner of the *George* was a woman and so, for a quarter of a century until her death in 1833 was the tenant. Her name was Susanna, or Susan, Wright, widow of Dennis Wright.

Susanna Blomfield married Dennis Wright, from Oxborough, at Forncett St Peter in 1796. They had a daughter, Elizabeth, in 1799 and two sons, Robert in 1801 and William in 1803. Dennis occupied mills by the turnpike road at Saxlingham Thorpe, south of Norwich, and owned over 170 acres of land. The young couple and their small children had a comfortable lifestyle.

But then, in December 1803, disaster struck. Dennis was declared bankrupt. On 25 February 1804, the watermills and windmills in Saxlingham Thorpe, with the granary, corn-drying kiln, stables and 'compact new-built sashed dwelling house', with its 'walled garden, well planted' were all put up for auction. Even worse, two days later, 'all the neat and modern household furniture, plate, linen, china, glass, waggons, carts, horses and other effects of Mr Dennis Wright' went under the hammer. It must have been heartbreaking for Susanna to part with her 'handsome mahogany chairs...set of mahogany dining tables...mahogany wardrobes and chests of drawers...four post and tent bedsteads, with chintz, moreen and other furniture, fine bordered goose feather beds', servants' beds and all the couple's other possessions, including the contents of the kitchen, riding and working horses and a 'brace of staunch pointers'.[26]

After Dennis's creditors had been paid off in January 1805, the couple moved to Watton. On 11 May 1805, the following announcement appeared: '*George Inn*: Dennis Wright respectfully begs leave to inform the nobility, gentry and the public in general, that he has taken the above inn, and fitted it up with every accommodation; gentlemen travellers may be assured of finding good beds, at all times, carefully aired. DW hopes the strictest attention to their comfort, together with a large stock of superior old wines and genuine spirits, which he has laid in, will ensure him their future support'. He also offered 'neat post-chaises, with able horses and careful drivers'.[27] He had invested heavily in the *George* but where had the money come from? Possibly from the owner, Isabella Sallitt, or from Matthew

Sallitt, as the Sallitt family came from Saxlingham. They must have known Dennis and Susanna Wright and installed them in their new position.

The following year, Susanna gave birth again. Her daughter, Susanna was baptised on 10 August 1806 but was buried only six weeks later, on 23 September. Two years later, twins were born, Susanna and Jane. Jane died in infancy but Susanna survived, did not marry and lived to the age of 70.

The *George* remained the regular venue for meetings of the subscribers to the Association for Apprehending and Convicting of Horse-Stealers. In 1807, the announcement of a committee meeting at noon on 19 November was followed by: 'NB a good ordinary [meal] at two o'clock precisely, by their humble servant Dennis Wright'.[28] Dennis knew how to look after his customers.

Eight months later, on 23 July 1808, they must have been surprised to read: 'Died: Tuesday last at Watton, Mr Dennis Wright, late of Saxlingham Mills'.[29] A week later, came a correction: 'We are happy to have it in our power to contradict the account (which appeared in our last, having been verbally communicated) of the death of Mr Dennis Wright, of Watton, who we have the pleasure to say, is fast recovering from a slight indisposition'.[30] An innocent mistake, a practical joke, or the malicious action of an aggrieved creditor?

An announcement that appeared just four months later, however, proved all too true: 'Died…Saturday last, sincerely lamented, in his 30th year, Mr Dennis Wright of the *George Inn*, Watton, whose obliging civilities will be long remembered by all who knew him, and the public [will] regret the loss of a most active and attentive landlord'.[31] Dennis had actually died two weeks earlier and had already been buried at Watton on 22 November 1808.

After the bankruptcy, the move and the deaths of two of her children, this must have been devastating for Susanna Wright. But she decided to take over the business and carry on. Barely a month later, she announced: '*George Inn*, Watton. Susan Wright returns her sincere thanks to the friends of her late husband, Mr Dennis Wright, for the many favours received, and hopes for a continuance of them, as her endeavours will be to accommodate and oblige her friends and the neighbourhood to the utmost of her power'.[32] On 23 November the following year, as her husband had done, she prepared 'a good ordinary' for the Association for Apprehending and Convicting of Horse-Stealers, and she continued to do the same in subsequent years.[33]

Business seems to have been good and in 1812 came another announcement: 'Susan Wright, impressed with a lively sense of gratitude for past favors [sic] from her numerous friends, humbly begs leave to solicit a continuance of their support, and to assure them and the public in general, she has spared neither pains nor expence [sic] in fitting up the [*George*] *Inn* with every suitable and requisite convenience, for the accommodation of commercial gentlemen and others who may honour her with their commands'. She concluded with a reminder about 'neat post chaises, able horses and careful drivers'.[34]

Susanna was alert to new business opportunities. In 1821, she announced that she had 'recently fitted up a neat hearse and mourning coach, with which she means to accommodate the public, on the lowest terms possible'.[35] In December 1824, she organised a ball at the *George*, offering tickets for gentlemen at five shillings (equivalent to nearly £15 today) and for ladies at four, 'tea and coffee included… dancing to commence at seven o'clock'.[36] Several more balls were organised at the *George* in subsequent years. It was the social centre for the district.

Another opening for Susanna was provided by the instigation, in 1828, of annual sheep, lamb and stock fairs in Watton, since the *George* could offer not only accommodation for the human attendees but also temporary pasture for the animals. The fair of July 1828, it was anticipated, would attract Scottish cattle drovers who had brought their animals to Norfolk for sale. Susanna announced that 'the Scotchmen and other salesmen can be accommodated with keeping for any quantity of bullocks, either before or after the fair, by applying to Mrs Susan Wright, at the *George Inn*, where the committee and subscribers intend to hold their first dinner that day, and most respectfully solicit the favour of those gentlemen who will please to honour them with their company'.[37] Similar arrangements were made successfully in subsequent years. The dinner following the sheep fair on 1 July 1829, for example, brought the praise already quoted for the 'excellent hostess'.[38]

Susanna Wright lived to see her daughter Elizabeth married to Robert Brasnett, steward to one of the principal landowners in Carbrooke, on 5 December 1822. One of the witnesses was Smith Wright, who was an important figure in Watton at the time and was probably a relative, perhaps a half-brother, of Dennis Wright.[39] Robert and Elizabeth Brasnett had eight sons and two daughters and Elizabeth, a widow from 1846, lived to the ripe old age of 79. Susanna, their grandmother, would have seen the first two of their children. Susanna's elder son Robert became a baker, occupying premises facing the market square in Watton, and her younger son William Wright became a farmer at Hall Farm in Ovington.

Susanna Wright died on 9 January 1828, aged 62, receiving the following posthumous tribute: 'Few indeed stood more highly and deservedly esteemed by all classes of society, added to which she was a kind and affectionate mother and a real friend to the poor; the remembrance of her amiable qualities will not easily be obliterated from the minds of all who had the pleasure of knowing and being acquainted with her'.[40]

Susanna Wright's sons may have kept the business going until her lease of the *George* expired, as it was not until March 1830 that the 'old-established and well-known inn and posting house…with about five acres of arable and pasture land' was offered to let. The inn was described as: 'a free house, with good brewing and other offices, and has an excellent bowling green'.[41] The new tenant, who announced himself on 24 April, was Robert Coe, formerly tenant of the *Crown*[42] and a farmer in Watton and Shipdham. The January after he had taken up the lease, the *George* hosted the 'Watton Annual Ball'.[43] The following year, Coe initiated a Saturday coach service from Watton to the Norfolk Hotel, Norwich, via Hingham and Barford, leaving the *George* at 6.30 am and setting off for the return journey at 5 pm.[44] A daily (except Sundays) coach service in the 'Holt Regulator' between Holt and London, in both directions, stopping at the *George*, began in 1833.[45]

Robert Coe invested in 'several new carriages, both for pair-horse and one-horse work' and claimed to have 'chaises, flys and gigs always ready, with steady drivers'. The hearse acquired by Susanna Wright continued to be available for hire. Coe also offered 'a large stock of old and superior wines, of the finest quality'.[46] The business seems to have been doing well.

Robert Coe's lease ended at Michaelmas 1842. During his tenure, extensive improvements had been made. 'Stabling, lock-up coach-house, gig houses, brewery, granary and other convenient outbuildings' had been erected, 'which, with the public inn, form a spacious inclosed yard'. The 'excellent bowling green' remained, and the property also included agricultural buildings and 13 acres of land.[47] Within a couple of months, with a recommendation from his predecessor, the new tenant was announced. He was William Allen, formerly of the *White Lion*, Eye. Allen undertook to continue all the services provided previously, and stated that the *George* 'will shortly undergo thorough repair, with such improvements to make it equal in comfort to any first-rate hotel'. He reminded his clientele that 'the stabling department is replete with every convenience, and any gentleman wishing for loose boxes during the hunting season, will find good accommodation'.[48] However, he was compelled to deny a rumour, possibly circulated by a rival, that 'has been insidulously [sic] represented, [that] post-horses are not kept at the *George*'.[49] Robert Coe, meanwhile, purchased (with a mortgage) the *White Hart* in Hingham and remained its proprietor until his death in 1849.[50] Perhaps he was the rival.

Both William Allen of the *George* and Robert Coe of the *White Hart* sought to take advantage of connections to the newly-built Norwich and Brandon Railway, opened on 9 July 1845. Four days before the service started, Robert Coe announced that he had been 'honoured with instructions from the railway company' to run a conveyance from Shipdham via Hingham to Wymondham, to connect there with trains for Norwich. William Allen trumped him, having 'the honour of announcing that he has been appointed by the railway company their agent for Watton, as the general booking office for all passengers, parcels and goods, for London and Norwich, via the Brandon, Thetford and Attleborough stations'. His advertisement went on to give details of the connections. The Holt Regulator coach, via Watton, would connect at Brandon with trains to and from London; the Royal Mail, leaving Watton at 5.45 pm, would take parcels and goods to London via Thetford; and the Prince of Wales Omnibus would leave Watton at 7.30 am on Monday, Wednesday and Saturday, connecting with the train at Attleborough at 9 am, which would get passengers to Norwich at 10 am, with similar arrangements for the return journey, leaving Norwich at 4 pm. The *Royal George* coach to Norwich via Barford would continue to run 'until further notice'.[51] It was still running in 1848 but the train was the transport of the future.

William Allen continued as the innholder of the *George* until Michaelmas 1848, one of the duties in his final year being the organisation of a banquet for W M Bagge to celebrate his election as a Conservative MP, with Lord Walsingham in the chair.[52] Allen had already taken over the carrying business of Swann and Sons, Railway Carriers of Cambridge, which ran daily vans leaving Shipdham at 1 pm, Watton at 2 pm and Stanford (now in the Battle Area) at three, to the railway station at Brandon, and he may have found that more lucrative than his tenancy of the *George*.[53]

ಇಂಡ

William Allen's successor at the *George* was Stephen Emerson, from Holkham. He and his wife Harriet had at least 15 children there, of whom four died in infancy. Two of the children were baptised Matthew Sallitt Emerson, suggesting that there may have been a family connection with the owner of the *George*. Stephen Emerson

Letterhead of Stephen Emerson, tenant of the George.
(Julian Horn)

had worked for Lord Leicester at Holkham Hall as a carpenter but by 1845, when he helped prepare the erection of the famous monument in the park there, he was described as 'Lord Leicester's architect'.[54] He left Holkham at the end of 1847, a sale taking place of his furniture and other effects, including about 100 books.[55] He moved to Watton and announced that he was ready to receive commissions as an architect and building surveyor, offering: 'Plans and estimates made and buildings superintended, on the most reasonable terms'.[56] His entry in Craven's Directory of 1856 refers to him as: 'Emerson, Stephen, victualler, "George" commercial & family hotel, and posting-house; architect, surveyor and valuer; agent for the English Cambrian Life Office, and Loan Society': an impressive CV.

It was probably at Michaelmas 1848 that Stephen Emerson took on the tenancy of the *George*. He held an opening dinner on 20 December, attended by 'between 40 and 50 gentlemen', with Thomas Barton of Threxton presiding, when 'the repast… was of a most recherche character, and the present of a fine haunch of venison, by the noble lord of Holkham and, also, the addition of champagne by the liberal proprietor of the hotel, added to the luxuries which the company enjoyed. The evening was much enhanced by the singing of many vocalists present; amongst whom, was the celebrated extemporaneous singer, Mr Charles Sloman, who contributed much to the mirth and hilarity of the evening by the introduction of some of his most excellent songs, in which he accompanied himself on the pianoforte'.[57] Emerson had connections, and his move to Watton had clearly been with the blessing of his previous employer, Lord Leicester.

Until now, on numerous occasions, the *George* had hosted auctioneers who used the inn as a suitable venue for their sales. Stephen Emerson turned auctioneer himself, conducting sales of property from 1858, sales of cattle and other stock at the 'Fairstead' on market days from 1860, and a 'repository' event for farming stock and furniture on the first Wednesday of the month from 1 February 1865. He gave up the tenancy of the *George* in 1863 and thereafter described himself as an auctioneer. He died in June 1870, aged 76. His was an interesting career, a story of social mobility, from estate carpenter to a pillar of Watton society. Two of his sons did well, too; Stephen Sallitt Emerson, the eldest, became an excise officer and Matthew Sallitt Emerson practised as a solicitor in Norwich.

ഈരു

The next tenant of the *George* was Leonard Tillott, or Tillett, who had previously been a publican in East Harling. It was during his tenure that events took place at the *George* that resulted in a case at the Norfolk and Norwich Assizes in March 1869.

Leonard Tillott had a daughter, Emma, who was said to be aged 22 in 1869.[58] She helped in the hotel's bar, where she attracted the interest of Henry Wrightup, aged 25, tenant of the Earl of Leicester's large farm at Panworth Hall, Ashill.

Wrightup was a regular at the *George*, visiting several times a week over a period of years. According to Emma's mother, Mary, giving evidence, he gave Emma several expensive presents, including a gold brooch costing five guineas (equivalent to about £330 today) and matching earrings. Emma's parents did not object to Emma and Wrightup being alone together, believing the latter to be a gentleman and trusting to his honour. However, while Mary had observed Wrightup 'paying attention to her daughter' she had also heard a report that he was engaged to a Miss Matthews. She confronted Wrightup with this information. He denied it, exclaiming: 'D____ Miss Matthews'.

Shortly after Christmas 1868, Emma was discovered to be pregnant. Her mother, Mary, was distressed but Wrightup reassured her that his intentions were honourable and that he would marry Emma. On 13 January, he announced that he had fixed the day of the wedding, which would take place in London, as he did not wish it to be in public. On 23 January, he came to the *George* for tea. Emma arrived while he was there, having been to buy a wedding dress, of which Wrightup, after some hesitation, stated his approval. On 27 January he visited again. This time, he met Emma's father Leonard Tillott, who had only learned of Emma's pregnancy from his wife on 20 January, and from whom Wrightup had wanted to keep news of the situation; perhaps he had feared a violent response (Tillott was shortly to appear at Dereham Petty Sessions charged with an assault there on 25 January).[59] However, the interview appears to have been civil; Tillott said that he could not provide Emma with a dowry and Wrightup replied that it didn't matter. He stated that the wedding would be in London the following Monday, 1 February. They would all set off together from the *George* at 6 am and catch the express train for London from Wymondham.

When 1 February arrived, Wrightup failed to turn up. Later in the day, he wrote to say that he had been compelled to go to Norwich to visit his father, who was ill.

During the court case, the evidence given by Mary and Leonard Tillott was corroborated by Ellen Tillott, Emma's younger sister, said to be aged 20.[60] She said that Wrightup had told her that Emma was pregnant and that he intended to marry her, and had asked her to be a bridesmaid. The two sisters and their parents had got up at 4 am on 1 February, expecting Wrightup to join them. Leonard Tillott's 'ostler and post lad' also gave evidence, confirming that he had prepared the horses and 'fly' to go to Wymondham station.

On Tuesday 16 February, at St Martin's in the Fields, London, Wrightup married Jane Elizabeth Matthews, a minor who was said to have 'large property'. Their son, Henry Boyce Wrightup, was baptised at St Peter Mancroft in Norwich two months later, on 21 April 1869. A month before that, on 20 March 1869, Emma Tillott had given birth to a son. He was baptised five days later as Palm Booty Tillott.

Emma Tillott prosecuted Henry Wrightup for breach of promise. The case was heard at the Assizes on Good Friday, 26 March 1869. Despite the best efforts of Wrightup's counsel,[61] who tried to show that the Tillott family had low moral standards, the jury, after an hour's deliberation, found in favour of Emma. The judge awarded her £700 (equivalent to about £44,000 today) in damages. According to a newspaper report, 'the announcement of the verdict was followed by applause, which was immediately suppressed'.[62]

Leonard Tillott was still the tenant of the *George* in February 1871, when he provided the annual 'market tea' to coincide with the opening of the cattle market, for a company of 60 to 70 people, comprising farmers, cattle dealers and 'a goodly number of the principal tradesmen of the town'.[63] Leonard, Mary, Emma, Ellen and Palm Booty were recorded at the *George* in the census on 2 April 1871 but they left later in the year, moving first to the *New Inn*, Attleborough and then, in 1874, to the *Royal Hotel* there, where Leonard became the general manager. Palm Booty was with his grandparents at the same hotel in 1881, and attending school. Leonard worked at the *Royal Hotel* until his death in 1884. His wife Mary and daughter Emma (referred to as Emma Jane) were his executors. Emma was still resident at the *Royal Hotel* when, eventually, she did get married, to John Harrison, a builder, in 1893.

∞CR

The owner of *The George*, Matthew Sallitt, died suddenly in 1866, aged 69.[64] Three years later, his executors sold the *George* and associated premises to William Rook, a farmer, for £2,000 (equivalent to over £125,000 today). In 1871, Rook, in turn, sold part of the property, including most of the hotel, to William Clubb for £800. The dividing line between the part sold and that retained by William Rook ran along the line of a former gable wall forming the west side of the entrance hall of the hotel and continued straight across the 'paved yard' behind it, where a new dividing wall was to be built. The ten-bay stables at the far end of the yard, together with the outbuildings beyond them, more stables on the east side of the yard and the house and shop 'with the bay window' (a confectioner's) and associated buildings were included in the sale to William Clubb.[65] Clubb was a baker and confectioner and was already the tenant of the shop and the four-bedroomed house and bakery attached to it, where, it was said, 'a good trade has been carried on...for forty years and upwards, and is now being carried on by the present occupier'.[66]

The properties that made up the *George Hotel* were much diminished, although the stabling, one of the hotel's principal assets, remained intact. A large ground-floor room and much of the sleeping accommodation had been lost. What remained on the ground floor were a 'coffee room', a smoking room, a bar and a kitchen. According to sale particulars of 1912,[67] the coffee room and part of the kitchen had by then been replaced by two 'commercial rooms' (each with bay window). On the first floor, according to later sources, was a 'club room', which was probably where dinners were served to the large gatherings that still assembled at the *George* from time to time. There was also a billiard room, two sitting rooms and six bedrooms on the first floor, and another six bedrooms on the second floor. The bedrooms on the first floor extended over the carriage entrance and the bakery and confectionery business next door.[68] William Clubb had been able, in 1876, to negotiate the grant by the lord of the manor of Watton Hall of two small areas of 'waste' in front of the building, on which were built the ground and first-floor bay windows mentioned in the 1912 particulars, which are prominent in old photographs of the *George*.

After the departure of Leonard Tillott and his family, William Clubb, having purchased the reduced premises, managed the *George* himself; or perhaps, in reality, it was his wife, Rebecca, who was in charge, as she was referred to as its 'landlady' in 1874.[69] One of Clubb's early decisions won approbation: 'Since the *George Hotel* has changed hands, the present proprietor…has issued notices stating that in future the house will be entirely closed every Sunday, except to any travellers who may be passing through the town'.[70]

William Clubb died in 1891 and ownership of the *George* passed to his widow, Rebecca and son-in-law George William Gentle. The *George* continued to function as a hotel and actually eclipsed the *Crown* for a time. A visitor in November 1896 commented that 'the *George and Dragon* with its grandiose sign, has almost a monopoly of the hotel trade here. It is a comfortable hotel of the average sort'.[71] The tenant was now Richard Guillard Holmes, assisted by his wife, Harriet, and, on the night of the 1901 census, there was just one guest, a commercial traveller.

Rebecca Clubb died in 1899 and her daughter, Sarah Clubb Gentle, in 1911. On 19 June 1912, in accordance with the terms of William Clubb's will, the entire property was offered for sale by auction. The *George Hotel*'s premises were bought by the Capital and Counties Bank Ltd (which was taken over by Lloyd's Bank in 1918)[72] while W S Hall, the auctioneer, purchased the confectionery shop and house next door.

The sale marked the end of over three centuries of history: the *George Inn* was no more.

But the building remained for another half century. According to a plan of 1952, the bank used what had been the hotel's two commercial rooms as its business area. The manager's office behind had a sloping ceiling and must have been part of the original, 16th century building. It was all swept away in the 1960s and replaced by the unattractive modern box which, until recently, housed Lloyd's Bank and is now derelict. All that remains of the original *George* is the part retained by William Rook in 1871, which was acquired by the Durrant family and is still relatively unaltered.

The *George* was the hub of Watton for over 300 years. It is, therefore, the best starting point for an imagined walk around the town as it was in 1841.

## Notes

1. NRO, WLS VII/3.
2. 1595 rental.
3. Inventory of Thomas Bettes, 1632; NRO, DN INV 38/82.
4. Will of Thomas Bettes, 1632; NRO, NCC 70 Morse.
5. British Library, Add Ms 70523.
6. Will of Susan James, 1689; NRO, ANW 1689 fo 255; will of Edward Harris, 1696; NRO, ANW 1695-96 fo 364.
7. Revd George Crabbe, 'Muniments of Merton Hall, Norfolk', in *Norfolk Antiquarian Miscellany*, vol II, part II (Goose, Norwich, 1883), quoted in the anonymous typescript, pre-1958.
8. Will of Richard Hamond, 1695; NRO, NCC Jones 87.
9. This and the previous two paragraphs are largely based on evidence from Hamont v Hamont, 1695; TNA, C 8/356/66.
10. The account in this and the previous paragraph is based on evidence in the court books of the manor of Watton Hall; Museum4Watton, M4W/2016/8A, 8B.
11. TNA, IR 1/17/f199, accessed via findmypast.com.
12. In 1776, Edward Crockley, maltster, employed John Ransome for a year. In 1787, still a maltster, he employed Ann Bales for the year, and continued to do so for the next 11 years. Settlement examinations of John Ransome and Ann Bales; NRO, PD218/12.
13. Crockley lost his only daughter, Sarah, and his son-in-law, Captain Sackville Turner, along with Susannah Crockley, who may have been his sister, when they were all drowned in the Bristol Channel while en route from Bristol to Cork in 1774, as recorded on a wall plaque in St Mary's Church.
14. NRO, MS19073 101x3.
15. NM, 10 January 1756.
16. NM, 22 November 1760; 25 April 1767.
17. Newcastle Courant, 25 November 1769.
18. Watton Overseers' accounts; NRO, PD218/3.
19. NM, 20 January 1770.
20. NC, 17 November 1781.
21. NC, 29 September 1792.
22. NC, 11 January 1784.
23. BNP, 16 January 1793.
24. BNP, 23 January 1793.
25. Abstract of title to the George, 1870; consulted by the author in 1995, with the permission of the then owners, Lloyd's Bank.
26. NC, 18 February 1804.
27. NC, 11 May 1805.
28. NC, 14 November 1805.
29. NC, 23 July 1808.
30. NC, 30 July 1808.
31. NC, 3 December 1808. Dennis Wright was actually 35 when he died.
32. NC, 24 December 1808.
33. NC, 18 November 1809.
34. NC, 8 August 1812.
35. NC, 17 March 1821.

36. NC, 11 December 1824.
37. NM, 5 July 1828.
38. NC, 4 July 1829.
39. Like Dennis Wright, he had been baptised at Oxborough; both of their fathers were named as William Wright but while Dennis's mother was called Elizabeth, Smith (who was baptised 13 years later, in 1786) was the son of William and Susanna Wright, who had married in 1779.
40. NC, 19 January 1833.
41. NC, 20 March 1830.
42. NC, 24 April 1830.
43. NC, 15 January 1831.
44. NC, 12 May 1832.
45. NC, 20 April 1833.
46. NC, 24 February 1838.
47. BNP, 20 July 1842.
48. NM, 19 November 1842.
49. NM, 7 January 1843.
50. NM, 18 November 1843, 28 July 1849.
51. NC, 5 July 1845.
52. NC, 18 September 1847.
53. NM, 3 April 1847.
54. NN, 16 August 1845.
55. NM, 4 December 1847.
56. NN, 25 March 1848.
57. NC, 23 December 1848. Charles Sloman (1808 – 22 July 1870) was an English comic entertainer, singer and songwriter, as well as a composer of ballads and sacred music (Wikipedia).
58. She was actually 23, having been born on 8 August 1845 and baptised at East Harling on 2 November 1845.
59. NC, 20 February 1869.
60. But she was actually 21, born on 15 July 1847.
61. He was Mr O'Malley, a campaigner against prostitution in Norwich – see Andy Reid, *Harriet Kettle: Pauper, Prisoner, Patient and Parent in Victorian Norfolk* (Poppyland, 2021).
62. NM, 31 March 1869; NN, 27 March and 3 April 1869; NC, 27 March and 3 April 1869.
63. NC, 11 February 1871.
64. NM, 1 August 1866; NN 4 August 1866.
65. Purchase agreement, 1870, and deed of covenants, 1871, between William Rook and William Clubb, consulted by the author in 1995, with the permission of the then owners, Lloyd's Bank.
66. NN, 8 July 1871.
67. Sale particulars, 19 June 1912; consulted by the author in 1995, with the permission of the then owners, Lloyd's Bank.
68. EDP, 24 July 1906.
69. NN, 3 October 1874.
70. NN, 2 December 1871.
71. NN, 28 November 1896.
72. Conveyance of 19 September 1913; consulted by the author in 1995, with the permission of the then owners, Lloyd's Bank.

# A Walk around the Town in 1841

What was Watton like at the time of the 1841 census, approaching 200 years ago? Starting at the *George*, we'll take an imaginary walk around the town.[1]

*The town centre as shown on the Tithe Map, 1839.*
*(Norfolk Record Office DN/TA 565)*

The map is dated 1839 but was produced in connection with the tithe apportionment of 1841.

In 1841, the owner of the *George* was Matthew Sallitt and the tenant was Robert Coe. Had we stayed there, we would have been looked after by Robert and his wife Elizabeth, and their three female and two male servants. We would probably have appreciated the quality of the upgraded facilities for both people and horses, and perhaps have played a game of bowls on the excellent bowling green at the rear of the inn.

Stepping out on to the gravelled surface of the street, sometimes known as 'Front Street' or 'the turnpike road' (because the turnpike road from Norwich continued as far as the windmill on the north side of Brandon Road), we would smell the piles of horse dung, and see and hear the clattering hoofs of many horses in the street and the yards of the inns.

Turning right (east), immediately next door to the buildings belonging to the *George* was the ancient property once known as the *Swan*. Owned by Richard

Callibutt, a landowner in Saham Toney and elsewhere, until his death in 1668, it then passed to his descendants and subsequently, in 1702, to the unfortunate Thomas Jarvis. Following his bankruptcy, the *Swan*, 'with the brewhouse, outhouses, barns, stables, backsides, yards, gardens, orchard' and two acres of land was sold in 1705.[2] It passed through several hands before being acquired by Francis Hicks (the elder) in 1716. He may have been responsible for the installation of a 'very striking staircase' recalled by a subsequent owner but removed in the 1970s. The massive timber beams that form the framework of the building may date back to the 16th century.[3] In 1841, like the *George*, it was owned by Matthew Sallitt. The occupier was Joseph Philo, a saddler.

If we now walked the few paces to the *Bull*, we would meet John Canham, who had been the innholder since 1831 and lived in the building with his wife, three children (one of whom was a dressmaker) and three servants. He specialised in Old Tom Gin and offered an annual market dinner for the townspeople, tickets 7s 6d each (equivalent to about £23 today), including a bottle of wine.[4] He was one of the proprietors of the Royal Blue coach, running on Saturdays from the *Bull* to the *Royal Hotel* in Norwich and, from 1845, providing a Wednesday service to Bury St Edmunds.[5] The yard behind the *Bull* contained a brewhouse and stabling for horses. In the field beyond the stables was 'Canham's cricket ground' which was 'said to be the best in the kingdom'. Several cricket matches were played on this ground every season and the team was 'supported by most of the gentlemen in the town and neighbourhood'.[6] In 1834, for example, it was the setting for the second of two matches between Watton and Wymondham, both of which were won by Watton. The second fixture saw Watton triumph by two wickets, 'to the great amusement of a large field of spectators'. Afterwards, 'the parties with their respective friends, 55 in number, sat down at seven o'clock to an excellent dinner in a spacious and handsome booth, belonging to Mr Canham, at the *Bull Inn*, where harmony and conviviality prevailed.'[7]

Beyond the *Bull* were the homes of 32 people, along with the commercial premises of a coachmaker and a currier and, at the corner of Thetford Road, the house and yard of Samuel Rice, a carpenter and builder, later to become the *New Inn*. That was the end of the built-up area. Along Thetford Road lay two short rows of cottages, nothing more. On Norwich Road were enclosed fields, including two called the Bull Closes, but, in 1841, very few buildings. The first, on the south side of the road, was the house, or row of houses, built on the site of a barn by Robert Dennis in 1834,[8] now the home of his widow Elizabeth and her family, together with four other small households.

After a gap came the second building: the large new vicarage, only just erected and occupied in 1841 by the Vicar of Watton, the Revd P B Jeckell, his wife Hannah, his four children, his mother, three visitors and a female servant. The new vicarage had been built on a piece of pasture land which was part of the glebe, or church land. It was described in 1845 as 'a new built red brick and slated vicarage house together with a clay-lump stable, chaise-house and offices adjoining covered with slate'.[9]

After the vicarage and the junction with Griston Road was a triangular piece of land called Garden House Close, first mentioned in 1771.[10] It was described as a 'piece of garden ground' in 1774 and so may have been a market garden or nursery.[11] The *Garden House* itself stood on the far side of the 'ancient lane'[12] called Wood Lane, which ran down the eastern edge of the close, crossed Griston Road, passed a couple of cottages and led ultimately to Wayland Wood. The *Garden House* was marked on Faden's map of Norfolk published in 1797, by which time the premises were licensed,[13] and the name remained in use alongside other names adopted subsequently: the *Flower Pot* and the *Rose*. After 1850, the inn was generally known as the *Rose*.

In 1804, the *Garden House* was owned and run by Robert Dennis and his wife Mary, the parents of Robert Dennis who erected the building in Norwich Road in 1834.[14] The property passed to their widowed daughter-in-law Elizabeth and then, after her death in 1847, to her son, Robert Willomatt Dennis, butcher. By 1841, the inn had been let to Daniel Waters who lived there with his wife Charlotte, four children and a servant. Daniel died in 1850, but his wife Charlotte may already have taken over the running of the public house and she continued as the publican at what was now called the *Rose* for some time after Daniel's death. Then, remarkably, she became the tenant of the *Green Man* in Watton, where she was recorded in 1869.[15] She died in 1875, aged 72. Her son, named, like her late husband, Daniel Waters, became an apprentice plumber and glazier and in 1853 established the building firm that developed into Waters and Sons.[16]

༄༅

We'll now turn back towards the town, this time walking on the north side of the gravelled road, past fields hedged with hawthorn. We would cross Church Lane, from which—as there were no other buildings in the area to block the view—we would be able to see Watton's parish church. The first building we would reach on this side of the road, about a quarter of a mile from Church Lane, would be the Willow House, the former vicarage, described in 1706 as 'the first [house] at the east end of the town, in good repair, a backhouse and stable in the yard, a hayhouse in the garden and candle house with a little piece of ground...three gardens and an orchard'.[17] As it was about to be superseded by the new vicarage, it was offered for sale in September 1839, described as being 'well situated at the entrance to the market town of Watton', and having two large parlours, four bed-chambers, kitchen and detached wash-house, gig-house and two-stalled stable, a good garden and a small paddock.[18] The references to the building in the documents which transferred its ownership to Lord Walsingham, the purchaser, in 1840 were less flattering. It was described there as 'an ancient small tenement or cottage built with

*Willow House.*
*(Noel Abel via Julian Horn)*

shed and clay and thatched with a small outbuilding and stable near thereto with the garden ground and pasture land contiguous thereto'[19] and the preamble to the conveyance commented that the 'vicarage house buildings with the offices thereto belonging are in a most dilapidated state and of very ordinary and inconvenient construction'; quite unfit for the residence of the vicar.[20]

In 1841, the Willow House housed a school for young ladies founded by Maria Ann Blade, in which, on the night of the census, ten girls aged ten to 16 were accommodated, taught by Miss Blade and an assistant, 20-year-old Martha Kett. Maria Ann Blade left in 1853 but the school continued to operate until 1858, when the Willow House was acquired by Richard Robinson, a solicitor. It remained in his family until the end of the century. In the garden stood the huge willow tree which gave the house its new name.

꼰ㅇ

Leaving the young ladies to their studies, we'll resume our walk westwards down the street. There would be a gap before the next buildings on the right, occupied by a pasture close, and then came the gated entrance to the yard behind the large property known in 2024 as the 'Manor House', through which we would see a coach house and stable. The next building on our right would be the home and workshop of James Pitts, plumber and glazier, a successful tradesman who, among other commissions, re-leaded the roof of Ashill church in 1833-34, for which he charged that parish £50 10s (equivalent to about £3,500 today).²¹ After Pitts' premises came those of the elderly Samuel Secker, basket-maker, on the corner of Bank Street, or Dereham Road as it is now.

Turning right into Bank Street, on the right-hand (east) side were buildings which had all been part of the Watton Hall estate, owned at the time of the Enclosure Award in 1803 by the trustees of the lady of the manor, Mrs Elizabeth Barker (formerly Elizabeth Hicks and originally Elizabeth Raby). Since at least 1796, she had lived at the 'Manor House', which was probably built in the 18th century, although the core of the front range may be older. After the deaths of Elizabeth Barker and her husband, the property changed hands twice before being offered for sale at an auction held at the *Crown* on 16 July 1834. It was described as 'a capital mansion, counting house, granaries, stables, coach-house, brewhouse, laundry, and all other suitable outbuildings, a large well planted walled-in garden, shrubbery, yards and a fine piece of pasture land adjoining, containing nearly three acres, with a circular stable standing thereon…The house contains breakfast, dining and drawing rooms, a suite of airy sleeping rooms, counting rooms, kitchens, store rooms, larder, pantries, cellars, and is replete with every convenience'.²² The successful bidder, at £1,430 (equivalent to nearly £100,000 today), was John Edward Hastings, wine and spirit merchant and, in the census returns of 1841 (identified only by his initials), he was recorded as a resident along with his father, Smith Hastings, and a nephew and niece.

Earlier in his life, Smith Hastings had been variously described as a miller, a baker and a farmer but now he was an agent for the East of England Joint-Stock Bank,²³ which is probably why Bank Street was so named. Hastings had been called to give evidence in a case of forgery at the Norfolk Assizes in August 1832, in which the defendant, John Tuck, a blacksmith from Scarning, had been accused of forging a cheque for £10 (equivalent to nearly £700 today). Tuck had visited the *King's Arms* and Goddard Buscall, the tenant, testified that Tuck had asked him who could cash cheques for him. Tuck had then called at Smith Hastings' house, where a servant, Lydia Howes, had observed him from a chamber window. It was Wednesday 25 July, Watton market was in progress between 6 and 8.30 pm and Smith Hastings was 'in the market'. Lydia was standing in the doorway when Tuck returned at about 7 pm; she spotted Hastings in the street and said, "there he goes". Hastings cashed the cheque but it was returned as a forgery a few days later and Tuck was arrested. He was sentenced to death, but with a recommendation for mercy.²⁴

Smith Hastings represented Watton on the Board of Guardians of Wayland Poor Law Union at its first meeting on 21 September 1835 and for several years was treasurer of the Association for the Apprehending and Convicting of Horse-Stealers. He owned the windmill on Brandon Road and various pieces of land. A major figure in Watton at the time, he died in January 1849, aged 72.

His son, John Edward Hastings, the owner of the 'Manor House', was aged

36 in 1841. He succeeded his father as treasurer of the Association for the Apprehending and Convicting of Horse-Stealers but then became insolvent. In 1859, held in a debtors' prison pending a hearing of his case, he was described as formerly of Watton, a wine, spirit, ale and porter merchant, and afterwards of various addresses in the London area, where he worked for a wine merchant.[25] He died in London in 1867.

Over 20 years earlier, John Edward Hastings had mortgaged his property in Watton and, in 1845, he sold it in two parts. The northern section, including the 'Manor House' itself, went to Edward Robert Grigson, solicitor, and remained a solicitors' office from then on, into the 21st century. The southern section, which comprised a dwelling fronting on to Bank Street (which was later to accommodate a girls' boarding school), a yard, a stable, a coach-house and the gated entrance on to the street to the south, was all acquired by Samuel Rice, the occupant of the carpenter's workshop where the *New Inn* stands today. Rice had to share with Grigson the cost of erecting and maintaining a nine-foot-high wall dividing the northern and southern parts of the property, which still stands (with a datestone, 'S R 1845').[26] Rice sold the coach-house, stable and yard to another builder, Jonas Frost, in 1852, and, by 1856, Frost had converted the buildings into a house and workshops.

The 'Manor House' and other buildings on the east side of Bank Street faced out on to what had been Watton's medieval market place, shown as the 'Square' on the plan attached to a deed of 1845,[27] which contained a mixture of temporary stalls and permanent buildings. The latter were detached from each other and did not present the almost continuous façade that they do in 2024. On the south side, facing the *George*, were two separate buildings, one of which may have been the post office, the responsibility of Sarah Blade, aged 58, mother of the schoolteacher Maria Ann Blade. Several other small detached buildings occupied the space in front of the *King's Arms*. The people who lived in the vicinity were mainly craftsmen and tradesmen—shoemakers, tailors, glovers, drapers and a baker.

ಸಂ

The *King's Arms* has a long recorded history, dating back to the 16th century, when it was known as the *Bull*. In 1595, Humphrey Mosse was noted as the owner of the inn and the 'brewhouse' attached to it.[28] It subsequently came into the possession of Thomas Bettes. By 1674, it was probably occupied by Roger Caudwell, 'beerebrewer' who, when he died, had debts owing to him for 'strong beere' and 'small beare' and for 'the carriage of letters and parcels to and from London'.[29] He left all his possessions to Anne Johnson,[30] widow, who was recorded as the owner in 1680.[31] The property was still called the *Bull* in 1700 but by 1712, when its then owner, Richard Tillett, made his will, it had become the '*Labour in Vaine*'. On the west side of the inn, where Wayland Hall stands now, separated from it by a passage, was Richard Tillett's own 'lately erected' residence and behind both properties were a yard and 'garden place...next the highway called the Backside' (now Harvey Street).[32]

When he died, Tillett bequeathed to his wife, Sarah, 'her dwelling in the parlour at the end of the house in which I dwell' for her lifetime. She also had the use of the rest of the house until her daughter Margaret reached the age of 21, when it was to pass to her. The *Labour in Vaine* itself went to Richard Tillett's son John when he reached the age of 21. When he did so, in 1719, the property had become '*le Half Moone*'. It was still called the *Half Moon* when John Tillett ('late of London, citizen, cabinet-maker') died in 1741 and his brother William Tillett became the owner.[33] He became a wealthy man, with property in various places in Norfolk and Essex, as well as in the City of London. St Mary's church contains a marble tablet to his wife, 'a tender and indulgent parent to her children' and 'in every circumstance a sincere friend and loving wife', who died in 1755. On William's death in 1770, his only son William became the owner of what was now called the *King's Arms*, together with the house on its west side erected by his grandfather Richard.

By 1788, the owner of the *King's Arms* was William Tillett's sister Arabella, wife of James Muller of the City of London. They sold the property to John Sparrow and, from the description given, it is clear that the brewhouse lay at the north end of the plot (next to the 'Backside'), with a yard containing a pump between it and the public house. The tenant in 1789 was John Thompson (the owner of the building used as a workhouse).[34] Following John Sparrow's death, in 1806, the ownership passed to Thomas Vipan, brewer, of Thetford. Two years after Vipan's death in 1835, it was bought for £700 (equivalent to over £47,000 today)[35] by the man who, for many years, had been his tenant, Goddard Buscall. 'A much-respected inhabitant of the parish', he was to remain the owner until his death, aged 69, 'after a long affliction, borne with Christian fortitude', in 1863.[36] If we were to go into the *King's Arms* in 1841, he is the man we would meet.

Next door to the *King's Arms*, on its east side, was Paines, the equally ancient property formerly held by Thomas Bettes, Ralph Ives, his son Thomas Ives, Thomas Younge and Edward Younge. After Edward Younge's bankruptcy in 1812, this was one of the properties acquired by the solicitor, William Lane Robinson, and by the later 1830s it was owned by Robert Baley, sheriff's officer and auctioneer, who conducted many of the sales that took place at the *George* and the *Crown* at this time. In 1841, as well as Paines, he also owned the former tollhouse and the property on the corner beyond it, facing Dereham Road.

ଚ୍ଚର

We could now walk a little way along Dereham Road, as far as the point where, in the 21st century, it joins Cadman Way, with Church Walk continuing straight ahead. Church Walk, which leads into the road to Carbrooke, was once a more important route than it is now; a few individuals in early-modern Watton left money in their wills to maintain it and a document of 1841 referred to it as 'Church Walk formerly the road leading from Watton to Dereham'.[37] Whoever wrote that must have had a long memory, because the enclosure award of 1803 referred to Church Walk only as a 'footway…for the use of the inhabitants of Watton as a way to their church'.[38] Perhaps, in the more remote past, the road over Neaton Fen was subject to flooding and travellers to Dereham had to follow Redhill Lane to Rockells Bridge and then proceed to Dereham via Ovington.

At the corner where Church Walk branched off Dereham Road was the manorial pound, where animals straying on the commons or anywhere else in the town were detained until their owners came to redeem them. The manor court books recorded, from time to time, the appointment of three pinders to superintend the pound. After parliamentary enclosure in 1803, the pound was less needed, although it was still shown, perhaps anachronistically, on a plan attached to sale particulars in 1861.[39] In 1841, a building owned by John Fox existed on the site and, in the second half of the 19th century, another public house, the *Live and Let Live*, stood there.

After that, we would see the enclosed fields which separated the market town from the hamlet of Neaton. Walking northwards, we would pass, on our left, the Independent Chapel (which later became Loch House). A few yards further on, on the right-hand side of the road was the entrance to Neaton Farm, owned by Charles Dorr, followed by a double cottage and the former premises of fellmongers (dealers in animal skins) called the Buxtons. In 1841, they were owned by Matthew Sallitt.

Successive generations of the Buxton family had carried on the related trades of fellmonger, glover, (leather) breeches-maker and collar-maker in Neaton for nearly three quarters of a century. A Robert Buxton had purchased the property, described as lying in 'Neaton Streete', in 1766. After his death in 1783, his wife Mary carried on the family business[40] for 17 years until she was bought out by her son Charles Buxton. He died in 1817, leaving the premises to all his children but his son Robert Buxton bought out his siblings. After Robert died in 1825, they were inherited by Matthew Sallitt, although they continued to be occupied by Robert's brother Charles Buxton, a glover, and his family. The story of glove-making in Neaton came to an end, however, in 1835, when Charles Buxton became insolvent.[41] Two years later, the 'old-established fellmonger's yard and premises… wherein a considerable trade has for many years been carried on, comprising drying houses, buildings, yards, vats', together with 'a double cottage, garden and about one acre of excellent arable land adjoining', went under the hammer[42] and, it appears, was bought back by Matthew Sallitt. By the time of the 1841 census, Charles Buxton had moved out and was living in the centre of Watton with his family.

Beyond the property formerly owned by the Buxtons was another ancient cottage which, before parliamentary enclosure in 1803, was surrounded by the common.

Its ownership can be traced back to 1653, when it was described as a 'mansion house or tenement' in Neaton Street. It may date from well before that.[43]

ఴఠ

We'll now turn round and walk back towards the town. At the beginning of the built-up area, after the pound, we would pass on the right-hand (north) side the house in which the unmarried Elizabeth Swallow lived, attended by a female servant. This residence, later to be known as Khyber House, had probably belonged to Robert Swallow, one of Watton's surgeons, and was later to become the home of Squire Sprigge, another surgeon. Turning into what in 1841 was Back Street, the next houses on the right, behind the *King's Arms*, were owned and occupied by, respectively, Henry Siggins, a plumber and glazier, and William Massey, a lawyer.

William Massey had bought his property from the executors of Robert Buxton, 'gentleman', formerly a baker, a successful businessman who had acquired a farm in Neaton and purchased lands and buildings in Back Street from the Revd Henry Say of Swaffham, whose family had, in turn, inherited them from Henry's great aunt and uncle, Thomas and Anne Ives. After Buxton's death in April 1835, Massey purchased his house in Back Street and 'several new created messuages, cottages or tenements'.[44] He mortgaged them and, in turn, 'laid out a considerable sum of money in additions and improvements'[45] necessitating a further mortgage in 1846. From a plan of 1854, it appears that he doubled the width of his house, creating the grand residence that later came to be known as Wayland House, and laid out extensive gardens behind it.[46]

Two barns, with an attached yard and garden, 'in Le Backside' of the *Angel*, were mentioned in the manor court book in 1679. They lay on the north side of Back Street and at some stage they were converted into houses. They were acquired by Robert Buxton in 1824 and by 1841 were owned by William Massey; they may have been the 'new created messuages' referred to above.

Beyond William Massey's house was a cottage inhabited by James Cornwell, a journeyman baker, and his family, followed by the *Red Lion* public house, the earliest known reference to which is from 1766, when it was offered to let.[47] In 1838, it was occupied by Robert Youngs and later, in 1861, when it had been acquired by Robert Stevens of Watton brewery and was tenanted by Edward Dalton, it was described as containing a parlour, two kitchens and four sleeping rooms, with a stable and gig house outside.

ఴఠ

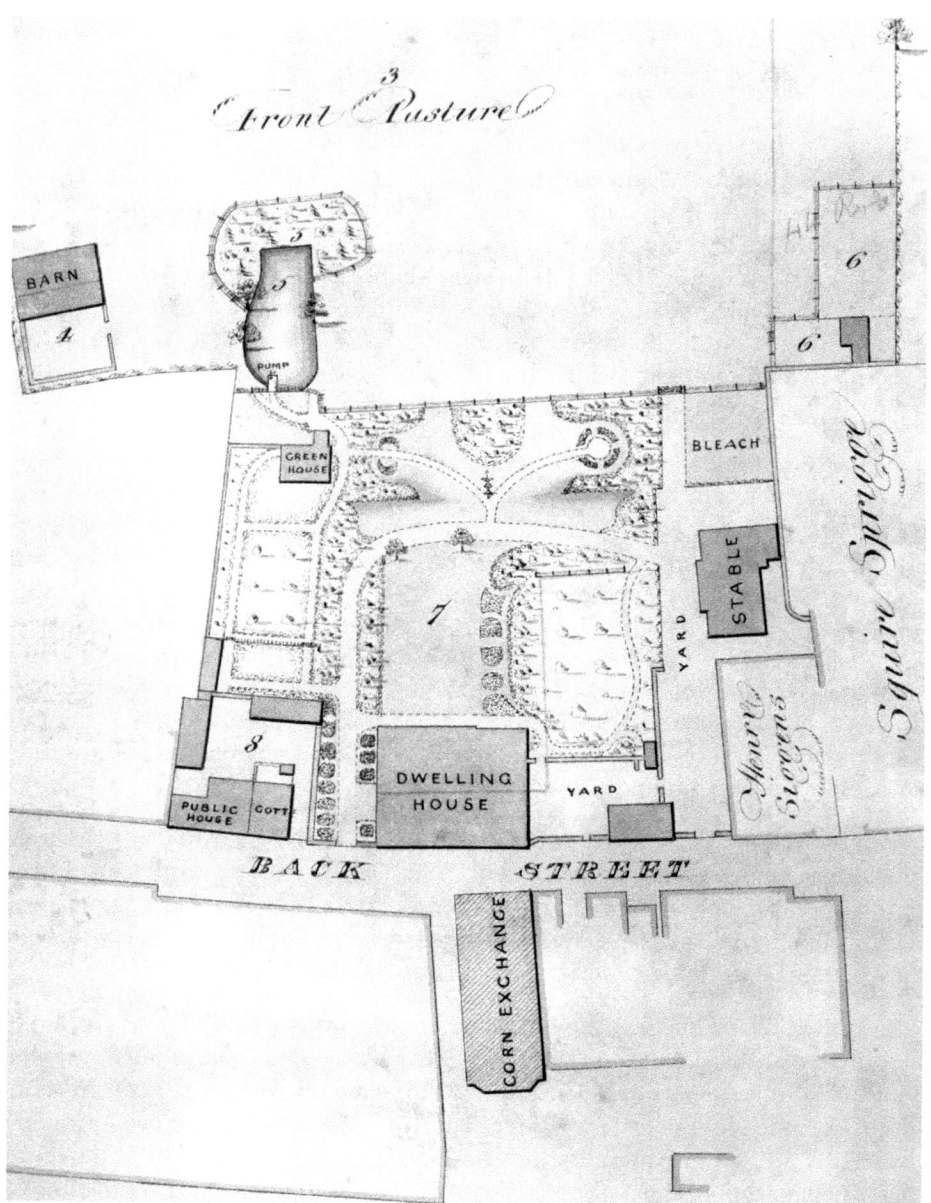

*The estate of William Massey, 1854.*
(Norfolk Record Office, DS 350)

Massey's residence was the former Wayland House; the 'public house' was the Red Lion and the 'corn exchange' was Wayland Hall.

The final house we would come to on the north side of Back Street is the residence now called Harvey House, a fine building of seven bays and three storeys, said to date from 1720,[48] with wings added in the 19th century. There was already a building here in 1695, called Godfreys, with an orchard,[49] and so the present house may be a rebuilding or replacement. It was to be described in 1879 as 'the capital messuage…formerly called Godfreys, wherein Robert Harvey formerly dwelt, with the outhouses, yards and gardens thereto belonging'.[50] Robert Harvey, a lawyer, died aged 71 in 1820 but his wife, Charlotte Harvey, survived him and was living in the house in 1841, aged 86. On the night of the census, her daughter (and only child) Charlotte M Harvey and grand-daughter Maria T Harvey were staying with her. Her household also included a 31-year-old companion, Marianne Gooch (who, two years after the census, married John Hargraves, a surgeon with a practice in Watton), a footman, a dressmaker and two female servants.

Further down Back Street, near the junction with Front Street and Cley Lane, were enclosures called Benn's Pightle and Naggs Close. In 1834, Charlotte Harvey gave Benn's Pightle to trustees, including her great nephew, the lawyer Edward Robert Grigson, for use as a playground. The trustees were to 'permit and suffer the said piece or parcel of land to be used and enjoyed as a play ground by the boys of Watton…not exceeding the age of fifteen years', at all times except 'on a Sunday during divine service at church'. Not only that: they were also to 'exclude and remove…all boys above the age of fifteen years and men and women who shall come thereupon for the purpose of playing any game or games whatsoever'; 'prevent any horses cows donkeys sheep pigs geese or other animals' from grazing there; and prevent the land from being used as a 'drying ground for linen' or for any purpose other than as a playground for boys. Girls were not mentioned.[51] The playground became known as the 'playpiece' and, many years later, the former Watton Youth Centre was built on part of it.

Charlotte Harvey was a remarkable woman. She outlived her deceased husband Robert by nearly 30 years, eventually dying in 1849, aged 95. Robert had made ample provision for her to live comfortably in her widowhood.[52] Charlotte got around in 'a superior well-built chariot, fitted with imperial and other travelling conveniences', along with a sedan chair and a 'garden chair on wheels'. Twelve bottles of brandy, stored in the house, no doubt helped to keep her spirits up.[53] Mrs Harvey was conspicuously generous, both in her lifetime and in her will. In 1826, the principal inhabitants of the parish, in their vestry meeting, resolved that they 'feel strongly impressed with the sense of Mrs Harvey's liberality in promoting the happiness and comfort of her neighbours and the general prosperity of the parish'; and wanted to thank her 'for the gift she has recently made to the church of a new and handsome pulpit, hanging cushion and tassals'. They sent a deputation to 'wait on' Charlotte and to present her with a copy of their resolution.[54] Charlotte Harvey was remembered fondly at a dinner of the Wayland Association at the *George* the November after her death, when Lord Walsingham 'passed a high and well-deserved encomium on the late Mrs Harvey,...a lady who was a firm supporter of this society, and one whom the poor, not only of this parish, but of the neighbourhood, would have great cause to lament.'[55]

Robert and Charlotte Harvey's daughter, Charlotte Mary, had married her cousin, Lieutenant Colonel Robert John Harvey, in a grand ceremony at St Peter Mancroft church in Norwich in 1815. Charlotte Mary's husband had played a significant role in the Peninsular War against Napoleon, and was later knighted and promoted to the rank of Major General.

సరు

On the south side of Back Street were several buildings. References to 'a barn and a newly built stable, part of a cottage called *Le Cock* with a garden in Middle Row' occurred in the court books of the Manor of Watton Hall from 1671 onwards.[56] The ownership of the barn and stable passed to Christopher Hey (they were near his residence next to the Clock Tower) and then to Sir John Wodehouse. At the end of the 18th century, they were acquired by Robert Buxton, the baker.

West of the barn and stable formerly belonging to the *Cock* lay two cottages later known as Hardinge Cottages, which in 1841 were owned by Charlotte Harvey of Harvey House. Further to the west, the space between Front Street and Back Street narrowed and was occupied by the line of houses known as Rotten Row. The houses faced the Front Street; walking down Back Street, we would be looking at the cottages, stables and other outbuildings in their back yards. Adjoining the yard behind the *Green Man*, for example, was a cottage with three bedrooms, stables and a carriage house. What is now 88 High Street, which was a blacksmith's shop in 1841, had a cottage in its back yard. The end of 'Rotten Row', where Front Street and Back Street joined and Cley Lane led off to the north, was referred to in the 1841 census returns as 'Walker's Corner', after Amos Walker, one of the census enumerators and at that time a 'traveller' (formerly a baker[57]), who lived there with his wife and family.

సరు

Before the enclosure award of 1803, if we had looked westwards from 'Walker's Corner', we would have been looking out over Mill Common. Now, in 1841, the land was all enclosed and houses had begun to appear on plots facing Brandon Road. One of them, on the north side of Brandon Road, just after the junction with Cley Lane, was a 'double cottage' which in 1818 was described as 'newly erected'. A short distance down Cley Lane, on the right, was the Wesleyan Methodist Chapel, built in about 1831.

Further west along Brandon Road, on the north side just past the junction with Swaffham Road, was a barn and what by 1841 was Watton's only windmill, owned by Smith Hastings. There had been a mill on this site in the 17th century when it appears (although the sources are confusing), that there were actually two mills standing in small enclosures on the common land. In 1680, one was owned by Robert Galland and the other by William Lance (a former tenant of Galland's mill).[58] The latter burned down before 1700 but was rebuilt, passing in 1730 to John Spurrill, who took possession of 'the sails, coombs, ropes and stones' as well as the windmill itself.[59] This was the mill that was shown on the enclosure map of 1803 and was acquired by Smith Hastings. Hastings made several attempts to sell it between 1832 and 1844. The mill was described in 1831 as a 'substantially well-built post windmill drawing 10 yards of cloth and driving two pair of French stones…with capacious brick roundhouse' and a 'comfortable dwelling house' adjoining. There was no buyer.[60] It was offered again, for sale or to lease, in 1839; and again, despite 'enjoying a full trade', it did not sell.[61]

In 1841, the mill's tenant was Thomas Mann, aged 35. Another miller aged 20 lived in his house, perhaps as an apprentice, and a third lived nearby. In 1843 and 1844, the mill was yet again advertised for sale or let, apparently with no result.[62] Ownership of the whole property passed to John Edward Hastings in 1845 and he erected on it a new house with outbuildings, which was known later as West End House. The mill did not survive for much longer; by 1859, it had been 'taken down'.[63]

Further on down Brandon Road, other buildings had appeared by 1841, including another public house: the *Jolly Farmers*, erected by 1832 on a plot south of the road and tenanted in 1841 by Robert Rice. In 1837 the land immediately to the west of it was sold, 'with the newly-built cottage…erected thereon' which, in 1875, was referred to as a double cottage.[64] Further west still, on the north side of the road near the parish boundary, the *Dog and Partridge* public house was soon to open. A few other cottages had now been built along both the Brandon and Swaffham roads. John and Mary Pitts, for example, built the house at 12 Swaffham Road in 1822.[65]

೩೦ಌ

Back at the Cley Lane, Front Street and Back Street junction, we'll now turn around and face east, up Front Street. On the right-hand side, in 1841, would have been the parish coal store with the National School above it; the new flint-faced school building that survives today was to be erected the following year. Further back from the road was the town house or 'common house' of 1719, due to be sold in 1842, when the building was described as a 'thatched double cottage'.[66] Next door were the Stevens almshouses, built in 1833 and conveyed in 1840 to trustees for 'the benefit of four poor married couples of the age of 60 years who have resided in the parish for not less than thirty years'.[67] Restored in 1975, they remain in situ in 2024. These were the only buildings on the south side of the High Street until, after passing two fields called Cinder Oven Close and Malthouse Close, we would reach a house owned and occupied by Mrs Alpe, a member of a family with close connections with the Stevens. Her house was followed by Goffe's almshouses and then the maltings, built by the Younge family and owned in 1841 by Edward Stevens, standing on the site occupied today by the Methodist Church. The malthouse probably replaced an earlier structure which, by 1808, had given its name to Malthouse Close.[68]

The north side of the street, known as Rotten Row, was, by 1841, an almost continuous series of buildings with only a few gaps. The people who lived in the section west of the brewery were mostly artisans and small traders. A shoemaker, three blacksmiths, a carpenter, a bricklayer, a butcher and a grocer were among the inhabitants. In 1841, John Lusher lived at what is now 90 High Street in what must have been very crowded conditions, with his wife, son, five daughters and four labourers who were lodgers. His next-door neighbour to the west was a public house called the *Chequers*,[69] owned by Sarah Eke, while to the east, at number 88, was a blacksmith's shop. After that came Watton's other 'town house', a brick and tiled cottage, with a yard at the rear, which, like the 'common house', was to be sold in 1842. The next building to the east was one of several owned by Smith Hastings.

A little further up Rotten Row, but not as far as the maltings on the south side, stood the new brewery. Robert Stevens and his large household lived there, and his unmarried uncle and aunt kept a separate establishment in an adjoining dwelling. Part of the ground occupied by the brewery and associated buildings had been the site of the *Three Fishes*, mentioned in 17th and early 18th century sources. Beyond that, alongside a butcher, a tailor and a blacksmith (a female blacksmith, Hannah Sturgeon), were professional men: veterinary surgeons Thomas Smith and James Worm (who later moved across the street to what became known as Worm's Yard and is now Beechwood Avenue) and Thomas Hargraves, a surgeon. Hargraves had been practising in the town for some time and shared his premises with his older son, George, also a surgeon; the younger son, John, was based on the other side of the street and he too was a surgeon. Thomas Hargraves died in in 1851 but his two sons continued to work in Watton; John (who served as the surgeon to the Foresters and was Medical Officer for the Saham Toney district of Swaffham Poor Law Union) until retirement in 1865, and George until his death in 1871. They both changed their residences and in 1861 were living either side of Richard Robinson, solicitor, in Dereham Road. John married in 1843 and he and his wife Marianne Gooch (formerly Charlotte Harvey's companion) had four children, while George remained single until 1860 when, aged 59, he married Emily Ann Robson, aged 35. They had a son and daughter but then died within 12 days of each other in 1871.

After Thomas Hargraves' house came the premises of Samuel Adcock, a 45-year-old watchmaker, who owned the property which is now 58 High Street and which older inhabitants of Watton may recall as 'Masons'. Adcock, the ancestor of the family who are still a prominent part of Watton's business community, shared the house with his wife, three sons and four daughters. Next door to the east was the *Green Man* public house.

The history of the *Green Man*, like that of several of the other hostelries in Watton, can be traced back to the 17<sup>th</sup> century. The property was referred to in 1761, as 'customary land with an house thereupon built…which piece of land did formerly consist of part of an old garden', lying 'in or near Rotten Row'. It had been purchased by John Muston in 1718 from the heirs of James Tooley. Tooley had acquired the plot from Mary Hornigold in 1699[70] (it had been part of her garden) and built the house sometime between 1699 and 1712. When he died, it was known as the *Queen's Arms*[71] but by the time of its acquisition by Muston, it was called the *King's Arms* (not to be confused with the *King's Arms* in what is now Middle Street) and was occupied by Peter Bacey.[72] The change of name must have been in honour of King George I, who succeeded Queen Anne in 1714. Edward Younge bought it from John Muston in 1745, and it was among the properties auctioned in 1812 following his grandson's bankruptcy. The purchaser was Edward Stevens.

In 1789,[73] and in 1792, the *Green Man* was occupied by Robert Dennis,[74] who later moved to the *Garden House* as its owner. In 1812, boasting 'new erected stables and brewing office',[75] its tenant was Samuel Rice, who moved on to the *Crown* in 1813. His furniture and other effects were offered for sale and give a good idea of what the interior of the inn must have been like at the time: '15 featherbeds and bedding, four-post and other bedsteads with moreen, checked and other hangings, eight-day clock in wainscot case, mahogany bureaus, chest with drawers, several dozen hollow and other seated chairs, dining, card, tea and dressing tables, the kitchen, back-house and dairy utensils, glass and earthenware; also two road carts, ploughs, harrows, luggage cart'.[76] The yard behind the inn must have been a busy place, and it would have become even busier, and noisier, on Wednesdays after a pig market was inaugurated there in July 1828.[77] What the rest of the accommodation was like can be imagined from a later description, when the property was put up for auction following the death of Robert Stevens, the owner, nephew of Edward Stevens, in 1866. It contained: 'bar, bar parlour, tap, large parlour, kitchen, club room, one front and three back bedrooms, four attics, pantry, excellent cellar, coal and knifehouse. In the yard at the rear is a room for travellers; lead pump, spacious carriage houses…three stables for fifteen horses; hay loft and corn chamber, fowl house, bin, etc, with an entrance to the back street'.[78]

John Warren, who was also a wheelwright, was listed in trade directories as the tenant of the *Green Man* in 1830[79] and 1836,[80] but then moved across the street to a house opposite, where he carried on his trade as a wheelwright and continued to keep a beerhouse.[81] His replacement was Edward Payne and, if we were to visit the *Green Man* in 1841, it is he who would greet us. We might also meet his wife and daughter, a female servant and two other guests, a labourer and a baker.

ଐଊ

The premises between the *Green Man* and the passageway leading through to Back Street, formerly possessed by the Hornigold family, were owned in 1841 by Charlotte Harvey. One of the tenants, possibly in the building occupied since the late 19th century by Edwards newsagents, was George George, bookseller and leather dealer. Other residents included a tailor (married to a straw-hat maker), a plumber and a boot and shoe maker, with their families and apprentices. On the other side of the passageway was another building owned by Smith Hastings, now 44-48 High Street, which older inhabitants of the town will remember as 'Carters'. Smith Hastings, then described as a baker, had purchased it from Edward Stevens in 1799, who in turn had bought it in 1788.[82] In the 17th century, it had belonged to Ambrose Dunn, miller and baker.[83] In the mid-18th century, it had been owned by Edward Dunn and occupied by John Spurrill, another baker. The owners of the property had the right to take water from 'the well lately belonging to the tenement lately called *Le Cocke* in Middle Row',[84] which was their next-door neighbour to the east. After acquiring the property, Hastings divided it into three tenements, which in 1841 were occupied by James Balls, a boot and shoe maker, with his wife and an apprentice; William Fox, a saddler, with his wife, five children, apprentice and lodger; and the man who must have been Watton's first representative of the newly established county police force, 30-year-old John Bates, his residence possibly being the cottage that lay at the rear of the main building.

The next house up Front Street (now 42 High Street), with three stories, is taller than its neighbours. This building can be identified with a reference in the will of John Payne, 'braser', who died in 1549. He had purchased this property, 'nowe the signe of the *Cocke*', from his father and referred to its 'soller', a solar being an upstairs chamber.[85] It belonged to John Candler in 1667, with two hearths, and passed to his grandson William Candler and his wife Martha before the fire of 1674, described as 'one parlour with a chamber thereupon built at the west end of a cottage...commonly called the *Cock*'. A small piece of land adjoining the parlour to the west probably gave access to the yard behind. The property remained in the Candler family for most of the 18th century. In 1725, John Candler was admitted to 'a messuage or tenement...called *Le Angel* and formerly *Le Cock*', bequeathed to him by his grandfather, William Candler, whose will referred to 'my messuage or tenement...commonly known by the sign of the *Angell*'. The *Angel* would have been the '*Angel alehouse*' mentioned in a document of 1756.[86] It was not listed among the alehouses for which recognisances were returned to the Clerk of the Peace in 1789[87] and so may have ceased trading at some point before then. This *Angel* alehouse was not the same as the *Angel* referred to in the rental of 1595, but it was close to the likely site of its eponymous predecessor, the memory of which may have influenced the choice of the name, The *Angel* for the former *Cock*.

The connection of the Candlers with the property ended in 1786, when William's grand-daughter Mary and her husband sold it to William Lane Robinson. It then passed to Robert Stebbing, collarmaker, to William Wenham, watchmaker and to

Samuel Fuller before being sold to Edward Platfoot, baker, in 1816. Edward died in 1827, aged 47, and the premises and business were inherited by his widow, Catherine.

Fifty years old in 1841, Catherine Platfoot was recorded in the census as a baker and confectioner. She was assisted by a younger journeyman baker who lived in her house, and also by a female servant. Her premises, when advertised for sale in 1851, were described as comprising 'an excellent baker's and confectioner's shop, bake-office and oven, keeping room, parlour, kitchen, wash-house, four sleeping rooms, attics, flour chamber, granary; a two-stall stable and gig-house, back yard, etc, with entrance into the back lane'. They were in the occupation of 'Mrs Platfoot, the proprietor, who has carried on the trade of a baker and flour merchant for many years'.[88] She must have retired from business after the sale but seems to have gone into property development, offering for sale by auction in 1864, 'a newly erected…public house called "The Golden Ball Inn" with outbuildings and 2.5 acres of land, on Swaffham Road, and 'a newly erected cottage, with large garden' next door, which she occupied herself.[89] The *Golden Ball* had, in fact, been open as a beerhouse for seven years. Its tenant, Robert Powley, was hauled before the magistrates later in 1864, charged with 'having his house, the *Golden Ball*, opened for the sale of beer at a quarter before eleven o'clock on Sunday morning';[90] this being his third such offence, he was fined £5, with costs. The Inn had changed its name to the *Carpenters' Arms* by 1870.[91] Catherine Platfoot died in 1873, aged 87, one of Watton's notable female entrepreneurs. By 1899, her former shop formed part of a property belonging to a butcher, George Chase, which, remarkably, was still described as 'formerly…called the *Angel* and formerly the *Cock*'.[92]

☙❧

We'll now cross the street again, to the south side. After the maltings and the associated buildings came a small house owned by Hannah Sturgeon, the blacksmith and then, at what is now called Beechwood Avenue, houses owned by Charles Russell who, in 1841, owned and worked one of the largest farms in Watton. Next, almost directly opposite the *Green Man*, was a house owned by John Took, which was where John Warren, the former publican, carried on his business as a wheelwright, assisted by his two sons. Behind it was a small Primitive Methodist chapel dating from 1836.

A little further up the south side of the street was the large establishment of Thomas Alexander, shopkeeper, at what is now 35 High Street. In 1841, Alexander was living with his wife Elizabeth Lane Alexander; three daughters and three sons. The household also included; a shopman and a shopwoman; an apprentice; and two female servants. The apprentice was John Scott, from Methwold, aged 15, who had been apprenticed to Alexander for five years just two months previously. According to his apprenticeship indenture, John was not allowed to 'commit fornication nor contract matrimony within the said term, he shall not play at cards or dice tables…

without licence of his said master…he shall not haunt taverns or playhouses nor absent himself from his said master's service day or night unlawfully'. In exchange for £24 paid by John's father (with a further £25 to follow two years later), Thomas Alexander would teach John 'the arts of grocer, draper and general shopkeeper' and provide him with 'meat, drink and lodging'. His clothing and washing were to be provided by his father.[93]

By 1841, Thomas Alexander had been in business for 15 years. He died in 1842 but his wife Elizabeth announced that she would carry on as a grocer and draper, 'for the benefit of herself and children, with the assistance of her brothers, whose experience in the trade will enable her to conduct it on the same liberal principles as hitherto, in buying the very best articles and selling them with a small profit'.[94] She seems to have done so very successfully. In April 1856, she advertised 'a varied assortment of shawls, mantles, silks, parasols, flowers, plain and flounced dresses, bonnets, etc, with every article in plain and fancy drapery. Millinery in all its novelties'.[95] As a woman, she may have enjoyed advantages in catering for a largely female market.

Elizabeth Alexander, like other members of her family, was a strong supporter of the Congregational Church. On her death on 11 February 1870, aged 69, an obituary noted that: 'her decease will be felt by the poor to whom her silent charities were often ministered in the time of need, and by whom she will be held in grateful and affectionate remembrance for loving words of Christian counsel and encouragement, as well as for her deeds of kindness. She was a humble-minded and sincere Christian, and by a life of active usefulness in the days of health, and of uncomplaining patience through a long and painful affliction, she "adorned the doctrine of God her saviour in all things"'.[96] All the shops in the town closed on the day of her funeral. Two of Elizabeth's sons, John Edmund and Henry, carried on the business in the same location until shortly after the 1881 census, when it was purchased by William Kendall.

Next door to Thomas Alexander's shop lived two elderly people, Dorothy Wright (a daughter of Thomas Younge, who had married Charles Wright in 1784), aged 75 and Philip S Youngs (perhaps her brother), aged 70, supported by a female servant. In the next house, where Chaston Place now (2024) stands, lived Edward Stevens, aged 74 and Susanna Wright, aged 69, with Elizabeth Wright, aged 29 and male and female servants. After their house came the *Crown*.

☙❧

Now we'll return to the north side of the street, to Catherine Platfoot's shop (now 42 High Street). Given that Catherine's premises were the 'west end of a cottage… commonly called the *Cock*' in the 17th and 18th centuries, the next property to the east (now 38 and 40 High Street) must have been the east end. This part, too was acquired by William Candler; it was granted to him, apparently as his wife's dowry, by her parents Abraham and Elizabeth Pooley. In 1841, it was owned and occupied by James Sampson, an elderly man of independent means with a younger companion, Ann Scott. The next house to the east (now 34 and 36 High Street) was owned by Charles Buxton, the former glover from Neaton, now a broker, with his wife, son and three daughters, and a clerk and female servant. Part of one of these properties was owned and occupied by George Wenham, watchmaker and jeweller. This was a family business, carried on for 50 years by William Wenham, including a period from 1793 when he owned the premises subsequently purchased by Edward Platfoot. William Wenham died in 1834 aged 76, and the business was carried on by his widow Charlotte and George, their son, who also 'held the office of postmaster 16 years' until his death in 1860.[97] The Wenhams were responsible for winding up the clock in the Clock Tower.

To the east of Charles Buxton's house, surrounding the Clock Tower on all sides apart from the south (where it faced the street), were the premises of Benjamin Chaston, druggist, and his wife and son, the latter working with him as an apprentice. The family was prosperous enough to employ two female servants. Chaston had purchased the house in which he and his family resided (on the east side of the Clock Tower), the recently-erected shop where he traded (on the west side), the associated outbuildings, yard and garden and the next house, on the corner of the High Street and the Market Square, in 1838. They had all belonged to Robert Buxton, the baker, until his death in 1835. In the 17th century, most if not all this property had belonged to Christopher Hey and at least some of it would have comprised part or all of the original 'Angel' mentioned in the 1595 rental.

Chaston's residence (now 30 High Street), when purchased in 1838, was

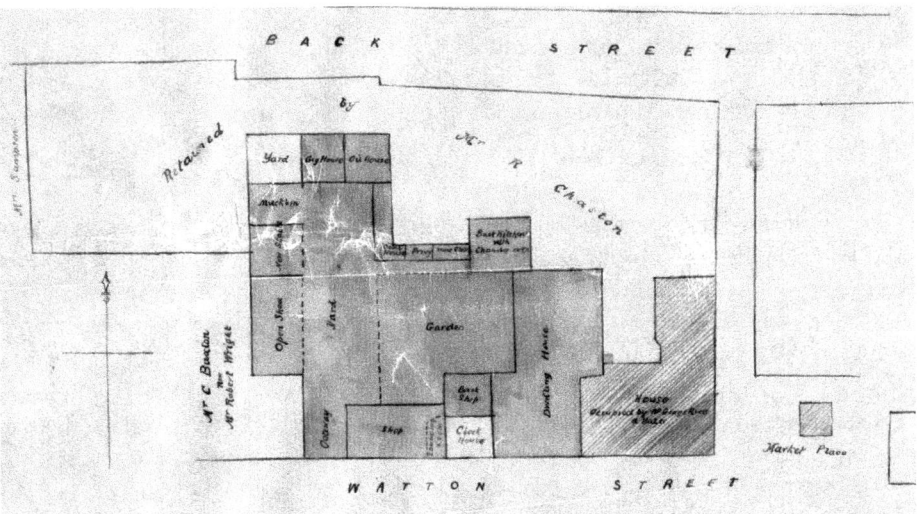

*Plan of the premises around the Clock Tower, from a conveyance of 1864.*
*(Norfolk Record Office, ACC 2023/12)*

advertised as 'substantial and well built'. It had an entrance hall, two parlours, six sleeping rooms, kitchen, cellar, store rooms, and 'commodious shop, counting house and warehouse' where an 'extensive and lucrative business' was conducted.[98] The shop (now 32 High Street) was probably built between 1803 and 1838, while in 1838 a gateway to its west (built over after 1864) still gave access to the enclosed yard in the centre of the property.[99] Among the products sold, as readers of the *Illustrated London News* in 1845 would have seen, were 'Chaston's India Rubber Elastic Corn Plasters' ('sent free [of postage] to any part of the Kingdom').[100] At the rear, in Back Street, was a house with a stable, lime-house and yard, owned by Chaston and occupied by a bricklayer, Ephraim Aldis. In front of the Clock Tower was the town pump, the source of water for many of the inhabitants of the centre of Watton.

The house on the corner, described as being in 'King's Arms Square', was occupied in 1841 by Robert Wright, another baker, son of the late Susanna Wright, the former landlady of the *George*, with his wife Alice, three children and two female servants. In a commanding position overlooking the market, it had been the 'mansion house' of Sir John Wodehouse and his wife Ann (formerly Ann Samwell), lord and lady of the manor of Watton Hall, at the end of the 17$^{th}$ century.[101] Previously, it had been owned by Peter George, son in law of Christopher Hey, and before him by Christopher Hey himself. When offered for sale in 1838, it was described as 'a spacious dwelling house…in the market place…opposite the *George* Inn, together with the baking office, shop, flour rooms, granaries, stable, gig-house, out-houses, yard' and wash-house. It had a frontage on the Market Place of 38 feet and contained 'an entrance hall, two parlours next the Market Place' and five bedrooms. 'An extensive business of a baker and flour merchant' had been carried on there for 'nearly half a century'.[102] Several cottages adjoined the house to the north, looking out on to the Market Square, including that owned and occupied by James Mallows, a butcher. There were several more cottages, including that occupied by Ephraim Aldis, around the corner in Back Street.

ഇരു

We are almost back where we started. We'll cross the street again, back to the *Crown*, and contemplate the buildings between it and the *George*. Prudence Nettleship, an independent woman of 56, lived with a 45-year-old female servant in a small house or, more likely, part of a house, although it did contain two sleeping rooms, a kitchen and a pantry and, in all likelihood, a parlour too. Prudence had only a year to live, dying in 1842, and making generous provision for annual payments to her servant, named as Mary Overton,[103] in her will, providing that Mary remained unmarried. Mary also received most of Prudence's furniture, utensils and clothing, but Prudence reserved her 'secretary' [desk] for her god-daughter, 'all my silk dresses and laces, rings and brooches and other ornaments of the person' for her nieces, 'a silver mustard pot, twelve dessert spoons, butter knife and cream jug marked PN' for her nephew and her plate and china, and the remainder of her goods, for her brother.[104] Prudence Nettleship was a woman of refinement.

Apart from Prudence's residence, we would be looking here at the impressive shop, house and associated buildings formerly owned by the Younge family. At the auction following Edward Younge's bankruptcy, they were bought by Hugh Boughen. When he died in 1825, the property was inherited by his son Hugh and Smith Wright, his son in law. Although it was mortgaged to the banker Anthony Hudson in 1838 (for whom Smith Wright had been an agent in 1822),[105] it was still occupied by Smith Wright in 1841, with his two daughters, a female visitor and a child of seven who was probably a grand-daughter. He had recently been discharged from bankruptcy but was still beset by financial problems. He could, nevertheless, afford to employ a groom and two female servants. Later in the same year, Hudson sold the property to Robert Overland George, who in turn sold in 1865 to William Rook, a farmer. In 1879, following William Rook's death in 1876, the property was conveyed by his daughter, Sarah Ann, to George Cubitt Durrant. It has remained in the ownership of the Durrant family ever since.

An area at the far end of the yard belonging to Smith Wright's premises was owned and occupied in 1841 by John Hicks Thompson, a 25-year-old carpenter and builder with a wife and two children. Two years previously, in 1839, Thompson had had financial problems of his own, necessitating an auction of his 'freehold dwelling house in two tenements, with carpenter's shop and large yard', which he shared with Henry Siggins.[106] He recovered quickly, however and the following year he bought the buildings in Smith Wright's yard, comprising four outhouses with a cart lodge and gig house with a chamber above, half of the adjoining 'ancient warehouse', part of a garden and the building formerly enjoyed by the Younges as a summerhouse.[107] John Hicks Thompson would have used these premises for his business but he also converted part of them into living accommodation for his family. He prospered for a while, employing ten men and a female domestic servant at the time of the 1851 census, but then, in 1857, hit further issues. These were exacerbated by his having guaranteed, eight years earlier, payment of a debt incurred by John Edward Hastings, the wine and spirit merchant and former owner of the 'Manor House'. He had to pay Hastings' creditor £321.[108]

Thompson had, once again, become an insolvent debtor and all his furniture, 'stock in trade, carpenter's benches and other effects' had to be sold.[109] Again, he survived and was able to re-establish his business. But then his eyesight began to fail and he had to sell up. His premises were auctioned in March 1871, advertised as 'a convenient brick-fronted and tiled dwelling house, carpenter's loft and low shops, wheelwright's shop with loft over, sawpit, shed, stable and other outbuildings and spacious yard. Also, a substantial brick and tiled building used as a carpenter's shop, with school room over' (the possible location of one of Watton's dame schools). John Hicks Thompson, the advertisement stated, was 'giving up business through failing health'.[110] He became almost completely blind, but lived on for another 30 years. He died on 3 February 1904, at the age of 89, 'probably the oldest inhabitant of the town'.[111] His wife Frances had predeceased him by only a few weeks; they had been married in 1836 and lived together for 68 years.

Now we're back at the *George*. Time for a drink before we return to the *Crown*…

**Notes**

1.  This chapter is based largely on two sources: the Watton tithe apportionment of 2 September 1841 (with a map dated 1839); NRO, DN/TA 565; and the 1841 census returns for Watton.
2.  Manor court book, Manor of Watton Hall, 1705; Museum4Watton, M4W/2016/8A.
3.  Thanks to Elizabeth Wright, daughter of Sydney Harvey, printer, for information about the building.
4.  NC, 1 December 1838, 18 February 1843.
5.  NM, 21 December 1844; NN, 14 June 1845.
6.  White's Directory of Norfolk, 1836.
7.  NC, 30 August 1834.
8.  Thanks to Anne Stimpson for this information.
9.  Watton glebe terrier, 1845; NRO, DN/TER 159/17.
10. Particular and rental of estate late Mr Thomas Younge, 6 June 1771; NRO, Bradfer Lawrence IXa.
11. Abstract of title of R W Dennis deceased, 1876; NRO, ACC 2023/12.
12. Abstract of title of Steward and Patteson, 1882; NRO, ACC 2023/12.
13. norfolkpubs.co.uk
14. Abstract of title of R W Dennis deceased, 1876; NRO, ACC 2023/12.
15. Post Office Directory, 1869.
16. Barry Waters, *Four Generations of Builders: A Memoir of the Waters Family* (privately published, 2016).
17. Watton glebe terrier, 1706; NRO, DN/TER 159/4.
18. NC, 28 September 1839.
19. Lease for a year, 20 April 1840; NRO, WLS XLII/8/1 423x5.
20. Conveyance, 21 April 1840; NRO, WLS XLII/8/2 423x5.
21. Ashill churchwardens' accounts 1795-1907; NRO, PD548/52.
22. Sale particulars, 16 July 1834; NRO, Spelman 404.
23. Pigot's Directory of Norfolk, 1839.
24. NC, 11 August 1832.
25. NC, 2 April 1859.
26. Deeds in private possession.
27. Deed in private possession.
28. 1595 rental.
29. Inventory of Roger Caudwell, 1674; NRO, ANW 23/3/159.
30. Will of Roger Cawdwell, 1674; NRO, ANW 1674-75 fo 155.
31. Rental of manor of Watton Hall, 1680-1704; NRO, BL/MC 25.
32. Will of Richard Tillett, 1712; NRO, ANW 1711-12 fo 382.
33. Manor court book, Manor of Watton Hall, 1741; Museum4Watton, M4W/2016/8C.
34. Alehouse recognizances, Wayland Hundred; NRO, C/Sch1/16.

# A Walk around the Town in 1841    159

35. *Suffolk Chronicle*, 3 June 1837.
36. Deeds of the King's Arms, Watton, in private possession; NC, 12 December 1863.
37. Abstract of title of George Hargreaves to a piece of land at Watton, 1847, reciting indentures of lease and release, 1841; NRO, ACC 2023/12. Julian Horn has argued that this road, which led to the commandery of the knights of St John of Jerusalem, was more important than Norwich Road in medieval times.
38. Watton enclosure award; NRO, C/Sca2/316.
39. Sale particulars, 1861; NRO, ACC 2023/12.
40. NC, 30 August 1783.
41. NM, 6 June 1835.
42. NC, 20 May 1837.
43. I am grateful to the owners of the cottages and former fellmongers' premises for sharing the deeds to their properties with me. This and the previous paragraph also draw on entries in the court books of the Manor of Watton Hall (Museum4Watton, M4W/2016/8A, 8B).
44. Indenture, Buxton trustees and Charlotte Pond to William Massey, 12 December 1838; NRO, ACC 2023/12.
45. Mortgage, William Massey to the Revd Edward Rigby, 1846; NRO, ACC 2023/12.
46. Map of the estate of William Massey, 1854; NRO, DS 350.
47. NM, 4 January 1766.
48. NHER 19202.
49. Manor court book, Manor of Watton Hall, 1695; Museum4Watton, M4W/2016/8A.
50. Deed of enfranchisement, 9 August 1879; Watton Parish Council mss.
51. Copy of deed of gift, Mrs C Harvey to Mr E R Grigson and others, 13 January 1834, in private possession.
52. Will of Charlotte Harvey, 1849; TNA, PROB11/2099/247.
53. These items were all auctioned after her death; NM, 1 September 1849.
54. Watton Vestry Minute Book 1821-29; NRO, PD218/88.
55. NC, 17 November 1849.
56. Manor court book, Manor of Watton Hall, 1671; Museum4Watton, M4W/2016/8A.
57. White's Directory of Norfolk, 1836.
58. Rental of manor of Watton Hall, 1680-1704; NRO, BL/MC 25.
59. Manor court book, Manor of Watton Hall, 1730; Museum4Watton, M4W/2016/8B.
60. NC, 17 March 1832.
61. NC, 7 September 1839.
62. NC, 4 November 1843, NM, 14 December 1844. See also norfolkmills.co.uk for more background about the windmill.
63. Manor court book, Manor of Watton Hall, 1859; Museum4Watton, M4W/2016/8F.
64. Deeds in private possession.
65. They mounted a plaque in celebration of the fact, as I was told by a former pupil in September 1983.
66. Handbill advertising property sale, 10 August 1842; NRO, ACC 2023/12.
67. Quoted in G Jessup (1985).
68. As shown on 'a map of an estate in Watton in Norfolk belonging to Edward Younge gent', surveyed by Thomas Starke and William Fendick, 1808; NRO, ACC 2023/12.
69. Manor court book, Manor of Watton Hall, 1854; Museum4Watton, M4W/2016/8F.
70. Manor court book, Manor of Watton Hall, 1699; Museum4Watton, M4W/2016/8A..

71. Rental of the manor of Watton Hall, 1712; NRO.
72. Deeds to the properties of Thomas Younge; NRO, Bradfer Lawrence collection.
73. Alehouse recognizances, Wayland Hundred; NRO, C/Sch1/16.
74. Deeds to the properties of Edward Younge of Watton; NRO, Bradfer Lawrence collection.
75. NC, 4 July 1812.
76. NC, 24 April 1813.
77. NM, 5 July 1828.
78. Sale particulars, Watton Brewery estate, 22 August 1866; NRO, ACC 12/2023.
79. Pigot's Directory of Norfolk, 1839.
80. White's Directory of Norfolk, 1836.
81. White's Directory of Norfolk, 1845. A beerhouse did not have a full licence and could not serve spirits.
82. Deeds to 44-48 High Street, in private possession.
83. His father, Thomas Dunn (died 1634) was also a baker. Will of Thomas Dunn, 1634 and of Ambrose Dunn, 1677.
84. Manor court book, Manor of Watton Hall, 28 March 1706, 25 November 1717; Museum4Watton, M4W/2016/8A, 8B.
85. Will of John Payne, 1549; NRO, ANW 1545-51, Aleyn fo 289.
86. NRO, PD218/100.
87. NRO, Sch1/16.
88. NC, 7 June 1851.
89. NC, 28 May 1864.
90. BNP, 20 September 1864.
91. NM, 29 January 1870.
92. George Chase to R Robinson, mortgage 25 March 1899 and conditional surrender 7 April 1899; NRO, ACCn 12/23. I am grateful to Julian Horn for drawing my attention to the significance of this and other sources relating to what is now 42 High Street.
93. Apprenticeship indenture, John Scott to Thomas Alexander, 17 May 1841; NRO, MC451/13 747x1.
94. NM, 17 December 1842.
95. NM, 26 April 1856.
96. NN, 26 February 1870.
97. NC, 28 June 1834, 24 May 1845; NM, 16 June 1860.
98. NM, 19 May 1838.
99. Enclosure map, 1803 (NRO, C/Sca2/316); tithe map, 1839 (NRO, DN/TA 565); conveyance and plan, 1864 (in private possession).
100. *Illustrated London News*, 28 June 1845.
101. Deeds in private possession.
102. NM, 19 May 1838.
103. She was listed as Mary Miller in the 1841 census returns.
104. Will of Prudence Nettleship, 1842; NRO, ANW 1840-43 (1842), fo 153, no 100.
105. Pigot's Directory of Norfolk, 1822.
106. NM, 7 September 1839.
107. Deeds in private possession.
108. NM, 4 April 1857.
109. NC, 21 March 1857.

110. LA, 25 February 1871.
111. DMG, 13 February 1904.

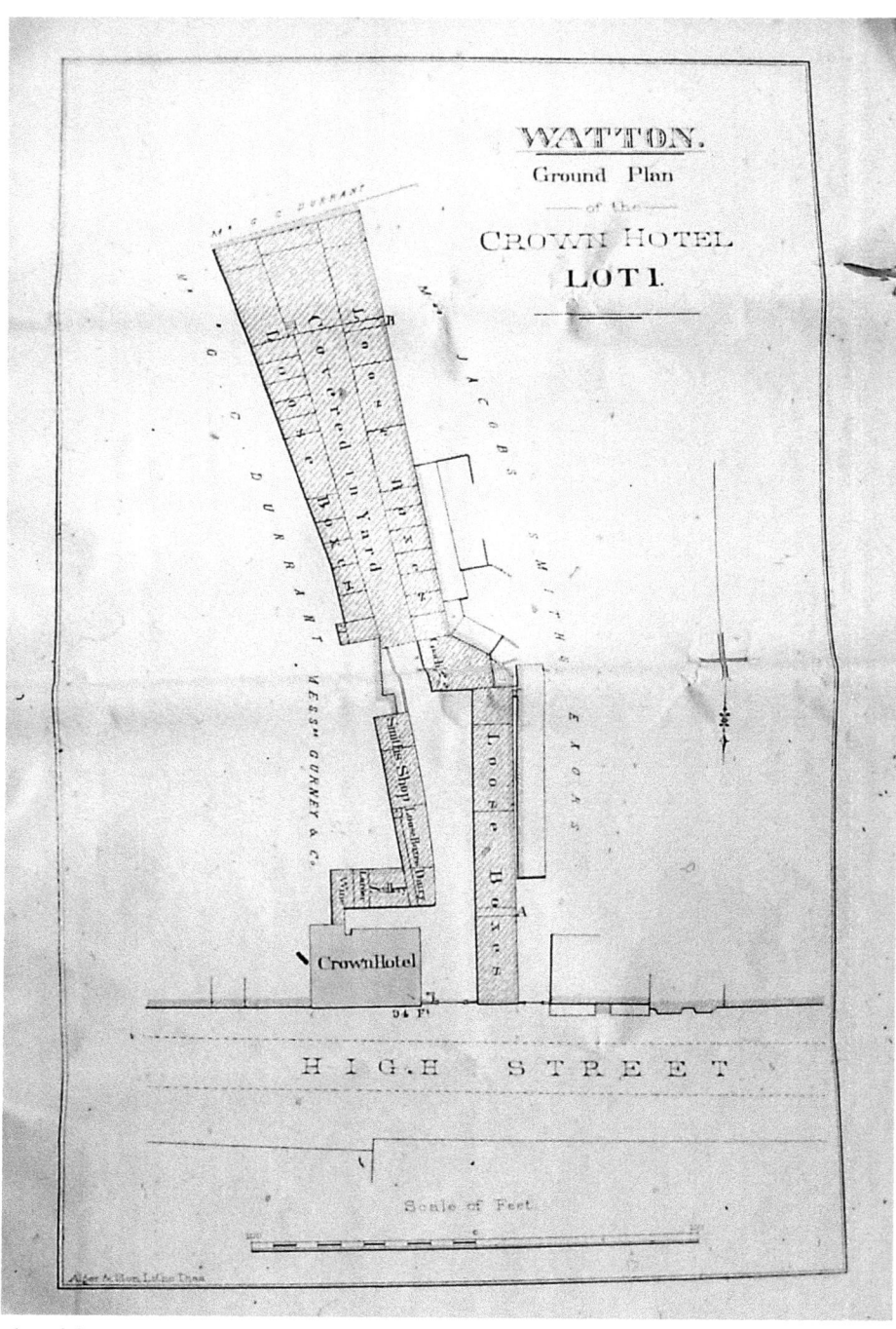

Plan of the Crown Hotel premises, 1890.
(Museum4Watton)

# George Jacobs and the Crown

The *Crown* was the most significant rival to the *George* throughout the 19th century.

The present building incorporated, or replaced, an earlier inn, the *Griffin*[1] and was erected in the 18th century. In 1763, the 'messuage or tenement…with the stables, houses, edifices, buildings, yard and garden to the same belonging and commonly…known by the name or sign of the *Crown*' was owned by Thomas Younge.[2] The tenant then, and until 1780, was John Flower. The *Crown* hosted the annual November meetings of the Association for the Apprehending and Convicting of Horse-stealers in 1776, 1778 and 1780, alternating with the *George*.

On 23 February 1782, the *Crown* was offered to let by William Younge, now the owner. It was described 'an old and well-accustomed inn', a stock phrase which nevertheless suggests that an inn had stood on the site for some time. It had a 'convenient brewhouse and offices, good stables for upwards of forty horses' and 'a good post chaise and horses'. The incoming tenant would be offered 'all the stock of liquors, furniture and fixtures…at a fair valuation'. The advertisement also mentioned that the 'the post office is kept at the above inn, and the excise duties and land tax are paid in there.'[3] On 3 April 1782 the furniture and effects of Robert Rising, who had briefly succeeded John Flower as tenant, were offered for sale by auction, including 'all the stock of liquors', the post-chaise and three horses, perhaps because the incoming tenant had declined to take them.[4]

William Darsley was the innholder in 1789;[5] he may have been a relative (or even the same person) as the owner of the *Crown* in Ashill, who died in 1830. Five years later, the Watton *Crown* was tenanted by George Bennett.[6] In 1803–6, the landlord was probably William Pearson, who was the postmaster in these years.[7] By 1807 the inn had been taken by Edward Taylor, who employed Charles Bowers of Ovington, 'colt breaker' there for two years around 1806–8, suggesting that horse-dealing was part of his business.[8] The *Crown* was still the post office and Taylor employed Erasmus Allcock as a 'post lad'.[9] Edward Taylor remained in occupation when the *Crown*, as one of the properties belonging to the bankrupt Edward Younge, was sold by auction, but he died later the same year, in December 1812.[10]

The next innholder at the *Crown* was Samuel Rice. He moved there in 1813 from the *Green Man*, on the other side of the street. Now in direct competition for business with Susanna Wright at the *George*, in November 1815 Rice hosted the Association for the Apprehending and Convicting of Horse-stealers and provided 'a good ordinary' for them. The *Crown* was also the venue for the celebration of the new clock installed in the Clock Tower in 1827. Samuel Rice died in November 1832 aged 66 but he had given up the *Crown* at least three years earlier. He retired to a 'substantial newly-erected brick and tiled dwelling-house (sash front)...near the mill in Watton...with a good brewhouse, stable, piggeries...commanding a very excellent wholesale and retail beer trade': the *'Jolly Farmers'*, in Brandon Road. One of his nine children, also named Samuel Rice, became a carpenter and builder, responsible for the erection of several buildings in the expanding town.

Samuel Rice's successor at the *Crown* was Robert Coe, who hosted the Association for the Apprehending and Convicting of Horse-stealers and provided 'a good dinner' for its members in November 1829.[11] The following year, Coe moved on to the *George*, illustrating the pecking order among Watton's hostelries at the time: Samuel Rice had left the *Green Man* for the *Crown*, but Robert Coe left the *Crown* for the *George*.

The *Crown* was described as an 'old-established independent commercial inn' with 'extensive stabling, coach-house, granaries, brew-house, yards, garden' when it was offered for sale by auction in February 1831.[12] By the time of the Watton sheep, lamb and stock fair in September of that year, the innholder was Robert Lusher. He remained the tenant for an uneventful 15 years until his death, after a short illness, on 27 June 1847. He was 47, 'greatly respected by a large circle of friends and acquaintances'.[13]

※※

A new tenant took over and, after several months, announced his arrival in the local newspapers on 9 August 1848. His name was George Jacobs, and he remained at the *Crown* for almost half a century, until his death in 1895.

George Jacobs was born in January 1814, the son of a 'shoeing smith'. He became a blacksmith too and practised his trade in Watton after his marriage to Mary Keziah Bennett in 1836. They had one daughter, Anne, but three months after her baptism, in June 1838, Mary Keziah died. George remained on his own for a decade but then married Sarah Lusher, the widow of his predecessor at the *Crown*, Robert Lusher, at St Peter Mancroft in Norwich in May 1848. Sarah, probably born in 1817, was the daughter of William Rackham, a currier (dresser of horses and/or tanned leather) in Watton, and so George may have known the family for some time. At the time the marriage took place he must already have taken over the *Crown* as he described himself as a 'hotel keeper'.

Jacobs assured his clientele that the hotel had 'undergone, in every department, a complete refitting'. He was already in the business of breeding and dealing in horses and called attention to his 'stud of horses, comprising hunters, saddle and harness horses' for sale at the *Crown*, and the forge which, he stated, would continue to operate, 'with every attention to the shoeing department'. Jacobs provided an opening dinner on 29 November 1848, to cement the 'support which was so liberally bestowed upon his late predecessor'.[14] It was attended by 'upwards of 50 gentlemen'. The 'dinner was served up with much taste; the wines were of the first quality and gave the most approved satisfaction'.[15] As the tenant of the *Crown*, George Jacobs had got off to a good start.

At the end of July 1857, the *Crown*, which had been mortgaged, was offered for sale by auction. Described as 'an old-established commercial inn and posting house', its accommodation included a 'commercial room', sitting room, smoking room and kitchens on the ground floor and a 'large dining or market room' and five bedrooms above. The stabling was extensive, including a new white brick five-stall stable, a four-stall posting stable and many other stables and loose boxes, along with accommodation for cows and pigs, the blacksmith's shop, where the shoeing would have taken place, and 'an excellent pit of water' in the yard. George Jacobs had a lease of the property for 14 years from October 1853. He also rented numerous small pieces of land adjacent to Brandon Road, probably as paddocks for his horses, as he was already an 'extensive horse dealer'.[16]

The *Crown* did not sell in 1857 and so was offered again in August 1859. It was bought by Jacobs himself, the purchase being completed in 1860.[17]

George Jacobs developed his equine business impressively. In 1858, he announced that he had 'selected 70 first-class horses from Downham Fair and from the best breeders in the county of Norfolk', which would be 'fit for show' in the week beginning 15 March.[18] As well as breeding, training and selling horses, he made a little extra money by endorsing 'Goatling's Condition Balls' for horses and, in 1860 by renting out a stallion, 'Fireking' to serve mares all over Norfolk, at £2 per mare (plus 2s 6d for the groom).[19]

In 1876, a reporter rhapsodised: 'The horse training establishment of Mr George Jacobs forms one of the most attractive features of this pleasant little town, and a walk through the extensive premises cannot fail to be interesting to the visitor. None but the most valuable horses are received here. They are trained for various purposes, some for government uses; some for single, and others for double, harness; some for ladies, others for gentlemen. A farm adjacent is specially adapted and set apart for breeding, and numbers of brood mares with their pedigree offspring are in the rich pastures. Other premises are provided for the safe custody of the entire horses, many of which will be remembered as carrying off valuable prizes from agricultural shows. In fact, the whole forms a complete business, and excites the admiration of every visitor, it being the result of many years' energy and perseverance on the part of Mr Jacobs'.[20] Jacobs now rented numerous pieces of land all over Watton — south of Brandon Road, as before, but also near Dereham Road, next to Cley Lane, near the church, and off Thetford and Merton Roads; all situated not too far from the *Crown*. A visitor to Watton in the second half of the 19th century would have seen many horses grazing in the fields near all the roads leading into the town.

As well as breeding and dealing in horses, George Jacobs bought Neaton Farm and held sales of cattle and sheep there in 1877, 1884 and 1886. When advertising the 1884 and 1886 events, he stated that lunch would be provided at the *Crown* an hour before the sale was due to start, which no doubt helped to put his customers in a good frame of mind.[21]

It was as a horse dealer, however, that George Jacobs earned world-wide renown, with customers in Europe and North America as well as in Britain. He had 'a reputation second to none as a breeder of Norfolk Hackneys and as a trader in the highest-class match horses, brougham horses, harness horses and cobs'.[22] In 1890, he received 'a distinguished honour' from King Umberto of Italy whose representatives had visited Jacobs' stud and purchased large numbers of horses. As a proof of his satisfaction with his purchases, the king 'ordered a very handsomely mounted copy of his royal arms to be sent to Mr Jacobs…accompanied by a very kind private letter' and by a royal warrant permitting him to 'adorn his premises with the royal arms of Italy'.[23] George Jacobs duly did so, commissioning an enlarged copy of the arms and warrant from Waters and Sons and hanging it in front of the hotel where it 'attracted a great deal of attention'.[24]

※

It may have been in search of horses that a Mr Hethrington of London came to Watton in February 1875. He stayed at the *Crown* but, after he had returned home, discovered that he had left behind his silver fusee (match) box and wrote to George Jacobs to enquire about it. Jacobs would not have known anything about it but two months later it came to light, in the following circumstances. Between 11 pm and midnight on Sunday 18 April, 'a man was seen by a gentleman living opposite the *Crown Inn*, to climb the sign-post, get upon the roof of the house, take a square of glass out of one of the attic windows, and get into the room. He informed Inspector Starke [of the local police] of what he saw, supposing the man was a burglar'.

The man was Charles Skipper of Watton, a butcher, and his motive was not burglary. He was interested in a servant at the *Crown*, Elizabeth Platfoot of Carbrooke, to whom he had 'paid his addresses'. After being alerted, the police officer 'at once went to the inn, called up the manager, Mrs Reeve, and went up into the bed-room, and found Skipper in bed with Platfoot and another domestic servant [!]. The officer took Skipper into custody and for the time left the two female servants. Upon searching Skipper, the officer found upon him a silver fusee-box, chased, and bearing the initials of Mr Hethrington. Skipper told the officer that his girl, Elizabeth Platfoot, gave it to him for a birthday present about last Valentine's time'.

The police officer then 'enquired of Platfoot if she had given it to Skipper, and how she came by it. After some hesitation, she said she took it out of the commercial bed-room. The officer took her into custody'. Elizabeth Platfoot had denied knowing anything about the article when questioned previously, after it had gone missing. She was charged with stealing the box, value 7s 6d, was found guilty and was imprisoned for 21 days. The charge against Skipper for receiving the box was dismissed, but he was fined for wilful damage to the window and had to pay costs to the court, as well as damages of two shillings to Jacobs.[25]

The story had a happy ending: Charles Skipper, aged 21 and Elizabeth Platfoot, aged 22, were married in Carbrooke on 3 June 1875.

ಸಾಂತ

George Jacobs' final years must have been lonely. His second wife Sarah had died in 1878, followed, barely a week later, by an old associate, Samuel Ward, 'for many years blacksmith…of the *Crown Inn*'.[26] Jacobs' daughter, and only child, Anne had married in 1861, given birth to eight children, one of whom had died, and had been widowed in 1881. She remarried in March 1890 but then died the following August. In 1892, George Jacobs, 'having reached old age' and beset by gout, decided to retire from his business. At the end of March 1892, he put his dairy herd of 117 shorthorn cattle at Neaton Farm up for auction.

The following week, on 6 April 1892, the whole of his stud was offered for sale by auction at the *Crown*, including horses named 'Watton Empress', 'Watton Princess', 'Watton Duchess', 'Watton Hero' and 'Watton Delight'. 'There was a good company and bidding was brisk', reported a local newspaper. The identity of the purchasers was indicative of George Jacobs' wide connections: they included Lord Egerton and Lord Acton; others with addresses in fashionable districts of London (Piccadilly, Hyde Park, Grosvenor Square, Brompton Road, and Kensington); and some from as far afield as Ascot and Brighton, as well from the locality and elsewhere in Norfolk and Suffolk. Horses sold for up to 185 guineas, and the total proceeds from the sale of 65 horses exceeded £4,000 (equivalent to about £330,000 today). Only two horses remained unsold.[27] The following year, Jacobs gave up the tenancy of Neaton Farm and put most of his remaining stock of animals up for auction.

George Jacobs died on 22 January 1895. On the day of his funeral, most of the shopkeepers and tradesmen in Watton closed their businesses for the day. There were wreaths from his sister, his five surviving grandsons and others, including Thomas Crawshay Frost, owner of Watton brewery.[28]

Two years later, on 23 July 1897, 'the family residence, with flower and kitchen gardens, also pasture land, for many years occupied by the late Mr George Jacobs and recently by the late Mrs Seal (Jacobs' sister)' came under the hammer, selling for £745.[29]

ಸಾಂತ

The *Crown* was offered for sale at an auction on 13 May 1895. The description of the premises was similar to that given in 1857, with coffee room, smoking room, commercial room and kitchen, plus service facilities, on the ground floor and a large market room ('46 ft long by 17½ ft wide') above, with a total of seven bedrooms on the first and second floors. Outside were a 'white brick and slated stable with loft and granaries above, coach house, wheelwright's shop, blacksmith's travis and forge' and 'a covered-in run, 210 feet long with clay and tiled loose boxes and stalls on each side; the whole affording accommodation for upwards of 70 horses'.[30] The *Crown* didn't sell on the day, but was subsequently bought privately by Bullard and Sons, the Norwich brewers. Within a month, the tenancy was offered and was taken up by Ethelbert Brunton Kent.[31] The 'entire household furniture for sitting and sleeping rooms', along with four posting horses, various road vehicles and the contents of the carpenter's shop, was auctioned on 7 August 1895.[32]

After that, the *Crown* was in the doldrums for a time. Ethelbert Kent was an elderly man and the property seems to have deteriorated. The pit of water, over which a large wooden carriage house had been erected, 'smelt bad' and the Rural District Council ordered (twice) that it be cleansed.[33] James Hooper commented in November 1896: 'We were sorry to find that the good old *Crown Hotel* has fallen upon evil days'.[34]

Yet the *Crown* survived, while the *George* did not. After the First World War, its owners adapted, converting part of the stabling into a motor garage. The garage burnt down, but the hotel survived, as it does to this day, although only as a public house as it no longer offers accommodation.

## Notes

1. As indicated by the details of properties to which Thomas Younge was admitted on 26 November 1761, in the court book of the manor of Watton Hall; Museum4Watton mss.
2. Abstract of title to properties in Watton, in private possession.
3. NC, 23 February 1782.
4. NC, 23 March 1782.
5. Alehouse recognizances, Wayland Hundred, 1789; NRO, C/Sch1/16.
6. The *Norfolk Pubs* website, drawing on the Wayland Licence Register, mentions William Parsley (1789) and George Bennett (1794) as tenants.
7. Settlement examination of Thomas Palmer, 1815; NRO, PD218/12.
8. Two settlement examinations of Charles Bowers, 1815; NRO, PD218/12.
9. Settlement examination of Erasmus Allcock, 1810: NRO, PD218/12.
10. Will of Edward Taylor, 1813; NRO, NCC Goodrum, fo 10.
11. NC, 7 November 1829.
12. NM, 29 January 1831.
13. NN, 3 July 1847.
14. NM, 12 August 1848.
15. NC, 9 December 1848.

16. NM, 11 July 1857.
17. Manor court book, Manor of Watton Hall, 1860; Museum4Watton, M4W/2016/8F.
18. NC, 13 March 1858.
19. NC, 28 April 1860.
20. NN, 9 September 1876.
21. NC, 13 October 1877, 11 October 1884, 23 October 1886.
22. NM, 9 April 1892.
23. NN, 19 July 1890.
24. NC, 18 October 1890.
25. NN, 24 April 1875.
26. NM 20 April 1878.
27. NN, 26 March 1892; NM, 9 April 1892. Extracts from the sale catalogue are reproduced in G Jessup (1985).
28. NM, 2 February 1895.
29. NN, 24 July 1897.
30. Sale particulars, 13 May 1895; copy in author's possession.
31. Kelly's Directory, 1896.
32. NC, 3 August 1895.
33. NM, 11 January 1896.
34. NN, 28 November 1896.

*The maltings, c 1908.*
(from a glass negative taken by F W Bird, from the clearance of Harvey and Sons via Julian Horn.)

*Watton Brewery c 1900.*
(copy in possession of the author.)

# Maltsters and Brewers

One of the most prominent landmarks in Watton's High Street is the former brewery. Its history dates back to the early 19th century.

When Edward Younge became bankrupt in 1812, one of the properties that had to be sold was his 'very substantial new erected and spacious malt-house'. The 'new erected' maltings almost certainly replaced an earlier building with the same purpose,[1] and stood on the south side of the street, on the site now occupied by the Methodist Church.

The maltings may have been occupied until 1810 by Christopher Dinmore, who was a maltster and also possessed another 'malting office', probably on the other side of the street. Christopher was a brother of Richard Dinmore, the surgeon and radical who emigrated to the United States. He was Edward Younge's brother-in-law, having married Younge's sister Pleasance in June 1791. Christopher probably shared his brother's (and his father's) political views, albeit more discreetly. He supported, and attempted to mediate for, another reformer, Lt Col W Tooke Harwood of Thompson, when Harwood (who had clashed with conservative elements at the *George* ten years previously) was accused of slander in 1803. Christopher and Pleasance Dinmore had seven children baptised in Watton between 1792 and 1803, all of whom survived infancy. The family lived comfortably, as was apparent when some of their 'bordered goose featherbeds' and mahogany furniture were auctioned in June 1810, after they had 'removed to Norwich'.[2] In Norwich, Christopher Dinmore owned a brewery in the parish of St Michael's Coslany, but he sold up in 1816[3] and at the end of the year was declared bankrupt.[4] He moved to King's Lynn and made a living as a bookseller in the High Street, although whether his stock included his brother Richard's publications is not known. Pleasance died in King's Lynn in June 1823. Three years later, Christopher, like his brother, was in North America. He died in Montreal, Canada, in March 1826.[5]

ඏᏣ

When Edward Younge's properties went under the hammer in 1812, the maltings and several of his other properties were purchased by Edward Stevens. Stevens was the second member of his family to play a prominent role in business in Watton. His father, also called Edward, was a grocer, a draper and (like the Younges and Francis Hicks) a butter factor, until his death in 1790. He and his wife Susanna (née Nobbs) had eight children, Edward being their third, born in 1766. Edward Stevens junior did not marry. His elder brother, Stephen Nobbs Stevens, married Elizabeth Fox in 1788 and they had several children including Robert Stevens, born in 1793, who was to be his uncle Edward Stevens junior's successor in business. The elder three of Edward's sisters married but his three youngest siblings remained single and two of them, Alice and Robert, were to live to a great age.

Edward Stevens junior went into partnership with his father and, on the latter's death in 1790, announced that: 'Edward Stevens, grocer, draper and butter factor, with gratitude, returns his sincere thanks to his friends and customers for their favours, while in co-partnership with the late Edward Stevens, his father, [and] respectfully informs them he carries on the same business'.[6] Like his father, he also served as treasurer of the Association for Apprehending and Convicting Horse-stealers for many years.

The properties Edward Stevens junior acquired at the auction of Edward Younge's estate included the 'very substantial new erected and spacious malthouse; comprising an excellent kiln, drying houses, working floors and twenty-two coombs steep, with the yard and land to the same adjoining...and including a new waggon-house standing thereon'. Also included were: Pit Close, south of the maltings, its name taken from the large pool of water which supplied the malting process; several pasture closes nearby; and two inclosures called Malthouse Close and Cinder Oven Close, with the cinder yard adjoining the latter. Stevens also bought several cottages in the street and 'the public inn, called the *Green Man*, with the new erected stables and brewing offices and yards thereto adjoining'.

With these purchases, Edward Stevens was able to go into the malting and brewing business in a big way. In 1814, he inserted an advertisement in the local papers: 'To maltsters. Wanted immediately, a sober steady man, who thoroughly understands his business, must bring an undeniable character with him, and will meet with constant employ and good wages, by applying to Edward Stevens. NB A comfortable cottage and garden will be provided adjoining the malting'.[7]

෧෬

Edward Stevens went into partnership with Smith Wright as grocers, drapers, butter-factors, ironmongers and tallow chandlers, but the partnership was dissolved in 1815.[8] Smith Wright then carried on the business of grocer, draper and general shopkeeper successfully for over 20 years. In 1825, in partnership with his father-in-law, he moved into the premises that had been the Younges' house and shop. He also became involved in freight transport by 'van' to London, the Midlands and the North,[9] and, in a mark of his status in the district, served as the treasurer of the Association for the Apprehending and Convicting of Horse-Stealers in many of the years between 1814 and 1837. Wright formed a new partnership with Henry Fiske in December 1828[10] but that arrangement was dissolved by mutual consent in December 1836.[11] The following month, Fiske was declared bankrupt.[12]

In 1838, disaster struck Smith Wright himself. Like Edward Younge before him, he encountered serious financial difficulties and, to pay his creditors, he was forced to sell his furniture and other effects; the stock, hay and implements on his farm in Saham Toney; and his stock in trade in Watton. The house and shop were put on the market but did not sell and on 30 April 1839 Smith Wright was declared bankrupt.

He seems to have weathered the storm and in October 1840 announced that he had 'again commenced business in a general line'.[13] But the respite was brief. Smith Wright's straitened circumstances had led him into wrong-doing. In 1841 he had to appear in court for retaining £800 with which, as the executor of a will, he had been entrusted and which he should have invested for the benefit of the deceased person's relatives. He was ordered to produce the sum and he and the other executors of the will had to pay costs.[14] In 1843, once again, he assigned all his goods to trustees (including Robert Coe, the former tenant of the *George*) so that they could be sold to pay his creditors. In 1845, described as, 'formerly of Watton, grocer, draper, dealer in ironmongery, general shopkeeper and farmer; then of Watton, farmer; late of Watton, out of business', Smith Wright was summoned to appear in court as an insolvent debtor.[15] He was ill, and could not appear. The case was adjourned four times, his brother testifying on the third occasion that he 'had not left his room for 33 weeks and could scarcely get from his bed to the chair'.[16] On 22 August, 1847, he died, 'after a long affliction', aged 61.[17] A sad story.

༄༅

Edward Stevens, on the other hand, seems to have prospered after the dissolution of his partnership with Smith Wright, and the malting business may have helped him to do so. Stevens became one of Watton's benefactors. On 6 July 1827, he presented the town with 'a new and elegant eight-day turret clock (by Nevill of Birmingham)…on which occasion the wardens and guardians of the parish , with a select party of the inhabitants, sate [sic] down at five o'clock, to an excellent dinner, at the *Crown* Inn, after which many loyal toasts and sentiments were given, accompanied with appropriate songs. The health of the highly esteemed and kind donor was drank with lively emotions of gratitude. The thanks of the parish were presented to him, and the party not paying that *minute* attention to the *object* they were met to commemorate, lost a stroke, and did not separate till an early hour'.[18] It sounds as though a good time was had by all and one can imagine the sounds of revelry echoing down the street. The clock remains to this day in the Clock Tower, with a brass plate recording Edward Stevens as its donor.

Another of Edward Stevens' philanthropic acts was the erection in 1831, under a single roof, of four almshouses. He stipulated that they were to be occupied by 'four poor married men and their wives…of the age of 60 years or upwards of good reputation for honesty, sobriety and industry and of the communion of the Church of England for not less than thirty years immediately preceding their election'. The married couples could not have children staying with them. The trustees were to 'remove and expel…any man or woman…who shall be in habit of drinking to excess or frequently brawling or quarrelling or be in other respects immoral or disorderly or who shall carry on any offensive trade or business in or upon any of the said almshouses…or who shall not attend the parish church of Watton or some other place of public worship according to the rites of the Church of England at least once every week'.[19] Edward Stevens, despite his strictures on the consumption of alcohol, cannot have been averse to the occasional tipple himself, as one of the bequests in his will was of 'all my wine, spirits, beer and other liquors'.[20] The Stevens almshouses were restored in 1975 and survive to this day.

In 1834, Edward Stevens decided to retire. He handed over the day-to-day running of his business to his nephew, Robert Stevens, son of his elder brother Stephen Nobbs Stevens. 'Having declined business',[21] and now in his late 60s, Edward wanted all accounts with his debtors and creditors settled. He died on 21 April 1847, 'in the 81st year of his age, highly and deservedly respected by all who knew him, particularly so from his many acts of benevolence and kindness'.[22]

෪෮

Robert Stevens, Edward's nephew, had married Ann Peck of Shipdham in 1819 and they had 11 children. The eldest was a son, Robert Edward, who was baptised in Beeston in 1820, where Robert was a farmer. The other ten were all daughters. The locations of their baptisms tell the story of the family's movements: Elizabeth and Anne were baptised in Beeston but by 1826, when Maria was baptised, the family had moved to Saham Toney and Robert was farming there. They had probably moved to Saham in 1825 because, when Robert's father, Stephen Nobbs Stevens was buried that year, his residence was given as Saham Park, which is where Robert farmed.[23] Robert and Ann's fifth and sixth daughters, Alice and Mary were also baptised in Saham Toney but, in September 1833, it was announced that Robert was 'retiring from the farming business' and a sale of his stock and implements took place on his premises at Saham Park Farm.[24]

By January 1834, Robert and his family had moved to Watton and he was described as a beer brewer.[25] When the next child, Martha Eleanor, was baptised in 1835, the ceremony took place in Watton and Robert was now stated to be a brewer and maltster, indicating that he had taken over all his uncle's businesses. The final three daughters, Emily Jane, Louisa and Clara, were all baptised in Watton, where the family now lived. The children all survived infancy and Robert Edward and eight of the daughters, in due course, married. The two oldest children, Robert Edward and Elizabeth, both married members of the Alpe family who were their first cousins.[26] Six of the other daughters married farmers, one of the husbands being married to two of the daughters in succession. Two daughters, Alice and Mary, died within a year of each other, aged 18 and 17 respectively; in both cases, the cause was consumption, or tuberculosis, a common cause of death in the 19th century.²⁷

Robert Stevens developed his uncle's business rapidly. In 1837 he bought a house with a yard, garden and stable in 'Rotten Row', on the north side of the street, the property extending through to Back Street. The premises comprised a former chairmaker's business, an adjacent dwelling and a 'baking office in full trade' with a garden and stable attached. They were sold by the executors of William Hubbard, the last chairmaker to occupy them. It was on this site that, in 1838, Robert Stevens erected a 'new brewery'.²⁸ The date is recorded on an inscribed stone on the façade of the building.

In 1840, Robert Stevens acquired more properties adjacent to the new brewery. They were conveyed to him by his uncle, Edward Stevens, 'in consideration of the true affection, esteem and regard which he had for his nephew', subject 'to the right of Robert Stevens the elder and Alice Stevens (the older Edward's unmarried brother and sister) occupying as tenants a tenement' paying rent to Robert Stevens the nephew of £16 per year.²⁹ Robert the elder was to die in 1865 but Alice Stevens, referred to as 'Miss Stevens', was still in occupation of part of the property when it was sold in 1866. She died five years later, on 6 January 1871, 'in the 97th year of her age; the last surviving member of the family of the late Mr Edward Stevens'.³⁰

The property Robert received from his uncle in 1840 included a cottage and brewhouse, 'then lately taken down' (having been replaced by the new brewery) and a 'malting office (then used as a store room)', which Edward had acquired from Christopher Dinmore in 1811, after Dinmore had moved to Norwich. The brewhouse 'lately taken down' may have dated from 1809, the date given by a later owner, Thomas Crawshay Frost, for the foundation of the brewery business which he took over in 1866.³¹ Edward Stevens also transferred to his nephew some of the properties that he had purchased in 1812 from the bankrupt Edward Younge's estate. The latter included the *Green Man*, another plot in 'Rotten Row' where the *Three Fishes* had stood and the site of an 'ancient cottage' now occupied by 'three new built messuages'. The process of transferring Edward Stevens' properties to Robert Stevens was completed after Edward's death in 1847.

In 1851, Robert Stevens was recorded in the census, aged 56, living in the house next door to the brewery with his wife, four as yet unmarried daughters, a grandson and several servants. Three years later, in 1854, the house and brewery were both offered for sale by auction at the *George*. The house had seven bedrooms and a nursery and—an ultra-modern feature for a country town at the time—two water closets. According to the sale particulars, the brewery was erected 'regardless of expense, upon an improved plan.' It was described as 'of handsome elevation, and fitted in the most complete manner, with the best approved machinery.' In the yard outside was a well, fifty feet deep, with 'a constant supply of the purest water, pumped up by horse works.' The purity of the water may help to explain the absence of infant mortality, so common at this time, in the Stevens family. The brewery supplied 19 inns and public houses within a 12-mile radius of Watton, including the *Green Man* in the High Street.[32] Despite all the stated merits of the property, it was not sold and so remained in the hands of the Stevens family.

Robert Stevens' wife Anne died in November 1855, aged 58, 'after a long and lingering illness'.[33] Robert Stevens himself, 'maltster, beer brewer and wine and spirit merchant' died in June 1857, aged 64.[34]

❧❧

Robert and Anne Stevens' only son, Robert Edward Stevens, had been working with his father in his business. He may have taken responsibility for the retail side, as he was described as a 'spirit merchant' on his marriage to Mary Ann Alpe in October 1845. The couple had four children and, when they were baptised, Robert Edward's occupation was given as 'brewer', although he also farmed at West Tofts, where he was residing at the end of his life, and at Wood Farm in Thompson.[35] Robert Edward's wife Mary Ann died suddenly, aged 28, in May 1851, 'deeply lamented by her family and friends, and has left a sorrowing husband and four small children to deplore the loss of an affectionate wife and mother'.[36] The eldest child had just had his fifth birthday. Robert Edward died on 19 June 1857, just eight days after his father, Robert, aged only 38. The orphaned children were looked after by his sister Susanna and her newly-wedded husband, Thomas William Sutton, a farmer.

The Stevens estate and the brewery were managed for a few years by other members of the extended family, acting as trustees. The 'capital residence' which had served as the home of Edward Stevens and afterwards of Robert Stevens, however, came on to the market immediately, and the details provide an indication of the family's lifestyle. The house had a 'spacious entrance hall, drawing room… dining room…kitchen, back kitchen, pantry, cellar and other domestic offices; five bedrooms, dressing room and good attics.' There were numerous outbuildings. 'The garden, in which is a large summer-house and a green-house, heated with hot-water apparatus, has loft brick walls on the north and west sides, is tastefully laid out, and planted with choice fruit-trees and bushes.' Adjoining the house was a paddock and a cottage, 'comprising two low rooms and two chambers over'.[37] The property did not sell.

At the time of the 1861 census, the main residence was occupied by Robert Stevens' daughter Susanna, her husband Thomas William Sutton, now described as a maltster's and brewer's clerk, and their one-year-old son, Thomas. Also resident were Susanna's youngest sister, Clara, performing the role of housekeeper (she was later to marry Thomas's brother, Margram Sutton), a niece, Elisabeth Alpe and three nephews, the children of the deceased Robert Edward Stevens, named as Robert, William and Nobbs.[38] A nursemaid, housemaid and dairymaid catered for the needs of the family. Next door lived the unmarried Robert and Alice

Stevens, now both in their eighties, assisted by a general servant, Elizabeth George.

Eventually, the entire estate was offered for sale by public auction on 22 August 1866. The 'capital residence', now described as a 'family residence', was included and a 'paved yard, with arcade and bottle house' were mentioned. Next door was another house, 'a very convenient dwelling house', with 'a yard, garden…stable and chaise-house', still occupied by the elderly Alice Stevens, Robert Stevens' unmarried aunt. The brewery, of course, was included, as were the 'capital brick and tiled malting office' and farm buildings on the other side of the street, and 45 acres of arable and pasture land in Watton, covering the whole of the area now occupied by the housing estate approached from George Trollope Road, between the High Street and Merton Road.[39]

༄༅

These properties were all purchased by the Revd William Frost, on behalf of his son, Thomas Crawshay Frost. He also bought 11 of the 14 public houses offered for sale.[40] They were the *Green Man* in Watton, the *Bell* at Saham Toney, the *Cock* at Ovington and others at North Pickenham, East and West Bradenham, Shipdham, Sporle, Necton (the *Good Woman*), East Harling and Westfield. The Revd William Frost's outlay amounted to £10,070 (equivalent to over £630,000 today).[41] The announcement in the local press advertising the sale noted that: 'An Act of Parliament has been obtained for making a railway from Watton to Thetford, which will open direct communication with London and the Eastern Counties, thus offering great facilities for the extension of trade both in brewing and malting'. The Revd William Frost had spotted a good business opportunity, which his son exploited to the full.

Thomas Crawshay Frost was born at Thorpe-next-Norwich in 1846, the second son, and fifth of six children, of the Revd William Frost and his much younger wife Caroline, the daughter of Sir Richard Crawshay of Honingham Hall and granddaughter of William Crawshay, owner of the Cyfartha ironworks at Merthyr Tydfil, South Wales. William was the owner of property in Pulham, Yaxham, Westfield, Scarning, Dereham, Norwich and Thorpe in Norfolk and Clopton in Suffolk. Although a 'clerk in holy orders' (as he was often described in the deeds) he was 'without the cure of souls' (was not the incumbent of any parish) and probably devoted himself mainly to the management of his estates and his investments in government stocks. His wife Caroline's family was very wealthy and, in a settlement agreed before her marriage, her father endowed her for life with the income from £5,000 invested in annuities, managed by a family trust. Thomas, therefore, grew up in affluent circumstances and his family's wealth enabled him to become the effective owner of the brewery and associated properties at an astonishingly early age: he was just 20. Brewing was one of the hobbies of Sir Richard Crawshay, while he resided at Honingham Hall and later at Ottershaw Park in Surrey. and he may have passed his interest, and his skills, on to his grandson before his death in 1859.

The Revd William Frost died in December 1875 and bequeathed the brewery and associated properties to Thomas, subject to the payment of an annuity of £300 to the widowed Caroline. Almost immediately, Thomas began to acquire additional properties. In 1876, he purchased the beerhouse called the *Dog and Partridge* on Brandon Road at the west end of Watton, and the *Horse Shoes* and an associated blacksmith's shop in Ashill.

The following year, Thomas invested heavily in the brewery, doubling its size and erecting the large chimney which became a landmark until eventually taken down in the 1970s. The date 1877, with Frost's initials, TCF, was inscribed on a stone in the wall, as they had been six years earlier on a row of houses on the south side of the street, east of the Methodist Chapel. Thomas installed a new boiler house and fittings in the brewery, 'bringing it up to date',[42] and erected a mineral water factory on the premises.

In 1879, Thomas Crawshay Frost acquired the *New Inn* in Watton, which had been a beerhouse owned by Barnabas Reeve, a basket maker, and before that Samuel Rice's carpenter's shop. An adjoining cottage was included in the purchase, which cost Thomas £1,020.[43] More land was purchased in subsequent years, along with several more public houses, including the *White Horse* in Carbrooke, the *Mill Inn* in Stow Bedon, the *Bird in Hand* in Caston, the *Bush Inn* in Yaxham and the *Horse Shoes* and Cator's beerhouse in Saham Toney. As well as owning 20 fully licensed public houses and beerhouses, Thomas also supplied beer to several more, including, in Watton, the *George* and *Crown* hotels, the *Chequers* and the *Carpenters' Arms* beerhouse.

෨෬

Thomas Crawshay Frost was not only a brewer of beer but also a maltster, a dealer in wines and spirits and a manufacturer of mineral water. The scope of the business was illustrated by an advertisement he placed in 1885 in the *Thetford and Watton Times*, the new local newspaper that had been launched five years earlier.[44] 'Light Bitter Table Ale (in eighteen and nine-gallon casks), Strong Ales and London Stout' were offered, along with 'ginger beer, gingerade, lemonade, soda, seltzer, etc'.

Throughout this period, Thomas Crawshay Frost remained single. In 1871, he had been described in the census returns as 'master brewer and malster' and was living with two servants including a housekeeper, Pleasance Ayers, who was still with him at the time of the 1881 and 1891 censuses. On 1 July 1891, however, Thomas Crawshay Frost sold the brewery and public houses (but not the farmland) to William Cann and Co. of Wymondham and, three years later, he married Druscilla (or Drucilla) Mary Fortescue, from Lincolnshire, who was almost 20 years his junior. At the time of his marriage, Thomas gave his (prestigious) address as 9 Brook Street in the parish of St George, Hanover Square in London.

However, he bought back the residence adjoining the brewery in Watton, now known as Clarence House, and he and Druscilla settled down there and had two sons, Thomas and Horace.

By the time of the 1901 census, Thomas described himself as a retired brewer, although he continued to farm. He had also become a JP and served as a trustee of the children's playground and a committee member of the Wayland Agricultural Association, allowing the committee to use the land that he had retained opposite the brewery for the annual Wayland Show. Druscilla, aged 35 in 1901, was assisted in bringing up the children and running the house by a governess and servants.

Thomas Crawshay Frost died on 14 December 1909, aged 63.[45] He was worth over £20,000 (equivalent to over £1.5m today). An obituary recorded: 'he was of a retiring disposition, but very precise in his habits and deportment. He was a good friend to the poor, and to all works of charity and benevolence.'[46] His coffin was taken to Watton station and thence by train to Pulham Market, where he was buried in the family vault. Thomas' wife, Druscilla, lived on as a widow for almost 40 years, dying in June 1948.[47]

The maltings were purchased by R Martin and Son, while the brewery was operated by William Cann for two years and was then put up for sale by auction. It was acquired by Morgans Brewery Company, who were recorded as the owners in Kelly's Directory of 1896 and in subsequent directories up to 1916. Brewing appears to have ceased in Watton after the First World War. Fortunately, the brewery building, one of the most unusual and distinctive in Watton, has survived and, along with the names of two roads, Stevens Close and Frost Close, stands as a memorial to two of Watton's more notable business people.

## Notes

1. Which gave its name to the area to the west called Malthouse Close on an 1808 map of Edward Younge's estate; NRO, ACC 2023/12.
2. BNP, 13 June 1810.
3. NC, 23 March 1816.
4. NC, 26 April 1817. The commission of bankruptcy was dated 24 December 1816. A Christopher Dinmore of Norwich, merchant or brewer, was declared bankrupt in 1825; he may have been the youngest son of Christopher and Pleasance.
5. NC, 20 May 1826. The news of his death had taken nearly two months to cross the Atlantic by sailing ship.
6. BNP, 1 September 1790.
7. NC, 8 October 1814.
8. NC, 8 April 1815.
9. NC, 25 February 1829.
10. NM, 20 December 1828.
11. NC, 17 December 1836.
12. NC, 21 January 1837.

13. NM, 17 October 1840.
14. NM, 20 November 1841.
15. NC 22 February 1845.
16. NN, 28 February 1846.
17. NM, 4 September 1847.
18. NC, 14 July 1827.
19. Quoted in the anonymous typescript, pre-1958.
20. Will of Edward Stevens, 1847; NRO, ANW 1844-47, fo50, no 40.
21. NM, 5 April 1834.
22. NN, 24 April 1847.
23. NM, 12 November 1831.
24. NM, 24 August 1833.
25. Deed pf gift, Mrs C Harvey to Mr E R Grigson and others, 13 January 1834: NRO, ACC 2023/12.
26. Thanks to Bronwen Tyler for this information.
27. NM, 15 July 1848; NN, 19 May 1849.
28. Deeds and papers relating to cottages purchased of the executors of William Hubbard; NRO, BR 156/2; draft abstract of title to Watton brewery 1866; NRO, ACC 2023/12.
29. Draft abstract of title to Watton brewery 1866; NRO, ACC 2023/12.
30. NC, 14 January 1871.
31. TWT, 1885.
32. NM, 29 July 1854.
33. NM, 17 November 1855.
34. LA, 27 June 1857.
35. NM, 22 August 1857, contains a notice of the sale of farm stock there.
36. NM, 24 May 1851.
37. NM, 29 August 1857.
38. The figures given for their ages were, in each case, lower than their real ages. Perhaps Thomas and Susanna Sutton did not know their real ages.
39. Sale particulars for the Watton brewery and maltings, 1866; NRO, ACC 2023/12.
40. NM, 18 August 1866.
41. Draft conveyance from the trustees of the will of Robert Stevens to the Revd William Frost, 2 February 1867; NRO, ACC 2023/12..
42. Obituary of Thomas Crawshay Frost, DMG, 18 December 1909.
43. Abstract of title to a messuage and carpenter's shop in Watton, 1879; NRO, ACC 2023/12.
44. TWT, 1885.
45. NN, 25 December 1909.
46. DMG, 18 December 1909.
47. Thanks to Bronwen Tyler for information on Thomas Crawshay Frost's family history, on which I have drawn in this and previous paragraphs.

# Piety and Scandal

Although it stood at some distance from the town, St Mary's Church was an important centre of Watton's life in the 19th century.

Religious observance played a significant part in the lives of the people. Most were affiliated with the Church of England and attended the parish church. They sat in box pews, for some of which rent had to be paid, and everyone had their appointed place. Music formed a part of the services. From 1827 until 1845, the church's possessions included a 'bass viol', two clarinets and two flutes, 'for the singers'.[1]

As the population of the town rose, it became necessary to expand St Mary's. In 1840, a petition was sent to the Bishop of Norwich, claiming that there was insufficient room for the inhabitants to 'sit, stand and kneel on the occasion of divine service' and that it had therefore been resolved to 'take down' the medieval north and south aisles and to rebuild them 'on a much larger scale'. The lead from the existing roofs would be sold and slate would be used to roof the new aisles, each having a separate roof structure. The nave arcades were retained and parts of the original windows were incorporated in the new aisles. A west door was added to the tower. The bishop sanctioned the work,[2] which was entrusted to Fuller Coker, a builder from Shipdham. It was completed in 1841 and the result was that 'two hundred and twenty additional sittings were obtained',[3] about three-quarters of them free. Uniquely for Norfolk, the width of the church was now greater than its length.

On Sunday 30 March 1851, when a census of church attendance took place, 148 people attended matins at St Mary's and 194 came to an afternoon service, a significant proportion of the adult population, although some people probably attended both services. Additionally, 53 children attended Sunday school in the morning and 50 did so in the afternoon.[4] The vicar at this time was the Revd Peter Blomfield (or Bloomfield) Jeckell, whose incumbency had begun early in 1839. He had taken over from the Revd Fairfax Franklin, vicar from 1803 until his death in 1838, who was also the rector of Attleborough and delegated much of his workload in Watton to curates. Jeckell it was who saw to the widening of the church, the building of the new vicarage and the erection of a new building for the National School in 1842. He was also present at the opening of the Wayland Hall in 1853. On 19 December 1853, he was presented with 'a handsome piece of plate and a purse of £136 10s from donors in the parish and neighbourhood, as a mark of their esteem and gratitude for his faithful and affectionate services during the fourteen years he has held the vicarage of this parish'.[5]

∞⌘

The Revd Jeckell's successor was the Revd William Henry Hicks, usually referred to as W H Hicks. He was the son of John Raby Hicks Esq and his wife Elizabeth and great-great-nephew of Elizabeth Barker, formerly Elizabeth Hicks and originally Elizabeth Raby, lady of the manor of Watton Hall until her death in 1813. W H Hicks was born at Caston on 24 October 1828, went to Corpus Christi College, Cambridge and in June 1850, before completing his degree, married Charlotte Louisa Bailey at St George's Chapel, Albemarle Street, Westminster. At the time of the 1851 census, the young couple were living at 4 Park Terrace, Cambridge, apparently in some style as they employed both a footman and a housemaid.

On reaching the age of 21 in 1849, Hicks had inherited the manor of Watton Hall from trustees appointed under the will of his great-great-aunt. He thought he should also have inherited certain lands that had belonged to the manor, which the trustees had sold in 1814, from which, he claimed, he should have been receiving the rents. Some of those lands had been bought by Matthew Sallitt, against whom Hicks launched (no doubt expensive) legal proceedings. In 1853, he secured a judgement in his favour. Sallitt appealed and the case went to the court of Chancery in 1854. Although the judge recognised that the outcome was hard on Sallitt, who had bought the lands in good faith in 1831, Hicks was not prepared to compromise on the rents he was owed and the judgement in his favour was upheld.[6]

Hicks had also inherited from his aunt the impropriate rectory of Watton, which carried the advowson or right to nominate the vicar. Following the retirement of the Revd Peter Blomfield Jeckell, Hicks nominated himself. And so, in 1854, at the age of 25, he became the vicar of Watton, although he employed a succession of curates who undertook much of the parish work. The Revd Benjamin Armstrong, diarist and vicar of Dereham, visited one of the curates, George Nelson, in September 1854 and noted in his diary that Nelson 'complains that his wealthy young rector does nothing but play cricket'.[7] Hicks did indeed play cricket and was still playing for the Watton team in 1858. Despite what he had heard from the curate, however, Armstrong subsequently preached with Hicks in St Mary's Church and enjoyed his hospitality at the Watton vicarage on several occasions, including on the day of the ambitious 'conversazione' which William Henry organised at Wayland Hall in 1859.

Hicks, like Armstrong, was probably of the 'high church' persuasion, a supporter of ceremony and ritual in services which, for some, were redolent of Roman Catholicism. This may be the background to a public meeting at the Wayland Hall in January 1858, advertised by placards proclaiming 'Protestantism in danger', whose object was to promote 'the exposition and defence of sound Protestant principles, now threatened by the open attacks of popery and by the insidious effects of formalism'. A banner proclaiming 'civil and religious liberty' was displayed and the hall was crowded, 'principally with the working classes'.[8]

Further investment took place at St Mary's Church during the Revd W H Hicks' tenure. In 1858, it was re-pewed and restored, its reopening on 16 June prompting the comment: 'a more earnest spirit is really existing amongst nearly all classes for the rendering our parish churches more fitting places for holy worship'.[9] Hicks, described as 'energetic and public-spirited',[10] was also active in the affairs of Watton, chairing meetings of the Mutual Improvement Society, supporting the formation of a Young Men's Institute in the town and chairing a meeting to discuss the introduction of gas lighting. He was also a magistrate and so, no doubt, had to devote time to the bench as well.

This may have helped him when he faced a claim in the County Court in 1860, from a Wymondham farmer, who alleged that while his son was driving a donkey cart containing eight pigs to Hingham Fair, the cart had been upended by Hicks' carriage and the pigs scattered across the turnpike road. The farmer's son stated that: 'when between Hingham mile-stone and Hingham town, an open carriage met him, on the front seat of which were a lady and gentleman, and a gentleman sitting behind, the wheel of the carriage caught the wheel of his cart which, in consequence, was dragged a little back and overturned'. The 'lady and gentleman' were subsequently identified as the Revd and Mrs Hicks, and it was alleged that their carriage had been travelling at 12 miles per hour. Hicks denied everything and was backed up by his passenger. He claimed that the farmer was drunk when he first made the allegation. The judge found in Hicks' favour and allowed him 'the costs of coming specially from London to defend the action'.[11]

The tenure of the Revd W H Hicks as vicar of Watton ended in scandal. His marriage with Charlotte Louisa Hicks was childless and, although William Henry conducted the weddings of two of Charlotte's sisters in London, relations with his wife were breaking down. The census of 7 April 1861 found the couple living at Gifford Lodge, Mortlake, Surrey. It would appear that they had moved out of Watton vicarage by then and that William Henry was no longer performing routine parish duties; the last baptism he conducted was in October 1860. By 29 May 1861, he had resigned the living and in June the 'entire contents' of the vicarage were auctioned.[12]

In July 1863, Charlotte petitioned for a divorce, using the provisions of the recently-passed Matrimonial Causes Act of 1857, which enabled a woman to seek a divorce in a civil court. Although divorce was now possible, it was still almost unheard of, especially from a clergyman. Two years later, in April 1865, Charlotte was granted a decree nisi, with costs, the decree being made absolute the following November.[13]

The story was as follows: 'Both the petitioner and the respondent belonged to families of good position and had independent property....After the marriage they lived for several years at Watton, and the respondent, who was a man of somewhat expensive habits, became embarrassed in his circumstances, and he had some disputes with the petitioner about money matters. In June 1861, he deserted her, and between that time and October 1862, he lived with a woman named "Julia" who passed as his wife at different places in and about London. He then went to New Zealand with the same woman'.[14] According to Charlotte's affidavit, William had never returned to her after 12 June 1861 but 'formed a connection with a person whose name is unknown to me but who styled herself "Mrs Hicks" and he resided with her [from April to October 1862] and subsequently [in early November 1862] left England with the same person in the clipper packet Gertrude occupying a cabin with her as man and wife'. During the months of April to October, Charlotte affirmed, Hicks had 'repeatedly committed adultery with the person styling herself Mrs Hicks and did in fact during such months live in open and flagrant adultery with her'. Hicks denied the allegations but offered no evidence.[15]

The vicarage of Watton was sequestrated until a new vicar was instituted on 6 August 1861, on the presentation of W H Hicks himself, who still owned the manor and the advowson. It seems unlikely that the people of Watton knew the full details of what had happened but, had they known, they would undoubtedly have been shocked.

ഈൡ

The incumbency of the new vicar, the Revd W C Hodgson, was relatively brief, lasting only until 1865, when he departed for a parish in Leicestershire. 'His care for his poorer parishioners', it was reported, 'has been unceasing and his treatment of all ever kind, courteous and considerate'.[16] He donated stained-glass windows for the south side of the church.[17] The living was purchased by the Revd G F W Wallis but his incumbency was even briefer, lasting under two years.

His successor, the Revd Dr Thomas Brookes Wrenford, was to have a much longer tenure, serving Watton for 23 years from September 1867 until his death in 1890. His background and character were very different from those of William Henry Hicks.

Thomas Brookes Wrenford was born in Bootle, Lancashire,[18] in 1822, the son of an excise officer. He married young; both he and his wife Elizabeth Booth were 21 when they were wedded at St Batholomew's Church, Wednesbury, in the West Midlands, Elizabeth's birthplace. Thomas was already resident in Wednesbury in 1841, working as a clerk to a shoe dealer. In 1851, he and Elizabeth were living in the market place there and Thomas was working as a printer, bookseller and stationer, perhaps having benefited from support from his father-in-law, who was a stationer. A daughter and two sons had been born and another son was born a month after the census. They were all baptised in Methodist churches in Wednesbury.

At some stage, Wrenford transferred his loyalties to the Church of England and decided that his vocation lay in the church rather than in business. In the 1850s, the family lived in Cumberland, where Thomas attended St Bees Divinity College and another daughter was born. On 11 June 1854, he was ordained as a deacon by the Bishop of Manchester and went to serve in a church in Preston. Two years later, he was 'minister of the chapel at Stockport Great Moor' in Cheshire and a final son was born while the family lived there. Thomas also served as incumbent of St James' Episcopal Church, Aberdeen in 1861-62, and as curate of a church in Newport, Monmouthshire. The Revd Thomas Brookes Wrenford's journey to the vicarage of Watton took him all over Britain but it seems clear that, for him, unlike for Hicks, it was a journey driven by conviction and commitment.

Three of Wrenford's four sons went into the church. One, Thomas Henry Wrenford, became curate of Great Cressingham. One daughter, Elizabeth Anne (known as Annie) remained unmarried and cared for her mother in her widowhood after 1890. The most problematic of Thomas Brookes Wrenford's offspring was his eldest son, Joshua Booth Wrenford, who seems, like W H Hicks, to have aspired to a lifestyle beyond his means. Like his father, he married young; in his case, most unusually, before his 20th birthday. He probably had to. His wife, Margaret, also a minor (meaning, at the time, under 21), came from Scotland and the wedding took place in Aberdeenshire. Their son, Basil Joshua Booth was born in 1869 and, when he was baptised at Watton, Joshua's occupation was given as 'gentleman'.

In the 1871 census, Joshua, aged 24, was again styled 'gentleman', with the qualification, 'no occupation', and the family was living in Islington with a nurse and cook. Later, Joshua acted as a locum for the vicar of St Clement's Barnsbury, Islington. In 1875, he was presented to the vicarage of St Mary's Church, Haverfordwest, Pembrokeshire[19] where, in 1881, he and Margaret were living as lodgers with a tailor and draper, while their son Basil and his younger sister Annette were staying with their grandparents in Watton. In 1882, considerably in debt, he moved back to Watton and became curate under his father there. Two years later, Joshua became the incumbent at Cransford, Suffolk and then, in 1887, rector of Knodishall in the same county. The following year, serious financial difficulties resulted in his bankruptcy, with liabilities of over £1,219 (equivalent to over £100,000 today). Most embarrassingly, no doubt, for his father, his creditors included several Watton people: Mrs Curl, schoolmistress; Thomas Crawshay Frost, mainly for wine and beer; William Kendall, draper; Mr L Langford, 'chinaman'; and Lacey Vincent, chemist. Joshua was also in debt to his father to the tune of £100.[20]

Despite the shenanigans of his son, the Revd Dr Wrenford was 'much respected' in Watton.[21] He enhanced the fabric and facilities of St Mary's Church in several ways. With his daughter, Annie, he successfully raised funds for a new organ and organ chamber for the chancel. They were installed in 1877 and Annie then both played the organ and trained the choir, bringing it to 'a high state of proficiency'.[22]

In 1878, the spire on the tower, which had become dangerous, was removed. About nine years later, a local artist, Thomas Waters, provided the designs for the painting on the ceiling of the chancel, of which one expert has written: 'The overall effect is remarkable and a fine example of Victorian design'.[23] It was probably also during Dr Wrenford's tenure that a mission hall was established at Watton Green.[24]

The town, also, benefited from Dr Wrenford's 'praiseworthy exertions' to rejuvenate the National School and to secure the construction of an extension to provide additional accommodation for infants.[25] His death in January 1890 caused, so it was said, 'grief and gloom [to be] cast over the whole parish'.[26]

Wrenford's successor was the youthful (28-year-old) Revd Wiliam Bertram Russell Caley. He and his wife Flora made an immediate impact, raising funds to build a parish room, erected within seven months of their arrival in Watton. Caley's tenure, however, was fairly brief, lasting only until 1898. His successor, inducted on 8 September 1898, was the Revd Charles Barnett Nash, who was also rector of Threxton. One of his first actions was to supervise the removal of the three existing bells from the tower and the installation of six new ones, which permitted 'change ringing'.[27] Nash served the parish as vicar until 1923, overseeing the re-glazing of the east window of the church as a war memorial in 1919. His own son, Captain Frederic Wybrow Nash, MC, was one of those who lost their lives during the war.

Throughout much of the 19th century, as well as attending church services, many of the inhabitants of Watton also participated in other meetings and social activities connected with the parish church, including, for example, meetings of the Society for the Propagation of the Gospel in Foreign Parts and the Church of England Temperance Society. The Loyal Walsingham Lodge of the Manchester Unity Oddfellows, founded in 1841, was linked closely with the church and its anniversary celebrations invariably included a church service as well as refreshments at one of the hostelries. Its membership included many of the prominent shopkeepers and professional men in the town, although not all: some supported the Ancient Order of Foresters, a rival friendly society.

ೞಬ

Not everyone subscribed to the Anglican church. Methodism also commanded significant support in Watton. A Wesleyan Methodist chapel was erected in Saham Road in about 1831, with room for 160 people. It was over half full for the afternoon and evening services on Sunday 30 March 1851, attended by 90 and 82 respectively, while 23 children came to the afternoon Sunday school.[28]

The Primitive Methodist movement broke away from Wesleyan Methodism in 1812. In 1832, Watton had been visited by a Primitive Methodist evangelist, Robert Key, who 'took his stand on the Market Place for the purpose of giving the people a sermon'. An uproar and confusion ensued, during which Key was 'twice thrown down from his stand'.²⁹ Despite this hostile reception, the Primitive Methodists were able to establish a chapel in what later became known as Worm's Yard in 1836, with room for 105 people. On 30 March 1851, it was almost filled by the 100 who attended afternoon service. The evening service attracted 70 worshippers and the steward, William Hart, reported that there was also 'a morning service for the members of this place of worship exclusively the number between 30 and 40'. Sunday school took place in both the morning and the afternoon and was attended by 32 children.³⁰ It would appear, therefore, that the Primitive Methodists and the Wesleyan Methodists commanded broadly similar levels of support in Watton. Twenty years later, however, attendances at the Wesleyan chapel had declined and the building was sold in 1870, only to be repurchased and revived in 1881.³¹ In the late-19th and early-20th centuries both the Wesleyan and the Primitive Methodists commanded influential support among the business people of the town. For example, Alexander Banham, the auctioneer, was a Wesleyan while Daniel Dunnett, owner of the 'Market House' was a strong supporter of the Primitive Methodists, a preacher for 58 years and founder of the church's Sunday school.

In 1862, the trustees of the Primitive Methodist chapel purchased a house and a small piece of land fronting the south side of the street, with the help of a generous loan from Mark Moore of Saham Hills. The following year, they erected the Central Hall on the land, and in 1874 they added a school room. A new school room was built in 1897, on adjacent land purchased seven years previously from Thomas Crawshay Frost. More land was acquired from Frost's estate in 1913 and 1915, the land on which the maltings, now disused, had stood, which became the site for a new Methodist church. A boundary wall was erected in 1915, commemorated by an inscribed stone laid by Miss M A Moore on 1 July 1915, but construction of the new church was not completed until 1926, at which point the Central Hall was redesignated as a school hall and institute. After the union of the Primitive Methodists and Wesleyan Methodists in 1933, the Wesleyan Chapel in Saham Road was closed and what had been the Primitive Methodist chapel and school room served the now-united Methodist Church.³²

೮ಂಜ

Longer established than Methodism in Watton was the congregation of the Independent denomination, which had been formed in 1818, and for which a chapel was erected in 1819. The first pastor, the Revd H E Robinson, was publicly ordained on 22 October 1822. After January 1827, however, according to the chapel's own account of its history, 'a great depression ensued. The cause of God languished, religious ordinances were neglected and the church greatly declined'. A recovery took place after May 1830, when 'it pleased God to grant a gracious revival of religion' under a new pastor.³³

On the day of the national religious census in 1851, 59 adults worshipped in the chapel in the morning, 58 came in the evening and 40 children attended a morning Sunday school. According to Alfred Griffin, the minister at the time, the average attendance at services was 120 in the morning and 75 in the evening, in a building which had seats for 200.[34]

The chapel was the building now known as Loch House, adjacent to Loch Neaton (which did not exist in 1819). The site was made available by Charles Dorr of Neaton Farm. Dorr was a notable breeder of sheep, his Leicester and Down crosses commanding high prices at the Watton fairs.[35] On the plot he provided, according to a deed of 1824, 'a chapel or meetinghouse with a vestry room and other erections had been built for the religious worship of a congregation of Protestants dissenting from the Established Church being of the Independent denomination'. Charles Dorr, it was stated, 'from a benevolent desire to promote religious worship amongst the Protestant Dissenters of the Denomination aforesaid' and also for 'the advancement of general good morals' had promised to convey the parcel of land concerned to trustees and he duly did so. There were 13 trustees from a surrounding area extending to Thetford in the south and Gressenhall in the north. Three Watton men were listed: Charles Dorr's son, Charles Dorr the younger, yeoman; Smith Hastings, miller; and, heading the list, George Andrews, shopkeeper. This was a church with a middle-class congregation.[36]

Charles Dorr the elder died in 1843 and Charles Dorr the younger followed him to the grave in 1850, leaving his properties to his son, also named Charles Dorr. The latter had been born in 1816 and married Sarah Ann Hodson in 1836, when they were both twenty-year-olds. They had two children, a son (called, predictably, Charles) and a daughter, but Sarah Ann died in 1851, aged only 35. Barely three months later, Charles remarried, his new wife being Rebecca Amas, aged 22.

Charles Dorr III, farming 118 acres and employing five labourers in 1851, seems to have lacked the stern moral principles of his father and grandfather. He raised money by a series of mortgages between 1851 and 1856, giving every indication of living well beyond his means. In 1854, a local newspaper reported that, on the evening of Saturday 11 October, 'a farmer, named Charles Dorr of Watton, accompanied a woman of the town[37] to the *Prince of Wales* public house in Common Pump Street; and while in her company was robbed of his purse, containing about £11 (equivalent to nearly £900 today). The woman has escaped apprehension up to the present time'.[38] This was a far from unique case of a farmer from rural Norfolk going into Norwich, perhaps selling his produce at the city's markets and then losing the proceeds in an inn or a brothel. History does not record what Charles' new wife, Rebecca, thought about all this but they were still together at the time of the 1861 census.

Charles Dorr's profligacy had a positive side, in the form of conspicuous philanthropy. When the country was hailing the end of the Crimean War in 1856, Alfred and Benjamin Chaston treated 50 of the oldest poor people of Watton to a dinner of roast beef and plum pudding, but 'the entire poor of the parish of

Newton [sic]³⁹ next Watton were also regaled in a similar way by the liberality of Charles Dorr…who provided a spacious booth upon his premises to celebrate the occasion, when about 160, including a great many friends and neighbours, sat down to the usual old English fare. A band of music was in attendance, and a variety of rural sports afterwards followed for their amusement'.[40]

As for the chapel, by 1855, only two of the original 13 trustees survived. A meeting was called on 21 June 1855, at which it was resolved to sell the building as soon as possible, 'and lay out the money arising from such sale in the erecting and building another chapel near and more convenient in the parish of Watton'. The new chapel, in Dereham Road, became the Congregational Church. When the foundation stone was laid, on 3 April 1856, in an atmosphere of celebration, a reporter reflected that: 'The present chapel is…unsightly and the exterior much dilapidated'.[41] The new chapel was opened on 10 August. A schoolroom was added in 1862 and a gallery, paid for by the Alexander family, in 1870.[42]

Charles Dorr bought back the site of the original building and then sold it. It became a private house.[43] In 1857, 1859, 1861 and 1862, parts of the estate assembled by Charles Dorr's grandfather and father were offered for sale.[44] Dorr defaulted on his mortgage payments and the mortgagee forced the sale of the mortgaged part of his property in 1863. Three years later, the whole of the 'substantial…dwelling house called Neaton Cottage', in which Charles Dorr still resided, came on to the market.

By 1871, Charles Dorr, working as an 'agent', was living as a lodger at the *Railway Hotel* in Norwich Road. Rebecca was not with him. She was working as a housekeeper to a farmer in West Rudham; the marriage had broken down. In 1881, Rebecca was housekeeper to James Miller at Uphall Farm in Ashill. She was still there ten years later but by 1901 had retired and was living alone in Church Street, Ashill. She died in 1907. Charles Dorr, meanwhile, was one of three boarders at the *Green Man* in Watton High Street in 1891 and still lived in the town in 1895.[45] His life ended in the workhouse of the Wayland Poor Law Union at Rockland, where he was buried, aged 87, in January 1900.

A pauper's grave for the man who had once treated 160 of his neighbours to roast beef and plum pudding.

ഌര

Relations between the Church of England and the 'nonconformists', the other denominations of Christians, were not always easy. When Robert Key, the Primitive Methodist evangelist was roughed up in 1832, it was alleged that beer had been distributed to the assailants and that the 'attack was directed by one or two principal persons in the town who had a Church of England parson as prompter behind the scenes'.[46]

The following year, friction developed between the Church of England and the Independent congregation. It was claimed that children who went to a Sunday school run by the Independents but also attended Watton National School, had been 'informed by the teacher of the National [School], that they were to be expelled if they went to the "Chapel Sunday School" any more'.[47] Watton National School was run by the National Society for promoting the Education of the Poor in the Principles of the Established Church of England and Wales but, as it was the only public elementary school in the town, it was also attended by the children of nonconformists, some of whose parents supported the school financially with their subscriptions.

In 1837, the curate of Watton, the Revd Stephen Jackson, refused to bury the child of a Dissenter (a member of the Independent congregation), who had not been baptised in the Church of England. The vicar (the Revd Fairfax Franklin) was consulted, probably at his residence in Attleborough, and eventually the interment, having been postponed by three days, was conducted by the incumbent of a neighbouring parish. The curate was the son of the owner of the Ipswich Journal who, it was reported, had been heard to remark: 'the Dissenters must be crushed'.[48]

A further controversy relating to Watton National School erupted in 1848. The pastor of the Independent Chapel, James Reading, complained that a member of his denomination had received a letter from Mr Groome, the schoolmaster stating: 'I am directed by the committee of the Watton National School to call your attention to the seventh rule, which states, "That all children do attend the church Sunday school and services, morning and afternoon, in their respective parishes", and I am also requested in inform you, that unless the attendance of your sons…be regular, they will be dismissed from the said school'.[49] Concerns about the denominational character of the National School became evident again in the debates about educational provision in the town that followed the passing of the Education Act of 1870.

By the second half of the 19th century, sectarian attitudes did not go unchallenged. In 1864, when the vicar, the Revd W C Hodgson, 'visited a young lady…with his displeasure because she had played the harmonium at a bazaar held for the benefit of a Dissenting Sunday-school in the town', he was censured because 'the country is getting too enlightened to submit to such hateful intolerance'.[50] His successor, the Revd G F W Wallis was more in tune with the spirit of the times when he announced that 'wherever he had laboured in the Lord's vineyard he always had the pleasure of co-operating with his dissenting brethren'.[51]

Nevertheless, all was not yet sweetness and light. In 1883, a dispute arose between John Alexander, a member of the Independent congregation and the Revd Thomas Brookes Wrenford, whom Alexander accused of reneging on an agreement to reserve a burial plot for his family. The case was brought before a

Select Committee of the House of Commons but restraint was urged on Wrenford by Lord Walsingham, who did not wish to damage relations with the dissenting community in Watton. Alexander, a strong supporter of the Liberal Party, was probably one of those behind a public meeting called at the Wayland Hall in March 1884 to discuss the disestablishment of the Church of England, which was disrupted by a 'disorderly contingent of boys and youths, organised for a rowdy defence of the church'.[52] Further disruption was attempted at another meeting with the same object a year later, which Alexander chaired.[53] In 1890, Alexander refused to sell a piece of land he owned that the church wished to acquire for an extension to the graveyard.[54]

However, much of the heat went out of the relationship between church and chapel after the passage of the Local Government Acts of 1888 and 1894, which created elected county, district and parish councils. Thereafter, the role of Church of England clergy in local politics and administration was much reduced. Increasingly, Anglicans and Christians of other denominations collaborated, for example in the Christian Endeavour Union formed for Watton and district in 1906.[55]

They now seemed to realise that more united them than divided them.

**Notes**

1. Watton glebe terriers 1827, 1834, 1845; NRO, DN/TER 159/23-25.
2. Bishop of Norwich to the churchwardens of Watton, 13 August 1840; Museum4Watton mss.
3. Wall tablet in the church.
4. Janet Ede and Norma Virgoe (eds), *Religious Worship in Norfolk: the 1851 Census of Accommodation and Attendance at Worship* (Norfolk Record Society, Vol LXII, 1998).
5. NM, 24 December 1853.
6. BNP, 9 March 1853; NM, 21 January 1854.
7. Christopher Armstrong (ed), *Under the Parson's Nose* (Larks Press, 2012).
8. Suffolk Chronicle, 16 January 1858.
9. NM, 30 June 1858.
10. NC, 4 June 1859.
11. NN, 23 June 1860.
12. NM, 29 May 1861.
13. TNA, Hicks v Hicks, divorce court file, J77/26/H168, accessed via ancestry.com.
14. NN, 6 May 1865.
15. TNA, Hicks v Hicks, divorce court file, J77/26/H168, accessed via ancestry.com.
16. BNP, 17 October 1865.
17. BNP, 1 May 1866.
18. Although this is uncertain: his place of birth was recorded as 'Lancashire, NK (not known)' in 1871 and Liverpool in 1881.
19. Monmouthshire Merlin, 6 August 1875.
20. Lynn News and County Press, 24 March 1888; Framlingham Weekly News, 24 and 31 March 1888.
21. NC, 26 February 1887.

22. NM, 1 March 1890.
23. Stephen Heywood, *The church of St Mary, Watton, Norfolk: Statement of Significance* (Norfolk County Council, 2009).
24. Mentioned in the EDP, 20 November 1890.
25. BNP, 11 August 1868.
26. Dereham and Fakenham Times, 1 February 1890.
27. Watton church guide.
28. J Ede and N Virgoe (1998).
29. *Bury Free Press*, quoted in K Chapman, 'Methodism' in WEA Watton Branch, *Watton in an Earlier Age* (1975).
30. J Ede and N Virgoe (1998).
31. G Jessup (1985).
32. K Chapman, 'Methodism' in *Watton in an Earlier Age 1700-1900* (WEA Watton Branch, 1975).
33. Watton Congregational Church book; NRO, FC44/1.
34. J Ede and N Virgoe (1998).
35. BNP, 10 July 1833 and 8 July 1835.
36. Deeds and other papers relating to Loch House, Neaton; NRO, ACC 2023/12.
37. A euphemism for a sex worker.
38. NC, 18 October 1854.
39. A double error by the newspaper: Neaton (not a parish) was intended.
40. NC, 7 June 1856.
41. NM, 9 April 1856.
42. J Roberts, 'The Congregational Chapel' in WEA Watton Branch, *Watton in an Earlier Age* (1975).
43. Deeds and other papers relating to Loch House, Neaton; NRO, ACC 2023/12.
44. Deeds of 'Ellington's'; NRO, ACC 2023/12; NM, 2 September 1857; NN, 21 June 1862.
45. NM, 11 April 1863; NC, 6 January 1866; NM, 29 May 1895.
46. *Bury Free Press*, quoted in K Chapman, 'Methodism' in WEA Watton Branch, *Watton in an Earlier Age* (1975).
47. BNP, 27 November 1833.
48. *Suffolk Chronicle*, 22 April 1837. Many thanks to Julian Horn for this reference.
49. *The Patriot* (London), 10 April 1848.
50. NN, 18 June 1864.
51. NC, 25 November 1865.
52. LNCP, 8 March 1884.
53. NN, 18 April 1885; *Nonconformist*, 23 April 1885.
54. Robert Lee, *Rural Society and the Anglican Clergy, 1815-1914* (Boydell, 2006).
55. DMG, 23 June 1906.

# Learning, Private and Public

The earliest record of free educational provision for the people of Watton dates from 1611.

In that year, Edward Goffe of Threxton wrote his will.[1] He left a house that he had purchased in Saham Toney for use as a school and an annuity to pay a schoolmaster, who was to provide free tuition for pupils from Saham, plus one from Threxton and six from Watton, 'if so many should be sent'. The school, located east of Saham church, was rebuilt by the Revd W H Parker of Saham in 1836 and evolved into what is now Parker's Church of England Primary Academy. It is not known how many boys were sent to it from Watton over the two centuries after the school's foundation but, by the first half of the 19th century, none were sent.

Until the early 19th century, the only schools in Watton itself were private establishments. One was conducted in the 1760s and 1770s by Clement Overton, a land surveyor, whose pupils included members of the Younge family. He advertised his services as follows: 'Youth are taught English writing in its various hands, vulgar and decimal arithmetic, mensuration, gauging, surveying of land, merchants' accompts, algebra, trigonometry and navigation, by Clement Overton, at Watton; where all people who like to entrust him with the care of their children, may depend upon having them properly instructed'.[2] Overton charged from five shillings to one guinea per quarter (equivalent to about £20 to £90 today), and also taught at 'the Rev. Mr Pigge's Grammar School', presumably conducted at the vicarage as Mr Pigge was the incumbent at the time.[3]

Provision for 'young ladies' was offered in 1780 by Mrs Pilgrim in a 'boarding and day-school' conducted in a house 'in a healthy and pleasant situation, near the church'.[4] The girls, announced Mrs Pilgrim, would be 'carefully taught the English language, with all kinds of needlework'.[5] She was still running a 'seminary for young ladies' in 1822.[6]

Clement Overton's and Mrs Pilgrim's schools were for those whose parents were wealthy enough to pay the fees, and they were probably very small. For the remainder of the population, there were schools, but their proprietors did not advertise in the local newspapers. A 'serviceable school dame' called Mary Funnell had worked in the parish for 40 years before her death in 1738, running a 'dame school' where a little, very basic instruction would be given, and she, no doubt, was followed by others.[7]

In 1819, a parliamentary enquiry was informed that Watton contained 'two schools [which would have been dame schools], containing on an average about 50 in each; and a school for girls, containing 30, who are not paupers' but that 'many of the poor are without sufficient means of education, but are desirous of possessing them'.[8]

Action followed immediately. On Town House Close, at the west end of the street, the parish built a coal house, for storing the coal purchased for supplying the poor and an engine house for storing the town's fire engine. Over the coal house, at the cost of £100 (equivalent to nearly £6,000 today) paid by a benefactor, William Lane Robinson, was erected a school room, 'for the teaching of poor children of Watton and adjoining parishes upon the National system'.[9]

The 'National' system was used in schools run by the National Society for Promoting the Education of the Poor in the Principles of the Established Church of England and Wales. Founded in 1811, the society, along with the non-denominational British and Foreign School Society, became one of major providers of elementary education up to and beyond the passage of the Education Act of 1870.

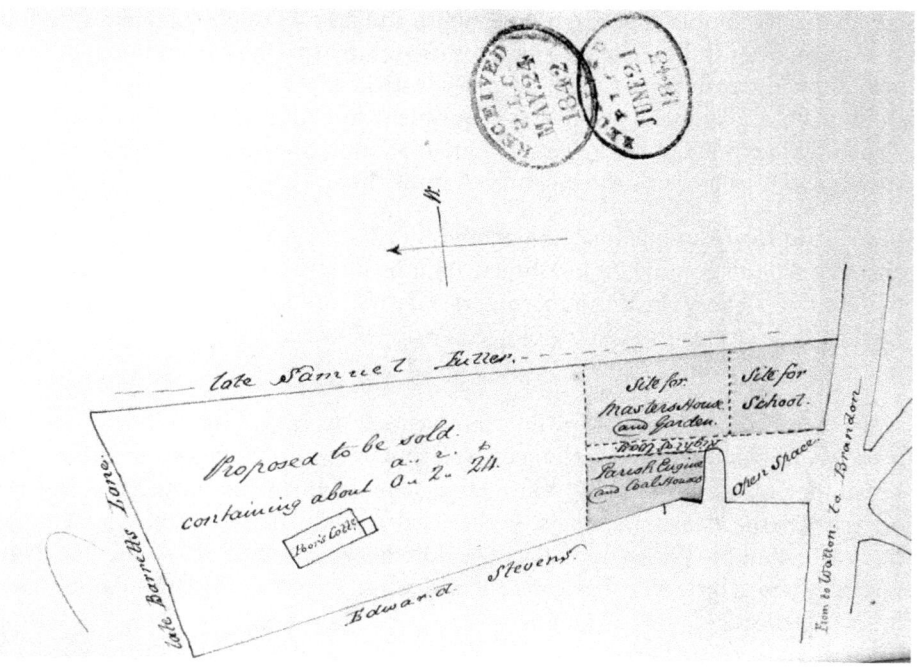

Plan of the site for the new National School, 1842.
(The National Archives, TNA MH12 8617)

Note that the arrowhead, which should point north, actually points south.

Watton's National School and the coal store beneath it were housed in a small structure, built end-on to, and a little back from the street, with an open space in front of it and the 'town house' of 1719 behind it.[10] The school, opened in 1819 and supported by voluntary donations, would undoubtedly have been welcomed, although its location in a room over a coal house does not sound ideal. However, from 1834, the boys (but not the girls) also had the benefit of the playground donated to them by Charlotte Harvey, on the other side of the street.[11]

The name of the National School's first schoolmaster is not known but by 1830 the person in charge was probably William Gedge.[12] He had left by 1834, when a new schoolmaster was sought at the very modest salary of £30 per year (equivalent to just over £2,000 today).[13] The successful candidate was probably William Took, as he and his wife Ann were recorded as the school's teachers in 1836, responsible for 120 pupils.[14] By 1839, the school was reported to be 'admirably conducted' and 'of great advantage to the children of the poorer classes'; the schoolmaster was Edward Legood and the schoolmistress Elizabeth Tooke, perhaps a daughter of William and Ann.[15] However, Legood appears to have left later in the year as, in November, the post of schoolmaster was again advertised and, this time, 'the salary will not exceed £40'.[16]

A major development occurred in 1842. At a meeting held in the parish church in January, the ratepayers and property owners of Watton agreed that the Board of Guardians of Wayland Poor Law Union should sell most of enclosure in which the old town house stood, but that the northern end fronting the street should be transferred to trustees and a new school building erected on it.[17] On the recommendation of the Committee of Council on Education (the national body responsible for education at that time), land south of the proposed school site was also conveyed to the trustees as the site of a schoolmaster's house.[18] There were still 120 pupils on the school's roll at the time.[19]

The vicar of Watton, the Revd Peter Blomfield Jeckell, co-ordinated the raising of money from voluntary subscriptions, 'for the purpose of erecting a new National School room…on or near the site of the present old and dilapidated school room'. Horace Darkins, of Watton, was contracted to erect the building and the first stone was laid by Charlotte Harvey on 18 May 1842.[20] The work cost £315 (equivalent to about £19,000 today) and the specifications were very precise, requiring for the school room foundations two feet deep, a projecting plinth and walls which were to be 14 inches thick with facings of 'riven flints squared and white brick quoins to the external angles of door and window openings'. The outbuildings, containing the privies, were to have floors of 'white hard lump'.[21] This was the building in which the Watton National School was now to be conducted, with the boys sitting on the left-hand side and the girls on the right.[22] It survives to this day, though no longer as a school.

The schoolmaster's house was built and in 1845 its occupant was Mr Groome, who was to incur the ire of the Independent congregation in 1848 by threatening to exclude a pupil who did not attend the Anglican Sunday school. Groome moved on shortly after the census of 30 March 1851. The following September, the vacancy was advertised: 'Wanted, a master and mistress for the National School, at Watton…The attendance of the mistress is required in the afternoon only [probably to teach the girls needlework]. Salary £50 per annum, with a house and garden'.[23] The appointees were probably Charles and Mary Smith, as they were in post by 1854.[24] They were still there two years later, teaching 65 pupils between them. An endowed infant school, supported by Lady Harvey of Norwich (Charlotte Harvey's daughter), had 48 pupils, taught by Charlotte Dye, almost certainly in the same building.[25]

Charles Smith was still the master in 1858.[26] It would appear, however, that the school deteriorated while in his charge as, according to a newspaper report of 2 June 1860, 'The appeal of the vicar [the Revd W H Hicks] to his parishioners to restore the National School-room, and place it in a thoroughly efficient condition, has met with a most cordial and liberal response from persons of all denominations. The school room has been restored at an expense of about £130. An able certificated master and his wife have been engaged. The school was opened last Thursday. Adult classes are intended to be established in connection with it'.[27] In 1861, the schoolmaster was 27-year-old James Neville; in January 1865, the master and mistress were Mr and Mrs Martin.[28] The school seems to have deteriorated again and, in March 1867, it was shut up completely and remained closed until the following January.[29]

The catalyst in improving the situation was the new vicar, the Revd Dr T Brooks Wrenford, instituted in September 1867. Supported by Squire Sprigge, the doctor, he threw himself into the resuscitation and improvement of the school. A new schoolmaster was appointed from January 1868; he was William Stovold Stace. Both he and his wife possessed certificates of competence granted by the government's education department on the recommendation of the inspectors, HMI, who were now deployed to assess and improve the work of all the schools that received government grants.

Watton was impressed by the change. 'We have had the pleasure on several occasions since the appointment of our present worthy vicar', wrote a correspondent, 'of noticing the great improvement which has taken place in the management and conduct of our National Schools. When he came to the parish these schools had been for some months shut up. Since then, however, two energetic and able certificated teachers, Mr and Mrs Stace, have been appointed, and very satisfactory progress has been made, both as regards the attainments of the children and the numbers in attendance'.[30] The Bishop of Norwich, after preaching at St Mary's, visited the school and 'expressed his pleasure and satisfaction at the ready answers given by the children, and with the intelligence they displayed'.[31]

When HMI visited on 5 May 1869, he found 118 pupils in standards 1 to 5 and 14 infants. The 'standards' contained pupils of similar levels of attainment, although their ages might differ. The inspector administered examinations in reading, writing and arithmetic for each standard. The pupils had to pass to progress to the next standard and their performance determined the government grant received by the school.[32] Most of the pupils passed. The inspector concluded that the school was 'well taught'.[33]

For the National School, this improvement happened just in time. An Education Act was passed in 1870, the intention of which was to create a national system of elementary education by filling the gaps in the provision made by voluntary societies such as the National Society. The number of school places required in each district was assessed by the Education Department in London and, where the provision currently made or that potentially could be made by the voluntary societies was insufficient to meet the needs of the district, a school board could be established, with the power to levy rates and construct new schools.

ಬಿಡಿ

Meanwhile, the private sector had been continuing to contribute to the educational provision in the town for those children whose parents could afford to pay for it. The private schools were small and, in most cases, did not endure for long.

One example was the 'seminary for young ladies and gentlemen' run by Miss Brock from 1820 to 1823, which moved to an 'excellently commodious situation in the most pleasant part of Watton' in 1821.[34] Another was the establishment of the three Misses Drew which, in 1836, offered an education for young ladies, including music, French and drawing, at 16 guineas per year (equivalent to over £1,000 today) for over-12s and 14 guineas for under-12s. Their 'ladies seminary' was recommended to 'those parents who wish to insure to their daughters a polite and useful education, their object being to win them to study by cultivating their affections and confidence rather than to urge by severity, and to inform their understanding rather than to burthen their memories'. It all sounds remarkably similar to the child-centred education advocated in more recent times.

Educational provision was also available for young gentlemen in Watton. Two schoolmasters recorded in the early 19th century were Thomas Starke, who was also active in various financial transactions and served as an overseer of the poor; and William Fendick, who was, at various times, a bookseller, stationer, tea dealer, insurance agent, surveyor of taxes and land surveyor.[35] In 1836, William Short was superintending a 'gentlemen's boarding' establishment providing a commercial education, at 18 guineas for over-10s and 16 guineas for under-10s.[36] In 1850, Short's 'commercial and classical school' was taken over by the Revd Alfred Griffin, 'late of Homerton College' and pastor of the Independent Church in Watton, who kept it going until he resigned from his ministry in 1855.³⁷ His prices were higher: 18 guineas a year (equivalent to over £1,500 today) for under-tens and 20 guineas for over-tens.

Another establishment for male pupils was founded by the Revd W H Parker, rector of Saham Toney, in 1852, housed in a large building he had erected in what is now Richmond Road in Saham. It was advertised as 'agricultural and commercial schools', and later renamed the 'commercial and boarding school'. At the time of the 1861 census, a headmaster, two assistant masters and a cook, housemaid and nurse were employed and 28 pupils were in attendance, including Edward Grigson and Benjamin Chaston, both of whom were to become prominent figures in Watton. Ten years later, there were only 13 scholars. The school had declined further by the time Parker died in 1876 and it had closed by 1881. It was revived in 1883, closed again in 1892 and reopened as 'the Saham middle-class school' in 1896, surviving until World War I, after which it closed for good.³⁸

A private school in Watton that kept going for longer than many was the establishment for girls conducted at the Willow House from 1841 to 1858. The teacher, Maria Ann Blade, was the daughter of Robert Blade, a tailor, and his wife Sarah, who kept the post office in Watton. Miss Blade ran a school for girls elsewhere in the town from 1836 onwards and moved into the Willow House after it had been acquired by Lord Walsingham. She had ten pupils aged ten to 16 in 1841 and appears to have invested in the facilities, referring in 1847 to 'alterations and improvements' for the 'increased accommodation' of her pupils.³⁹ Maria Ann Blade got married on 7 October 1850, to George Woodhouse Kett, a draper in Watton, but, contrary to the contemporary expectation, she announced that, as Mrs Kett, 'it is still her intention, with the aid of efficient teachers, to conduct her school on the same liberal system as before'.⁴⁰ In 1851, she was employing a 21-year-old music teacher and had seven pupils aged 12 to 18, from Norfolk, Suffolk, Essex and Lincolnshire. Two years later, Maria Ann Kett moved to Norwich and took over a well-established school there. The 'course of instruction' to be followed there embraced 'a useful and an accomplished routine, with a kind regard to domestic comfort, assimilated to the indulgences at home', the key selling point being that 'young ladies [were] speedily prepared for governesses'.⁴¹ Presumably, the school in Watton had been conducted on similar lines.

The establishment at the Willow House, 'lately conducted by Mrs Kett', was taken over by Miss Ursula Wightwick, who was 'experienced in tuition, having for some years resided as private governess in families of distinction'.⁴² Evidently, however, Miss Wightwick's skills in the tuition of future governesses were not matched by abilities in financial management. By November 1856, she was insolvent and the following month her furniture and effects were offered for sale by auction. The premises were taken over in 1857 by Miss E Wright, an experienced teacher and probably one of the 'Misses Wright' who had been running a boarding school in

Watton since 1843, mostly, as appears from the 1851 census returns, for their cousins. Miss Wright, however, stayed for only a year, after which her household furniture and effects were auctioned on 22 December 1858. As well as school desks and forms, three pianos, books and maps, they included 'eight four-post and other bedsteads and bedding', for her boarders.[43] That seems to have been the end of the school founded by Miss Blade.

A very different kind of private provision was offered by the 'dame schools', which catered for the young children of the poorer inhabitants of Watton and provided them with a little basic education. They did not advertise in the local press and so much less is known about them but, in the discussions about how Watton should respond to the requirements of the Education Act of 1870, it emerged that there were two such schools in the town. One of them, run by Caroline Bicker, was considered 'above the average, in point of instruction' but, like the other, 'was held in premises unsuitable for a school'.[44] Mrs Bicker obtained a certificate of competence as a teacher and she and her pupils were moved into the National School after 1870. The other dame school may have been founded by Elizabeth Targett, wife of a small landowner and farmer, and operated with the support of her daughters Mary Ann, Hannah and Jane, all of whom were listed in census returns as teachers. Between 1851 and 1861, they moved from Front Street (High Street) to premises in Thetford Road, where they were still to be found in 1871. Mary Ann and Jane were still working as schoolmistresses in 1881, although it is not known where they were employed.

ಸಂ

After the passage of the 1870 Education Act, the ratepayers of Watton began to consider whether a school board should be established in the town. The decision had already been taken to expand the National School building by erecting a new room to house an infant department, for which funds had been raised and the government's Education Department had promised a grant. The new room, with a gallery, lay behind and at right angles to the original building, and was about two-thirds its size. It was designed by the Norwich architect, R M Phipson, who took the opportunity to modify the original structure and make further additions. The original porch was removed; girls and boys would now use separate entrances at the east and west ends of the main building, and the girls were to have a separate, enclosed yard with 'necessaries' and a room for 'caps and bonnets' opening off it.[45] The new room was opened in 1871.

Watton was declared a school district, with Merton a contributory district, and the Education Department determined the number of school places required, concluding that the 187 places at the expanded National School were insufficient to meet the needs of the district and that a new infant school would be required for 60 children at the east end of the town.[46]

The question was: should a school board be created to build the additional accommodation? A meeting to consider the issue was held at the Wayland Hall in October 1874. Some may have welcomed the idea because a school board would be non-denominational; in 1870, it had been asserted in a vestry meeting that the management committee of the National School 'ought to be confined exclusively to members of the Church of England',[47] despite a number of Nonconformists having been subscribers to the school and having thitherto exercised their right to be members of the committee. However, the dominant opinion was against forming a school board because, it was argued, high rates would have to be paid and education could be provided much more cheaply by voluntary effort. The need for additional school accommodation was questioned but on this point the Education Department in London was unyielding: a new infant school was needed and if it could not be built by voluntary effort, a school board would be established. But, unlike those in Hingham and Dereham, the ratepayers of Watton were determined not to have a school board.

A further meeting was held in April 1875, at which Henry Woods, Lord Walsingham's agent, who had experience of building schools on the Walsingham estate, counselled that 'the best thing would be to do what they were commanded to do, and meet it with the best face they could'.[48] His advice was taken: a new infant school would be built, and it would be funded voluntarily. A suitable site, owned by Lady Walsingham, was found at the east end of the town, behind the *'Live and Let Live'* public house on Church Walk. Lord Walsingham paid for it and provided some of the materials for the building. His proposal that the new school should be non-denominational, managed by a committee comprising three churchmen and three dissenters, was accepted. Plans were produced and the tender of a local builder, Jonas Frost, 'being the lowest' was accepted. The funds required were raised by subscription and a voluntary rate. By the autumn of 1877, the new building was complete.[49]

ಬಂ

William Stovold Stace and his wife Martha, the schoolmaster and schoolmistress appointed to Watton National School in 1868, remained in post until 1878. Their places were then taken by Charles and Emily Lintott, who were to serve the school for a considerable time and maintain it in a satisfactory state.

Elementary education was made compulsory under legislation passed in 1876 and 1880 and an attendance officer prosecuted parents who did not send their children to school. At the same time, parents had to pay fees, which were set as follows in 1890: for tradesmen and farmers, 3d per week (equivalent to £1 today); for mechanics and journeymen, 3d for the first child and 2d for each subsequent child; and for labourers, 2d each for the first two children with no charge for subsequent children.[50] The following year, however, elementary education was made free.

Following the passage of the Education Act of 1902, responsibility for maintained schools in Norfolk passed to the county council, which established an education committee and, on 30 September 1903, sent out a form to every maintained school to gather information about its teachers, pupils, accommodation and furniture. The headteacher of Watton mixed school was still the college-trained and now long-serving Charles Lintott, who had completed 25 years at the school and was paid a salary of £110 per year (equivalent to about £8,600 today). He was a widower, his wife Emily having died in 1902, but he carried on and was still in post in 1911. According to George Jessup, 'Charles Lintott was loved and respected by some pupils, disliked by others and feared by all'.[51] Cecil Chapman commented that Charlie Lintott was 'a name remembered by some of his pupils for many years after they left school'.[52]

In 1903, Lintott recorded that the school had 168 pupils on roll, the average attendance being 149. The children were now organised in seven standards. The higher standards were taught in the main room by Lintott himself, with the assistance of another certificated teacher, Mrs Louisa Toombs, who had worked in the school for seven years but was paid only £45 per year. A third certificated teacher had just left, and so the younger children were taught by pupil teachers (pupils who were training 'on the job' to be teachers). Their lessons took place in the extension at the rear, built in 1871. The desks were arranged in parallel rows and the resources available to the teachers comprised four blackboards with easels and the contents of four cupboards. The school had a museum, its collections probably being used in the 'object lessons' provided as part of the curriculum. As well as the traditional 3Rs (reading, writing and arithmetic), the curriculum also included singing.[53]

The headteacher of the infant school on Church Walk was Mrs A E Edwards. Although not college-educated, she had a teaching certificate and was paid £55 per year. Her only assistance came from Dora Stringer, a monitor. The school's roll was 58 in 1903 but the average attendance was only 44. In the school room, the 'babies' were accommodated in a 'gallery' on one side and the other children in parallel desks on the other.[54] In September 1913, Mrs Edwards was succeeded as headteacher by Mary Ann Sykes, formerly schoolmistress at Ashill.[55] In February 1919 the east end of the building and part of its north wall collapsed and temporary arrangements had to be made for the accommodation of the pupils, who eventually transferred to the former National School.[56]

Over the period 1900-1915, the number on roll at Watton's mixed school varied between 137 and 168. Theoretically, there was room for 187 pupils but there were only the two rooms: the 'main room' and the 'class room'. Of the premises, an unsigned report submitted to the Board of Education in March 1913 noted: 'Since the last report, several improvements have been carried out. A partition has been erected in the main room; a new floor has been laid down in the class room, and suitable desks have been provided for the junior scholars. The school has an untidy appearance for various reasons. The internal walls are dirty and discoloured in places; much of the wood-work requires painting or varnishing; the maps, pictures and diagrams are not dusted and cleaned as frequently as they should be, and the cupboard accommodation is inadequate. Brown paper, paints and odds and ends stored on the tops of cupboards, miscellaneous stacks of books and papers, and numerous boxes of all shapes and sizes, not only give the school an untidy appearance but they prevent the floors being properly swept, collect dust, and possibly spread infection.' Somewhat surprisingly, in view of the foregoing, it was noted that: 'This school has improved steadily of recent years. The staff has recently been strengthened and all the teachers appear to take a great interest in their work. In the lower part of the school, which is now organised as a junior section with two women teachers, some remarkably good work is being done. The recently provided partition facilitates instruction in the upper part of the school'.[57]

༄༅།

Other educational opportunities continued to be available to those who could pay for them. In 1871, the Misses Knopwood, 'who have for some time past been residing on the Continent',[58] announced that they had moved into Harvey House, in which 'they intend opening a Ladies' Boarding and Day School [where] pupils entrusted to their charge will receive a sound and liberal education, including careful moral and religious training'.[59] The school seems to have operated a four-term year, sessions beginning in January, March or April, July or August and October. From October 1873, the announcements referred to only a single Miss Knopwood. A clue to the school's curriculum came in a subsequent advertisement: 'Miss Knopwood receives young ladies as boarders and educates them in thorough English and the usual accomplishments. The vicar of Watton [the Revd Dr Wrenford] kindly gives a Bible lecture once a fortnight'.[60] The school was still functioning in July 1877 but may have closed after that. The Misses Knopwood moved out of Harvey House in 1879.[61]

A few years later, another girls' boarding school was opened in White House, Thetford Road, by Elizabeth Curl, a widow whose husband, a 'gentleman' and retired farmer almost 30 years older than herself, had died in August 1882. Mrs Curl began by advertising, in 1884, that she was 'desirous to receive 2 or 3 children to educate with her own. Maternal care, and every comfort'.[62] Aged 33 at the time, she had three young children, the youngest of whom had been born after her husband's death. In 1885, her project had developed into a school for young ladies, offering instruction in English, French, music, drawing, dancing and calisthenics, with 'every home comfort and careful training'. Private lessons in French and music were offered, and a dancing class was organised at the *George*.[63]

At the end of the year, Mrs Curl 'gave her breaking-up party in the large room at the *George* Hotel…The programme consisted of recitations, French and

English, in which the pupils acquitted themselves in a manner that reflected the highest credit on the training given them by Mrs Curl. A variety of pianoforte music was also given by the pupils, in all of which they displayed a remarkable degree of intelligence'. The vicar of Watton, the Revd Dr Wrenford, and his wife, whose grandchildren were probably among the participants, attended the event. Afterwards, the vicar gave a speech of thanks, the memory of which would not have lessened his embarrassment when, in 1887, his eldest son became bankrupt, owing money to Mrs Curl.[64]

At the beginning of 1886, Mrs Curl was able to announce that her school was 'under the patronage of the right honourable Lady Walsingham' and by the end of the year she was assisted by 'a lady holding first-class certificates with honours'. Pupils were 'prepared for public examinations' and the private lessons now also included drawing and lustra [oil] painting. A 'preparatory class for boys under ten' was added from the beginning of 1887.[65] The school continued to operate for another ten years but, in 1897, Mrs Curl moved to Harvey House and, either then or shortly afterwards, she retired. The 1901 census recorded her, aged 50 and described as 'retired principal of school', living in Enfield with her two sons and daughter.

With the demise of her school, private educational provision in Watton appears to have come to an end.

## Notes

1. Will of Edward Goffe, 1612; NRO, ANW Dewpleet fo 66; extracts in PD 566/152.
2. NM, 27 September 1766.
3. NC, 2 January 1773.
4. It is unclear where this was: there were no houses near the church at this time.
5. NM, 1 January 1780.
6. Pigot's Directory of Norfolk, 1822.
7. Watton parish register, 1730-1799; NRO, PD 218/28.
8. Parliamentary Papers, *A Digest of Parochial Returns made to the Select Committee appointed to inquire into the Education of the Poor*, 1819.
9. Collection of papers relating to Watton charities and description and tenure of parish property, November 1841; NRO, ACC 2023/12.
10. Correspondence of the Poor Law Commissioners with Wayland Poor Law Union, 1842; TNA, MH12 8617.
11. White's Directory of Norfolk, 1836.
12. Pigot's Directory of Norfolk, 1830.
13. NM, 14 June 1834.
14. White's Directory of Norfolk, 1836.
15. Pigot's Directory of Norfolk, 1839.
16. NC, 30 November 1839.
17. Watton vestry minute book, 1842-83; NRO, PD218/89.

18. Correspondence of the Poor Law Commissioners with Wayland Poor Law Union; TNA, MH12 8617.
19. Ibid.
20. NC, 21 May 1842.
21. Bundle of papers regarding Watton school and church; NRO, ACC 2023/12.
22. Watton National School, building grant plans; NRO, P/BG 126.
23. NM, 20 September 1851.
24. Francis White's Directory of Norfolk, 1854.
25. Craven's Directory of Norfolk, 1856.
26. Post Office Directory, 1858.
27. NC, 2 June 1860.
28. NN, 21 January 1865.
29. NM, 11 January 1868.
30. NN, 10 April 1869.
31. NN, 10 April 1869.
32. Under the 'Revised Code' of 1862.
33. NM, 12 May 1869.
34. BNP, various dates, 1820-23.
35. Pigot's Directories of Norfolk, 1822, 1830, 1839; White's Directory of Norfolk, 1836. Fendick was described as 'for many years a schoolmaster and surveyor at Watton' after his death in 1866. He left a legacy of £10 for the poor of Watton, which was distributed in coal and bread; NC, 5 January 1867. Starke and Fendick drew a map of the estate of Edward Younge in 1808, four years before the latter's bankruptcy.
36. White's Directory of Norfolk, 1836; Pigot's Directory of Norfolk, 1839; NM, 9 January 1836 and 2 June 1836.
37. NN, 23 February 1850. According to the NC, 1 March 1851, Griffin was 'late of Somerton College, London'. His school was listed in Craven's Directory of 1856 but he had already resigned his ministry by April 1855, his intention to do so being reported in British Banner 1848, 14 February 1855.
38. Robin A Brown with John Newton and Andy Reid, *Shadows on the Summer Grass: some essays on aspects of a Norfolk parish from prehistory to the 20th century* (Woodcock Hall Publications, 1998).
39. NM, 17 July 1847.
40. NM, 19 October 1850.
41. NN, 12 November 1853.
42. NN, 29 October 1853.
43. NM, 11 December 1858.
44. NM, 10 October 1874. Fifteen children from dame schools who were admitted to the National School were described as 'all very backward'; perhaps they came from the other dame school (quoted in E Farrall, 'Education in Watton, 1812-99' in WEA (1975).
45. Watton National School building grant plans; NRO, P/BG 126.
46. NC, 24 June 1876. These figures had been revised from those provided in 1873, 203 and 53 respectively, as reported in the NM, 1 March 1873.
47. NN, 15 October 1870.
48. LA, 17 April 1875.
49. Watton vestry minute book, 1842-83; NRO, PD218/89. The school building bears a plaque bearing the date 1876.
50. E Farrall, 'Education in Watton, 1812-99' in WEA (1975).

51. G Jessup (1985).
52. Cecil F Chapman, *More about Grandad's Watton* (1985).
53. Survey of Norfolk schools, 1903; NRO C/ED 183/1.
54. Ibid.
55. DMG, 4 October 1913.
56. The collapse is recalled vividly by George Jessup (who was a pupil at the time) in G Jessup (1985).
57. Documents submitted to the Board of Education; TNA 21/13105.
58. NN, 25 March 1871.
59. NC, 1 April 1871.
60. NN 24 July 1875.
61. NN, 27 September 1879.
62. LA, 2 August 1884.
63. TWT, 23 May, 13 June 1885.
64. NM, 26 December 1885.
65. TWT, 11 December 1886; NC, 15 January 1887.

# Celebrating and Campaigning

The people of Watton knew how to put on a show, especially to mark event connected with the royal family. Such celebrations had a long history, as the account of the proclamation of King George II in 1727 shows.[1] Many simila events took place in the 19th century.

One occasion that was celebrated with great enthusiasm was the wedding o the Prince of Wales, the future Edward VII, in 1863. A dinner 'of the usual old English fare' was provided for 'between 700 and 800 poor persons'. They sat a 'tables situated in the centre of the principal street…ranged in three rows, with a triumphal arch crossing the street at each extremity'.[2]

The prince passed through Watton on several occasions on his way to visi his friend, Lord Walsingham, at Merton Hall to enjoy a few days' hunting and shooting. In January 1865, having arrived from Sandringham at Swaffham station he travelled to Merton in a carriage drawn by four horses and was greeted by people in Ashill, Saham and Watton on his way. In Watton, as he passed the Nationa School, 'the children…stood outside and greeted the Prince, who appeared particularly to notice the salutation, and very graciously acknowledged it. When passing the Market-hill and the *George* Inn, the very large number of people who were congregated there warmly greeted him. The principal shops were closed, an evident token that the Watton tradesmen determined to make the Prince's visit a holiday'.[3] A great crowd of people followed him but those on foot were turned back at the gates of Merton Park, where members of the county aristocracy had been assembled. The following day, many birds were shot and a fox was chased with hounds. The fox escaped.

The Prince came to Merton again in November 1870 and November 1873. On the latter occasion, he arrived after dark and was greeted by a series of 'coloured fires', one on Saham College, followed by another on the bridge over the Little Wissey. In the town, people 'were able to get a view of His Royal Highness by the light of some burning torches held by men and boys on each side of the street.'[4] Another visit took place in November 1882; this time, the Prince arrived by train at Watton station, to be greeted by Lord Walsingham on the platform, and passed through triumphal arches erected outside the station and across the road by the police station.[5]

After the death of Queen Victoria in January 1901, arrangements were made to celebrate the coronation of King Edward VII on 26 June. The ceremony in Westminster Abbey had to be postponed until 9 August as the king had been taken ill with an abcess but Watton, like most other places, went ahead with the planned celebrations anyway. The Watton Town Band assembled in the market place at 10 am and led a procession to St Mary's Church for an inter-denominational service, a sign of the improved relationships between the Church of England and the Nonconformists. Afterwards, 250 children were given dinner in the Wayland Hall, while the band played outside. Next, the band, who worked hard that day, led another procession to the cricket ground off Norwich Road, where marquees had been erected and dinner was served to the adults, accompanied by the usual toasts and speeches. The day ended with a variety of sports on the field.[6]

The following year, on 24 May (the late Queen's birthday), 'Empire Day' was celebrated for the first time. It became an annual event and was marked in Watton by a parade up the High Street, in which children from the school participated, waving flags, supervised by their teachers.

The celebration of the coronation of Edward VII left a lasting legacy for Watton. During the autumn of 1901, the funds left over from the events of 26 June were devoted to purchasing over 130 lime trees and planting them in Church Walk to form an avenue which remains to this day. At the end of the year, Lord Walsingham presented the town with 'a handsome set of gates and palisades' which were 'erected at both ends of Church Walk to take the place of the...unsightly chains'.[7] The gates became known as the Walsingham Gates. The piers and railings installed in 1902 were listed in 1983 and remain *in situ* but the gates are no longer the originals. They were recreated at Wayland Prison in 1999—2002 and are of tubular metal,

*Empire Day parade passing the Green Man, 1907.*
(George Jessup family collection via Julian Horn)

whereas the originals were of cast iron.⁸

༄༅

In 1857, the landowners and farmers of Watton and district formed the Wayland Agricultural Association and organised the first-ever Wayland Show. The association had grown out of, and in co-ordination with, the Association for Promoting and Rewarding Good Conduct and Encouraging Industrious Habits among Servants, Cottagers and Labourers, then in its 23rd year. The first show took place on a field behind Back Street, owned by the solicitor, William Massey. It featured 'an exhibition of stock, which had never before been attempted'. Horses, bulls, cows, sheep and lambs were displayed, along with roots and a few agricultural implements. An exhibition of fruit and vegetables from cottage gardens was held at the same time in the Wayland Hall.

The show was successful. 'The ground was visited by several hundred persons, including a large number of ladies and', added a newspaper, 'the weather being exceedingly fine, the scene was one of animation such as is but occasionally witnessed at Watton'.⁹ A band played and everyone enjoyed themselves. Also admitted, at 6d per head, were 600 members of the 'working classes'.¹⁰ Lord Walsingham presented prizes and provided venison for the evening dinner in the Wayland Hall, at which he presided, which was attended by 'upwards of a hundred gentlemen'.¹¹ The meal was prepared at the *George* and carried across, which must have been a tricky operation.

The following year's meeting, on 22 September 1858, was an even greater success. The morning saw 'a very excellent cottagers' show of fruits and vegetables in the Wayland Hall'. At noon, Lord Walsingham 'distributed prizes to the successful competitors at this exhibition, and also to agricultural tradesmen's servants, shepherds, yard-men, team-men, laborers [sic], cottagers, ploughmen, etc, who had been commended for industry and good conduct'.¹² The show of stock took place in the afternoon and was followed by the dinner in the evening, again presided over by Lord Walsingham who, with his agent, Henry Woods¹³ (secretary of the association), played an active role in supporting the show. The following year's show was blighted by poor weather but that held on 26 September 1860 in 'a spacious field occupied by Mr Jacobs'¹⁴ was, again, very successful, attracting about 2,000 visitors in the course of the day.

By 1864, the Wayland Agricultural Association was being hailed as 'this admirable association'; the show of that year, it was stated, 'fully upheld its well-known reputation as one of the best district societies in the Eastern Counties'.¹⁵ It was now held on the old cricket ground behind the *Bull Inn*, 'the approach to which, as well as the main street in the vicinity of the Wayland-hall, was gaily decorated with evergreens and flags, and the thronged avenues and bustling crowds showed that the meeting was evidently considered the great event of the year, and worthy

*Wayland Show day, c.1910.*
*(Norfolk Record Office, ACC 2015/277)*

The sports took place on the field opposite the brewery, owned by Thomas Crawshay Frost.

of being made a general holiday'.[16] Owing to an epidemic of cattle plague, no shows were held in 1865 or 1866 but they were resumed thereafter.

On show days, numerous sideshows to the main event were staged and carriages and carts of all descriptions flooded into the town, causing traffic congestion. During the show of 1868, 'the town of Watton was quite lively… presenting all the appearance of a fair. Booths [and] stalls…lined the streets, flags floated from the windows, and everyone seemed to be bent on holiday-making'.[17] Not everyone was thrilled by the 'usual collection of shooting galleries, steam hippodromes, etc…in the market place'[18], nor by the 'host of nondescript individuals'[19] who came to the town. Nevertheless, the Wayland Show had become a highlight of the year in Watton and its surrounding district, and was to remain so.

*Hurdles for the Wayland Show, c.1910.*
*(Norfolk Record Office, ACC 2015/277)*

*Wayland Show exhibition of poultry in Wayland Hall c.1910.*
*(Norfolk Record Office, ACC 2015/277)*

಄ೋ

Lord Walsingham was a great supporter of the Wayland Show but he was certainly not supportive of the agricultural labourers' campaign for better terms and conditions.

In the early 1870s, the first trade unions for agricultural labourers were established in Norfolk. A branch of the Swaffham district of Joseph Arch's National Agricultural Labourers' Union was set up in Watton. The idea of combining to secure improvements in their wages, or to prevent their reduction, quickly caught on among the Norfolk labourers; 'Trades unionism swept the county like some massive religious revival'.[20] In the Watton area, the movement reached its peak in 1873. On 22 January: '500 labourers assembled in the Wayland Hall, to hear addresses upon the labour question.' By the end of the meeting, the Watton branch had about 100 members.

The union had already had an impact, as 'it is stated that all the men on one of the farms in this neighbourhood struck last week, as their master had dropped their wages to 12s (equivalent to about £40 today) per week, under the impression that the other farmers in the district would do the same. He had given the men notice that he should do so a week previous, whereupon they struck, but when he found that the step he had taken was not general, he immediately agreed to the men's terms, and to show them that he had no wish to wrong them, gave them 13s

6d per week instead of 13s'.[21] The men's victory, no doubt, helped to encourage other labourers in the Watton area to join the union.

The landowners and farmers hit back. On 20 February 1873, at a meeting in Watton, they agreed to establish a Wayland Farmers Defensive Association. Lord Walsingham presided, stating his objection to 'the system of compulsion by which labourers sought to enforce advances in their wages'. He had himself tried to persuade the labourers of Merton and Tottington not to join the union but had been rebuffed: not one had accepted his offer to reimburse them for their membership fees and a few more labourers joined the Watton branch of the union afterwards, the membership of which 'now number[ed] about 250 men'.[22] On 24 February, Lord Walsingham tried, unsuccessfully, to persuade the Board of Guardians of Wayland Poor Law Union to deny poor relief to labourers who were on strike.[23]

The labourers held a further meeting at the Wayland Hall on 26 February and, again, the hall was 'crowded to excess', with over 500 said to have attended. On this occasion, the General Secretary of the union presided and another speaker presented a petition for all labouring men to have the vote, declaring that: 'They wanted men in Parliament who would look after their rights, and did not want men who went shooting bulls with the Prince of Wales'. He had probably had a rough reception when he arrived for the meeting, commenting that 'he could say from experience that afternoon in the Corn Hall, that the labourers were not the only persons who could use abusive language'.[24]

Further meetings were held at the Wayland Hall from time to time over the following two years, and other methods of campaigning were tried. On 23 July 1873, the union organised an open-air 'public tea' in a field. 'Between 300 and 400 labourers, most of whom wore blue ribbons or rosettes on their hats, marched through the streets of the town, a band of music and a labourer carrying a large blue and white flag leading the way'. Blue and white were the colours of the Liberal Party. The report continued: 'On reaching the field, their wives joined them, and the company, upwards of 600 in all, partook of tea. After tea, another march round the town took place',[25] followed by an evening meeting in the Wayland Hall.

In January 1874, the membership of the union's Watton branch had slipped slightly, to 230.[26] The next few months were quiet but on 22 September, 'there was a little excitement in the town, a "Great Demonstration" having been announced freely in the town and neighbourhood'. Several hundred people paraded through the town, proceeded by a band, and then sat down to tea in a field as they had done the previous summer. Joseph Arch, the founder and leader of the union, was expected but arrived later than scheduled, giving the very modern excuse that he had missed his train to Swaffham (the line from there to Watton had not yet opened). Another modern form of communication did work successfully for Arch: he sent his message by telegram, a telegraph office having opened in Watton at the end of 1871.[27]

Union activity subsided for a few years after 1874 but meetings continued to take place from time to time in Watton. The union's motto was 'Live and Let Live' and routine gatherings continued at the public house of that name, at the corner of Church Walk and Dereham Road, although occasionally the *Jolly Farmers* in Brandon Road was used instead, as it was for a branch meeting of 2-300 people in January 1876.[28] There was a revival in the early 1890s and in 1892 Joseph Arch, now a Liberal MP, did manage to address a meeting of the labourers in Watton.[29] Unsuccessful strikes followed and many of the farm labourers involved were evicted from their cottages. A new union, led by George Edwards, developed from 1906 onwards but, by now, the focus was largely on securing improvements through political rather than strike action

ೞಣ

The labourers' campaign for the vote achieved success in 1884, when the Conservative government of Benjamin Disraeli extended the franchise to all male householders and men who paid £10 a year in rent. A large meeting in support of the Act took place at the Wayland Hall on 2 July 1884, chaired by the Liberal MP for King's Lynn and attended by the local Liberal candidates who, no doubt, hoped that the votes of the newly enfranchised agricultural labourers would help them to win seats at the next election.

Their hopes were not to be realised immediately. Watton had been a Conservative town since the 18th century, voting solidly for Tory candidates in contested elections up to the Great Reform Act of 1832 and then for the Conservatives up to 1865, the last contested election before the Ballot of Act of 1872 ended the practice of open voting.[30]

The success of the Conservative, William Bagge, in the Western Division of Norfolk in the general election of 1847 was celebrated in Watton with a banquet at the *George* (tickets 10s 6d), with Lord Walsingham in the chair.[31] Five years later, a similar event took place at the *Crown*, again chaired by Lord Walsingham, to celebrate the return, unopposed, of William Bagge and George Bentinck for the two-member seat of West Norfolk.

An even more extravagant celebration followed the election of the Hon Thomas de Grey, son of Lord and Lady Walsingham, who partnered William Bagge for the Conservatives in the general election of 1865 and for whom 'the enthusiasm manifested by the people of Watton was very great'.[32] People lined the street to cheer him, flags were hung from windows and 'a temporary triumphal arch, of oak boughs and small flags, was erected across the road, opposite the *Crown Inn*'. When De Grey's carriage approached from the direction of Swaffham, cheers went up and a band played. At the National School, 'they halted, and the horses from the carriage in which Mr De Grey...was riding were immediately detached and the ropes fastened to eight or ten men, who drew the carriage after the band through the town of Watton'. At the Market Place, de Grey stood on the seat of his carriage and made a speech, greeted with more cheers. He then resumed his journey to Merton Hall, still pulled by the men who had drawn him through the town and preceded by the band.

One of the local newspapers detected signs of impending change in the 1880 general election, the first time Watton had been a polling place. The polling station was the boys' school-room at the National School. The Liberal committee rooms were at the *George* and those of the Conservatives at the *Crown*, giving a new twist to the rivalry between Watton's two premier inns. The town was decorated with bunting and placards in the colours of the two parties: blue and white for the Liberals and pink and purple for the Conservatives. There was no violence or acrimony, although 'about 50 or 60 boys, with old tin kettles, tin whistles, a drum, and tin trays, etc, marched up and down the town during the afternoon and evening making a most discordant noise, occasionally stopping and "beating up" with renewed vigour immediately under the committee room windows of each party'. While conceding that, as a result of the introduction of the secret ballot, the local results were 'mere conjecture', the newspaper nevertheless concluded that: 'Considering the very few Liberals there are even now in this place, the results... show that Liberalism has gained ground here'.[33] But not enough to change the overall result.

The 1885 general election, the first after the extension of the franchise in 1884, was keenly contested. Watton was part of the newly-created South-West Norfolk single-member constituency. The polling place for the district was, again, the boys' schoolroom, where 'van and waggon loads of voters arrived from the villages' from early in the day, giving rise to 'a considerable amount of good-natured banter... between the parties on either side as the laden vehicles of their friends, displaying their colours, passed down the town'. The following day, a crowd gathered outside the post office, where the result (a Conservative victory) was announced to cheers.

One of the leading Liberals of the town was John Edmund Alexander, retired shopkeeper and mainstay of the Congregational Chapel, whose views had been condemned as 'objectionable' by Lord Walsingham two months previously.[34] When he, Stephen Gowing (of the printing firm) and two other prominent Liberals arrived from Swaffham by road, they were mobbed. Alexander's hat was knocked off and 'quickly kicked to pieces by the crowd' and, when their vehicle reached Alexander's house (Gladstone Villa), 'through fear of being molested, Mr Alexander was obliged to take refuge in the police-station and Mr Gowing managed to escape up the Thetford Road'. Later, Lord Walsingham was greeted enthusiastically when he arrived at the station and 'during the evening, a number of men amused themselves by carrying a burning effigy through the streets'.[35]

*The Liberal Club, 1910.*
(Lesley Cowling)

The posters supported the Liberal MP, Richard Winfrey, who held his seat in both elections in 1910.

Watton continued to be represented by Conservative MPs until 1906, when the Liberal Party swept to power nationally and the Liberal, Richard Winfrey, won the South-West Norfolk seat, defeating the sitting member, Sir Thomas Hare. The election took place on 25 January and, after the declaration of the result the following day, the successful candidate met his enthusiastic supporters in the Wayland Hall. Over five months later, on 4 June, a large celebration was organised: the town band played in the market place and then

*The Conservative HQ at Wayland Hall, 1910.*
(Norfolk Record Office, ACC 2015/277)

Hare was the Conservative candidate and the party's committee rooms were in Wayland Hall from January 1910.

600 people sat down to a 'monster tea' in three marquees pitched on W S Hall's auction ground. In the evening, a thousand crammed into the largest marquee to hear speeches from Winfrey and others.[36]

The Liberals held the seat in the two general elections of 1910 and continued to do so until 1920 when it was won for the Labour Party, in a by-election, by George Edwards, the agricultural labourer and union activist.[37]

෪෬

Norfolk County Council came into existence in 1889, following the passage of the Local Government Act the previous year. Five years later, in 1894, another Local Government Act created urban and rural district councils, and parish councils. Watton came within the jurisdiction of Wayland Rural District Council and acquired an elected parish council. These measures transferred the administrative responsibilities of the magistrates to the new elected bodies and greatly reduced the role of the Anglican clergy in local administration.

Watton Parish Council met for the first time on 4 January 1895. Its members were William Meek, harness maker; George Minns, farmer; Alexander Banham, auctioneer; John Edmund Alexander, 'gentleman'; Henry Mallins, doctor; Robert James Waters, painter; Daniel Dunnett, grocer and draper; Matthew Rae, tailor and draper; William Whalebelly, butcher; George Cubitt Durrant, grocer and draper; and James Leggate, agricultural labourer.[38] They represented a good cross-section of Watton society and a balance of religious and political affiliations. Among the matters the parish council discussed in the period up to World War I were the management of the town's property, for which they took over responsibility, and, in conjunction with the rural district council, the provision of services—sewerage, water supply, installing pavements and watering the street with the parish water cart, and securing allotments for the inhabitants to cultivate.

They were cautious about making decisions, especially if they entailed spending the ratepayers' money, and so their impact on the town was not as great or as rapid as it might have been.

But progress was made, if slowly.

**Notes**

1. See Chapter 7.
2. NM, 14 March 1863.
3. NN, 21 January 1865.
4. BNP, 15 November 1873.
5. NN, 25 November 1882.
6. NN, 28 June 1902.
7. NN, 27 December 1902.

8. Thanks to Kathryn Stallard of Watton Town Council for this information.
9. NN, 26 September 1857.
10. NM, 26 September 1857.
11. NN, 26 September 1857.
12. LA, 25 September 1858.
13. Henry Woods retired in 1888 and died in 1890. He resided at Rokeles Hall, which Lord Walsingham had purchased.
14. NC, 29 September 1860.
15. NN, 1 October 1864.
16. NC, 1 October 1864.
17. NC, 19 September 1868.
18. NM, 16 September 1876.
19. NM, 29 September 1888.
20. A Howkins, *Poor Labouring Men: Rural Radicalism in Norfolk 1870-1923* (History Workshop Series, Routledge and Kegan Paul, 1985).
21. BNP, 28 January 1873.
22. BNP, 25 February 1873.
23. Robert Lee, *Rural Society and the Anglican Clergy* (Boydell Press, 2006).
24. NM, 5 March 1873.
25. NM, 26 July 1873.
26. *Lowestoft Journal*, 31 January 1874.
27. NM, 26 September 1874.
28. LA, 22 January 1876.
29. NM, 15 October 1892.
30. Poll books, 1768, 1806, 1817, 1865.
31. NC, 11 September 1847.
32. NM, 29 July 1865.
33. DMG, 17 April 1880.
34. In a letter to the NM, 2 September 1885. Lord Walsingham insisted, however, that 'the last thing…I wish to see is an antagonistic feeling between Churchmen and Dissenters', and he consented to Lady Walsingham opening the Congregational Chapel's bazaar.
35. DMG, 12 December 1885.
36. DMG, 9 June 1906.
37. Wikipedia.
38. Watton Parish Council, minutes, book 1, 4 January 1895.

# Connections and Diversions

In 1869, in a significant development for the town, Watton was connected to the national railway network.

Watton may have been a somewhat isolated place, but it had never been entirely unconnected with the rest of the country. Coaches and waggons plied regularly between Watton and Norwich, London and elsewhere, and carts connected the town with the navigable waterway at Narborough. However, Watton did not acquire a railway until 20 years after Thetford (on the Norwich to Brandon line, in 1845), Dereham (via Wymondham, in 1846) and Swaffham (via King's Lynn, in 1847). Watton, in the centre of the triangle formed by those three towns, had to wait.

Various schemes were proposed from time to time but did not come to fruition. In 1860, however, a plan to build a railway from Thetford to Watton was canvassed[1] and, at last, in 1866, an Act of Parliament was passed authorising the construction of a line from Roudham Junction, east of Thetford on the Norwich to Brandon line, to Watton. The proposal benefited from the influential financial and political support of Lord Walsingham, which probably helped to persuade the local

Watton railway station, c.1908.
*(From a glass negative taken by F W Bird, from the clearance of Harvey and Sons via Julian Horn.)*

landowners to invest in the line. The Thetford and Watton Railway Company was formed in July 1866 and J S Valentine was appointed as its engineer. The land required for the route was acquired and rails were purchased from the Crawshay Bailey Company of South Wales, owned by a relative of Thomas Crawshay Frost's. Valentine surveyed the line and Richard Walker of Ipswich was contracted to construct it. The work got under way at the end of May 1867.[2] Contracts were let for the construction of the stations and, at Watton, a goods shed, engine house and tank-house.[3]

On 14 October 1868, 'an engine, to which was attached a first and second-class carriage belonging to the Great Eastern Railway, ran for the first time along the entire length of line from Thetford to Watton…bringing with it T Barton Esq, one of the directors, Mr Valentine, the company's engineer, Mr Stevenson, district superintendent of the Great Eastern Railway, and other gentlemen. A large number of the townspeople were down to witness the arrival of the 'first train', as they called it, and gave hearty cheers as it came into the station-yard'.[4]

The line opened for regular freight traffic at the end of January 1869. However, arrangements for the connection with what was now the Great Eastern Railway at Roudham Junction were not completed until July and time-tabled passenger trains did not begin running until mid-October.

Meanwhile, discussion about extending the line to Swaffham had begun in 1867, offering the prospect of 'direct communication with the sea-side at Hunstanton and with the Northern coal ports' via King's Lynn.[5] The route was surveyed and the necessary Act of Parliament secured. A public meeting was held at the Wayland Hall on 2 March 1869 to consider how the railway should cross Norwich Road in Watton, the general view being that a level-crossing would be preferable to a high arch to carry the road over the railway. So Norwich Road did not acquire a hump-backed bridge.

Construction of the line to Swaffham was managed by a separate company, the Watton and Swaffham Railway Company (in which the Thetford and Watton company had a major stake) The section opened for goods traffic in September 1875 and to passengers two months later.[6] It was also hoped that the Watton to Thetford railway would connect with a line from Thetford to Bury St Edmunds and that did eventually happen in March 1876.

By 1878, when the whole route from Bury St Edmunds to Swaffham was served by passenger trains, there were three departures from Watton to Thetford on each weekday, with an extra service on Tuesday and Wednesday, and three for Swaffham, with two extra trains on Tuesdays. It was also noted that 'for the convenience of passengers attending Watton market on Wednesdays, a carriage will be attached to the goods train due to leave Swaffham at 1.40 pm and Holme Hale at 2 pm'. The passenger trains, pulled by tank engines, usually took between 50 minutes and an

*Thetford and Watton Railway poster, 1877.*
*(The National Archives, TNA, RAIL 1016/1)*

hour to reach Thetford, and 20 minutes to complete the journey to Swaffham.[7] Later, the number of trains rose to a maximum of five a day in each direction every day except Sunday, when there were two. An additional school service ran on weekdays.[8]

The railway opened up new possibilities for the people of Watton. In 1877, large posters were printed (by 'Gowing, steam printer, Watton') advertising fortnightly return tickets to Hunstanton, Great Yarmouth, Lowestoft and Cromer from 21 May onwards. They were not cheap; from Watton to Cromer, for example, the fares were 16s 9d first-class (equivalent to over £55 today), 12s 6d second-class and 8s 6d third-class. However, the farmers and larger shopkeepers were probably able to afford first-class while the third-class tickets were affordable for artisans and tradespeople. The following year, the offer was expanded to include more distant destinations: Aldeburgh, Harwich and Walton-on-the-Naze. If they could find the money, the people of Watton could now travel more quickly and easily to the seaside and spend a week or two there.[9]

After a modestly profitable start, the companies got into financial and operational difficulties. In 1879, the Thetford and Watton and Watton and Swaffham companies amalgamated and agreed to lease the whole line from Thetford to Swaffham to the Great Eastern Railway. The GER purchased the line outright in 1897.[10]

Before then, in 1877, a scheme had been proposed by a company called the Norfolk Central Railway for a line from Norwich to Downham Market and Wisbech, via Watton, which might have resulted in Watton becoming a major railway junction, the Crewe, or at least the Melton Constable, of Breckland. It would also have created a direct connection to Norwich, the lack of which led one Norwich-based writer to lament Watton's inaccessibility: 'To get there by railway involves a journey through a considerable part of west or mid-Norfolk, either by way of Thetford or of Dereham and Swaffham'.[11] But the projected east-west line was never built.[12]

Instead, Watton remained one of the five intermediate stations on the Thetford to Swaffham route. It did, however, become the operational centre of the line, boasting workshops and a turntable for the locomotives. The line became known as the 'Crab and Winkle', a name it shared with the Canterbury and Whitstable line in Kent and the Tollesbury and Kelvedon Light Railway in Essex.[13] It closed to passengers in 1964 and to freight the following year, a victim of the 'Beeching Axe'.

෩෬

The opening of the railway had an immediate impact on the local economy. Within days of the inauguration of Watton station for goods traffic, a local paper reported: 'A large number of trucks of coal have been brought to the station and seem to meet with ready sale. The public have already begun to feel the advantage of the railway in this respect particularly'. Coal which previously would have cost £1 5s or £1 6s could 'now be brought from the station for a pound per ton' (equivalent to over £60 today).[14] The following winter, those of the poorer inhabitants of the town who were entitled to free coal were required to take tickets signed by the trustees of the 'poor's allotment charity' to the railway station between nine and 12 o'clock on alternate Mondays to receive the coal from merchants who had contracted with the parish for the supply of '120 tons of the best Wallsend house coal'.[15]

The railway carried much agricultural produce and its opening sparked a plan to establish a cattle market in Watton. The initiative, proposed in December 1868, gained support, including from Lord Walsingham.[16] Matters proceeded rapidly and a fortnightly cattle market, behind the *George*, was inaugurated on 3 February 1869. It appears to have been very successful; 'There was a much better supply of cattle of all kinds than was expected, and they met with ready sale...Between twenty and thirty pens of sheep were sold...There was an unusual number of strangers in the town during the day'.[17] It was reported that animals had been sent to London by train although the lack of a satisfactory connection with the Great Eastern Railway at Roudham Junction remained an issue for a time.

The introduction of the fortnightly market for animals, and transport by rail, meant that the traditional fairs were no longer needed. The Fairs Act of 1871 gave the Home Secretary the power to abolish fairs if petitioned to do so. The magistrates of the Wayland Petty-Sessional Division promptly sent a petition, arguing that, at the fairs held since medieval times on 10 July and 11 October, 'considerable trade was formerly carried on in cattle and sheep [but] of late years no business has been transacted at those fairs and ...the remaining three fairs have ceased to be observed'. Furthermore, they claimed, using the wording in the Act, the 'customary annual fairs have become unnecessary, are the cause of grievous immorality and are very injurious to the inhabitants of the town'. The abolition order was issued on 6 November 1871.[18]

The sales of cattle, held on alternate Wednesdays, became a fixture in the town. In 1896, for example, they were conducted by Alexander Banham in the yard behind the *Bull*[19], while in 1899 the *Crown* was the venue. From 1899, sales of stock in Watton became competitive, when H G Barnham began holding a fortnightly sale of cattle, horses, sheep, pigs and poultry.[20] W S Hall entered the fray in 1902 and by 1903 both he and Barnham were conducting weekly sales, Hall on a site adjacent to Thetford Road and Barnham at the *Bull* before moving out in 1912 to a site on Norwich Road later acquired by Abels.[21]

The opening of the railway station encouraged building in its vicinity and along Norwich Road between the station and the town centre. In 1841, only one house stood between the recently-built new vicarage and the Willow House. In 1876, however, three plots immediately to the west of that one house were offered for sale as 'excellent pasture land or building ground'[22] and were promptly built upon.

By 1884 four more cottages had been built on the south side of Norwich Road.[23] Houses soon appeared on the north side of Norwich Road as well, and in Griston Road.

ಐಾ

For the first three-quarters of the 19th century, mail travelled to and from Watton by cart. It was received and distributed by a postmaster. That role was performed by the tenant of the *Crown* from 1782 until 1806 but from 1807 the postmaster was Edmund Oldfield. In 1822, his duties included supervising the arrival of mail from London and points south at 10.15 in the morning and its dispatch at 4.15 in the afternoon.[24] Oldfield died in July 1833 at the age of 84, having been 'for many years master of the post office [in Watton], and inspector of corn returns'. He seems to have done his work well: 'To a steady, temperate and well spent life, his lengthened years may be attributed – his peaceable demeanor gained him the esteem of his neighbours. His aged partner still lives to lament the loss of a kind husband, and his offspring a tender and effectionate [sic] father'.[25]

His successor, as the person in charge of the post office, was his daughter, Sarah Blade.[26] Sarah had married Robert Blade, a tailor, in 1803. They had at least six children, one of whom was named Edmund Oldfield Blade in honour of Sarah's father. Another was Maria Ann Blade, the teacher who was conducting the school at the Willow House in 1841. Sarah was widowed in 1827 but continued as postmistress until a month before her death in September 1841. During her tenure, the mail arrived earlier and departed later than in her father's time, reflecting the

*Watton Post Office 1906–14.*
(Steve Easter)

increasing speed of travel.²⁷

Sarah Blade's successor was her son, Edmund Oldfield Blade, tailor and draper, and the post office moved to his premises.²⁸ He had, however, become an insolvent debtor earlier in 1841²⁹ and his tenure of the post office appears to have lasted only until 1844.³⁰ In 1847 he was convicted on two counts of fraud and was sentenced to a month in prison for each offence.³¹

By 1851 the post office was located at the residence of George Wenham, watchmaker, his wife Elizabeth and their family. Now, with the Norfolk Railway operational, the mail from London was arriving even earlier: at 5 am in 1854 and 4.30 am in 1858.³² The business of the post office had expanded to include the issue and cashing of money orders. George died in 1860 but Elizabeth took over as postmistress and was still performing that role, which now included custodianship of the Post Office Savings Bank, in 1869.³³ By 1871, she had probably relinquished her responsibilities as postmistress, although, with the assistance of two daughters, she still had a jewellery and silversmithing business on the south side of the High Street.³⁴ In 1872, the postmaster was another watchmaker and jeweller: Richard James Johnson. The post office was also, from Christmas Day 1871, a telegraph office³⁵ and so the people of Watton were now able to send telegrams and benefit from instant communication over the whole country.

On 25 May 1872, during Richard Johnson's brief tenure as postmaster, his servant of six weeks, Mary Ann Lusher, was charged with stealing various items out of letters that passed through the post office: 'a photographic portrait, a piece of black lace, a piece of black gimp [trimming], a neck-tie and certain patterns of dresses.' Johnson stated that 'after the arrival of the mail cart from Thetford, which reaches Watton at a quarter past four in the morning, [he] sorted the letters and placed the town letters on a table in the hall for the boy to deliver'.³⁶ He had already received complaints about letters not being received and suspicion fell on Mary Ann. A police officer was called, her boxes were searched (servants invariably had boxes in which they kept their possessions) and several stolen items found. She was sentenced to twelve months' imprisonment with hard labour.³⁷ The episode may have occasioned the sale of Johnson's 'watchmaker's and jeweller's shop and residence (now used as a post office)' in 1873 and his discharge as postmaster for 'grave mismanagement'.³⁸

The new postmaster was William Stovold Stace, the schoolmaster at the National School. He was to run Watton's post office for over 30 years. Initially, it was housed in the shop of George Adcock, watchmaker, and it may have been while he was operating from there that, in 1875, Stace was appointed as a dispenser of gun licences and game certificates and a distributor of postage stamps, which, as a local paper noted, would 'be a very great public convenience, as hitherto no stamp office has existed within ten miles of Watton'.³⁹

By 1878 Stace had left his post at the school and acquired premises in the High Street, two doors east of the *George*, which he was to share with the Harvey family (no relation to the Harveys of Harvey House). He and his wife Martha and two daughters were recorded there in the 1881 census, William styling himself as postmaster and stationer. A directory entry two years later was more expansive: 'Stace, William Stovold, printer (Stace and Harvey), postmaster, stamp distributor, stationer, bookseller, news agent, agent to the Alliance Insurance Company, clerk to the poor's allotment charity, post, money order and telegraph office'.[40] By 1891, in a sign of the times, he was employing his two daughters as telegraph clerks. William Stovold Stace eventually retired in 1906, by which time wall letter boxes had begun to appear in Watton, initially in Watton Green and outside the gasworks and later at the railway station and in Brandon Road.

When a new postmaster was appointed, the post office moved once again. Its new location was at the east end of Middle Street, in premises owned by Robert Waters, the builder, who applied successfully to extend the building out into the street and, in December 1906, persuaded the Parish Council, of which he was a member, to agree to rename the street Post Office Street.[41] Immediately before World War I, the postmistress was Lydia Maud Stibbon whose husband, Arthur, was a Relieving Officer for Wayland Poor Law Union.

The possibility of establishing a telephone exchange for Watton had been raised initially in 1903[42] but nothing happened because the expense was felt to be too great. What was claimed to be the first telephone line in Watton was a private one connecting the premises of Waters and Sons in Thetford Road and the High Street.[43] Meanwhile, other towns acquired telephone exchanges. Wymondham got one in 1907, for example, and even Caston was connected. Eventually, in 1913, a public meeting was held at the Wayland Hall and the decision was made to go ahead.[44]

Now Watton really was connected.

ഌൟ

As well as being more connected with the rest of the country, the people of Watton were finding new ways to enjoy themselves.

The creation of Loch Neaton, a long-term consequence of the building of the railway, opened up new possibilities for recreation. The Watton and Swaffham railway had purchased a piece of land west of the Dereham Road, from which soil was excavated to make the embankment that carried the line across Neaton Fen. Once the railway had been opened, the company no longer required the rest of the land and sold it back to its original owner, Mary Beets. She leased it to the Revd A T Crisford, rector of Ovington, who allowed it to flood, creating 'an artificial lake, to be known as "Loch Neaton"'. The main purpose was to provide 'a skating rink for the townspeople', but, the press report added, 'it is proposed to stock the water with fish, and also to make it available for bathing'.[45] Volunteers sealed the bottom of the hollow with clay and a pump was installed to convey the water supply from a nearby spring.[46] Trees were donated, 'to ornament the shores of the Loch'.[47]

On 10 June 1893, it was reported that Loch Neaton had been opened formally as a 'summer resort' and that 'great attractions and extensive improvements have been made during the past few months, every effort having been made to give the lake and its surroundings as pleasing an appearance as possible…The shallow parts have been deepened and the "heading" raised at the outlet so as to deepen the water all over the lake. Walks have been cut on the sides down to the water's edge and along the higher parts of the banks, these forming a very pleasant promenade for visitors.' The loch would be 'a nice little summer retreat for the people of the town and neighbourhood' transforming 'what was only a few months ago a huge ballast pit' into a pleasant place for picnics.[48]

When Mary Beets died in 1893, the loch, along with the former congregational chapel, 'now known as Loch House', came on to the market, described as 'an attractive piece of ornamental water…with promenade, now used for boating, fishing, bathing and skating and known as Loch Neaton'.[49] It was acquired 'for the benefit of the Town of Watton' by George Cubitt Durrant of the 'great shop' and Samuel Short, a baker and, in 1906, was conveyed, together with the shelters standing on it and a watermill at its north end, to trustees who had subscribed the funds for its purchase. A bandstand was presented by Elsie Buscall of London later in the same year. The conveyance stipulated that the trustees 'shall not under any circumstances whatever permit or allow the said recreation ground to be used on a Sunday for any other purpose than as a promenade, nor at any time for the sale of intoxicating liquor or for any political meetings whatsoever'. The restriction on Sunday use was dropped but the prohibitions regarding the sale of alcohol and political meetings remained, even when the recreation ground was transferred from the trustees to Watton Parish Council in 1962.[50]

൸൫

By the late 19th and early 20th century, the people of Watton were participating in an increasing number of team sports and recreations. The sport with the longest history in the town, from the 17th century onwards, was bowls. It remained popular and the pleasure grounds around the Loch Neaton incorporated a bowling green, which became the home of the Loch Neaton Bowls Club from 1900.[51]

Cricket had long been established and the town's team continued to play matches against sides from other towns and villages up to and beyond World War I. In May 1906, for example, a reporter noted: 'The season's fixtures of the Watton Cricket Club are just issued and already during the past few evenings passers-by on the Norwich Road have heard "the crack of the willow" on the cricket meadow',[52] this

*Watton cricket team c.1890—95.*
(George Jessup family collection via Julian Horn)
The player holding the bat is Charles Lintott, schoolmaster.

being the field on which the northern part of Charles Avenue was to be built later.

In the last two decades of the 19th century, association football was added to the sports practised in the town. In November 1884, 'a meeting was held at the *George Hotel*…to form a football club for Watton and district'. Those interested included the vicar's son, the Revd Joshua Booth Wrenford, who took the chair, along with Thomas Crawshay Frost, Dr Alexander and Frederick Robinson, the solicitor. The attendees 'decided that play should be according to Association rules',[53] reflecting the novelty of organised football in England: the original Football League was not to be formed until four years later, in 1888, although the first F A Cup final had taken place in 1872. The Watton teams, up to World War I, were not part of a league. The arrangements for matches were ad hoc, with fixtures against other local sides being arranged at the beginning of each season. The facilities for matches at Watton would have been rudimentary too, the pitch no more than a pasture field near the railway station.

When the players gathered at 2.30 pm on Saturday 15 November 1884, they played against each other 'with much spirit till dusk'.[54] The new year saw at least one competitive game, when Swaffham visited Watton and thrashed the hosts 4-0. The solicitor, Frederick Robinson, was the 'umpire'.[55] The following season, the

*Watton football team, 1897.*
(Museum4Watton)

Percy Vincent, who went on to become Lord Mayor of London, is in the middle row, on the left.

Watton team suffered an even worse defeat, 5-0, away to Thetford in December,[56] but they got their revenge in the return fixture the following March, winning 2-1. After another heavy defeat, 1-6, at home against Thetford in 1886,[57] interest seems to have lapsed for ten years.

In 1896, a new outfit, called the Wayland Club, was formed in Watton, playing in green and gold.[58] For the 1898-99 season, it changed its name to Watton FC but enjoyed little success; of 12 matches played, ten were lost and only one won.[59] Watton FC appears to have folded but in 1899-1900 a new club, Watton Rovers, emerged, and managed to win four of the eight matches it played.[60] It kept going for a few years; for 1902-03, the team turned out in a new strip, described as 'black shirt with yellow star and blue knickers',[61] but nothing was heard of it after that.

In November 1905, a meeting was held to re-start, yet again, a football club in the town, to be called Watton Town FC. It had influential support: Charles Robinson was elected president, Cubitt Durrant captain, Arthur Julnes vice-captain and H Harvey secretary.[62] This time, the club survived, if tenuously. In 1907-08, 16 fixtures were arranged but only two were actually played (both of which Watton lost); the other 14 were scratched because too few players turned up.[63] It was a similar story the following year[64] but 1909-10 saw a big improvement: the team, playing in red, won half the 14 matches they played. Competition from within the town may have spurred this improved performance: from 1911, the Watton Liberal Club also fielded a football team—and a cricket team, too. This was the state of play as World War I began in 1914.

೫෬

Indoor recreations and entertainments were also becoming available in Watton. In 1882, 'for the pleasure and instruction of the young men of the town during the winter evenings', two of the ground-floor spaces in the Wayland Hall were converted into 'reading and amusement rooms'. Newspapers were supplied and a bagatelle board, a 'Norfolk Billiard board', chess and draughts were provided.[65] The *Thetford and Watton Times*, the new local newspaper founded in 1880 was, no doubt, one of the titles taken, and in April 1883 it celebrated the success of the initiative, reporting that many young men had been 'kept from temptation' by the opportunities for 'social intercourse, combined with mutual instruction and amusement'.[66]

Thirty years later, in June 1913, Watton acquired its first cinema, the 'Royal Picture Palace'. According to a contemporary report, 'the opening of the Royal Picture Palace by Mr Fred Garner...elicited much enthusiasm on the part of the townsfolk...At the inaugural performance, many influential residents were present. Watton has hitherto known no other illumination save that of gas and oil lamps, and in consequence, the electric light used to illuminate the interior and exterior of the picture palace has caused no small amount of comment'.[67]

The 20th century had arrived in Watton.

## Notes

1. NM, 3 March 1860.
2. NM, 25 May 1867.
3. NC, 6 June 1868.
4. NC, 17 October 1868.
5. NC, 14 November 1868.
6. *Bury Free Press*, 20 November 1875.
7. Photocopy of a timetable in the author's possession.
8. G Williamson,'"The Crab and Winkle", the Railway', in WEA (1975).
9. Thetford and Watton Railway posters 1877, 1878; TNA, RAIL 1016/1.
10. R S Joby, *Rails across Breckland* (Klofron, 1976); G Williamson (1975).
11. NN, 28 November 1896.
12. R S Joby (1976).
13. Wikipedia.
14. NC, 6 February 1869.
15. NN, 1 October 1870.
16. NN, 26 December 1868.

17. NN, 6 February 1869.
18. TNA, HO 45/10231/B37096.
19. TWT, 11 July 1896.
20. DMG, 29 December 1900.
21. G Jessup (1985).
22. Sale particulars, 1876; NRO, ACC 12/2023.
23. Deeds in private possession.
24. Pigot's Directory of Norfolk, 1822.
25. NM, 20 July 1833.
26. Although, on her baptism, Sarah's father was named as Edward rather than Edmund Oldfield, the newspaper report of her son Edmund's appointment as postmaster in 1841 stated that the role had 'been in the family 34 years; NC, 28 August 1841.
27. White's Directory of Norfolk, 1836; Pigot's Directory of Norfolk, 1839.
28. NC, 28 August 1841.
29. BNP, 10 March 1841.
30. Although Edmund Blade was still listed as postmaster in White's Directory of 1845, George Wenham, who died in 1860, was said to have been postmaster for 16 years: NC, 16 June 1870.
31. Register of persons charged with indictable offences in 1847, accessed via findmypast.co.uk.
32. Francis White's Directory of Norfolk, 1854; Post Office Directory of Norfolk, 1858.
33. Post Office Directory of Norfolk, 1869.
34. Later, Elizabeth Wenham moved to Norwich. She died there, aged 80, in 1892 and was buried in Watton.
35. NN, 30 December 1871.
36. NN, 1 June 1872.
37. NM, 7 August 1872.
38. NC, 26 April 1873; NN, 10 October 1874.
39. *Lowestoft Journal*, 12 June 1875.
40. White's Directory of Norfolk, 1883.
41. DMG, 3 November and 15 December 1906; NN, 15 December 1906.
42. NN, 29 August 1903.
43. B Waters (2016).
44. DMG, 6, 13 September 1913.
45. NC, 19 November 1892.
46. G Jessup (1985).
47. NM, 24 December 1892.
48. DMG, 10 June 1893.
49. NN, 16 September 1893.
50. Watton Town Council documents; G Jessup (1985).
51. G Jessup (1985).
52. DMG, 12 May 1906.
53. NM, 15 November 1884.
54. NN, 22 November 1884.
55. NN, 31 January 1885.
56. DMG, 5 December 1885.
57. BNP, 19 October 1886.

58. EDP, 14 October 1896.
59. DMG, 9 September 1899.
60. DMG, 19 May 1900.
61. DMG, 13 September 1902.
62. DMG, 25 November 1905.
63. DMG, 5 September 1908.
64. DMG, 21 August 1909.
65. NM, 30 September 1882.
66. TWT, 7 April 1883.
67. *The Kinematograph and Lantern Weekly*, 19 June 1913.

# A Walk around the Town in 1911

Watton had changed in the 70 years since our previous imaginary walk around the town, in 1841.[1]

It had acquired a railway station, which was now the point of entry for many visitors to the town, and is the logical starting point for a second imaginary walk, around Watton, in 1911.

Watton in 1883.
(from the first edition of the Ordnance Survey 25-inch map)

Watton station, now operated by the Great Eastern Railway, had two platforms, with the 'up' (to London) and 'down' tracks lying between them. We'll arrive at the 'down' platform, the one nearer the town. To the south of it were sidings and goods sheds; to the north, beyond the level crossing on Norwich Road, was the cottage of the long-serving signalman, William Morley Rolfe, aged 67 in 1911. On alighting, we might see the station master, Alfred Page, aged 52, and a porter might offer his services. If we had travelled a long way, our first port of call might be the *Railway Hotel*, built on the north side of Norwich Road, right next to the level crossing, to coincide with the opening of the railway in 1868. The hotel had nine rooms, including a hall used for functions. In 1911, its landlady was Sarah Wright or, to give her full name, Sarah Maria Ann Wright.

ಸಂಬಂ

Sarah was a widow, her husband Richard William Wright having died in February 1896, aged only 40. Both Richard and Sarah were born into innkeeping. Richard's parents were tenants of the *Unicorn Inn* in Great Hockham, while Sarah came from the East End of London, her father being the licensee of hotels, first in Canning Town and then in Stratford. Perhaps they met through the hospitality trade. Having married in London in June 1882, they moved to Watton. Three children were

39. *Railway Hotel, c.1908.*
(*from a glass negative taken by F W Bird, from the clearance of Harvey and Sons via Julian Horn*)
Standing in the doorway is the owner, Sarah Wright.

born to the couple: Emily (1884), Elizabeth (1887) and Samuel Watkins Wright (1889). After her husband's death, in her widowhood, Sarah became another of the notable female publicans of Watton. She continued to run the *Railway Hotel* for almost a quarter of a century, until her death in April 1920. She was assisted by John Ward who, in 1891, as a 17-year-old, had been an ostler at the hotel and from 1899 was employed as its manager until, in 1910, he branched out and opened a fish and fruit shop next to the station.

Like her namesake, Susanna Wright, tenant of the *George* in the early 19th century, Sarah Wright showed enterprise in exploiting business opportunities. She provided 'good accommodation for horses, traps and bicycles',[2] which would have been advantageous for those travelling to and from the railway station, especially on Wayland Show days, when the Great Eastern Railway ran special trains for the many visitors who came to the town. On those occasions, Sarah also advertised refreshments, 'one shilling dinners from 1 o'clock. Tea from 4 o'clock'.[3] The *Railway Hotel* also hosted property sales. The Watton Town Band (formerly known as the Volunteer Band) met there, a room being provided for its rehearsals free of charge. Sarah promoted a successful concert by the Town Band in a packed Wayland Hall in January 1902, to raise funds for the Victoria Cottage Hospital.[4] Her younger daughter Elizabeth (Betty) may have been involved; she was an accomplished pianist and was active in organising concerts in Watton. As a result, on her marriage in September 1909 (to a 'gentleman' from Brixton, then a fashionable district of London), she was hailed as a 'popular figure' in the town.[5] The elder daughter, Emily, followed her parents' vocation; after her marriage, she and her husband took on the *King's Arms* in Swaffham.

Sarah Wright's son Samuel did not go into the hospitality trade. Instead, he worked as the booking clerk at Watton railway station for several years, played the drums in the town band, was involved in the Volunteer Force (an earlier version of the Territorial Army), which held meetings at the *Railway Hotel*, and was secretary of the town cricket club.[6] While working at the station, he rented a first-floor room at the hotel from his mother, for 4s a week. He was 'one of the most popular young men in the town and district', highly esteemed for his courtesy and kindness.[7]

When World War I broke out in August 1914, Samuel Wright immediately enlisted in the 4th Norfolks, 'one of the first Watton men who volunteered' and was to become 'the first man to give his life for his country'. On 17 June 1915, in a 'khaki wedding', he married Fanny Goward at St Mary's Church.[8] Two months later, on 13 August 1915, Corporal Samuel Watkins Wright was killed at Suvla Bay in the Dardanelles. He was one of the 29 young men from Watton who lost their lives in action during World War I.

ഌരു

The *Railway Hotel* was not the only example of development in the vicinity of the railway station. Behind the 'up' platform, in Griston Road, 14 houses had been built by 1911, four occupied by men whose work was connected with the railway. Development was also evident around the level-crossing where Norwich Road crossed the tracks. Immediately to the west of the railway line was Frederick Garner's carriage and cycle works and west of that was Hunton's iron and brass foundry. Clustered around the station were the premises of coal merchants, Charles Knott, Thomas Howlett and Arthur Julnes.

*Norwich Road and the level crossing, c.1908.*
(from a glass negative taken by F W Bird, from the clearance of Harvey and Sons via Julian Horn)

Garner's coach works is on the left, with Goodrick's (later Hunton's) ironworks out of shot further to the left.

*Customers at the Rose Inn c.1886.*
*(George Jessup family collection via Julian Horn)*

To the east of the station, the scene remained overwhelmingly rural. One ancient landmark had disappeared: the *Rose* public house. Its owner, Robert Willomatt Dennis, had died in 1869 and eventually, under his will, it was offered for sale by auction on 19 July 1876. The accommodation included a parlour, bar parlour, 'good club room' service rooms and four bedrooms, together with 'the stable and other outbuildings, yards, garden and land thereto adjoining'. The gardens were 'well stocked with good fruit trees and there are some good walnut trees standing thereon'.[9] The property was purchased by James Hook, the tenant, who sold it on to Steward and Patteson, the Norwich brewers. Hook remained in occupation until succeeded as tenant by Jeremiah Jessup.[10]

On the night of 14 August 1889, Jessup had to watch as the *Rose*, described at the time as 'one of the oldest houses in the town', caught fire and burned down. The adjoining building, still known as the Garden House, survived and Jeremiah Jessup continued as its tenant, together with the garden, land and 'cucumber house'.[11] A collection was organised for him by the Revd Dr T Brookes Wrenford, the vicar of Watton, assisted by Charles Lintott, master of the National School, and the sum raised more than covered his losses.[12] In 1911, the Garden House was occupied by Albert Semmence, a mineral water manufacturer.

In the 25 years before 1911, a few spacious new houses had been erected on this section of Norwich Road. Beyond them lay Rokeles Hall and Watton Green, the latter still comprising two farms and a scatter of cottages, mostly occupied by farm

*The Rose Inn after the fire.*
*(George Jessup family collection via Julian Horn)*

labourers and their families and elderly, retired people. A few cottages, almost entirely occupied by farm labourers, were also recorded in Redhill. Not much had changed here.

But walking west from the station, along Norwich Road towards the town, it was a different story. The vicarage, which in 1841 was a brand-new building, had seen several vicars come and go since then, and was now, in 1911, the home of the Revd Charles Barnett Nash, aged 54, with his wife, two daughters, two sons and two domestic servants. After the vicarage, starting about half way between the station and the Willow House, we would see new houses, first on the north side of the road and then on the south. Some of these were built in the 15 years after the opening of the railway; others had been erected subsequently.

A visitor to Watton in 1896 wrote: 'The houses on each side

*Threshing at Redhill Farm, early 20th century.*
*(George Jessup family collection via Julian Horn).*

A reminder that Watton was still, in part, a rural community, with several farms.

Norwich Road, looking towards the town centre, c.1908.
(from a glass negative taken by F W Bird, from the clearance of Harvey and Sons via Julian Horn)

[of Norwich Road] are mostly of the cottage variety, some of them looking very poor, until we get into the more central broad street of the old town'.[13] By 1911, however, especially on the north side of the road, there were also substantial Victorian and Edwardian villas, comprising from six to nine rooms. Some were occupied by people whose business premises were in the town centre, such as Alexander Banham, auctioneer; Herbert Adcock, grocer and cycle dealer (owner of the West End Stores at the west end of the High Street); and Sidney Tennant, builder (a former employee of Robert Waters, who had taken over Waters' former premises). Four of the dwellings on the north side of the road, with 'nice front gardens with palisadings and at the rear good kitchen gardens' were known as Beaconsfield Terrace.[14] The more modest dwellings in Norwich Road had a bricklayer, charwoman and laundress among their inhabitants.

On the corner of Norwich Road and Thetford Road stood the police station, opened in 1856, which also served as the residence of Police Inspector Robert John Clipperton, his wife, four daughters and two sons. Facing it on the north side of Norwich Road was the house with distinctive stepped gables, built by Samuel Rice between 1845 and 1851 and sold by him in 1851 to the surgeon, George Hargraves, in exchange for Hargraves' former premises in Front Street, west of the brewery, and a cash balance. Hargraves, in turn, sold the house to Henry Alexander in 1866 and it was Alexander, whose family were pillars of the Congregational

*New Inn corner, c.1908.*
(*from a glass negative taken by F W Bird, from the clearance of Harvey and Sons via Julian Horn*).
Part of the new police station of 1855 is on the left.

Church and strong supporters of the Liberal Party, who named it 'Gladstone Villa' in honour of the Liberal Prime Minister. Following Henry's death, the house was inherited by his brother, John Edmund Alexander, JP, who moved in in 1885 and was still the owner in 1911. After his death two years later, it was sold, renamed 'Elm Cottage'.[15]

Next door to Gladstone Villa was the Willow House, the home of Richard Robinson, solicitor, until his death in 1905 and now, in 1911, the residence of his son Frederick and his family. The willow tree which inspired its name had gone. On the evening of 19 November 1875, a 'destructive gale' had proved fatal to the splendid tree, which 'spreading as it did its beautiful and gracefully shaped branches far and high over the public road, was a familiar object of admiration to the passer-by'. The willow 'fell with a loud crash about nine o'clock, during the height of the gale, and reached quite across the road to the *New Inn*, and completely blocked the passage of the road for a time. The beauty and grandeur of this old tree on a frosty night', the report continued, 'with the gaslight shining through its branches, has frequently drawn forth expressions of admiration from those who have witnessed its beauty...and its untimely downfall is a subject of general regret'.[16]

White House Thetford Road, 1902.
(Julian Horn)

We'll now turn into Thetford Road. The first building on the right-hand (west) side was the former residence of Horatio Goodrick, agricultural implement maker, who had died in 1907; in a sign of the times, it was to become a motor garage. From here, looking south, we would get a view down Thetford Road. On the west side, a row of small, single-storey cottages was followed by a two-storey building occupied by a baker and confectioner, and then White House, a large building of white brick, at least part of which had been occupied by Mrs Curl's girls' boarding school in 1885-7. To the east of Thetford Road was the cattle sale yard.

In the angle of the Thetford and Merton Roads was a 'substantially built' five-bedroomed house erected before 1872, with a two-stall stable and chaise house, in which Eunice Taylor, a lady of private means, lived with two daughters and a servant. Beyond it were two notable buildings which had not been erected 70 years previously: the premises of Robert Waters, builder, and the Victoria Cottage Hospital.

Robert Waters, son of Daniel Waters, plumber and glazier, bought land on which an iron foundry had stood, probably in 1896 when the manager of the foundry, Horatio Goodrick, moved his business to Norwich Road. Waters moved in with his firm of building contractors, Waters and Sons, established in 1853 and erected a four-bedroomed house on the site. Waters was a parish councillor and captain of the Watton fire brigade at the turn of the century but it was as a builder that he left a permanent mark on the town, constructing many of the new houses on Griston

Road and Norwich Road.[17]

The Victoria Jubilee Hospital (Watton Cottage Hospital) stood a little further out of town on the west side of Thetford Road. It was built in 1899 at a total cost of £740 (equivalent to about £58,000 today), the funds being contributed voluntarily by subscribers in Watton and the surrounding parishes, a further example of Wattonians 'doing it for themselves'. Patients whose weekly income did not exceed £1 were not charged for their board and nursing.[18] The first patient arrived on 14 August 1899: William Bennett, who had been carting barley and was thrown from the cart, sustaining bruising but no broken bones. Up to 31 December 1899, eight patients had been admitted, 'of whom eight were discharged cured'. One had an arm amputated and two others had other operations. One case of typhoid had been treated successfully.[19]

Thetford Road, looking north.
*(from a glass negative taken by F W Bird, from the clearance of Harvey and Sons via Julian Horn)*

The 1901 census returns recorded two members of staff (a nurse and a servant) and two patients. An operating room was added to the hospital in 1904 and a children's ward in 1907.[20] In 1911, the medical officers were the local doctors, Panting, Alexander and Mallins and the superintendent nurse was Amelia Pritchard, aged 39, from New Cross in south-east London. With the support of a general domestic servant, she was responsible for the care of four patients on the census day: a married woman from Watton, a 60-year-old farm labourer, and two boys aged 11 and 12.

We'll make a quick detour into Merton Road, which now boasted 11 brick and tiled cottages, described as 'newly-erected' in 1874. Six, known as Walsingham Cottages, had been built by 1872; they had an 'iron palisade' at the front and walled gardens at the back. Another five clay-lump cottages, also built by 1872, adjoined them.[21] In 1874, both they and Walsingham Cottages were offered for sale as rental properties, 'let to good tenants'.[22] In 1911, several were occupied by skilled tradesmen and one was a lodging house. There were no other houses in Merton Road: the road ran through fields for several hundred yards to the turn-off for Wick Farm, which, when offered for sale in 1869, comprised 275 acres of land with a farmhouse and a range of agricultural buildings. The farmhouse was a substantial structure with seven bedrooms. Stables, two barns, cowsheds, piggeries and a double cottage stood nearby.[23] In 1908, Wick Farm had been divided up into ten smallholdings.[24] Today, it remains a name on the map but the only building on the site is a large warehouse.

༄༅

Returning to the junction of Thetford Road and Norwich Road, we'll turn left into the High Street, as it was now called.[25] On the north side, the next building to the west after the Willow House was Clematis House ('The Gables'), the home since before 1881 of the physician and surgeon, Thomas Arthur Alexander. After that came the house and workshops created by Jonas Frost in 1856 by converting the former coach-house and stable of the 'Manor House'. These were now, in 1911, occupied by an ironmongery business. The premises may have been extended, before or after 1911, as in 1919 the ironmonger's shop was described as 'recently erected'.[26] On the other side of the gateway to the yard behind the shop, the premises that had belonged to James Pitts had been taken over by the Waters family of builders and, in 1911, were occupied by Hannah Waters, house decorator. On the corner of High Street and Dereham Road was a saddler's business.

On the south side of the street was the *New Inn*, now in the occupation of Fred Jessup. It was followed by 'The White Shop', a gents' outfitting business managed by George Self, who also offered his services as a 'ladies' tailor'. Next came the *Bull*, a 'family and commercial hotel', owned and occupied by Edward Sayer, and now the headquarters of the Cyclists' Touring Club. From 1874 to 1891, the tenant of the *Bull* had been a woman who, unusually for a pub landlady, was neither married nor a widow. Sarah Spanton took on the tenancy in 1874, following the deaths, successively of her father and mother. Her tenure was very successful. In January 1875, she provided, for the first time, 'a public market tea and evening party... when between thirty and forty gentlemen sat down to an excellent and substantial repast, ably served by Miss Spanton the hostess'. The market tea became an annual event and in 1876 Sarah Spanton was described as a 'very obliging hostess'.[27] On leaving in 1891, she moved into a four-roomed cottage in Dereham Road, where she offered lodgings. She died, aged 78, in 1910.

A couple of doors west from the *Bull* was the shop and residence of William Whalebelly, a butcher and farmer. He was the county councillor for Watton and district, having been elected for a second time, with an increased majority, in 1910.[28]

The next building, the former *Swan*, had for some time hosted a printing works.

The name of James Warden Gowing, steam printer, appeared on many handbills in the second half of the 19th century. Gowing, originally a bookseller, and the creator of a 'public circulating library',[29] died in January 1893 and the property was offered for sale by auction, described as an 'excellent shop, with printing offices, outbuildings, paved yard, small garden and domestic offices, together with the 6-roomed dwelling house, now known as the post office, stationery, and printing works, in the occupation of Messrs Stace and Harvey'.[30] By 1911, the post office had moved to what is now Middle Street but the census of 1911 was to find Edward Harvey, aged 60, letterpress printer and stationer, still living on the premises with his wife, two daughters, two sons and a domestic servant. The family continued to trade there until recent times.

Next door, between Harvey's premises and the *George*, was a bakery and confectionery business. In 1911, we would find it occupied by Samuel Balls but until 1906 the tenant was William Alfred Brookbank. A former ship's steward, Brookbank, born in Blyth, Northumberland, had opened up in partnership with his father in 1896, advertising that they had been 'appointed sole agents in the district for the finest bread in the world, "Bermaline malt extract bread"...as used in the Queen's household'.[31]

The partnership was dissolved in 1902 and William continued on his own, until he became bankrupt in 1905. He hadn't kept any accounts and his trade had decreased owing, he claimed, to increased competition. Creditors received only about 12 per cent of the money they were owed.[32] An inventory of the

East end of High Street, pre-1906.
(Julian Horn)

furniture, utensils and stock was compiled. Brookbank, his wife Eliza and their four children occupied accommodation on the second floor (the first floor formed part of the *George* Hotel) and some private spaces on the ground floor, and much of the furniture there belonged to Eliza, inherited, she said, from her deceased grandmother.

The equipment and ingredients in the 'baking office', however, were William's responsibility. The latter included '50 stone of parish flour of Watton, Brookbank allowed one penny [per] stone for weighing same out weekly', a reminder that the parish continued to supply flour to the poor. The contents of the shop, facing the street, included: 49 bottles containing sweets, about half full; 62 small bottles of sweets (eight full, 54 half full); 22 full boxes of sweets; two glass show cases; cakes; two tins of biscuits, partly full (and five empties); four boxes 'containing a few Christmas toys'; 17 pounds of tea; paper bags; one pair of small scales and weights; and two wooden stools and a chair.[33] The scene can be imagined. Brookbank's must have been a favourite haunt of the children of Watton at the time.

ೞಚ

Now we'll turn into Dereham Road. On its east side, after the saddler's shop on the corner, were the former premises of the school run by the Misses Wright, which had been conveyed from Alexander Banham, auctioneer, to Frederick and Charles Robinson in 1904, thus reuniting this building with the 'Manor House', which had been bought by Edward Robert Grigson, solicitor in 1845. Grigson went into partnership with Richard Robinson and after Grigson's retirement and subsequent death in 1897, and the death of Richard Robinson in January 1905, the business became known as Robinson and Sons.

In 1911, the sons, Frederick and Charles Robinson, conducted the business in partnership and, as individuals. performed many public offices in Watton: Frederick, the elder, was clerk to both Wayland Rural District Council and the Board of Guardians of Wayland Poor Law Union, as well as secretary to the gas company and the Wayland Hall company; Charles, the younger, was clerk to the magistrates and commissioners of taxes and secretary to the Victoria Jubilee Hospital. Frederick was the registrar of Wayland district and Charles was the deputy registrar.[34] Charles, who was single, lived in the eight-roomed premises in Dereham Road with a 61-year-old housekeeper.

On the west side of Dereham Road were the buildings between the High Street and Middle Street which occupied the sites of stalls in Watton's medieval market place. By 1911, they had been transformed by the Dunnett family, drapers and grocers, who created a new façade across the west side of the block, facing what remained of the market place.

Daniel Dunnett, from Rockland St Peter, had established a grocery and drapery

*Wayland Hall and Dunnetts, 1910-14.*
*(Lesley Cowling)*

business in Watton by 1861, working until 1863 in partnership with William Rook, the owner of the *George*. By 1871, Daniel and his wife Ann had three sons and four daughters, the youngest son being Burton Samuel Dunnett, who was to take over the Watton business after the death of his father. Four live-in assistants were employed in the shop, and a nurse and two domestic servants in the house. Daniel advertised regularly in the *Thetford and Watton Times* from 1880 onwards, referring to his premises as the 'Market House'. In 1891, the recently-improved shop front was described as 'handsome and attractive, and also fitted with patent polished plate glass and handsome half-glass entrance door. One of the rooms of the house', the report continued, 'has been added to this part of the shop'.[35]

By the end of 1895, Daniel Dunnett had also acquired the post office and stores in Ashill, which were managed, and in due course inherited, by his son Ernest Jabez Dunnett. As well as his commercial activities, Daniel Dunnett was a prime mover among the Primitive Methodists, for whose church he had acted as a trustee since 1862. He was a lay preacher and his daughter Edith was the organist and Sunday school teacher. Dunnett was also an active supporter of the Liberal Party.

When Daniel Dunnett died in May 1899, aged 74, he was worth over £1,700 (equivalent to £133,000 today). The shop in the Market Place was taken on by his son Burton Samuel Dunnett and his wife Ann, who had spent time in Australia, where their eldest child was born, before returning to Watton. Burton Samuel, like his father, was an active supporter of Primitive Methodism and Liberalism. In 1911, he was aged 43 and still living at the Market House, which had 13 rooms,

*Burton Samuel Dunnett and family.*
*(George Jessup family collection via Julian Horn)*

enough to accommodate himself and his wife, two sons, two daughters, two grocery assistants and two domestic servants. The eldest son and eldest daughter worked in the shop on the drapery side of the business.

ಸಂಡ

Facing the market place on its north side was, of course, Wayland Hall. The Conservative Club had established itself there in January 1910, in what had previously been the reading room. The premises had been redecorated and the room 'well provided with a liberal supply of comfortable armchairs and the walls with attractive pictures'.[36]

The market place had become a subject of controversy in 1899. Its surface was of 'rough flints or cobble stones' and it was in a poor state of repair, a 'blot' on the town as one member of the new parish council put it. The issue was: who was responsible for its maintenance? If the Wayland Rural District Council was to take responsibility, it had to be shown that the market place was a thoroughfare and had been used as such for over 60 years, or previous to 1836.

A committee was set up to investigate and heard evidence from some of the oldest parishioners. John Hicks Thompson, aged 83, the carpenter and builder who had occupied premises behind what was now Durrants' shop, testified that the market place had always been used as a thoroughfare. He continued: 'The Rev. J Hicks [he meant the Revd W H Hicks] came to reside in the town some 45 years ago, and was then the lord of the manor. A stone obelisk was then fixed in the centre of the market place, and this was taken down during Mr Hicks' time'. Thompson explained that he had managed the bailiwick (manorial rights) in the parish for 32 years, from 1839 to 1871, and 'used to provide stalls for those who came to sell their goods…The stone cobbles now down in the market place were there when he had charge of the bailiwick, which he hired from the lords of the manor as a man hires a farm. When any repairs required to be done…on the stalls, he did them… The tradesmen of the town did the repairs to the market place, with instructions of the parish surveyor, who had charge of the work.'[37]

John Hicks Thompson's evidence was corroborated by other witnesses, including Daniel Dunnett. However, William Sayer, a former parish surveyor, said that 'he had never repaired the market place because it was pebbled'. He had driven across it but 'thought it belonged to the lord of the manor'. The current parish surveyor, George Minns, opined that it belonged to the district council, adding that: 'The drains and cesspits around the market place he always had emptied at the cost of the district council'. The current lessee of the bailiwick continued to collect tolls, not only from stalls in the market place but also on those 'down the High Street as far as the old brewery'.[38]

Wayland Rural District Council maintained that the market square was not a highway. Watton Parish Council appealed to Norfolk County Council, which held a public meeting at Wayland Hall on 11 October 1899. Edward Harvey, the printer, clerk to the parish council,[39] put the case that the market place was a public highway, noting that: 'The cement pavement alongside of the stone part of the market place was laid by order of the parish surveyor and paid for by the rural district council'.

The district council argued that the market place was blocked by stalls and could not be used as a thoroughfare but the parish council maintained that a space was left for carts to pass through. George Minns 'remembered the post office being near where the *King's Arms* now stood [perhaps when Richard Johnson was the postmaster], and the mail cart used regularly to cross the [market] hill to get to the office'; nor, in his view, had the obelisk ever been a 'hindrance to the free passage of carts…as there was plenty of room on either side of it'.

Thomas Edwin Adcock, a member of the parish council, noted that Lord Walsingham 'always drove across it whenever he came to the petty sessions' which were held in Wayland Hall. Robert Waters, the builder, another member of the parish council, earned applause when he pointed out that, 'on several occasions the numerous vans of wild beast shows which had visited Watton were so placed across the main street opposite Mr Alexander's shop as to entirely obstruct the passage of vehicular traffic and all carts have been obliged to go by way of the back street', which, of course, did not mean that the High Street was not a public highway. William Sayer, however, reaffirmed that he had never repaired the market place: 'After a public fair had been held on the hill, the people who had pulled up the stones put them down again'.⁴⁰ Actually, they were not meant to lift the stones at all, and handbills had been ordered from Gowing the printer in 1858 by W H Hicks and 1880 by John Remington Mills, as lords of the manor, forbidding them from doing so.⁴¹

The outcome was that the county council found in favour of Watton Parish Council, and an order was issued to the rural district council to maintain the market place as a public thoroughfare.

෩෬

Let's resume our walk. From the market place, we'll proceed along Post Office Street (Middle Street, as it is now). After Wayland Hall, the first building on the north side was the *King's Arms*, tenanted in 1911 by Ernest Cook. It was to be rebuilt 12 years later.⁴² Other properties were occupied by a watchmaker and jeweller, bootmaker, tinsmith and 'jobbing gardener'. The post office was at the end of the street, on the north side. A post office clerk lived there with the postmistress, Lydia Maud Stibbon, and her husband Arthur.

Adjacent to the post office, on the corner of Dereham Road and Harvey Street, were the premises of the International Stores and Watton's Temperance Hotel. The latter reflected a campaign against alcohol consumption, supported enthusiastically by the churches, and particularly by the Primitive Methodists, which was in full swing in 1911.

A dramatic event was to occur at the International Stores in the summer heat of Wednesday 8 July 1914: 'At ten minutes to three, just at the busiest time in the market and town, two men riding into town on the Dereham-road entrance observed smoke issuing from the roof of the International Stores...One of these men immediately ran to Mr Ernest Adcock, who has charge of the clock house, and the fire alarm bell was rung, and the fire brigade turned out...With remarkable rapidity, the fire gained headway, until in a few minutes the whole length of the roof was blazing furiously, and it was soon evident that the whole premises were doomed.'

The shop had a new front but was housed in very old buildings. The fire threatened to cross Back Street and affect the premises of Siggins and Sons, painters and decorators but this was prevented by the Watton fire brigade, which had stationed their pumping engine 'at a pit some 400 feet distant belonging to Mr L[acey] A Vincent at the rear of Wayland House'. The fire brigade also managed to save much of the adjacent Temperance Hotel (although two bedrooms were lost), while volunteers removed the furniture and deposited it in Post Office Street.

The fire continued to burn for several hours. After the roof of the stores had fallen in, 'the front shop and its contents became an easy prey to the flames. The great heat had the effect of exploding several of the bottles and canned goods, that were

*The International-Stores on fire, July 1914.*
*(George Jessup family collection via Julian Horn)*

hurled from the seat of the fire for some considerable distance. In the midst of the fire, a cat was seen to rush from the burning stores. The poor animal was singed and burnt, and had been forced from its position by the action of the hose, and in a half-drowned condition rushed across the road and took shelter amongst some greenery growing beneath the windows of Khyber House, whence it was removed and placed in a sack and cared for'.[43]

A temporary home was found for the International Stores (and perhaps for the cat) in vacant premises in Middle Street and replacement stock was rushed to Watton; amazingly, the shop opened again the following morning. The fire led to urgent calls to improve Watton's water supply, an issue that had been raised previously, in 1885, in connection with a suggestion that the streets should be watered to lay the dust.[44] It was not to be until 1937-38, however, that Watton benefited from mains water.[45] Until then, water was drawn from wells and the pumps outside the Clock Tower and the National School. A shallow, polluted well in Norwich Road had been the source of an outbreak of typhoid in 1899.[46]

෴

Now we'll return to 1911 and continue our walk, along Dereham Road. The first building on the left, the imposing 10-roomed residence in white brick, now known as Khyber House, was the home of Henry Mallins, one of Watton's doctors in 1911. He came from Ireland and in 1872 became a surgeon in the Indian Medical Department, serving with the 'Khyber Column' in the second Afghan War of 1878-

*Khyber House and Dereham Road.*
(Stephen Easter)

80;[47] hence the name he gave to the house that he shared with two of his sisters when he came to Watton in 1881. Dr Mallins remained unmarried and devoted himself to his work and the affairs of the town. He was appointed as a magistrate in 1911, served as the medical officer and public vaccinator for the Watton district of Wayland Poor Law Union, and had been the chair of Watton parish council.

Dr Mallins' predecessor as the occupant of the house was Squire Sprigge, another doctor. Sprigge was practising in Watton in 1851 and had taken possession of the property by 1854, the year in which he married. Four children of Squire and Elizabeth Sprigge were baptised in Watton, including a son, Samuel Squire Sprigg,[48] who is one of Watton's more notable sons. After graduating from Gonville and Caius College, Cambridge in 1882, Samuel trained as a doctor and then worked in London, including at Great Ormond Street Hospital. He wrote several books and articles and edited the medical journal, *The Lancet*, from 1909 until 1937. His father, Squire Sprigge, continued to live in Watton until his death in 1877.

After Dr Mallins' house, facing the wall of the garden belonging to the Manor House, was a line of four-roomed cottages whose inhabitants were mainly artisans, clerks and retired people but also included 34-year-old George William Trollope, clerk and groom, his wife, three sons and daughter; he was to become a significant figure in Watton between the wars and is commemorated in the name of the road leading south off the High Street, opposite the old brewery building.

At the corner, where Dereham Road swung north and Church Walk branched off to the east, stood Rose Cottage, a delightful early-Victorian house. First mentioned in 1854,[49] it was offered for sale in 1861 as 'newly erected' and had a stable and gig house, a groom's cottage adjoining and a 'garden or pleasure ground'.[50] After the sale, it was occupied by Robert Barnard, a butcher with a shop in Middle Street, as a 'pretty spot to reside in' but less than six months later it was the scene of a ghastly tragedy when the clothes of Mrs Barnard, who was alone in the house at the time, caught fire and she was burned to death.[51] Rose Cottage was offered for sale again in 1862 and 1869 and must have been purchased by Robert Barnard, as he was the owner and occupier when he died in 1884.[52] In 1911, its occupants were an elderly couple, James and Mary Augusta Ellis, supported by a niece and nurse.

Across the road from Rose Cottage was the *'Live and Let Live'* public house, the rendezvous of members of the National Agricultural Labourers Union.[53] It was here that 'a large number of labourers and other new voters met the assistant overseer' and registered to vote in February 1885.[54] In 1911, Thomas William Tennant was the landlord. Behind the inn, on Church Walk, was the infant school built in 1876.

Fields still lay between the town and the hamlet of Neaton, further north along the Dereham road. Neaton remained a rural, predominantly agricultural, community. Of the 20 houses in the hamlet, ten were occupied by farm labourers and their families and three by farmers, two of whom were retired. The farm formerly owned by Charles Dorr remained, but there were no longer any glove-makers in Neaton: that industry had died. On the site of what had been the fellmonger's yard and premises was now a brick-built dwelling of 1861 known as Neaton Villa.

We'll now retrace our steps, back to the junction of Dereham Road and Harvey Street (or Back Street, as it was still called by some of its residents in 1911). Henry Siggins, a 'house decorator', owned the property next door to Khyber House that had been owned by his eponymous father in 1841. Beyond it was Wayland House, the large residence that had been occupied by William Massey in 1841. It was offered for sale in 1861, the advertisement boasting of its 'lofty dining and drawing rooms…hall, two sitting rooms or offices, an upper sitting room, seven bed and two dressing rooms, bath room, and water closet', along with its 'stable, chaise house, pleasure grounds, garden, vinery, barn, cow house' and eight acres of pasture and arable land.[55] The pleasure grounds contained the pit from which the Watton fire brigade was to draw water to quench the fire at the International Stores in 1914.

In 1881, this desirable estate had been occupied by Lacey Andrews Vincent, a chemist or, to give him his full credentials: 'chemist, druggist, oil and colourman, dealer in cigars and tobacco, manufacturer of Wood's mixture for sheep,[56] agent for W and A Gilbey's wines and spirits, Burton ales and stout, in casks or bottles, and for Bury ales'[57]. Vincent's business was carried on in his shop next to the Clock Tower in the High Street, where the family had been living, with two servants and two shop assistants, ten years previously, in 1871. Vincent and his wife Susan had 11 children. Their third son, Percy, left home at the age of 13 to become apprentice to a draper in Stratford in the East End of London. Ten years later, he started a business of his own as a draper and textile warehouseman. He prospered and, as Sir Percy Vincent, baronet, became Lord Mayor of London in 1935-36; 'London's latest "Dick Whittington"', as the New York Times dubbed him.[58]

When the 1911 census took place, Lacey Andrews Vincent was a widower of 73, still living in his large house but now accompanied only by one son, one daughter, two female domestic servants and a visitor of private means. Following his death on 4 June 1915, the contents of Wayland House were offered for sale by auction. In addition to 'brass, Parisienne and other bedsteads' and much mahogany furniture (including a telescope dining table and 'massive' sideboard), they included books and 'framed oil paintings, engravings and prints'.[59]

Two doors along the street from Vincent's residence was the *Red Lion* public house, described in 1861 as a 'beer house...held by Mr Stevens, or his undertenant'. The landlord in 1911 was Charles Stebbing, who was also a house painter.

Further to the west, Harvey House remained the property of the Harvey family after the death of Charlotte Harvey in 1849. From 1871 to 1877, it had been rented by the Misses Knopwood, who ran the school for young ladies there. Two years after the closure of the school, on 3 April 1879, the house was offered for sale, described as: 'an excellent residence...containing entrance hall, dining and breakfast rooms, lofty drawing room, with bow, school-room, ten sleeping rooms, one dressing room, w.c., kitchen, scullery, pantry, store rooms, cellar, brew house etc.' The house was 'approached by a carriage drive' and had 'a good vegetable garden, walled in from the road, containing a fish pond, also a cottage and garden adjoining...' It didn't sell and was offered again for sale or rent in September 1879. Also offered for sale were the household furniture and effects: the Misses Knopwood were 'giving up the occupation'.[60]

Either then or a few years later, Harvey House was purchased by George Jacobs, of the *Crown* Hotel, but he did not reside there. After his death in 1895, it came on to the market again and was described in the sale particulars as 'dilapidated, being unoccupied for several years'.[61] It was purchased by Alexander Banham, auctioneer and valuer, for the knock-down price of £240 (equivalent to about £19,000 today).[62] In 1911, it was occupied by John Panting, one of Watton's doctors, with his wife, daughter and two servants.

సౌరి

And so we reach the junction of Harvey Street, High Street, Brandon Road and Cley Lane, a location now, in 1911, dominated on the north side by the gas works erected in 1859 and the adjacent house, occupied by Edward James Mason, 'gas manager', his wife and five children. Cley Lane still contained only the Wesleyan Methodist Chapel and a couple of cottages but Brandon Road now had a considerable population.

The section as far as the junction with Swaffham Road, largely built up on its north side but bounded by fields to the south, was still called Mill Road, or Mill Street, by its inhabitants, although the windmill had gone by 1859. In 1841, there had been just one double cottage here. By 1847, another cottage had been built on to it and four more dwellings, described in 1858 as 'under one roof', had been added between it and the corner of Cley Lane.[63] At the far end of this row, from the mid-19th century onwards, was a public house, the *Black Horse*.

Other terraces were mentioned in the census returns: Brandon Terrace, Brandon Villas and Rosedale Terrace. The people who lived in these houses were small farmers, craftsmen, tradesmen and labourers. Brandon Terrace was a row of four brick and tiled cottages, while Brandon Villas comprised a pair of slightly more spacious semi-detached brick and tiled houses.⁶⁴ Just before Swaffham Road was Burleigh House, a residence with five bedrooms, drawing and dining rooms with bay windows and iron 'palisading' along the road frontage, belonging to William Salkeld Hall, one of the founders of W S Hall and Palmer, auctioneers, valuers and estate agents in Watton from 1902 until the 1980s. Hall had purchased the house in 1903 and lived there with his sister and a servant.

In the angle formed by Brandon and Swaffham Roads stood Disraeli House, the name honouring Bejamin Disraeli, Conservative prime minister and providing political balance to Gladstone Villa, next to the Willow House, named in honour of Disraeli's Liberal rival, William Gladstone. Disraeli House was the eight-roomed home of Thomas Edwin Adcock.

Building had taken place along Swaffham Road, called 'Saham Road' or 'College Road' by most of its residents in 1911. The houses included Saham Cottages, a row of five brick and tiled cottages and the *Carpenters' Arms* (formerly the *Golden Ball*) public house, where Harry Semmence, the landlord, like his brother Albert at the *Garden House*, was a manufacturer of mineral water.

೧೦೦೩

In Brandon Road, west of the Swaffham Road junction, 38 houses were recorded in 1911. The largest, West End House or West House, with ten rooms, was the residence of Bernard William Blomfield, a veterinary surgeon. His wife Susan Florence was a daughter of Lacey Andrews Vincent, the chemist. Blomfield was the great-grandson of William and Margaret Blomfield of Forncett St Peter who were very likely related to Susanna Wright of the *George* Inn, who also came from Forncett St Peter and whose name before her marriage was Blomfield. It may not be a coincidence, therefore, that Bernard William Blomfield was occupying the very house in which the two surviving daughters of Susanna Wright, Elizabeth Brasnett (a widow since 1846) and Susannah Wright, had been living in 1871. They died in December 1878 and April 1879 respectively.

After West House, all the houses apart from the *Dog and Partridge* Inn, near the parish boundary, were on the south side of Brandon Road. About a quarter were occupied by farm labourers and the occupants of many of the remainder were artisans and

*The West End.*
*(Museum4Watton)*

small businessmen. An exception was James Abbey, senior, 'retired foreman on metropolitan water board, London' at 6, Kitchener Terrace, a recently-built row of dwellings. Further west was 'Northview', said to be the first bungalow in Watton, occupied by James Abbey's son, James, and his wife and daughter. In 1911, James Abbey junior gave his occupation as 'painter and decorator' but he was to earn distinction during and after the First World War as the proprietor of an engineering works.[65]

There were two public houses in Brandon Road. The landlord at the *Jolly Farmers* public house, which already existed in 1841, was now, in 1911, Edmund G Leggett. The *Dog and Partridge* had opened shortly after 1841 and was now owned by Morgan's Brewery. Frank Sharman, the landlord, combined running the inn with a butchery business. In 1910, at a hearing before the magistrates, renewal of the licence of the *Dog and Partridge* was opposed on the grounds that it was 'not required for the wants of the town', which had 14 licensed houses, one to every 93 of Watton's population of 1,335 in 1901, and that the *Jolly Farmers* was only 546 yards away. The *Dog and Partridge* had stabling for three horses and a coach house to accommodate one four-wheeled vehicle but, unlike the *Jolly Farmers*, did not take lodgers. However, it was argued, renewal of the licence was justifiable because 'a number of waggoners and others coming from the parishes…on that side of Watton were accustomed to call there for bread and cheese and other refreshments, also that the house catered for cyclist parties.' Frank Sharman added that there had been no complaints about the house, that there was a good space in front of it for waggons and carts to draw up and that 'in the summer, the men from the surrounding farms got their beer supply there'.[66] The *Dog and Partridge* survived until 1964, the *Jolly Farmers* until 1983.

ೲಌ

We'll now retrace our steps to the junction of Brandon Road, Cley Lane, High Street and Harvey Street. On our left (to the north) is the gasworks, on our right, the school and Stevens' almshouses, the latter comprising four dwellings of two rooms each, inhabited by elderly people. We'll begin by looking up that side of the street, the south side. A new development here was West End Terrace, comprising substantial houses of seven or eight rooms. Goffe's almshouses followed; they were even smaller than Stevens', each of the four dwellings having only one room occupied by an elderly widow, the youngest being 78 and the oldest 92. The next building was the Primitive Methodist Central Hall of 1863 and the schoolroom behind it, built in 1874. Immediately next door to the east were the maltings, which still stood in 1911 but were disused. The land on which they stood was to be sold by Thomas Crawshay Frost's widow in 1913 and 1915. All that survives of the maltings today (2024) is their back gable wall, built in flint and brick, which now divides the Methodist church from the car park off Goddard's Court. Joined to it is a curved, then straight wall, behind which formerly lay a pit, which provided the

*West End Terrace and the Chequers.*
(Julian Horn)

water for the malting process.

Returning to the school and crossing the road there, the first building on the north side of the High Street, on the corner with Harvey Street, was formerly the home of Amos Walker, the census enumerator of 1841 and 1851. He had come to an unhappy end; described as formerly a wine and spirit merchant and brewer, he had been declared bankrupt in 1862 and had also become paralysed. He died in 1865, having, as a founder member of its Watton branch, benefited during his illness from the financial support of the Oddfellows friendly society.[67]

In 1911, what had been Walker's house was now the West End Stores, the emporium of Herbert Adcock. He was a prolific advertiser in the local papers; on 2 September 1893, for example, he had advertised a 'great harvest sale', featuring: raisins, currants and sultanas, hams, pure malt and hops, finest cheese, lard and butter, 'and last but not least, H Adcock's wonderful 1s 6d tea, the best in the county of Norfolk'.[68] Also belonging to Herbert Adcock was a cycle shop, further up the street, on a site later occupied by a motorcycle showroom.

The section of the north side of the High Street between West End Stores and the *Green Man* public house, formerly but no longer called Rotten Row, was now, in 1911, almost entirely built up. The inhabitants were mainly working people. A blacksmith's shop still stood about half way to the brewery building, the associated premises now occupied by Thomas Garner, coach builder and shoeing and general smith and Alfred Reynolds, general smith, and their families. Reynolds' residence

*Clarence House and High Street.*
*(Julian Horn)*

was the former *Chequers* public house. The brewery was no longer in operation but a 'brewer's manager', Herbert Carley Watson, still lived there, and next door was Clarence House, the residence of Thomas Crawshay Frost's widow, Druscilla Mary Frost.

A few doors further up the street was York House, whose occupants were Samuel Smith, a retired Primitive Methodist minister and his family. His house was followed by those of John Rowe, tailor and Lionel Julnes, coal and corn merchant, this being the first property in the High Street owned by the Julnes family. Next came the property occupied by Elizabeth Augusta Adcock, watchmaker, daughter in law of the Samuel Adcock who had carried on the same trade in 1841, and, immediately next door, that of her son Ernest A Adcock, watch and clock repairer, whose descendants are a prominent part of the Watton business community to this day.

We would now reach the *Green Man*, still one of Watton's more frequented public houses. William Johnson was its landlord in 1911. Three doors on from the *Green Man* were the premises of John Edwards, stationer and picture-frame maker, whose descendants still own the same shop. On the east side of the passage leading through to Harvey Street, the building owned by Smith Hastings in 1841 was now divided between William Meek and William Clubb, and probably occupied by John Jackson, a butcher, William Benjamin Taylor, a saddler and Edwin Tyson Toombs, a hairdresser, whose wife Louisa was a teacher at the elementary school.

The three-storey building that had been Catherine Platfoot's bakery and residence in 1841 was still occupied by George Chase, butcher, with his wife and an adopted daughter. Next door to the east were the premises of William Sayer, tobacconist and former parish surveyor. Previously, they had been occupied by Frederick Adcock, a member of the family of watchmakers and jewellers, who was now an elderly man, and had moved up the street into what had formerly been Lacey Vincent's residence. To visit him there, we would pass the premises of a retailer of boots, another hairdresser and Lacey Vincent's chemist's shop.

*High Street, pre-1912.*
*(Julian Horn)*

*The building on the right had been the manorial 'mansion house' in 1689.*

At the corner of the market place, in the former manor house facing Dunnett's shop, were the premises of George Butcher, ironmonger. Butcher was a prolific advertiser in the local papers, offering 'household furniture, ironmongery, china, glass and earthenware; mangles, trunks, bassinettes, powder, shot and cartridges'.

ଛଓ

Now, we'll cross back to the south side of the High Street and pick up the story from the Methodist Central Hall and schoolroom eastwards. A row of houses here had been built by Thomas Crawshay Frost, a stone tablet ('TCF 1871') commemorating the fact. Next to them, set back from the street, was Beechwood, a substantial residence in which Jane Bricknell Gage lived with her maid and four sisters, all, like her, spinsters. On the other side of what is now Beechwood Avenue was Worm's Yard, three small dwellings named after James Worm, a veterinary surgeon, behind the larger house occupied by Worm himself. He had married Lydia Stebbing of Watton in 1824 and settled down here. Having started out as a 'cow leach and farrier',[69] by 1836 he was trading as a veterinary surgeon. In 1851, his son, James Stebbing Worm, born in 1826, had joined him in that profession. James Worm senior died in 1859 but his son continued to practise as a veterinary surgeon until his death in 1891. His premises were taken over by George Greengrass, described as a castrator; he died in 1910 and, in 1911, his house was occupied by his widow Mary Greengrass, aged 78, and their son.

Three doors on from James Worm's house was the extensive grocery and drapery shop of William Kendall (formerly Alexanders), occupied in 1911 by Kendall himself, his wife and daughter, a housekeeper, two further servants, four shop assistants and an apprentice. Kendall had purchased the Alexanders' business in 1881 and, like them, was a supporter of the Independent Chapel.[70] William

*Kendall's and the building that became the Liberal Club, pre-1909.*
*(Julian Horn)*

Kendall advertised extensively in the local press over the next few years, styling his shop the 'West Norfolk Supply Stores' and offering grocery, drapery, boots and shoes, millinery and a 'mantle and dressmaking department'.[71]

To the east of Kendall's establishment was the shop of Elizabeth Moss, recorded in her census return as a 'tobacconist and fancy business'. Next to her, on the other side, was the building which in 1841 had been the residence of Edward Stevens and from 1909 onwards, housed the Liberal Club and its resident caretaker, Albert Ernest Piper. The opening of the Liberal Club on 5 August 1909 was a major event, with over a thousand people from the town and surrounding villages being treated to a 'meat tea…served in relays in large tents erected in the paddock adjoining the bowling green, while there were several tables in the open air and under the shade of the trees'. Banners celebrating free trade and old age pensions (introduced by the Liberal government the previous year) were displayed and the local Liberal MP, Mr R Winfrey, gave a speech.[72] The Liberal Club was as much a social as a political organisation. A new billiard room had been erected before it opened and the club supported cricket and football teams, and had its own bowling green. It was also the headquarters of the Watton Rifle Club.[73]

After the Liberal Club came the *Crown*, the landlord in 1911 being Herbert William Wicks. To its east was Bank House, residence in 1883 of Mr and Mrs H Alexander and in 1911 of Edward Pratt, bank manager. His neighbour to the east was a widow, Julia Regester, her daughter and a brother, John Durrant.

※ ※

Now, we come to the 'Great Shop', formerly the premises of the Younges and, later, of the unfortunate Smith Wright, which had been owned and occupied since 1879 by George Cubitt Durrant, grocer and draper.

Both the facade and the interior of the 'Great Shop' were impressive. The facade had been embellished in 1891 with 'spiral oak columns and French-polished and carved caps and bases, with stall board plates of brass engraved, extending all along the bottom of each window, while the door in the centre is of handsomely embossed plate-glass with the words 'show-room' burnt in'. As for the interior, 'the general show-room on the ground floor…is handsomely fitted with mahogany counters…The gas fittings are elaborate, and several large mirrors adorn the walls and inner ends of each of the front windows…The jacket and millinery show-room

*East end of the High Street, with Durrant's 'Great Shop' on the right.*
*(Julian Horn)*

above is reached by a broad and conveniently-constructed staircase...Behind this [department] is a spacious 'fitting room', ladies lavatory and private room, also the milliners' room and a work-room...'[74] Quite a place.

Two years previously, readers of a local newspaper had been advised: 'for a new dress, jacket, bonnet and hat, we recommend Geo C Durrant's great shop, Watton. He is noted for the latest styles, great variety, and lowest prices. The milliner has just returned from a visit to London, and is now prepared with all the newest ideas. A staff of dressmakers on the premises, charges most moderate, fit and finish guaranteed. New books of fashions in dresses, jackets and mantles. Wedding and mourning orders receive prompt attention'.[75]

George Cubitt Durrant had married Sarah Elizabeth Barnard, daughter of a blacksmith in the town, in 1876. Sarah died in 1888, aged only 40, leaving three young children, a daughter and two sons. In 1911, George Cubitt, now aged 67, was assisted in the business by the elder of the sons, Cubitt Richard, now aged 29. Two years later, Cubitt Richard Durrant, married Margaret Pratt, literally the girl next door, as she was the daughter of the bank manager who lived at Bank House. After George Cubitt's death in 1929, Cubitt Richard took over the business.

George Cubitt Durrant was a conscientious businessman who sought to provide a good service for his customers'. George Jessup recalled: 'I can still picture George Durrant standing at the shop door in a bowler hat, long coat and slippers. He opened the door in his friendly manner for each customer and as they were about

High Street, c.1910.
(Norfolk Record Office, ACC 2015/277)

The picture was probably taken on a Wayland Show day.

to leave he always asked if they had been suited and, if not, would endeavour to obtain whatever they required as quickly as possible'.[76] George Cubitt was also a staunch supporter of the Church of England and was active in the affairs of the town. He was one of those who developed Loch Neaton for the benefit of the people of Watton.

In 1911, four draper's assistants, two dressmakers and a milliner, all living on the premises, were employed in the shop, along with three servants who catered for the needs of the family. The live-in staff slept in the attics above the shop and some of them wrote their names in pencil on the plaster of the walls and ceiling. Bertha Hewson, born in Stoke Ferry and aged 19 in 1911, was a draper's assistant. She wrote: 'Came Sept 18 1905, left Sept 29 1912'. Hilda Childerhouse, aged 14, an apprentice milliner, lived across the street with her adoptive father, George Chase, butcher, but managed to write her name, with the date: March 6 1911. Another draper's assistant who lived on the premises was Elsie Sillett, aged 21, from Cratfield in Suffolk; she did not write her name on the plaster but her younger sister, Mabel, was to do so, with the dates of her employment: Jan 6 1913 to Jan 7 1924. Mabel was probably the person responsible for one of the spicier contributions to the graffiti in the attic: 'Mabel & Billy will soon be doing the trick, getting well on the way rather', followed by 'Now they've done it'. No surprise, then, that, a year after she left Durrants, Mabel married William J Stebbings, a butcher with a shop in the High Street.[77]

ഔര

Finally, we arrive at the *George*, which was to have only one more year of its existence before its sale in 1912. Frank George Steel, the manager, employed no staff apart from members of his own family. Perhaps the writing was already on the wall for Watton's once premier hostelry.

It was soon to be the end of an era, not only for the *George*, but for Watton and the country as a whole. World War I began in August 1914.

## Notes

1. This chapter draws heavily on evidence in the 1911 census returns, supplemented by that from early Ordnance Survey maps and contemporary trade directories.
2. DMG, 24 September 1910.
3. TWT, 8 September 1900.
4. NN, 18 January 1902.
5. DMG, 25 September 1909.
6. *Diss Express*, 10 September 1915.
7. DMG, 4 September 1915.
8. DMG, 19 June 1915.
9. Sale particulars, 1876; NRO, ACC 2023/12.
10. Grandfather of George Jessup, author of *Watton through the Ages* (1985).
11. Rental agreement, Steward and Patteson to Jeremiah Jessup, 15 September 1890; NRO, ACC 2023/12.
12. TWT, 31 August 1889.
13. James Hooper in NN, 28 November 1896.
14. NC, 22 July 1893. They were named in honour of the Earl of Beaconsfield (Benjamin Disraeli, Conservative prime minister who was ennobled in 1876).
15. Deeds in private possession.
16. NC, 27 November 1875.
17. B Waters (2016).
18. Cecil F Chapman, *Grandad's Watton* (1985).
19. First report of the Victoria Jubilee Hospital, 1899, in private possession; TWT, 19 August 1899.
20. A K Chapman, 'Social life' in WEA (1975).
21. LA, 14 September 1872.
22. NC, 28 March 1874.
23. Sale particulars, manor of Watton Hall, 13 May 1869; NRO, HIL 1/256 875x3.
24. NC, 31 October 1908.
25. Watton's main street was sometimes called the High Street from the 1871 census onwards, but as late as the 1901 census it was referred to as Front Street. What is now Harvey Street was still 'Back Street' in 1901.
26. Deed in private possession.
27. NN, 9 May 1874, 30 January 1875, 29 January 1876.
28. EDP, 5 March 1910.
29. NC, 17 September 1853.
30. NC, 22 July 1893.
31. TWT, 26 September 1896.
32. DMG, 28 October 1905.
33. Inventory of the goods of W A Brookbank, Watton, 23 February 1905; NRO, ACC 2023/12.
34. Kelly's Directories of Norfolk, 1908 and 1912.
35. NM, 12 September 1891. It is not clear whether the whole of the new façade was created at this time, or earlier.
36. DMG, 1 January 1910.
37. NM, 21 October 1899.

38. TWT, 6 May 1899.
39. He served in this role from 1895 to 1927 and was succeeded by Mr E A Harvey (parish clerk 1927 to 1948), followed by Mr W E Harvey (1948-1974), all three being members of the same family, a remarkable record. See C F Chapman, *Grandad's Watton* (1985).
40. DMG, 14 October 1899.
41. NRO, HIL2/60/1-3.
42. G Jessup (1985).
43. Thanks to Julian Horn for alerting me to this reference.
44. NM, 2 May 1885.
45. G Jessup (1985).
46. NN, 4 November 1899.
47. DMG, 28 October 1911.
48. Thanks to Julian Horn for drawing my attention to the career of Samuel Squire Sprigge.
49. Francis White's Directory of Norfolk, 1854.
50. NM, 3 August 1861.
51. NM, 29 January 1862.
52. NM, 22 March 1884.
53. NM, 25 July 1874.
54. NM, 28 February 1885.
55. NM, 20 July 1861.
56. Claimed to be an antidote for fever in sheep. Vincent also sold a 'sheep dipping composition'; TWT, 12 November 1881.
57. Harrod's Directory of Norfolk, 1877.
58. A K Chapman, 'Social life' in WEA (1975); LNCP, 26 January 1943; New York Times, 10 November 1935.
59. TWT, 4 September 1915.
60. NN, 27 September 1879.
61. Copy of sale particulars, 13 May 1895, in possession of the author.
62. NN, 18 May 1895.
63. Deeds in private possession.
64. EDP, 25 June 1903.
65. G Jessup (1985).
66. EDP, 3 March 1910. See also norfolkpubs.co.uk.
67. NM, 22 July 1865.
68. TWT, 2 September 1893.
69. Pigot's Directory, 1830.
70. TWT, 12 November 1881.
71. Examples of his advertisements in the *Watton Almanac and Advertising Medium* (1891) were reproduced in G Jessup (1985).
72. DMG, 14 August 1909.
73. G Jessup (1985).
74. NM, 12 September 1891.
75. DMG, 11 May 1889.
76. G Jessup (1985), which also contains examples of Durrant's advertisements in the *Watton Almanac and Advertising Medium* (1891).
77. I am grateful to Julian Horn for sharing with me his photographs of the graffiti, taken with the permission of Kate Durrant.

# The Last Hundred Years

Watton has changed more in the last hundred years than in the whole of its previous history but it will be for others with greater knowledge than this author to write a detailed account of the town's development since World War I.

The population of Watton, as counted in the decennial censuses, has grown exponentially since World War II. From 1,331 in 1921 and 1,413 in 1931, it ballooned to 3,104 in 1951.[1] In that year, more than twice as many men as women were recorded, indicating that a large part of the increase was attributable to the presence of male servicemen, who, like this author's father, were stationed at RAF Watton. The population dropped again in the 1950s but the presence of the base helped to ensure that it remained above the pre-war totals. In 1961, the inhabitants of the town numbered 2,462, with marginally more women than men.

After that, Watton's population has increased relentlessly, by large increments from census to census: 3,343 in 1971; 4,789 in 1981; 5,492 in 1991; 6,819 in 2001; 7,202 in 2011; and (the biggest jump ever) 8,967 in 2021.[2]

The increase in its population has been accompanied by the transformation of the shape of Watton's built-up area. Infilling and ribbon development took place between the two world wars, especially along the Brandon, Swaffham, Norwich and Dereham roads, although gaps remained, where the land continued to be used for agriculture. The hamlet of Neaton was no longer completely separated by fields from the rest of the town. The first council-built houses, a crescent on Merton Road, appeared.

However, it was the building of Watton airfield from 1936 onwards, its opening in 1939, and the development of the housing areas associated with it, that completely changed the geography of the town, extending the built-up area eastwards by over a mile. The economy of Watton changed too: the 'base' was a major employer of civilian labour and brought, not only an influx of young men from all over the country but also, from 1943, servicemen from the United States.

After World War II, further construction took place. Wayland Rural District Council erected numerous houses on what had been five fields lying between the High Street and Merton Road, approached by a new road named after George Trollope, the auctioneer. By 1981, 14.67 per cent of the 1,800 households in the town occupied houses rented from the council.

Later, in the 1960s, new housing estates developed off Harvey Street and Thetford Road. They were supplemented by further building off Brandon Road, Norwich Road and Merton Road in the 1970s and 1980s, and the expansion of the built area has continued unabated in the 21st century.

New public buildings appeared in Watton between the wars. The old National School was finally replaced by the 'Watton Senior Mixed Council School' (now Watton Junior School) in 1926 and the new Methodist Church opened the following year.

Development continued after World War II. The Queen's Hall was opened in 1956. In 1958, Watton Secondary Modern School opened on a greenfield site off Merton Road and in 1976, with the addition of a new sports hall and other facilities, became the all-ability Wayland High School (now Wayland Academy). The Sports Centre adjacent to Loch Neaton was opened in two stages, in 1974 and 1976.

In the High Street, many of the shops were extended to take in what had previously been the living accommodation behind them: far fewer people actually live in the High Street today than did so in 1911. After World War II, some familiar landmarks disappeared, notably the *George* and the *Green Man*, to be replaced by unsightly modern buildings housing banks. The railway station fell victim to the Beeching Axe and closed in 1964/5. A large abattoir was erected at the west end of the town and the Abels removals business developed into a large undertaking. The RAF station closed, its housing was sold off and its administrative buildings were occupied by small businesses.

Wayland Rural District Council ceased to exist in 1974, when Breckland District Council became the local government body responsible for Watton. At the same time, Watton Parish Council became Watton Town Council, with a town mayor as its chair.

And, appropriately, the Wayland Hall now houses a museum, run by volunteers, with a wonderful collection of artefacts, photographs and documents celebrating Watton's fascinating past.

**Notes**

1. Owing to World War II, no census took place in 1941.
2. I am grateful to staff at the Census Customer Services at the Office for National Statistics for making recent census data available and for guidance on its interpretation. It is important to stress that the nature of census data changed over time and so the results of successive censuses are not always strictly comparable. For example, in 1961 and 1971 (as in all previous censuses from 1841), the census recorded the persons who were present at an address on census day, whereas from 1981 onwards the numbers of 'usual residents' at each address were counted.

# A Watton Bibliography

Francis Blomefield, *An Essay towards a Topographical History of the County of Norfolk*, volume 2 (William Miller, 1805).

Thomas Barton, *Notices of the Town and Parish of Watton*, in Norfolk Archaeology, Volume 3 (1852).

W G Clarke, *A Guide to the Town of Watton and the Country adjacent thereto* (George Self, 1909).

Anon, *The History of Watton* (undated, pre-1958; unpublished typescript, preserved by Wilfrid Harvey from the clearance of Harvey and Sons).

WEA Watton Branch, *Watton in an Earlier Age* (1975).

George Jessup, *Watton through the Ages* (1985).

Cecil F Chapman, *Grandad's Watton* (1985) and *More about Grandad's Watton* (1985).

Julian Horn, *Watton: Some Snapshots of its History* (The Wayland Partnership Development Trust, 2011)

# Index

Abbey, James, father and son  254
Adcock family
   Elizabeth Augusta (wife of George)  256
   Ernest (son of George and Elizabeth Augusta)  248, 256
   Frederick (cousin)  257
   George (son of Samuel)  225
   Herbert (son of George and Elizabeth Augusta)  238, 255
   Samuel (1791-1850)  150, 256
   Thomas Edwin (cousin)  247, 253
Alden, Mary  67
Alden, Robert  56, 58, 67, 80
Aldis, Ephraim  156
Aldreda, a freewoman  15, 16
Alexander, Dr Thomas Arthur  228, 241, 242
Alexander family  191
   Elizabeth Lane (wife of Thomas)  153, 154
   Henry (son of Elizabeth Lane and Thomas)  238
   John Edmund (son of Elizabeth Lane and Thomas)  192, 215, 217, 239
   Mary Diana (wife of Henry)  258
   Thomas (1796-1842)  153, 154
Alice  172
Allcock, Erasmus  103, 163
Allen, William  129, 130
Almshouses, Goffe's and Stevens'  42, 47, 57, 80, 149, 150, 173, 174, 254
Alpe, Mary Ann  149, 176
Ames, Alexander  49
Andrews, George  190
Angel alehouse  152
Angel, The  42, 67, 69, 70, 76, 79, 87, 105, 145, 152, 153, 155
Anne  164
Anowe Furlong  37
Arch, Joseph  212, 213, 214
Armstrong, Revd Benjamin (Vicar of Dereham)  56, 115, 184
Ashill  12, 109, 113, 131, 140, 158, 163, 178, 191, 203, 208, 245
Attleborough  130, 133, 181, 192
Avenall, Francis  46
Ayers, Pleasance  178
Bacey, Peter  151
Backside, The  143, 145
Back Street  46, 145, 147, 148, 149, 152, 156, 175, 210, 248, 251
Bagge, William H  130, 214
Balding's Pightle  95
Baley, Robert  143
Balls, James  152
Balls, Samuel  243
Banham, Alexander  189, 217, 223, 238, 244, 252
Bank House  258, 259
Bank Street  141, 142
Barker, Benjamin  85
Barker, Elizabeth (née Raby, previously Hicks). *See* Raby, Elizabeth (daughter of John; later Hicks, Barker)
Barkham, Sir Edward  43, 77
Barnard, Robert  250
Barnham, H G  223
Barrell, Le (tenement)  46, 63, 72
Barton, Thomas  38, 71, 81, 82, 115, 131, 220
Baskerville, Thomas  73, 76, 122
Bates, John  152
Baxterwong  37
Beaconsfield Terrace  238
Beauchamp, Lady Philippa de  21, 24
Beechwood  257
Beechwood Avenue  150, 153, 257
Beeston  174
Beets, Mary  226, 227
Bell, the (Saham Toney)  177
Bennett, George  163
Bennett, Mary Keziah  164
Bennett, William  241
Ben's, Benn's Pightle  147
Bentinck, George  214

266

Berry, John (Vicar of Watton, 1691-1730) 99
Berys Pece 37
Besowthe, Margaret 53
Bettes family
   John I 42, 45, 119
   John III (probably son of Thomas) 119
   John II (probably son of John I) 69, 87
   Thomas (probably son of John I) 44, 45, 48, 49, 87, 119, 142, 143
Bicker, Caroline 201
Bigod/Bigot, Roger 16
Black Horse, The 252
Blade family
   Edmund Oldfield (son of Robert and Sarah) 224, 225
   Maria Ann (daughter of Robert and Sarah) 140, 142, 200, 224
   Robert (1780-1827) 200, 224
   Sarah (née Oldfield, wife of Robert) 142, 200, 224, 225
Blomefield, Francis 15, 17, 70, 71, 78, 89
Blomfield, Bernard William 253
Blomfield, Susan Florence. *See* Wright family (at the George): Susanna I, Susan (wife of Dennis)
Blumfeilde, Thomas 43, 48
Borgopp (Burgopp), Isabel 52, 53
Bougeon, Agnes 52
Boughen, Hugh (father and son) 157
Bougion, John 33
Bowers, Charles 163
Bowgeon (Bougeon/Bowgen), John 45
Bowls, game of 137, 227
Bradfresshe, Long- and Short- 38
Brame, John 124
Brandon 130
Brandon Road 12, 36, 110, 111, 117, 137, 141, 148, 149, 164, 165, 178, 214, 226, 252, 253, 254, 263
Brandon Terrace 252
Brandon Villas 252, 253
Brasnett, Elizabeth (née Wright) 128, 253
Brasnett, Robert 128
Breckland District Council 264
Brett, John 122

Brett, Robert (blacksmith) 122
Brett, Robert (butcher) 35, 45
Bridge Wong (Brygwong, Brigwong) 35, 37
Broadmere Field 37
Broadmere Lane 37
Brock, Miss (schoolmistress) 199
Brookbank, Eliza 244
Brookbank, William Alfred 243
Browne, Thomas 44
Bullard and Sons 168
Bull Closes 138
Bull, The (became the Labour in Vain, the Half Moon and the King's Arms) 42, 44, 45, 79, 142
Bull, The (in High Street) 84, 106, 138, 210, 223, 242
Burleigh House 253
Bury St Edmunds 138, 220
Buscall, Elsie 227
Buscall, Goddard 141, 143
Bushy Close 35
Butcher, Francis 122
Butcher, George 257
Butchers' stalls, Shambles, Butchery 45, 70, 71, 73, 84
Buxton family (fellmongers) 144
   Charles II (son of Charles I) 144
   Charles I (son of Robert and Mary) 144, 155
   Isabella. *See* Sallitt family: Isabella
   Mary (wife of Robert I) 144
   Robert I (husband of Mary) 126, 144
   Robert II (son of Charles I) 144
Buxton, Robert (baker) 145, 148, 155
Bywater, Katherine 43
Bywater, Thomas 43
Cadman Way 143
Caley, Flora 188
Caley, Revd William Bertram Russell (vicar of Watton 1890-98) 188
Callibutt, Richard 42, 137
Cambridge 17, 68, 73, 76, 86, 89, 98, 106, 130, 184, 250
Candler family

John I (grandfather of William) 152
John II (grandson of William) 152
Mary (grand-daughter of William) 152
Thomas (probably son of William) 123
William (d.1736) 122, 152, 154

Canham, Thomas 49
Cann, William and Co 178
Canon, Matilda 26
Canoun, Nicholas 25
Capital and Counties Bank 134
Carbrooke 24, 25, 83, 84, 85, 109, 128, 143, 166, 167, 178
Carpenters' Arms, The 153, 178, 253
Case, Philip 94, 95
Caston 83, 84, 178, 184, 226
Cattle market 133, 223
Caudwell, Roger 48, 142
Chapman, Cecil 203
Charity Commissioners 57, 105
Charles Avenue 228
Chase, George 153, 160, 257, 260
Chaston, Alfred 190
Chaston, Benjamin 190, 200
Chaston Place 154
Chequers, The 150, 178, 255, 256
Childerhouse, Edward 59
Childerhouse, Hilda 260
Childerhouse, John 45
Chirnell, Thomas 59
Chrashell, William 59
Christian Endeavour Union 193
Christopher, The 42, 48
Church Lane 139
Church of England 173, 174, 181, 186, 191, 192, 193, 195, 202, 209, 260
Church, Parish Church of St Mary/St Giles 12, 13, 14, 15, 20, 21, 53, 67, 85, 143, 181, 182, 184, 185, 187, 198, 209, 235
Church Walk 28, 56, 143, 144, 202, 203, 209, 214, 250, 251
Churchwardens 54, 55, 56, 57, 58, 62, 67, 72, 75, 100, 101, 103, 104

Cinder Oven Close 149, 172
Clarence House 179, 256
Clematis House 242
Cley Lane (Saham Road) 35, 67, 116, 147, 148, 149, 165, 252, 254
Clipperton, Robert John 238
Clock Tower, Clock House 33, 41, 42, 64, 67, 68, 73, 75, 76, 77, 78, 148, 155, 156, 164, 173, 248, 249, 251
Clubb family
Rebecca (wife of William) 134
Sarah (daughter of Rebecca and William; married George Gentle) 134
William (husband of Rebecca) 133, 134, 256
Coaches 83, 219
coal house 77, 105, 106, 196, 197
Cock, Cocke, Nicholas 55, 60, 61, 62, 64
Cock, The 79, 148, 152, 153, 154
Coe, Elizabeth 137
Coe, Robert 112, 129, 137, 164, 173
Coker, Fuller 181
Coke, Thomas W 111, 112
College Close 16
Common / Town House 99, 105, 149, 150
Congregational (Independent) Church 154, 191, 238
Conservative Club 246
Conservatives 130, 214, 215, 216, 246, 253
Cook, Ernest 248
Cornwell, James 145
Cranworth 122, 123
Crawshay, Sir Richard 177
Cricket 227
Crisford, Revd A T (Rector of Ovington) 226
Crockley, Edward 104, 123, 124, 126
Crown, The 42, 84, 95, 103, 104, 113, 114, 124, 129, 134, 141, 143, 151, 154, 156, 158, 162, 163, 164, 165, 166, 167, 168, 173, 178, 214, 215, 223, 224, 252, 258
Crundle (Crown Hill), Nether- and Over- 37
Cuffard, Francis 49
Curl, Elizabeth 187, 204, 205, 240

Curle, William  122
Curson, Francis  122
Curson's Cross  20, 87
Curson's, 'manor' of  20
Dalton, Edward  145
Darkins, Horace  77, 197
Darsley, William  163
Davy, Thomas  27
Delfe, William  52
Delpyt Furlong  37
Deney, George  45
Dennis family
    Elizabeth (wife of Robert II)  138, 139
    Mary (wife of Robert I)  139
    Robert I (husband of Mary)  139, 151
    Robert II (husband of Elizabeth)  138, 139
    Robert Willomatt (son of Robert II and Elizabeth)  139, 236
Dereham  144, 177, 202, 219, 222
Dereham Petty Sessions  132
Dereham Road  141, 143, 144, 150, 165, 191, 214, 226, 242, 244–245, 248, 249–252
Dillingham, Brampton Gurdon  125
Dinmore family
    Christopher (son of Richard I)  171, 175
    Jane (wife of Richard II)  102
    Richard II (son of Richard I, husband of Jane)  101, 102, 125, 171
Disraeli House  253
Dog and Partridge, The  149, 178, 253, 254
Doket, John  19
Domesday Book  9, 15, 16, 19, 23, 24, 33
Dorr family
    Charles I (d. 1843)  78, 144, 190
    Charles III (son of Charles II)  190
    Charles II (son of Charles I)  190
    Rebecca (née Amas, second wife of Charles III)  190
    Sarah Ann (née Hodson, first wife of Charles III)  190
Dovehouse  19
Dove, The  42, 79
Downham Market  40, 73, 89, 222
Drew, Misses (schoolmistresses)  199
Drynkins  54
Duffield, Reuben  122

Duke's Head, The  87
Dunche, John  24
Dunche, William  24
Dunn, Ambrose  35, 152
Dunn, Edward  152
Dunnett family  244
    Ann (wife of Daniel)  245
    Burton Samuel (son of Ann and Daniel)  245, 246
    Daniel (d. 1899)  189, 217, 244, 245, 247
    Ernest Jabez (son of Ann and Daniel)  245
Dunsburgh (Dunsburrowe)  38
Dunthorne, William  79
Durrant family  134, 157
    Cubitt Richard (son of George Cubitt)  229, 259
    George Cubitt (d. 1929)  157, 217, 227, 258, 259
    Margaret (née Pratt, wife of Cubitt Richard)  259
    Sarah Elizabeth (née Barnard, wife of George Cubitt)  259
Dye, Charlotte  198
East Bradenham  177
East Harling  28, 131, 177
East of England Joint-Stock Bank  141
Edrich, William  27
Education Act, 1870  192, 196, 199, 201
Education Act, 1902  203
Education, Committee of Council on; Board of; Government Department of  203
Edwards, Cissie A E  203
Edwards, George  214, 217
Edwards, John  256
Eke, Sarah  150
Ellington, Samuel  85
Ellis, Edward  124, 125
Ellis, James  250
Ellis, Mary Augusta  250
Elm Cottage  239
Emerson family
    Harriet (wife of Stephen)  130
    Matthew Sallitt (son of Harriet and Stephen)  130, 131
    Stephen (husband of Harriet)  116, 130, 131
    Stephen Sallitt (son of Harriet and Stephen)  131
Empire Day  209
Engaine, William d'  19

Everard, Thomas 25
Fairs 27, 47, 111, 112, 128, 164, 165, 185, 211, 247
Fendick, William 199
Ficket (Feket) family 26
  George (brother of Thomas and Henry I) 62
  Henry I 35, 55, 62
  Henry II (d. 1650, son of George) 35
  Margaret (wife of Henry I) 62
  Mary (wife of Henry II) 62
  Thomas (d. 1572) 52, 62
Fire Brigade 240, 248, 251
Fire engine 100, 105, 114, 196
Fish stalls, Fishmarket 45, 67, 79, 87
Fiske, Henry 172
Fitzwalter, Ranulf 16, 19, 33
Fitzwilliam, Elizabeth 31, 32, 44
Fle 23
Fleming family
  Sir William (son of William Henry's second marriage) 78, 84
  William Henry (husband of Anne) 78
Flower, John 84, 163
Flower Pot, The 139
Football 228–230, 258
Foresters, Ancient Order of 114, 150, 188
Forncett St Peter 126, 253
Foster, Revd William (Vicar of Watton 1632-60) 53, 54
Fox, Elizabeth 171
Fox, John 144
Fox, William 152
Franke, George 54
Franklin, Revd Fairfax (vicar of Watton 1803-38) 181, 192
Front Street 137, 147, 148, 149, 152, 201, 238
Frost Close 179
Frost family
  Caroline (née Crawshay; wife of William) 177
  Druscilla Mary (née Fortescue; wife of Thomas Crawshay) 178
  Horace (son of Thomas Crawshay and Druscilla) 179
  Revd William 177, 178
  Thomas Crawshay (son of Revd William and Caroline) 20, 167, 175, 177, 178, 179, 187, 189, 211, 220, 228, 254, 256, 257
  Thomas (son of Thomas Crawshay and Druscilla) 179
Frostick, Sarah 85
Frost, Jonas 142, 202, 242
Fuller, Samuel 153
Funnell, Mary 195
Gage, Jane Bricknell 257
Galland, Robert 149
Game Furlong 38
Garden House 139, 151, 236, 253
Garner, Frederick 230, 235
Garner, Thomas 255
Gas lighting 117
Gas works 116, 252
Gawdy family 69
Gedge, William 197
Gentle, George William 134
Gentle, Sarah Clubb. *See* Clubb family: Sarah (daughter of Rebecca and William; married George Gentle)
George family (17th century)
  Anne (daughter of Peter and Jane) 76
  Jane (née Hey, wife of Peter) 76
  Peter (husband of Jane) 76, 156
George family (19th century)
  Elizabeth (wife of George) 177
  George (1806-75) 152
George II, proclamation of 208
George, Robert Overland 157
George, the 42, 45, 71, 79, 83, 84, 85, 87, 101, 109, 110, 111, 112, 113, 114, 116, 117, 119–136, 137, 138, 142, 143, 147, 156, 158, 163, 164, 168, 171, 173, 175, 178, 204, 208, 210, 214, 215, 223, 226, 228, 234, 243, 244, 245, 253, 260, 264
George Trollope Road 12, 177
Girth, Elizabeth 52
Gladstone Villa 215, 239, 253
Goddard's Court 254
Godfreys 147
Godwyn, John 48
Goffe, Edward 42, 47, 57, 195

Golden Ball, The  153, 253
Gooch, Marianne  147, 150
Goodrich, Thomas  49
Goodrick, Horatio  240
Goward, Fanny  235
Gowing, James Warden  243
Gowing, Stephen  215
Great Cressingham  41, 187
Great Eastern Railway  220–224, 233–234
Great Ouse  73
Great Spicers Close  37
Great Wong, the  23, 67
Green Croft Furlong  37
Greengrass, George  257
Greengrass, Mary  257
Green Man, The  46, 72, 87, 139, 148, 151, 152, 153, 163, 164, 172, 175, 176, 177, 191, 209, 255, 256, 264
Gressenhall  190
Gressenhall, House of Industry  103
Grey, de, family, of Merton Hall
    Edmund (great nephew of Thomas I)  76
    Thomas I (1531-62)  34
    Thomas (MP for West Norfolk)  214
    William (grandfather of 1st Baron Walsingham)  122
Griffin (Gryffen), The  79, 163
Griffin, Revd Alfred  190, 199
Grigson family
    Edward Harvey  109
    Edward Robert (son of Edward Harvey)  142, 147, 244
Grimes, Susan  101
Griston  25, 37, 57
Griston Road  37, 139, 224, 235, 240
Groome, John  192, 197, 198
Half Moon, the (later King's Arms)  42, 44, 104, 114, 141, 142, 143, 145
Hall Close  33
Hall, William Salkeld  253
Hamond family
    Charles (son of Frances and Richard I)  122, 123
    Frances (wife of Richard I)  71, 122
    Judith (probable relative)  122
    Richard I (husband of Frances)  55, 122

    Richard III (son of Jane and Richard II)  123
    Richard II (son of Frances and Richard I)  122
Hardinge Cottages  148
Hare, Sir Thomas  216
Hargraves family
    George (son of Thomas)  238
    John (son of Thomas)  147
    Thomas  150
Harp Pightle  37
Harris, Edward  122
Hart, William  189
Harvey family (of Harvey House)
    Charlotte Mary (daughter of Charlotte and Robert; wife of Robert John)  147, 148
    Charlotte (wife of Robert)  147, 148, 150, 152, 197, 198, 252
    Maria T (daughter of Charlotte Mary and Robert John)  147
    Robert (husband of Charlotte)  57, 125, 147
    Robert John (cousin and husband of Charlotte Mary)  148
Harvey family (printers)
    Edward  243, 247
Harvey House  79, 147, 148, 204, 205, 226, 252
Harvey Street  46, 143, 248, 251, 252, 254, 255, 256, 263
Harwood, W Tooke  125, 171
Hastings family
    John Edward (son of Smith)  141, 142, 149, 157
    Smith (d. 1849)  103, 141, 148, 149, 150, 152, 190, 256
Hatley, Elizabeth  59
Heighmere  37
Heighoo family
    Edward (son of William)  61
    James (son of William)  61
    William (d. 1632)  48, 60, 61, 68
Hethrington, Mr (visitor to the Crown)  166
Hewson, Bertha  260
Hey family  67–82
    Alice (née Wilks, previously Fuller, second wife of Christopher III)  73
    Ann (née Scott, wife of John I)  68
    Charles (son of Christopher I)  33, 35, 45, 61, 67
    Christopher I (alias Hethe, son of Thomas I)  33, 35, 42, 45, 46, 55, 56, 67

Christopher III (son of John and Ann) 68–77
Christopher II (son of Christopher I) 67
Edward (son of Christopher I) 33, 35, 67
Jane (daughter of Christopher III and Mary) 68
John II and III (sons of Christopher III and Mary) 68
John I (son of Christopher I) 67, 68
Lucy (daughter of Christopher III and Mary) 68
Mary I (first wife of Christopher III) 68, 69, 70
Mary II (daughter of Christopher III) 76
Robert (son of Christopher I) 67
Thomas I (alias Hethe) 67
Thomas III (son of Christopher III) 68, 76
Thomas II (son of Christopher I) 67

Hicks family 83–85
Burden (son of Francis I) 84
Elizabeth (née Raby, wife of Thomas). See Raby, Elizabeth (daughter of John; later Hicks, Barker)
Francis I (d. 1743) 83
Francis II (d. 1783) 78, 84, 85
Henry (son of Francis I) 85
Jane II (daughter of John) 85
Jane I (wife of Francis I) 84
John (son of Francis I) 84
Robert (son of John) 85
Thomas (son of Francis I) 84, 85
William (son of Francis I, Vicar of Watton, 1779-84) 84

High Street 12, 20, 40, 46, 71, 115, 116, 149, 171, 177, 201, 209, 226, 238, 242, 243, 244, 247, 256, 257, 260, 264
Hill Close 33
Hill (Hylle) Furlong, Hill Close 37
Hill, William 122
Hingham 37, 61, 72, 89, 129, 185, 202
Hobbys, John 26
Hodgson, Revd W C (vicar of Watton 1861-65) 186, 192
Holkham 111, 130, 131
Holkham Hall 131
Holme Hale 61, 220
Holmes, Richard Guillard 134
Hook, James 236
Hooper, James 168
Hornigold family 46, 152
Edmund (son of William and Margery) 63
Elizabeth (daughter of William and Margery) 63
John (son of Edmund and Mary) 72
Margery (wife of William) 63
Mary (wife of Edmund) 72, 151
Thomas (brother of William) 63
William (d. 1630) 63

Horn, Julian 115
Hothemore 37
Howard, John 42, 71
Howard, Mary 123
Howard, William 62
Howes, Lydia 141
Howlett, Thomas 235
Hubbard, William 175
Hudson, Anthony 157
Hundred Oak 15
Hunton's iron and brass foundry 235
Hurthaunt, Robert 24
Iceni 11
Incendiarism 112
Infant School 188, 198, 201, 202, 203, 251
International Stores 248, 249, 251
Isaak, Joseph 76
Isaak, Mary 76
Ives family 69
Anne II (wife of Thomas) 145
Anne I (née Betts, wife of Ralph) 44, 68
Ralph (husband of Anne I) 44, 55, 68, 69, 71, 143
Thomas (son of Ralph and Anne I) 87, 143, 145

Jackson, John 256
Jackson, Revd Stephen 192
Jacobs family
George 117, 163–170, 252
Mary Keziah (née Bennett, wife of George). See Bennett, Mary Keziah
Sarah (nee Rackham, second wife of George, previously Lusher) 164, 167
James, Susan 122
Jarvis (Jarvys) family
Edmund 71
Thomas 71, 85–86, 138
William I 45
William II (probably son of William I) 45
Jeckell, Peter Blomfield (vicar of Watton 1839-53) 138, 181, 184, 197

Jenney, John 32
Jessup, Frederick 242
Jessup, George 203, 259
Jessup, Jeremiah 236
Jessup, William 104
Johnson, Anne 142
Johnson, Penelope 103
Johnson, Richard James 225
Johnson, William 256
Jolly Farmers, The 117, 149, 164, 214, 254
Julnes, Arthur 229, 235
Julnes, Lionel 256
Kendall, William 154, 187, 257
Kent, Ethelbert Brunton 168
Kett, George Woodhouse 200
Kett, John 84, 85
Kett, Maria Ann. *See* Blade family: Maria Ann (daughter of Robert and Sarah)
Kett, Martha 140
Kett's Rebellion 1549 33
Key, Robert 188, 191
Khyber House 115, 145, 249, 250, 251
Kiddall, Robert 122
King's Arms Square 156
King's Arms, the. *See* Half Moon, the (later King's Arms)
King's Arms, the (Middle Street) 151, 247, 248
King's Arms, the (previously Queen's Arms, later Green Man) 87, 151
King's Arms, the (Swaffham) 235
King's Lynn 123, 171, 214, 219, 220
Kitchener Terrace 254
Knopwood, Susan and Eleanor (schoolmistresses) 204, 252
Knott, Charles 235
Knotts Lane 37
Labour in Vain, the (previously Bull, later Half Moon and King's Arms) 79, 142, 143
Lance, William 149
Langford, L 187

Leggate, James 217
Leggett, Edmund G 254
Legood, Edward 197
Leicester, Lord 131
Letton 25, 122, 123
Letton Hall 125
Liberal Club 216, 230, 258
Liberal Party 193, 213, 216, 239, 245
Lincolne, Thomas 56
Lincoln, Richard 35
Lintott, Charles 202, 203, 228, 236
Lintott, Emily 202
Little Wissey 9, 11, 16, 23, 26, 31, 35, 36, 37, 116, 208
Live and Let Live, The 144, 202, 250
Live and Let Live (Union motto) 214
Local Government Act 1888 217
Local Government Act 1894 217
Loch House 144, 190, 227
Loch Neaton 190, 226, 227, 260, 264
London 47, 73, 77, 89, 124, 125, 129, 130, 132, 142, 143, 166, 167, 172, 177, 178, 185, 186, 219, 223, 224, 225, 227, 233, 235, 241, 250, 251, 254, 259
London, butter market 94
London, Great Fire of 72, 77
London, Poor Law Commissioners 106
Longlond 28
Long, Short Long, Long Long Furlong 38
Lord's Meadow, the 33
Lusher, John 150
Lusher, Mary Ann 225
Lusher, Robert 164
Magges, Richard 59
Magistrates/Justices of the Peace 70, 73, 185, 250
Maidswell 36
Main drainage 115
Mallins, Henry 217, 249
Mallows, James 156
Malthouse Close 149, 150, 172

Maltings, Malthouse 91, 150, 153, 170, 171, 172, 179, 189, 254
Mann, Thomas 149
Manor Farm 78
Manor House 85, 140, 141, 142, 157, 242, 244, 250
Margisson, Richard 85
Marie 61
Market Cross 40, 41, 45, 76, 83
Market Hill 12
Market House 189, 245
Market Place 13, 40–51, 115, 156, 188, 215, 245
market stalls 28, 41, 45
Martin, Mr and Mrs (schoolmaster and schoolmistress) 198
Mason, Edward James 252
Massey, William 106, 145, 146, 210, 251
Matthews, Jane Elizabeth 132
Mayes, William 55
Mayses Close, Closes 35, 67, 69
Meek, William 217, 256
Mere Meadow 32, 44
Merton 16, 23, 24, 35, 36, 37, 38, 91, 112, 201, 208, 213
Merton Hall, Park 16, 34, 36, 76, 122, 208, 215
Merton Road 117, 165, 177, 240, 241, 242, 263, 264
Methodist Church, Methodism 42, 47, 148, 150, 171, 178, 186, 188, 189, 191, 252, 254, 257, 264
Middle Row 46, 47, 72, 148, 152
Middle Street 27, 40, 42, 44, 46, 115, 151, 226, 243, 244, 248, 249, 250
Mill Common 58, 110, 148
Mill Corner 117
Miller, James 191
Mill Field (Myllefeld) 26, 28, 36, 37, 61, 110
Millington, Thomas 15
Mill, Over Mill, Newther Mill Furlong 37
Mill Road, Mill Street 110, 111, 252

Mills, John Remington 248
Minns, George 217, 247
Minns, Thomas 103
Mirrill, John 59
Monk's-Wick 19
Montagu (Monte Acuto), de, family
   Alice 24
   Edward 24
   William 24
Moore, M A 189
Moore, Mark 189
Moore Meadow, Close 33
Mosse, Humphrey 142
Moss, Elizabeth 258
Muller, Arabella (née Tillett) 143
Muller, James 143
Muston, John 86, 87, 151
Muston, Reuben 83, 87
Mutual Improvement Society 113, 114, 185
Naggs Close 147
Nash, Captain Frederic Wybrow 188
Nash, Revd Charles Barnett (Vicar of Watton, 1898-1923) 188, 237
National Agricultural Labourers' Union 212
National School 77, 114, 117, 149, 181, 188, 192, 196, 197, 198, 199, 201, 202, 203, 208, 214, 215, 225, 236, 249, 264
National Society for promoting the Education of the Poor in the Principles of the Established Church 192, 196, 199
Neaton 12, 23, 31, 36, 37, 40, 100, 126, 144, 145, 155, 251, 263
Neaton Cottage 191
Neaton Farm 78, 144, 166, 167, 190
Neaton Fen 36, 110, 144, 226
Neaton Street 12, 56, 144, 145
Neaton Villa 251
Nelson, George 184
Nelson, Richard 43
Nettleship, Prudence 156, 157
Neve, John 26
Neve, Thomas 25, 26

# Index

Neville, James  198
New Inn, the  133, 138, 142, 178, 239, 242
Nonconformists  202, 209
Norfolk Central Railway  222
Norfolk County Council  217, 247
Norwich  12, 14, 15, 25, 27, 37, 72, 88, 89, 101, 102, 103, 104, 110, 112, 126, 129, 130, 131, 132, 137, 138, 148, 164, 168, 171, 175, 177, 190, 191, 198, 200, 201, 219, 222, 235, 236
Norwich and Brandon Railway  129
Norwich Assizes  131
Norwich, Bishop of  181, 193, 198
Norwich Castle  25, 26
Norwich Consistory Court  122
Norwich Court of Mayoralty  72
Norwich Road  11, 12, 13, 110, 116, 138, 139, 209, 220, 223, 224, 227, 233, 235, 236, 237, 238, 240, 241, 242, 249, 263
Norwich Union Fire Insurance Society  112
Oake Close  58
Oak Furlong  37
Obelisk  41, 108, 246, 247
Oddfellows, Loyal Walsingham Lodge of the Manchester Unity  114, 188, 255
Oldfield, Edmund  224
Olley, John  69
Overgate Furlong  37
Overseers of the Poor  56, 100
Overstede Furlong  37
Overton, Clement  36, 91, 195
Overton, Mary  156
Ovington  23, 25, 26, 27, 128, 144, 163, 177, 226
Page, Alfred  233
Paines, Paynes  44, 45, 62, 68, 71, 87, 143
Palmer family
    Henry (nephew of Thomas)  34
    Henry (son of Henry)  33, 34, 35
    Matilda (wife of Thomas)  56
    Thomas (vicar of Watton, 1528-57)  34
Palmer, Lydia  101
Palmer, Thomas (of Bawdeswell)  103

Panting, Dr John  241, 252
Parker, Revd W H (rector of Saham Toney)  195, 200
Parliamentary enclosure, 1801  109
Parliamentary enclosure, 1803  23, 35, 58, 100, 124, 144
Parry, Sir Edward  105
Patriotic Society  102
Pattrick, William  122
Payne, Edward  151
Payne, Paine family
    Alice (wife of Thomas)  44
    Henry (son of Thomas and Alice)  44
    John (d. 1549)  44, 56, 152
    Thomas (son of John)  44
Payn, John (1381 rebel)  25, 32
Pearson, William  103, 163
Pentney, Prior of  26
Philo, Joseph  138
Phipson, R M  201
Pigge, Revd Thomas (vicar of Watton 1730-79)  195
Pilgrim, Mary  195
Piper, Albert Ernest  258
Pit Close  172
Pitts, James  140, 242
Pitts, John  149
Pitts, Mary  149
Platfoot, Catherine  153, 154
Platfoot, Edward  153
Platfoot, Elizabeth  166, 167
Platfoot, Ralph  27, 28
Plowlets  54
Poaching  112
Police Station  116, 208, 238, 239
Pooley, Abraham  155
Pooley, Elizabeth  155
Pooly, Widow  122
Poor Box  56
Poor Rates  57, 105
Population of Watton  21, 40, 43, 49, 64, 109, 111, 181, 252, 254, 263

Porter, Robert 37
Posterlond (Postellon), Upper, Lower Furlongs 37
Post House, Le 72
Postle, Possell Pyssel, Bridge 55, 115
Post Office, postmaster/mistress 142, 163, 200, 215, 224, 225, 226, 243, 245, 247, 248
Post Office Street 226, 248
Pound, the 28, 56, 144, 145
Powley, Robert 153
Pratt, Edward 258
Primitive Methodism, Primitive Methodist Chapel, Hall 153, 188, 189, 245, 248, 254, 256
Prince of Wales (became King Edward VII) 208, 213
Prince of Wales Omnibus 130
Prince of Wales, the 190
Pritchard, Amelia 241
Protestantism 52, 53, 184, 190
Puritans 63
Pyman, Elizabeth 103
Pyman, William 103
Queen's Arms, the (later King's Arms, Green Man) 79, 87, 151
Queen's Hall 264
Rabies 88
Raby, Elizabeth (daughter of John; later Hicks, Barker) 85, 141, 184
Raby, John 85, 184
Rackham, William 164
Rae, Matthew 217
Rafmen 27
RAF Watton, airfield 9, 263
Railway Hotel 233, 234, 235
Railway Hotel, Norwich 191
Railway Station 130, 219, 223, 226, 228, 233, 234, 235, 264
Reading, James 192
Redhill Lane 23, 37, 55, 144
Redhill (Rockolls) 36, 100

Red Lion, The 145, 146, 252
Reeve, Barnabas 178
Reeve, Mrs (manager at the Crown) 166
Regester, Julia (née Durrant) 258
Reynolds, Alfred 255
Rice, Robert 149
Rice, Samuel 138, 142, 151, 163, 164
Rice, Samuel (son of Samuel) 164
Rising of 1381 (Peasants' Revolt) 16, 25, 26
Rising, Robert 163
Robinson family
  Charles (son of Richard) 229, 244
  Frederick (son of Richard) 228, 244
  Richard (1824-1905) 140, 150, 239, 244
Robinson, Revd H E 189
Robinson, William Lane 143, 152, 196
Robson, Emily Ann 150
Rockland St Andrew 105
Rockland St Peter 84, 244
Rokele (Rupella) de, Richard 20
Rokeles Bridge 23, 37
Rokeles Green 36, 37
Rokeles Hall 20, 23, 26, 27, 28, 33, 36, 37, 48, 60, 68, 236
Rokeles Manor 20, 26, 27, 28, 61, 67
Rokeles Meadow 23, 28, 37, 61
Rolfe, William Morley 233
Roman Catholicism, Roman Catholics 53, 60, 184
Rook, Sarah Ann 157
Rook, William 133, 134, 157, 245
Roos (Ros) de, family
  John 23, 31
  Margery (wife of William II) 19, 24, 25
  Maud (née de Vaux, wife of William I) 19
  Thomas (son of William II and Margery) 25
  William I 19
  William II (possibly grandson of William I) 19
Rose Cottage 250
Rosedale Terrace 252
Rose, The 139, 236, 237
Rotten Row 47, 72, 79, 87, 99, 106, 148, 150, 151, 175, 255

Roudham Junction  219, 220, 223
Rowe, John  256
Royal Picture Palace  230
Russell, Charles  112, 153
Rust, Robert  31, 32
Rutland, Earl of  31
Saham College  208
Saham Cottages  253
Saham Park  174
Saham Road  23, 188, 189, 253
Saham Toney  11, 12, 19, 21, 25, 31, 32, 57, 109, 150, 173, 174, 177, 178, 195, 200
Saham Toney Free School  57
Saham Waite  61
Sallitt family
   Isabella  125, 126
   Matthew  126, 144
   Thomas  125
Salteresmoor  28
Salter, Richard  86
Salter, Rose  55
Sampson, James  155
Samuel Rice  238
Samwell family
   Anne (daughter of William and Anne)  78, 99. *See* Woodhouse, Anne (previously Samwell)
   Anne (wife of William). *See* Woodhouse, Anne (previously Samwell)
   Anthony  78
   William (son of Anthony)  78
Sandwade  23
Saxlingham  126, 127
Saxlingham Mills  127
Saxlingham Thorpe  126
Sayer, Edward  242
Sayer, William  247, 257
Say, Revd Henry  145
Scarning  103, 141, 177
Scott, Ann  155
Scott family, of Rokeles Hall
   Thomas I  58
   Thomas II (possible grandson of Thomas I)  61
   Thomas, Revd (descendant)  125

Scott, John  153
Secker, Samuel  141
Self, George  242
Semmence, Albert  236
Semmence, Harry  253
Sexiswong  28
Sharman, Frank  254
Shipdham  83, 85, 95, 122, 129, 130, 174, 177, 181
Shorne Hill Bush  35, 37
Short, Samuel  227
Short, William  199
Siggins, Henry  145, 157, 251
Sillett, Elsie  260
Sillett, Mabel  260
Skipper, Charles  166, 167
Sloman, Charles  131
Smallpox  86, 87, 101, 104
Smith, Charles  198
Smith, Mary  198
Smith, Samuel  256
Smith, Thomas  150
Smythe, Anne  52
Smyth, Thomas  25
Society for the Propagation of the Gospel in Foreign Parts and the Church of England Temperance Society  188
Sondehill  37
Spanton, Sarah  242
Sparrow, John  143
Spicer, Thomas  45
Sporle  84, 177
Sports Centre  264
Sprigge family
   Elizabeth (wife of Squire)  250
   Samuel Squire (son of Elizabeth and Squire)  250
   Squire  145, 198, 250
Spurrill, John  149, 152
Stace, Martha  198, 202
Stace, William Stovold  198, 202, 225, 226
Stagg, Nathaniel  46

Stalworthy family
   Elizabeth (daughter of Thomas I) 86
   Mary (daughter of Thomas I) 87
   Thomas I 86, 88
   Thomas II (son of Thomas I) 86, 88

Stanford 130

Starke, Police Inspector 166

Starke, Thomas 199

Stebbing (builder of Town House) 99

Stebbing, Charles 252

Stebbing, Lydia 257

Stebbing, Richard 123, 124

Stebbing, Robert 152

Stebbings, William J 260

Steel, Frank George 260

Steppellz, the 23

Stevens Close 179

Stevens family
   Alice (daughter of Edward I and Susanna) 177
   Ann (née Peck, wife of Robert II) 174
   Clara (daughter of Robert II and Ann) 176
   Edward I (d. 1790) 171
   Edward II (son of Edward I) 171, 172–174
   Elizabeth II (daughter of Robert II and Ann) 174
   Elizabeth I (née Fox, wife of Stephen Nobbs). *See* Fox, Elizabeth
   Mary Ann (née Alpe, wife of Robert Edward). *See* Alpe, Mary Ann
   Robert Edward (son of Robert II and Ann) 174, 176
   Robert II (son of Stephen Nobbs and Elizabeth) 171, 174–176
   Robert I (son of Edward I and Susanna) 172
   Stephen Nobbs (son of Edward II and Susanna) 171, 174
   Susanna I (née Nobbs, wife of Edward I) 171

Stibbon, Arthur 226, 248

Stibbon, Lydia Maud 226, 248

Stocks 41

Stokes Avenue 12

Stow Bedon 178

Strange, Robert 33

Stranguage, Peter 85

Street, the 40

Stringer, Dora 203

Sturgeon, Hannah 150, 153

Surveyors of the Highways 56

Sutton family
   Margram (brother of Thomas William) 176
   Susanna (née Stevens, wife of Thomas William) 176
   Thomas (son of Thomas William and Susanna) 176
   Thomas William 176

Swaffham 67, 212, 213, 215, 219, 220, 222, 228

Swaffham Poor Law Union 150

Swaffham Road 36, 110, 116, 117, 148, 149, 153, 252, 253

Swaffham Station 208

Swallow, Elizabeth 145

Swallow, Robert 103, 145

Swan, the 42, 71, 79, 85, 86, 137, 138, 242

Sykes, Mary Ann 203

Targett family
   Elizabeth 201
   Hannah (daughter of Elizabeth) 201
   Jane (daughter of Elizabeth) 201
   Mary Ann (daughter of Elizabeth) 201

Taylor, Edward 103, 163

Taylor, Eunice 240

Taylor, Robert (vicar of Watton 1626-32) 54

Taylor, William Benjamin 256

Tebold, Robert 44

Temperance Hotel 248

Tennant, Sidney 238

Tennant, Thomas William 251

Thetford 69, 89, 103, 124, 130, 143, 190, 219, 220, 222, 225, 229

Thetford and Watton Railway 116, 177, 220, 221, 230

Thetford and Watton Times 178, 245

Thetford Priory 15, 19, 33, 34, 35, 36, 45

Thetford Road 138, 165, 201, 204, 215, 223, 226, 238, 240, 241, 242, 263

Thetford Way 37

Thickpenny, Joseph 124

Thompson family
   Frances (wife of John Hicks) 158
   John (d. 1803) 104, 143
   John Hicks (probably grandson of John) 49, 157, 246, 247

Thompson, Henry  123
Thompson (village)  14, 16, 47, 125, 171, 176
Thompson, William  46, 79
Thorpe-next-Norwich  177
Three Fishes, The  79, 150, 175
Threxton  11, 12, 57, 115, 131, 188, 195
Threxton Nab  16
Tillett family, at the King's Arms
   John (son of Richard and Sarah)  143
   Margaret (daughter of Richard and Sarah)  143
   Richard (d.1712)  142, 143
   Sarah (wife of Richard)  143
   William II (son of William I)  143
   William I (son of Richard and Sarah)  143
Tillett, Richard (chairmaker)  79
Tillott, Tillett family, at the George
   Ellen (daughter of Leonard and Mary)  132, 133
   Emma (daughter of Leonard and Mary)  131, 132, 133
   Leonard  131, 132, 133, 134
   Mary  132, 133
   Palm Booty (son of Emma)  132, 133
Tolisepytt  23
Tollhouse, The  27, 41, 87, 143
Took, Ann  197
Tooke, Elizabeth  197
Took, John  153
Took, William  197
Toole, Philip  48
Tooley, Henry (vicar of Watton 1660-81)  54
Tooley, James  79, 151
Tooley, John  79
Toombs, Edwin Tyson  256
Toombs, Louisa  203
Tottington  213
Town House Close  196
town house, the  99, 105, 149, 150, 197
Trendill, Gregory  31
Trollope, George William  250
Tuck, John  141
Turner, Edmund  122
Turner family
   Henry  58
   Hugh (son of Henry, vicar of Watton,1571-1608)  58
   Margaret (wife of Richard)  52, 53
   Richard (son of Henry)  58
Turner, John  123
Turnpike Road  89, 126, 137, 185
United States
   emigration  102, 171
   servicemen  263
Valentine, J S  220
Vaux (Vallibus), de, family
   Ada  19
   John  19
   Oliver  20
   Robert  19
Vicarage  54, 84, 138, 139, 140, 181, 184, 185, 186, 187, 195, 223, 237
Victoria Cottage Hospital  234, 240
Vincent family
   Lacey Andrews  187, 248, 251, 253, 257
   Percy (son of Lacey and Susan)  229, 251
   Susan  251
Vincent, John  48
Vipan, John  143
Volunteer Force  235
Wada  9, 12, 15
Waite Farm (Saham)  14
Walker, Amos  148, 255
Walker, Dr Samuel  122
Walker, John  103
Walker's Corner  148
Wallis, Revd G F W (Vicar of Watton 1865-67)  186, 192
Walsingham Cottages  117, 241
Walsingham Gates  209
Walsingham, Lady  112, 114, 202, 205, 214
Walsingham, Lord  vii, 37, 111, 113, 115, 130, 139, 147, 193, 200, 202, 208, 209, 210, 212, 213, 214, 215, 219, 223, 247
Ward, John  234
Ward, Samuel  167
Warner, Thomas  25
Warren, John  151, 153
Wasshbek  23, 24
Wasshbrygg  23, 24

Watermill  16, 23, 24, 227
Waters and Sons  139, 166, 226, 240
Waters family
   Charlotte (wife of Daniel I)  139
   Daniel I (d. 1850)  139
   Daniel II (son of Charlotte and Daniel I)  139, 240
   Hannah (wife of Daniel II)  242
   Robert (son of Daniel II and Hannah)  226, 238, 240, 247
Waters, Robert James (painter)  217
Waters, Thomas (artist)  188
Watson, Herbert Carley  256
Watton and Swaffham Railway Company  220
Watton Brewery  20, 72, 170
Watton Fen  100
Watton Green  9, 11, 12, 23, 24, 36, 37, 40, 61, 110, 112, 188, 226, 236
Watton Hall, Manor  19, 20, 24, 25, 26, 27, 28, 31, 32, 33, 34, 42, 44, 47, 77, 78, 84, 85, 119, 134, 141, 148, 156, 184
Watton Junior School  264
Watton Mere  23, 26, 31, 36
Watton Mixed School  203
Watton Parish/Town Council  vii, 82, 217, 218, 227, 231, 247, 248, 264
Watton Rifle Club  258
Watton Secondary Modern School  264
Watton Town Band  209, 234
Watton Wick  13, 23, 33, 34, 36, 37, 38, 40
Wayland Agricultural Association  179, 210
Wayland Association for Apprehending and Convicting Horsestealers  89, 172
Wayland Association for Promoting and Rewarding Good Conduct and Encouraging Industrious Habits among Servants, Cottagers and Labourers  112, 210
Wayland Farmers Defensive Association  213
Wayland Field  36, 37, 38, 61
Wayland Hall  46, 106, 108, 114, 115, 116, 142, 146, 181, 184, 193, 202, 209, 210, 212, 213, 214, 216, 220, 226, 230, 234, 244, 245, 246, 247, 248, 264

Wayland High School/Academy  264
Wayland Hospital  105
Wayland House  145, 146, 248, 251
Wayland Hundred  14, 15, 17, 76, 112
Wayland Poor Law Union  105, 141, 191, 197, 213, 226, 244, 250
Wayland Prison  209
Wayland Reede  37
Wayland Rural District Council  217, 244, 246, 247, 263, 264
Wayland Show  179, 210, 211, 212, 234, 260
Wayland, Wayland Smith  15
Wayland Wood  9, 11, 12, 14, 15, 16, 36, 37, 139
Webster, John  42, 48
Wenham family
   Charlotte (wife of William)  155
   George (son of William)  155, 225
   William (c. 1758-1834)  152, 155
Wesleyan Methodists, Wesleyan Methodist Chapel  188, 189
Westell, Wassell, The  42
West End House, West House  149, 253
West End Stores  238, 255
West End Terrace  254, 255
West Harling  69
West, Isabella (née Buxton, previously Sallitt). See Sallitt family: Isabella
West, John  126
West Norfolk Militia  103
Westonne, John  52
West Road  12
West Tofts  176
Wetlond, Wetlond Furlong, Wetlands Close  28, 38
Weyland, John  105, 113
Whalebelly, William  217, 242
Whisker, Nicholas  41
White Hart  79, 129
White House  204, 240
Wick Common  110
Wick Farm  19, 33, 35, 36, 242

Wicks, Herbert William  258
Wightwick, Ursula  200
Wilkinson, John  63
Williamson, Dr Tom  17, 18, 20, 29
Willow House  139, 140, 200, 223, 224, 237, 239, 242, 253
Windmills  37, 89, 110, 137, 141, 148, 149, 252
Winfrey, Richard  216
Wingfield, Sir Robert  28
Wolbyswong  23
Wollydam  23
Wong Close. *See* Mayses Close, Closes
Wood Field. *See* Wayland Field
Wood Furlong  38
Woodhouse, Anne (previously Samwell)  78, 99, 156
Woodhouse, John  78
Woodhouse, Manor, in Saham and Ovington  27
Wood Lane  37, 139
Woodrising Hall  105, 113
Woods, Henry  202, 210, 218
Workhouses  103, 104, 105, 143, 191
World War I  200, 217, 226, 227, 228, 230, 235, 260, 263
World War II  263, 264
Worm family
    James  150, 257
    James Stebbing (son of James and Lydia)  257
    Lydia (née Stebbing, wife of James). *See* Stebbing, Lydia
Worm's Yard  150, 189, 257
Wrenford family
    Annette (daughter of Joshua Booth and Margaret)  187
    Basil Joshua Booth (son of Joshua Booth and Margaret)  187
    Elizabeth II (daughter of Thomas Brookes and Elizabeth)  187
    Elizabeth I (née Booth, wife of Revd Thomas Brookes)  186
    Margaret (wife of Joshua Booth)  187
    Revd Joshua Booth (son of Thomas Brookes and Elizabeth)  187, 228
    Revd Thomas Brookes (vicar of Watton, 1867-90)  186, 187, 188, 192, 192–193, 236
    Revd Thomas Henry (son of Thomas Brookes and Elizabeth)  187
Wright, Dorothy (née Younge)  154
Wright, Elizabeth  154, 200
Wright family (at the George)
    Alice (wife of Robert)  156
    Dennis (d. 1808)  126–127
    Elizabeth (daughter of Dennis and Susanna I)  126. *See* Brasnett, Elizabeth (née Wright)
    Jane (daughter of Dennis and Susanna I)  127
    Robert (son of Dennis and Susanna I)  126, 128, 156
    Susanna II (daughter of Dennis and Susanna I)  127, 253
    Susanna I, Susan (wife of Dennis)  111, 126–128, 163, 183, 234, 253
    William (son of Dennis and Susanna I)  126, 128
Wright family (at the Railway Hotel)
    Elizabeth (daughter of Richard and Sarah)  234
    Emily (daughter of Richard and Sarah)  234
    Richard (husband of Sarah)  233
    Samuel Watkins (son of Richard and Sarah)  234, 235
    Sarah (wife of Richard)  233–234, 234
Wright family (Smith Wright)
    Smith (d. 1847)  128, 157, 172, 173, 258
Wright, John (overseer)  104
Wrightup family
    Henry  131, 132
    Henry Boyce (son of Henry and Jane)  132
    Jane Elizabeth (wife of Henry). *See* Matthews, Jane Elizabeth
Wymondham  27, 89, 129, 132, 138, 178, 185, 219, 226
York House  256
York, Robert de  24
Younge family
    Dorothy (wife of Thomas I)  88, 94–95. *See* Wright, Dorothy (née Younge)
    Edward I (d. 1761)  86–88
    Edward II (son of Thomas I and Dorothy)  95
    Elizabeth (née Stalworthy, first wife of Edward I). *See* Stalworthy family: Elizabeth (daughter of Thomas I)
    Hester (daughter of Edward I and Mary I)  88
    Mary II (daughter of Edward I and Mary I)  88
    Mary I (née Stalworthy, second wife of Edward I). *See* Stalworthy family: Mary (daughter of Thomas I)
    Pleasance (daughter of Edward I and Mary I)  88
    Thomas II (son of Thomas I and Dorothy)  94–95

    Thomas I (son of Edward I and Elizabeth, d. 1770) 88–94
    William II (cousin of Thomas I?) 94–95

Youngs, Philip S 154

Youngs, Robert 145

Youth Centre 67, 147

www.ingramcontent.com/pod-product-compliance
Ingram Content Group UK Ltd.
Pitfield, Milton Keynes, MK11 3LW, UK
UKHW021930160125
453778UK00004B/106